P

John Allison
Paul Emmerson
Jon Hird
Chris Murray
Mark Powell
Rosemary Richey
Nicholas Sheard
Jeremy Taylor
Anne Watson
Jon Wright

in company

Upper intermediate
Teacher's Book

Contents

A business English classroom

As Stephen crosses the bridge over the River Main, the towering skyscrapers of Frankfurt's commercial district glitter with lights in the distance. 'Mainhattan' the locals call it, referring to a certain resemblance to New York. Stephen is on his way there now, to his last lesson of the day. But he's not happy.

The class itself is great. Otto, Wolfgang, Ernst and Liesl are a lot of fun. They often take Stephen for a drink at a nearby bar after the lesson and he sometimes thinks they learn more English there than in the class.

And that's where the problem lies. The group speaks pretty good English already and, having had a succession of English teachers over the last three years, there doesn't seem to be a lot they haven't done before. The language of meetings, telephoning, presentations, negotiations – you name it, they've studied it. Stephen did a fluency activity with them last week only to discover they'd done it the year before with a different teacher. They laughed about it, but it was clear one or two of them felt they couldn't be making much progress.

Looking at the upper intermediate business English materials in the teachers' room at his school, Stephen decides that most of them are really just going over old ground again, teaching the same basic functions and topics they taught at intermediate, but sometimes introducing unnecessarily complicated language to justify the continued effort. 'What is upper intermediate business English, anyway?' he wonders. 'What more is there left to teach?'

Then Stephen remembers a lesson he did with them a few weeks back. It was a roleplay in which they had to visit their boss's home for a meal, make a good impression and raise a rather delicate work issue without offending their host. They found it really challenging and liked the mixture of social and business language that came out of doing the activity. They said they felt this was more the kind of advanced English they needed. So, as Stephen catches his bus into the city, his mood is already brightening and he's beginning to think, 'Maybe I'm on to something here ...'

In Company is Macmillan's skills-based business English series, aimed at professional, adult learners seeking to realise their full potential as speakers of English at work – both in and out of the office – and in social settings.

In Company Upper intermediate takes students through eighteen progressively more challenging units, ranging from entertaining clients and colleagues, exchanging information and problem-solving on the phone to higher-level skills such as leading meetings, team-presenting and negotiating. The course reflects the need for students at this level to review and explore in more depth previously studied areas of grammar and to increase their grasp of idiom and lexical range. Above all, the course aims to boost students' communicative power as self-reliant speakers of English in both professional and social situations.

Ten key observations on the teaching of English to professional learners underpin the course:

1   Professionals like to be regularly reminded why they are studying and what's in it for them.
2   They are used to goal-setting and time constraints and tend to welcome a fairly fast pace.
3   They are motivated by topics which directly relate to their own personal experiences.
4   They expect to see an immediate, practical payoff of some kind at the end of each lesson.
5   It is English, not business, they have come to you for help with (but see 7).
6   They want to be able to actually *do* business with their English rather than just talk about it.
7   They appreciate texts and tasks which reflect what they have to do in their job.
8   They also appreciate texts and tasks which allow them to escape from what they have to do in their job.
9   They don't regard having fun as incompatible with 'serious learning' (but see 1 and 4).
10 They like to see an overall plan and method behind the classes they attend.

The upper intermediate learner of business English

At this level, learners can fairly easily cope with most everyday situations in English and, unless they have very special needs, there's a danger they may not be sufficiently motivated to continue their studies. Those who are motivated are driven by more than the need to be competent. They are already competent. They want to excel, to really 'look good' in English. Having worked for so long at improving their English, they think it's time their English started working for them.

For the upper intermediate learner, therefore, telephoning is less about learning set telephone expressions and more about solving problems on the phone; presenting is less about facing forwards and making sense and more about impressing and delighting the audience; meetings are less about coming in here and there with constructive remarks and more about taking the initiative and influencing the outcome. Social English in a real business context, where the boundaries between work and pleasure are not so clearly defined, is likely to be a priority. So too is the ability to talk perhaps only superficially, but articulately, about a number of topical issues.

Much so-called advanced English is really rather simple English used in advanced ways. So, as well as increasing the complexity of their utterances, upper intermediate learners need to learn that particular stresses, pauses and intonation can make simple expressions like 'Yes, but ...' and 'Well, OK, but look, ...' serve them very well in many business situations.

Skills-based approach

In Company is a practical course in *how* to do business in English. Each unit is a fast track to excellence in a particular business skill. Recognising that people need more than just phrase lists and useful language boxes to operate effectively in real-life business situations, each unit provides a substantial amount of guided skills work to give students the chance to fully assimilate the target language and 'make it their own', before going on to tackle fluency activities.

Target skills developed at this level include:
*   making a strong impression on clients, colleagues and business partners in social situations
*   introducing important business issues into general conversation
*   expressing informed views on topics of general business interest

- leading and influencing the outcome of cross-cultural meetings
- tackling everyday problems on the phone
- acquiring a professional e-mail writing style
- using the voice and visuals to their full potential in business presentations
- employing a range of rhetorical skills to get the message across
- dealing with crises and emergencies face to face and by teleconferencing
- being persuasive but diplomatic in negotiations

Why are the units divided into categories?

In Company Upper intermediate contains five types of unit: *Networking, Meetings, Presenting, Desk work* and *Talking points*. Categorising the units in this way means that you can teach the course in:

- *either* a **linear fashion**, starting at Unit 1 and finishing at Unit 18, selecting the most relevant material as you go, but knowing that you are varying your skills focus from lesson to lesson and covering all the key grammatical structures for this level.
- *or* a **modular way**, doing all the units in one category before moving on to the next, thereby ensuring that students see some real improvement in one area before going on to another.

The approach you choose will largely depend on your needs analysis with your class. Some students will have very clear ideas about their priorities and be able to agree in their group on the areas they would like to address first. Others may have no specific objectives but simply wish to improve their overall performance in English. The course is designed to cater for both types of student.

Within each category, you may want to consider the following:

Networking

Given the choice, most of us would prefer to do business with people we like. Networking and building business relationships are, therefore, important business skills and the focus of these units. Unit 1 is a good place to start with a new group because it addresses the difficulties of keeping up a conversation with relative strangers on whom you want to make a good impression. The other units in this category can be studied in any order.

Meetings

Meetings are endemic in business, but, of course, a lot will depend on the kind of meetings your students take part in. Unit 2 is the best one to start with as it provides communication techniques your students will certainly need later on in the course. Unit 6 increases students' communicative repertoire to include the necessary skills to chair a meeting and steer it to a successful conclusion. Unit 10 tackles the one fundamental skill all business people require: taking decisions. Unit 17 is more specialised, but nonetheless useful to anyone in business, not just professional negotiators.

Presenting

Thirty million business presentations are given every day and the ability to present effectively is a clear advantage in the competitive world of work. Unit 4 lays the foundations,

helping students to capitalise on the immense power of their voice and refer succinctly to any visual aids they wish to use. Unit 8 teaches them how to structure and sequence a team presentation, whilst Unit 13 shows them how to reorganise points and use rhetorical techniques to maximum effect.

Desk work

Business people now spend many hours on the phone and online, taking messages and sending e-mail. This places a new importance on listening acuity and writing skills. The units in this category can also be studied out of order. However, it is probably better to leave Unit 16 until last, as it brings together phone, e-mail and meeting skills.

Talking points

In these units the emphasis is on using the English students already have to discuss a topic of general business interest. These units tend to rotate around a text or texts, usually with accompanying listening work. There is some lexical input but no grammar focus. The topics, which include attitudes to money and success (Unit 3), information overload (Unit 7) and the ongoing globalisation debate (Unit 11), have been selected to generate animated conversation amongst learners from a wide range of business backgrounds. There is often an element of controversy to increase the level of involvement.

Lexical syllabus

In Company Upper intermediate devotes a lot of attention to lexis, showing students how to build words, many of which they may already know, into larger, multi-word items they may not know. For example:

- compounds – *search engine, help menu*
- collocations – *sharp rise, go out of production*
- noun phrases – *cost of living, rate of exchange*
- phrasal verbs – *sell out, buy up, cut back*
- discourse markers – *above all, by the way, to sum up*
- fixed expressions – *Leave it with me, I'll do my best, I'm afraid we'll have to break off here*
- idioms – *do your homework, don't get carried away*
- partial frameworks or scripts – *(a month) ago we were having difficulties with ..., which was also affecting ... and ..., not to mention ... . So, what was going wrong? Well, the problem we were facing was not ... but ... . Have a look at this ...*

Pre-constructed lexical chunks, like those above, are a crucial part of native-speaker interaction and, if carefully selected, can significantly speed up the language processing time of non-native speakers too, allowing them to sound more fluent and confident in situations they can predict they are likely to encounter.

Lexis, therefore, is given a prominent place in the units themselves and, in addition, students are referred to optional Lexis links, which effectively double the lexical input in each unit and can either be set for homework or made the basis of vocabulary-building lessons.

Throughout *In Company Upper intermediate* rather more attention is paid to the teaching of phrasal verbs and common idioms than was the case in the lower levels of the series. The aim here is to gradually build up students' ability to 'decode' phrases and expressions whose meaning cannot simply be worked out from their constituent parts, but which are, nevertheless, a common feature of natural spoken English. Students may not actually need to be able to produce such expressions themselves. Indeed, where they are working with other non-native speakers of English the occurrence of phrasal verbs and idioms will, of course, be much less frequent.

The reality is, however, that many students at upper intermediate level may be required to do business with native (or near-native) speakers, while having had little exposure to the idiomatic English such speakers use every day. There is much talk these days of aiming in the language teaching classroom for a less complex, more error-tolerant and essentially de-cultured 'international English'. While this makes a lot of sense at lower levels where the students simply want to get by, we can safely assume that 'international English' is precisely the kind of English our upper intermediate students already have. And, surely, one of the reasons people continue studying English at advanced levels is to start to engage with native speakers on their own terms. If this was not their aim, they would only need to maintain the English they have. At higher levels, therefore, a grasp of idiom and natural conversational English is an important part of maximising lexical power.

Some of the more difficult lexis in the skills material has been highlighted for pre-teaching. There is a variety of ways to approach this including: group discussion, peer teaching, definition/synonym matching, contextualisation, real-life examples etc.

Grammar syllabus

Of course, lexical chunks (be they collocations, fixed expressions, phrasal verbs or idioms) are only useful in so far as our students are able to produce them in real time, as and when they need them. When, for whatever reason, they are unable to do so, they will fall back on the generative power of grammar and the simplest words in their vocabulary to get the job done.

The approach in *In Company Upper intermediate* is to highlight target grammar as it naturally emerges in the activities, but there are no long detours in the units themselves into structural matters. The reasoning behind this is that students at this level have probably studied grammar quite extensively before, and the sort of short review that would comfortably fit into the units would not be sufficiently thorough to deepen their understanding. This is where the Grammar links come in. Thirteen Grammar links, cross-linked to the thirteen main skills-based units, systematically address the usual questions of time, tense, aspect, voice, clause structure, modality and conditionality, as well as broader areas such as reporting, rhetoric and diplomacy, where grammar becomes as much a matter of choice as of rules.

In the Grammar links students are encouraged to explore grammatical use and, to some extent, work out the rules for themselves. Where the formula was *teach–test* at lower levels of the *In Company* series, here a more challenging *test–teach* approach is taken. Grammatical features are usually presented contrastively. Practice exercises are more commonly text- or dialogue-based (rather than simply sentence-based) to give a feel for the discoursal role of different structures.

Class Cassettes and CDs

Throughout the course, substantial use is made of audio recordings both to input business expressions, target lexis and grammatical structures and to demonstrate subtler

communication skills in action. Indeed, very little of the language work is not presented or recycled in a recording.

In Company Upper intermediate contains a wealth of listening extracts for teachers to choose from – everything from business conversations and documentaries to interviews and vox pop, screenplays and famous speeches. We chiefly learn to speak by listening and it is important for students to realise that, whilst they should sometimes be listening for content, sometimes for language and sometimes just for pleasure, they are not expected to understand every word they hear or even to hear every word they listen to! Bearing this in mind when playing the listening material will keep your students motivated and engaged and allow the extracts to serve their purpose – to act as a bridge to listening to authentic spoken English in the real world.

The recordings feature both native and non-native speaker accents, providing the students with extensive exposure to real spoken English. There is frequently an element of humour in the recordings which, besides entertaining the students (and teacher), motivates them to listen again for things they missed the first time round. The target language in the units is printed in bold in the recording scripts.

How can I exploit the dialogues further?

Play some of the dialogues a second time and:
- pause the cassette after questions for students to recall or predict the response (if they write these down as they go, you can ask them to recall the questions as well at the end)
- pause the cassette after responses to questions and ask students to think of other possible responses
- pause the cassette in the middle of lexical chunks (collocations, fixed expressions) for students to complete them either orally or by writing them down
- ask students to speculate about the personalities of the speakers in the dialogue
- ask students if they have ever met/done business with anyone like the speakers
- ask students if they would have reacted differently to the speakers in the dialogue

Reading texts

The reading texts in *In Company Upper intermediate* have been chosen to involve, entertain and provoke students into lively discussion, as well as to contextualise key target vocabulary. Squeezing a text completely dry of all useful language usually demotivates a class, but many of the longer texts in *In Company Upper intermediate* are informationally and lexically rich and can usefully be revisited.

How can I exploit the texts further?

Try some of the following:
- students set each other questions on a text
- students set you questions on a text, and vice versa
- give students several figures from a text and ask them to recall the context in which they were mentioned
- read the text aloud but slur certain words/phrases and students ask for repetition/clarification
- students read/listen to a text and complete sentences to reflect their own reaction to it e.g. *I thought the point about … was interesting*; *I'm surprised that …*; *I'm not sure I agree with what it says about …*; *I'm not convinced that …*; *I completely disagree with the idea that …*

- give students the first half of 8–16 collocations and a time limit in which to search for the collocates
- give students a set of miscollocates and ask them to correct them by referring to the text
- students find expressions which mean the same as e.g. *incidentally = by the way, moreover = in addition; generally = by and large* or the opposite of e.g. *in practice/in theory, in general/in particular*
- give students a set of prepositions and ask them to scan the text for noun phrases/phrasal verbs/idioms which include those prepositions
- read out the text pausing in the middle of collocations/fixed expressions/idioms for students to predict the completions either by shouting out or writing down the answer

Fluency work

Each unit culminates in at least one fluency activity which draws on both the specific language presented in the unit and the wider linguistic resources of the students. Activity types include:

1 skills workouts, where students practise a specific micro-skill (such as paraphrasing or voice projection) in a semi-guided way
2 roleplays and simulations, where students are given a scenario to enact and perhaps some kind of 'personal agenda'
3 case studies, where students are confronted with an authentic business problem and then compare their solution with that of the actual company concerned
4 'framework' activities, where the students decide on the content for a presentation, e-mail or short report and the Student's Book provides them with a linguistic framework to help deliver that information

Thorough preparation is essential for types 2–4 and it may sometimes be advisable to carry out the actual fluency activity in a subsequent lesson, allowing plenty of time for feedback. And even in shorter pairwork activities, where an 'information gap' is not a vital element, you may find that your students perform much better if allowed to discuss and rehearse what they are going to say before they say it.

Care has been taken in the selection of fluency activities in *In Company Upper intermediate* to keep interest levels and motivation high by including two quite different kinds of task.

The first kind is the 'high content reality' task – one which closely resembles the sort of thing students routinely have to do in their work (solve problems on the phone, 'fight their corner' in a meeting, strike up a conversation with a fellow passenger on a plane, team present a new project). This kind of activity has the advantage of being immediately relevant to students' needs and can be further personalised and fine-tuned to even more closely match their real work situation. It is less roleplay than what Adrian Underhill has called 'realplay'.

The second kind of task is the 'low content reality' task – one which, though the scenario may be unfamiliar to the students (for example performing a scene from a movie, acting as politicians for a developing country, taking life-and-death decisions or negotiating a record deal for a rock band), nevertheless requires language and cognitive processing skills which are very much part of what they have to do in their work. The advantage of this kind of activity is that it encourages a greater degree of creativity and, being quite different from what students usually do, does not run the risk of being similar to a real work situation, but not quite similar enough – a common problem when you attempt to simulate real life in the classroom.

Some students will have a definite preference for one kind of activity over the other, but, in general, a balance of the two will prove most effective. Many management training courses are programmed so that participants progress from low content reality activities in the early stages to high content reality simulations at the end. For those of you who wish to follow this pattern, a wide range of alternative fluency activities are included in the Resource materials section at the back of this teacher's book.

A feedback sheet is also included to allow you to provide written feedback to individual students/groups (see page 185). The following aspects of students' performance can be highlighted in the 'good use of language' section:
- accurate use of grammar
- use of new vocabulary/expressions
- successful interaction/communication
- awareness of register
- good pronunciation
- accuracy in wrtitten work

Mark Powell
July 2004

Contents: Student's Book

3

1 Business or pleasure?

All things being equal, people will buy from a friend. All things being not quite so equal, people will still buy from a friend.

Mark McCormack, What They Don't Teach You at Harvard Business School

Discussion

1   Work with a partner and discuss the following questions.

   a   Is it easier to work with friends or more complicated?

   b   Would you be worried about doing business with a member of your family?

   c   How many of the people you work with do you mix with socially?

   d   When was the last time you had to attend an office party or business function? Did you have a good time?

   e   The Japanese spend $40 billion a year on corporate hospitality – almost as much as the country's annual defence budget! In what ways can entertaining clients and colleagues be good for business?

2   Complete the following extract from a corporate entertainment company's website using the words in the box. Are you persuaded by what it says?

service	team	experience	clients	seats	relationships
box	reception	setting	office	members	viewing

What better way to build and maintain (a) <u>relationships</u> with key (b) <u>clients</u> and to reward star (c) <u>members</u> of your (d) <u>team</u> than to offer them a unique and unforgettable (e) <u>experience</u> far away from the pressures and constraints of an (f) <u>office</u> environment? Whether it's front row (g) <u>seats</u> at the Metropolitan Opera in New York, a VIP (h) <u>box</u> at the World Cup Final, a private (i) <u>viewing</u> at the Guggenheim Gallery in Bilbao or a champagne (j) <u>reception</u> at the Paris Ritz, we can provide the ideal (k) <u>setting</u> and first-class (l) <u>service</u> that will leave your guests simply saying 'Wow!'

3   Work in two groups. Group A read about corporate events **a** and **b**, Group B events **c** and **d**.

Networking

1 Business or pleasure?

This unit is about corporate entertaining and making conversation. There is a strong focus on fluency and students practise the business skill of socialising. This will be especially appropriate with a new group.

Students first discuss socialising and study related lexis. They read short texts on corporate events and then share information in order to select an appropriate event for specific clients.

Students listen to business people socialising at corporate events and study the functional language from the recordings. They get fluency practice in the form of a game in which they have to avoid saying 'no'. Another two recordings provide further listening practice and the students study the language used in making conversation. The students then practise giving and receiving compliments and, in a final fluency activity, they use suitable topics of small talk to start and keep a conversation going.

The grammatical focus is on tenses and the lexical focus is on aspects of conversational English.

In this first section, students discuss socialising in business and then complete a gapped text taken from a corporate entertainment company's website. They read different texts about corporate social events and then pool their information in order to recommend an event for particular clients.

Warm-up

If this is a new class, have students interview each other about their job and free-time interests and list three memorable facts e.g. an interesting aspect of their job etc. Students then give a short presentation on their partner, including job title. This will act as an ice-breaker and help establish the professional role and interests of the students.

As a lead-in to the unit, get students to brainstorm what is important in establishing a business relationship e.g. the time to build up a rapport before doing business, frequent socialising etc.

Check/Pre-teach: *All things being equal*. Ask students to read the quotation by Mark McCormack. Ask if they agree that friendship is important in the commercial world in general.

Discussion

1 Lead in to the discussion by finding out who organises corporate entertaining in the students' company. Elicit a list of typical ways in which business visitors are entertained at local and national level e.g. lunch/dinner, theatre trips, sporting events. Ask students what their annual entertainment budget is and if they think it is worth spending the money. Then get the students to guess how much is spent on corporate hospitality in Japan in a year.

Students work in pairs or small groups to discuss questions a–e. Hold a feedback session, asking pairs to report back on anything interesting which they discussed. Elicit students' reaction to the Japanese budget figure in question e.

2 Write the following on the board: *service, environment, champagne*. Elicit some collocations e.g. *first-class/valet service, working environment, vintage champagne*.

Explain why collocation is important – it is a key feature of English and is essential in the development of fluency and so forms an important part of the lexical content of the course. Point out that collocation will help students do the gap-fill task. Elicit *to maintain relationships* as the answer for gap (a) and then get students to complete the task. Check the answers with the whole class. Ask students if they would use the corporate entertainment company and which event they would choose.

As a follow-up activity, write some of the collocations on the board and get students to use as many as possible in an anecdote: *to maintain relationships, key clients, star members, unforgettable experience, office environment, ideal setting, first-class service*.

3 Find out which students have made business or holiday trips to the UK. Elicit what impressed them as visitors and where they were entertained. If no-one has been to the UK, brainstorm some famous venues for leisure and sporting events. Include the following examples from the texts on page 5 if students don't give these: Silverstone – venue of the world-famous racing car event; Wimbledon – home of the lawn tennis championship; the London Eye – a high-tech ride which gives great views over London; Britannia – the former royal yacht now a tourist attraction in an Edinburgh dock; Tate Modern – a modern art gallery on the South Bank in London.

Before setting up the jigsaw reading activity, point out that the reading material in the course contains a wide range of lexically-rich and challenging texts. Encourage students to decide which words/expressions from each reading text they want to use as part of their *active* vocabulary and make a note of these, and which can be part of their larger, *receptive* vocabulary.

Focus attention on the texts on page 5. With stronger groups, tell students not to expect to know every word when they read, but remind them of useful strategies such as predicting the content and vocabulary, reading the text quickly first for gist and deducing meaning from context. With weaker groups, check/pre-teach: *to descend on, to soak up, glamorous, breathtaking, to clash, awesome, to roll out the red carpet* (give special treatment to a guest), *capsule, cutting-edge*.

Divide the class into AB groups. With larger classes, divide the class into two or more A and B groups. Ask students to read their texts and make notes of the key information about each of their events to use in the following task. Set a time limit to ensure students only focus on the main points.

Fluency

4 Check if any of the students organise/have organised corporate entertainment. If so, elicit what they need to think about first e.g. budget, finding out about the likes and dislikes of the visitors in advance, organising a guide/interpreter. Most students will have experienced corporate entertaining. Ask them which events they enjoyed and which were most successful and why.

Set up new groups, mixing A and B students, and rearrange the classroom seating to facilitate the meetings. Appoint or let students choose a chairperson for each group. Write the following agenda on the board:

Agenda

Aim: to choose corporate entertainment for different groups of visitors
1 Short presentations of the four possible events
2 Discussion of each event and final choice
3 Brainstorming and choice of suitable gifts

With weaker students, brainstorm the pro and cons of the four events before students start the meeting. Point out the factors which the students will need to consider e.g. cost, the fact that entertaining sales reps doesn't generate income but creates motivation, your current relationship with different clients, the value of potential business. Set a time limit for the meeting, encouraging students to move on if they cannot reach a consensus. Monitor and take feedback notes.

Ask the chairperson for each group to report their decisions to the rest of the class. While there are no 'correct' answers, students should justify their choices e.g. the Chinese delegation may enjoy a cultural event, the Dutch customer would need to go to a 'family' event etc. Similarly, there are no set answers for gifts, but possible options include: (a) a travel voucher for a weekend away for each rep, (b) a bottle of malt whisky for each engineer, (c) tickets for the theatre for the Chinese officials, (d) tickets for another sporting event or a guided city tour for the Dutch customer and family. Feed back on overall fluency before highlighting any important or common errors.

5 Ask the students to work with a new partner and discuss the questions. When students have completed the activity, elicit the most popular choice for the class as a whole.

a British Grand Prix, Silverstone

Engines roar, tyres squeal and sparks fly as two-million-dollar supercars accelerate from 0 to 250kph in under seven seconds. 200,000 spectators descend on Silverstone for this fabulous sporting occasion that attracts a worldwide TV audience of 350 million. From your trackside seat you'll soak up all the atmosphere of one of the most glamorous and spectacular events in the motor-racing calendar. VIP treatment; breathtaking action!

VIP box and hospitality tent: €1,000 per person

b All England Lawn Tennis Championships, Wimbledon

Experience the nail-biting climax to the world's premier international tennis tournament as the true giants of the game clash in the men's Wimbledon final. All the tradition of vintage champagne and strawberries and cream combine with 140-mile-an-hour serves and awesome cross-court shots to make what many consider to be the greatest sporting event on Earth. Game, set and match!

Men's final, lunch, champagne, music: €3,000 per person

c Banquet on board the Royal Yacht Britannia

Dinner on board Britannia is a once-in-a-lifetime experience – oysters and aperitifs, tables decorated with ice sculptures, waiters in white gloves and music played on the very piano Princess Diana used to practise on. You'll be seated in the state dining room where the Queen once entertained world leaders like Boris Yeltsin, Bill Clinton and Nelson Mandela. Why not really roll out the red carpet for your guests and make your corporate hospitality event a truly 'royal' occasion?

5-course dinner, military band, fireworks: €500 per person

d London Eye and Private Tour of Tate Modern

Your evening begins 130 metres above London in your very own capsule on the London Eye. A waiter serves champagne. On a clear day you can see for 25 miles – all the way to Windsor Castle. You are then transferred to the Tate Modern for a private tour of one of the world's most cutting-edge contemporary art galleries, followed by a superb dinner in the tasteful surroundings of the Level 2 Café. High altitude; high culture!

London Eye, tour of Tate Modern, dinner: €1,600 per party of 20

Fluency 4 Team up with people from the other group. You all work in the PR department of a British engineering company. Using the information you read in 3, hold a meeting to decide which would be the best event to invite each of the following to:

  a your top fifty sales reps and their partners

  b six Finnish engineers with whom you have just completed a very successful two-year project

  c a delegation of twelve Chinese government officials with whom you are currently negotiating an $80 million contract

  d the CEO of your biggest Dutch customer, her husband and teenage son

  Also think of a suitable gift you could give to each of your guests.

5 Which of the events would
  a you **b** your partner **c** the people in your department
  most enjoy?

Making conversation

1 ▭ 1.1 Listen to some business people chatting at two of the corporate events on page 5 and answer the questions.

Conversation 1

a What's the connection between Helen Keating, James McRae and Alan Sullivan?
They were all at a dinner together in Riyadh.

b When Helen asks James 'Mind if I join you?', how does he reply?
N _ot_ a _t_ a _ll_ . Be _____ my _____ guest .

c What excuse does Helen make for leaving the rest of the party?
She complains about the music.

d Two of the following mean 'That can't be true.' Which two?
You're joking! ☑   You're fooling! ☐   You're kidding! ☑

e Helen and James use several expressions to refer to memories. Can you remember the first three words of each expression? Contractions (_it's_, _you're_, etc.) count as **one** word.

1 _Have_ _we_ _met_ somewhere before?
2 _It's_ _not_ _like_ me to forget a face.
3 _I_ _thought_ _I_ recognised you.
4 _It's_ _all_ _coming_ back to me now.
5 _I_ _seem_ _to_ remember spending most of the evening fighting off some creepy little guy called Alan.

Conversation 2

a How would you describe relations between Mr Ishida and Mr Thompson?
warm ☐   amicable ☐   cordial ☐   cool ☐   strained ☑   frosty ☐

b Mr Thompson uses the word 'so' five times during the conversation:
So, Mr Ishida, let me freshen your glass.
So, how are you enjoying the match?
So, tell me, have you been to one of these big tournaments before?
So, do you still play?
So, shall we return to our seats?
Why does he need to use it so often? _to introduce a change of topic_
What's the equivalent word or expression in your own language?

c Mr Ishida says he's too old to play table tennis now. Mr Thompson replies 'Oh, I'm sure that's not true.'
Is he: paying Mr Ishida a compliment? ☑   calling him a liar? ☐

d Mr Thompson tries to use his background knowledge to keep the conversation going. Complete his remarks below.
1 I h _ear_ you're quite a tennis fan.
2 I u _nderstand_ the Japanese are world table tennis champions.
3 I s _ee_ the Nikkei's looking strong. That m _ust_ be good news for you.
4 I r _ead_ somewhere that things were improving. Or a _m_ I mistaken?

e What word is Mr Ishida avoiding by saying the following? _no_
Not at the moment, thank you.   Not really.   Not especially.
Not any more.   As a matter of fact, …

Making conversation

In this section, students listen to two recordings of business people socialising at two of the events on page 5 – the yacht Britannia and a Wimbledon tennis match. They focus on and practise the functional language used in the recordings. Students then play a game in order to say avoid saying 'no'.

Two recordings of business people socialising at Tate Modern and the British Grand Prix provide further listening practice. The students focus on some of the useful expressions used when making general conversation. They then practise giving and receiving compliments. The unit ends with a fluency activity in which students practise keeping up a conversation.

1 ▣ **1.1** Lead in to this section by asking students how they rate themselves as socialisers on a scale of 1–10. Ask if they are generally relaxed at corporate parties and events, or tense and a bit insecure.

Conversation 1

Get students to read through the questions for conversation 1 first. With weaker students, ask the following gist questions and play the recording through once to check: *Where are the speakers?* (on the yacht Britannia), *How do they know each other?* (they met at a conference), *What is the tone of their conversation?* (friendly). Play the recording and get students to note down their answers to questions a–e. If necessary, play the recording again, pausing at intervals to allow students to listen for anything they missed. Students check their answers in pairs and then check the answers with the whole class.

Conversation 2

Give students time to read through the questions for conversation 2. Check they can paraphrase *amicable, cordial, strained* and *frosty*. For weaker students, ask the following gist question and play the recording through once to check: *What is the main mistake made by Mr Thompson's marketing staff?* (they told him Mr Ishida likes tennis when he in fact never watches it). Repeat the same procedure as for conversation 1, pausing the recording and allowing the students to check their answers before doing a whole class check.

Focus students' attention on the recording script on page 140. Check pronunciation and intonation of the key language in bold in each of the scripts. Get students to practise some of this language by writing cues on the board and getting students to complete the expressions e.g. *Have we...?, It's not like me to ..., I thought I ... / I hear..., I understand ..., I read somewhere ...* Set up a mingling activity with a time limit of two minutes. Ask students to talk to as many of their classmates as possible using the key language from the recordings. Monitor and take feedback notes. Feed back on language errors and highlight intonation problems by marking the correct intonation over the sentence in a different colour.

▣ **1.1**
Conversation 1
A: Hi, mind if I join you?
B: Er, **not at all. Be my guest**.
A: Only if I have to sit through 'Rule Britannia' by the Band of the Royal Scots Dragoon Guards once more I think I'll scream.
B: And I thought you Americans were supposed to like all that traditional British stuff.
A: Yeah, well, you can have too much of a good thing. Thought I'd come out here and enjoy the view. I must say, though, it was an excellent dinner. Fabulous ship too.
B: Yes, isn't it? I'm James McRae, by the way. BP, engineering division.
A: Hello, James. I'm ...
B: Helen Keating. Exxon Mobil.
A: Yes, how did you ... oh ... ? **Have we met somewhere before?**
B: We have indeed, but I obviously failed to make much of an impression.
A: Wait a minute. **It's not like me to forget a face**. I know – Riyadh. The Petrochemicals Conference. **I thought I recognised you**.
B: As matter of fact, we had dinner together.
A: **You're kidding!** Now, I think I would have remembered that.
B: Well, there were rather a lot of us in the group. At least forty. I don't think we actually spoke.

A: Aha. OK. Yes, **it's all coming back to me now. I seem to remember** spending most of the evening fighting off some creepy little guy called Alan.
B: Alan Sullivan. My boss.
A: Oops! I'm sorry. I didn't mean to ...
B: No problem. He's not my favourite person either. Anyway, Helen, looks like we've got the best part of the Royal Yacht to ourselves this evening. How about another drink?
A: OK. Why not? I'll have another Armagnac. Oh, look, the fireworks are starting!
B: So they are. I'll be right back.

Conversation 2
A: **So, Mr Ishida, let me freshen your glass**.
B: Thank you. I'm fine.
A: Some more strawberries, then, perhaps?
B: Er, **not at the moment, thank you**.
A: I am sorry about this weather. Typical English summer, I'm afraid. The forecast did say we might have showers. But I'm sure it'll blow over in half an hour or so. **So, how are you enjoying the match?**
B: Ah, very entertaining, I'm sure ...
A: Good. Splendid ... **So, tell me, have you been to one of these big tournaments before?** The American Open perhaps?
B: Ah, no, I haven't.
A: Ah. But **I hear** you're quite a tennis fan, though.
B: Er, **not really**. In fact, I never watch tennis normally.

A: Oh, ... I see. My marketing people must have made a mistake.
B: Maybe they meant table tennis. I used to play for my university in Tokyo – many years ago.
A: Table tennis! Ah, yes. **I understand** the Japanese are world table tennis champions, isn't that right?
B: **As a matter of fact**, that's the Chinese.
A: Ah, yes, of course ... Erm, **so, do you still play?**
B: **Not any more**. Much too old for running around now.
A: Oh, **I'm sure that's not true**.
B: I assure you it is true, Mr Thompson. Bad heart, you see. Doctor's orders.
A: Oh, right. Sorry. Erm, ... **I see** the Nikkei's looking strong. **That must be** good news for you.
B: **Not especially**. For Japan economic recovery is still a long way off.
A: Oh? **I read somewhere** that things were improving. **Or am I mistaken?**
B: Over-optimism, I'm afraid.
A: Ah, well, I suppose, er ... Oh, look, the rain's stopped! Yes, the players are coming back on. Excellent. **So, shall we return to our seats?**
C: Quiet, please. Hewitt to serve. Hewitt leads by three games to two and by two sets to love.

Fluency

2 Ask the following questions as a lead-in: *What effect does saying 'no' have in your language? Is it acceptable, or considered over-direct? What is your experience with the way native speakers use 'no'? Have you noticed a difference between say UK and US speakers?* Point out that when you do not know someone well, 'no' is sometimes too direct in British English, whereas this can be less of a problem in American English.

Before playing the game, give students three minutes to write down their eight sentences. Monitor and be ready to help weaker students with examples/ideas e.g. *I've lived in (Mexico City), I've worked in (advertising all my life)* etc. Focus students' attention on the useful expressions. Explain that these are all alternatives to saying 'no'. Model the intonation of each of the expressions and get students to repeat, checking they don't sound flat/uncommunicative. If appropriate, record the students and play them back to highlight how they sound.

Demonstrate the game with a confident student first. Divide the class into pairs and get them to swap their lists of statements. Students play the game, working with a new partner when someone loses. Monitor and take feedback notes.

Get students to feed back on the task. Ask how successful they were in avoiding saying 'no' and how they felt – awkward or quite confident. Then give feedback on overall fluency before highlighting any important or common errors.

3 🔲 **1.2** Before playing the recording, remind students of the other two corporate events on page 5 – the Grand Prix and a visit to Tate Modern – and explain that these are the contexts for the following two recordings.

Conversation 1

Check that the students know what the Turner prize is (the controversial prize awarded in the field of modern/contemporary art. Radical prize winners have included a sculpture which was a pile of bricks! Many people are not convinced this is art.) Check/Pre-teach: *laundry, heap, dying to do something.*

Use question a as a pre-listening question. Play the recording through once and let students compare their answers. Elicit the difference in attitude between Fiona and Alistair (neither of them is enjoying the exhibition but Fiona says what she thinks and is somewhat sarcastic; Alistair wants to give a good impression and is more tolerant.)

Ask students to read the questions b–e and answer them as far as they can from memory. Play the recording again and allow students to complete their answers. They then check their answers in pairs before checking with the whole class.

Ask students why they think native speakers can do exercise b quickly. Explain that these expressions exist as 'chunks' which native speakers can access automatically; non-native speakers frequently need to build these up step-by-step.

🔲 **1.2**

Conversation 1

A: Alistair, we've been here nearly three hours! Can't we just make our excuses and go? You know how I hate these things.

B: Look, Fiona, I'm not enjoying myself any more than you are, but this is business. Besides, I need to speak to Julian about this Internet advertising idea of his.

A: Oh, all right. Where is Julian, anyway? We haven't seen him all evening …

C: Hello! You must be Julian's guests. I don't think we've met. I'm Dan Wilson, Creative Director at JJK Advertising. I work with Julian.

B: Ah, pleased to meet you, Mr Wilson. No, we've not met. **Julian's mentioned your name, of course**. Alistair Hamilton. And this is my wife, Fiona.

C: **A pleasure to meet you both at last.** And **please call me Dan.**

A: **We were just wondering** what this pile of dirty laundry was doing in the middle of an art gallery.

B: Fiona!

C: So, you're not a fan of contemporary art then, Fiona – **you don't mind me calling you Fiona, do you?** Actually, this, er, 'dirty laundry', as you call it, came second in this year's Turner Prize, believe it or not.

A: Doesn't surprise me in the least, but, er, still just looks like dirty laundry to me, I'm afraid.

C: Well, yes, but I don't think that's what the artist would call it.

A: What does he call it, then?

C: Erm, I'm not sure. I'll check the catalogue for you … Here we are – erm, exhibit 12, oh, 'Dirty Laundry'.

A: What did I tell you?

C: Yes, quite. Erm, Alistair, **I wonder if we could have a word?** Julian tells me you're not very happy with the new Internet campaign.

B: Er, yes. **Would you excuse us a moment, Fiona?** Dan and I need to talk.

A: Oh, don't mind me. There's the heap of broken glass in the room next door I'm just dying to see.

B: Er, right. Well, **I'll catch you later**, then … Now, look, Dan, the thing is …

2 Work with a partner. Practise avoiding saying 'no'.

The no-no game

Prepare
- Write down eight false (but believable) statements about yourself, your job, your family, your interests, your company or your country. When you are ready, swap lists with a partner.

Play
- Imagine the two of you are chatting at a conference or corporate event. Take it in turns to make wrong assumptions about each other using the lists as a starting point but adding remarks of your own if you can.

  e.g. **I hear** you're based in Rotterdam.

  I understand you're a keen golfer.

  I believe your company's about to be involved in a merger.

  I read somewhere that Russia will be joining the EU soon.

- Your objective is to get the other person to say 'no'. Their objective is the same. Use the expressions opposite to help you avoid saying 'no'.
- Whoever says 'no' first loses.

Useful expressions
- Not very.
- Not really.
- Not especially.
- Not exactly.
- Not yet.
- Not any more.
- Not at the moment.
- Not as far as I know.
- Actually, ...
- As a matter of fact, ...

3 1.2 Listen to some business people chatting at the other two corporate events on page 5 and answer the questions.

Conversation 1

a What sort of people are the Hamiltons? Compare your impressions with a partner. (suggested answer) posh, irritating, she's fussy, he's long-suffering

b Put the words in the following greetings and introductions in the correct order.

1 Dan call please me

Please call me Dan.

2 meet last to both pleasure at a you

A pleasure to meet you both at last.

3 mentioned name Julian's course your of

Julian's mentioned your name, of course.

4 Fiona calling me mind do don't you you you?

You don't mind me calling you Fiona, do you?

c It's common when someone joins a group at a party to tell them a bit about the conversation you've just been having. Complete the following:

talking	wondering	discussing	saying	trying

We were just

- saying what a marvellous party this is.
- discussing these new tax laws they're bringing in.
- talking about you – how are things?
- wondering what this pile of dirty laundry was doing in an art gallery.
- trying to work out what this whole thing must have cost.

d Why does Dan say to Alistair 'I wonder if we could have a word?' when they're already talking? He wants to speak to him in private.

e All the expressions below mean 'I'm going'. Which also mean 'but I'm coming back'? Some of them were in the conversation you just listened to.

It's been nice talking to you. ☐   Would you excuse me a moment? ☑

I'll have to be going. ☐   I'll be right back. ☑

If you'll excuse me. ☐   Is that the time? ☐

Don't go away. ☑   I'll catch you later. ☑

Conversation 2 **a** Do Tom and Ricardo do a deal? _No_____

b What expression does Tom use to switch from discussing motor racing to discussing business?

T_alking___ o_f_____ races, how's the South African bid going?

c Complete the expressions below. They were all in the conversation you just listened to. Contractions (*I'd, wouldn't, who's,* etc.) count as **one** word.

1 Glad __you____ _could_____ make it.

2 I _wouldn't__have_____ missed it for the world.

3 There's _someone_ _I'd_____ like you to meet.

4 Can't _have____ _you_____ standing there with an empty glass.

5 So, _who's____ _this_____ person you wanted me to meet?

6 I _see_____ _you_____ two know each other already.

7 I'll _leave____ _you_____ two to chat. See you later.

d What do the following remarks tell you about Ricardo and Élise's relationship?
_They used to have a very close friendship._____

Lexis link

for more on conversation see page 101

Long time no see.

You haven't changed a bit.

Neither have you. Charming as ever.

Ricardo and I go back a long way.

I'll have whatever you're having.

Fluency **4** Work with a partner. Practise paying and receiving compliments.

The mutual appreciation game

Prepare
- Spend a few minutes thinking of compliments you could pay your partner. Use the expressions opposite to help you.

Play
- When you are ready, start exchanging compliments with your partner. Respond to each compliment you receive in an appreciative but modest way. See who can give the most compliments in under two minutes!
- Join the rest of your group and report some of the compliments you've been giving. e.g.

I was just saying how nice Alain's new haircut looks.

I was just telling Yvonne what a marvellous tan she's got.

Useful expressions
- You're looking as ... as ever/usual today!
- What a brilliant/fantastic/fabulous ...!
- You know, that/those ... really suit(s) you!
- I (really) like your ...! Where did you get it/them?
- By the way, you did a great job in the meeting/presentation the other day.
- In fact, I must say you're one of the ...*est* people I've ever met. And I'm not just saying that. I (really) mean it!

Discussion **5** They say 'Flattery will get you everywhere.' How important is it in your culture to

a pay people personal compliments?

b compliment them on their work?

Does it depend on how well you know each other? Is it different for men and women?

Conversation 2

Again, use question a as a pre-listening question. Play the recording once and elicit the answer. Ask students to read the questions b–d and answer them from memory. Play the recording a second time and allow students to complete their answers. Allow students to check in pairs and then check answers with the whole class.

As a follow-up activity, refer students to the recording scripts of conversations 1 and 2 on pages 140–1 and point out that the key language is in bold. Play the recording again while students listen and follow the script. Get them to focus in particular on the stress and intonation of the language in bold. Write some of the expressions on the board and have the students mark in the stress and intonation.

Direct students' attention to the Lexis link on page 101 for more practice on conversational English.

Fluency

4 Ask students the last time they were paid a compliment. Tell students they are going to play a light-hearted game, practising giving and receiving compliments. Give students time to think of compliments they could pay their partner. With weaker students, brainstorm ideas e.g. colours/style of clothes/hair, personality traits, attractive belongings, abilities/skills, and elicit specific examples relevant to the group.

Focus attention on the useful expressions and check stress and intonation. Ask two confident students to demonstrate the game first. Then divide the class into pairs, getting students to work with a new partner if appropriate. Set a time limit of about two minutes and get students to play the game. Elicit examples of some of the compliments students gave or received.

Discussion

5 Check/Pre-teach: *flattery* and get students to read the questions. Do the activity as a whole-class discussion or with larger classes, divide the students into groups. If appropriate, ask follow-up questions e.g. *How genuine do you think compliments are when given at work? Would you compliment your boss? What 'rules' on giving compliments would you give to a visitor to your country?* Point out that in Britain, it is not usually acceptable for a man to compliment a woman on her figure or even what she is wearing unless they are close friends and/or longstanding colleagues. It is fine for a woman to compliment another woman on the way she looks, or to comment in a fairly neutral way on a man's appearance.

▭ 1.2

Conversation 2

A: Ricardo! **Glad you could make it.**

B: Hello, Tom. **I wouldn't have missed it for the world.** It's not every day I get invited to something like this. I hear Schumacher's out, so it should be a good race.

A: Yes, it certainly evens things up a bit with Ferrari down to one car. **Talking of** races, how's the South African bid going? I heard it was just between you and Swedish Steel now.

B: Hm, yes, the negotiations are still going on, but we're hopeful. I don't think the Swedes can beat us on price.

A: Well, let me know how it goes. We'd be happy to organise the transportation if you need it. We'd do you a good deal.

B: Sure, I'll certainly keep you in mind if we win the contract.

A: Great … Ricardo, **there's someone I'd like you to meet.**

B: Oh, really?

A: Yes, but first let me get you something to drink. **Can't have you standing there with an empty glass.** What are you on? Champagne?

B: Just mineral water for now, thanks.

A: Oh, dear … Here you go.

B: Thanks. **So, who's this person you wanted me to meet?**

A: Ah, yes … Oh, here she is now. Élise, this is Ricardo Piquet. Ricardo, Élise de Cadenet. Élise is …

C: Hello, Ricardo. **Long time no see.** What is it, five years?

B: Hello, Élise. Must be five at least. **You haven't changed a bit.**

C: **Neither have you. Charming as ever.**

A: Ah, **I see you two know each other already.**

C: **Ricardo and I go back a long way**, Tom. A very long way.

B: Yes, actually, we first met in Monaco – at the Grand Prix, funnily enough … So, Élise, last I heard you were getting married again.

C: And divorced again. I'm between husbands at the moment. Far too busy setting up this new business in Biarritz.

A: Er, well, **I'll leave you two to chat. See you later.** Don't forget the race starts at three.

B: Yes, see you later, Tom. So, Élise, how about a drink?

C: Mm, sounds good. **I'll have whatever you're having.**

B: Er, waiter, two champagnes, please.

Fluency

6 Ask students if they have heard of Dale Carnegie's famous book *How to win friends and influence people?* (This people skills book was first published in 1937 and sold about 15 million copies. Carnegie's advice is to make people feel important and appreciated. The implication for business is that financial success has as much to do with these people skills as with professional knowledge.) Elicit students' reaction to the statement from the book.

Set the scene for the activity by creating a space for the party and putting on some background music. Bring in glasses of water for students to hold/serve if appropriate.

Ask students to brainstorm acceptable 'small talk' topics and write up the subjects on the board. Students then check their ideas against the list on page 9. Divide the class into AB pairs. Student A reads page 126 and student B reads page 128. If you have an odd number of students, assign two students the same role. Check with the A students that they understand that they have to initiate the questions and with the B students that they have to appear unenthusiastic apart from when talking about their 'hot buttons'. Note that the students will change roles in the next activity.

Focus attention on the conversation starters and give the A students a short time to formulate some ideas. With weaker students, check they know how they can continue each question by eliciting examples as a whole-class activity.

Get students to mingle as if at a real party and play the game. Monitor and take feedback notes. Leave the feedback until after exercise 7.

7 Make sure students keep the same partners as in exercise 6. Student A reads page 126 and student B reads page 128. Check with the A students that they understand that they want to talk about their favourite 'hot button' topic and with the B students that they want to move the conversation on to different topics. Students mingle again to do the activity. Monitor and take feedback notes.

Before giving feedback, ask students to evaluate how successful they were at keeping the conversation going. Ask which topics the students found were easiest to talk about and why. Elicit examples of what they did when the conversation dried up and if they felt embarrassed.

Give feedback on overall fluency and how successful students were in keeping the conversation going. Then feed back on any important or common errors.

Direct students' attention to the Grammar link on page 100 for more information and practice on tenses.

If you're short of time

Omit exercises 3–5 on pages 4–5.

Omit *The mutual appreciation game* on page 8.

6   According to Dale Carnegie, author of the all-time best-selling people skills book *How to Win Friends and Influence People*, 'You can make more friends in two months by becoming interested in other people than you can in two years by trying to get people interested in you.' Work with a partner to practise keeping up a conversation.

Speaker A see page 126. Speaker B see page 128.

The hot buttons game

Conversation starters	Topics
1 How are you enjoying ...? Do you attend a lot of these things?	the event
2 Isn't this weather ...? Apparently, the forecast is for ...	the weather
3 How's business? I hear ...	work
4 Have you heard about ...? ... news, isn't it?	recent news
5 I see the stock markets are ... It's probably a good time to put your money into ...	the economy
6 Are you into (sport) at all? Did you see the game/match on ...?	sport
7 What kind of music are you into? Have you heard ...'s latest album?	music
8 Do you know ..., by the way? S/he's a bit/very ..., isn't s/he?	mutual friends
9 Have you seen any good films lately? I quite liked that one with (actor) in ... oh, what was it called?	movies
10 Do you get to do much travelling? Have you ever been to ...? I've always wanted to go there.	travel
11 Have you seen those new ...? I wonder if they're any good? Because I heard ...	gadgets
12 I like your ..., by the way. Where did you get it/them? I suppose it/they must have cost you ...?	clothes/jewellery
13 Have you been away on holiday this year? Anywhere nice? I was/We were planning to go to ...	holidays
14 Shall we get ourselves ...? What do you fancy? How about ...?	food/drink

Grammar link

for more on tenses see page 100

7   Have the conversation again – this time the situation has changed a little. Speaker A see page 126. Speaker B see page 128.

Meetings are called by **managers** who get lonely. *Sue Gaulke, management trainer*

1 Roughly how much of your working week do you spend in meetings?

Discussion **2** Which of the following attitudes is closer to your own? Indicate your position on the scale below and compare with a partner.

Meetings: where the real work gets done! ⟷ Meetings: a practical alternative to work!

3 Read the article below. Would you have liked to work for Harold Geneen? Is he anything like your boss?

THE MEETING MAN

Harold Geneen

The average executive spends half their life in meetings. If there was a king of meetings, it would have to be former ITT chief, Harold Geneen, a remorselessly driven workaholic who believed that facts and analytical rigour could – and surely would – conquer all.

Every month more than fifty ITT executives flew from all over the world to Brussels to spend four days poring over the figures. Clocks in the meeting remained resolutely on New York time. The room housed a 90-foot long table. The curtains were drawn and the executives survived on a diet of hamburgers and statistics.

The shareholders didn't complain. Between 1959 and 1977, when Geneen was chief executive, ITT's sales went from $745 million to nearly $28 billion.

Business Life magazine

Collocations **4** Some of the things you might discuss in an information-sharing meeting are listed below, but the second word in each collocation has been switched with another. Switch them back. The first two have been done for you.

production **margins**
balance **appraisals**
market **channels**
staff **sheets**
profit **methods**
distribution **trends**

quality **campaigns**
sales **chains**
advertising **control**
cost **development**
supply **projections**
product **cutting**

customer **budgets**
recruitment **setting**
salary **support**
training **relations**
price **procedures**
IT **reviews**

Discussion **5** Use the template below to help you talk about the meetings you attend. Use some of the phrases in 4 or choose others that are more relevant to your own line of business.

> Well, a lot of the meetings I go to these days tend to be about _____ and usually that will involve discussing things like _____. The most important figures we look at are _____. So I'll probably have to prepare _____ and issue copies before the meeting. If there's any real disagreement, it will generally be about _____. But, frankly, the worst thing about the meetings is _____.

Meetings 2 Exchanging information

This unit is the first to focus on the language of meetings. Most business English students attend meetings at work. Many will attend meetings in English, with native speakers and also non-native speakers. Students may need to draw on a range of language and skills to ensure a successful outcome to a meeting, so the sequence of four units on meetings provides a wide range of language input and encourages students to develop key communication skills.

Students start with a discussion of their personal views on business meetings and then read a short article about Harold Geneen, the somewhat controversial former boss of American giant ITT. They focus on key collocations related to information-sharing before discussing the content of their own meetings.

Students focus on the language used in paraphrasing and also practise expressing vague language more directly. A listening task gives practice in spotting discrepancies, followed by a fluency task with the same aim. Students then practise using complex numbers.

The students then focus on complex question/sentence forms with the aim of probing for further information, listen to a recording of part of a meeting and work on collocations and conditional forms. In the final sections, students listen to extracts from a further meeting and then study the language used. They personalise and practise these expressions through a dialogue-building task before participating in a final fluency activity.

The grammatical focus is on conditional forms and the lexical focus is on the language of meetings.

In this first section, students think about their own involvement in meetings. They read a short article about 'the king of meetings', Harold Geneen, and focus on a range of useful collocations.

Warm-up

Read out the quotation from the management trainer, Sue Gaulke. Ask students what they think she means and if they agree that meetings are often more of a social occasion than a way to achieve things.

Discussion

1   Ask students how much time they spend in meetings in a week. Then ask *What exactly is a meeting?* and elicit ideas from the students e.g. some people feel that informal discussions with colleagues count as meetings; others think that meetings should always have an agenda and always finish with an action plan.

2   Ask students to mark their position on the line and then compare with a partner. Elicit a range of answers to establish the general class view. Alternatively, draw a

line on the board and write the phrases from the book at each end. Invite the students to come out to the front of the class and mark their cross on the scale. Then ask some of the students to justify their viewpoint.

3   Tell students the short article is about someone who could have been called 'the king of meetings' whose recipe for success was 'the old-fashioned virtues of hard work, honesty and risk-taking'. ITT (International Telephone and Telegraph) embarked on an ambitious buying spree under Geneen, making more than 250 acquisitions – some hostile – in the 1960s and 1970s.

Check/Pre-teach: *remorselessly, rigour, to conquer, resolutely.* Students read the article and then discuss their reactions to Geneen's working methods. Ask follow-up questions e.g. *Do you agree that executives spend half of their life in meetings? Do you know of any other workaholics who are as driven as Geneen? Do you know of similar approaches to business, where profits are all?*

As an optional follow-up activity, ask students to work in small groups to choose another leader who achieved a remarkable change in company fortune. They can search the Internet for information, briefly report back to the class and justify their choice.

Collocations

4   Write *production margins* and *profit methods* on the board. Ask students to say what is wrong with the expressions (the second word in each pair has been switched round) and to give the correct collocations. Get students to continue finding the correct collocations in exercise 4. Then check the answers with the class.

Tell the students that many of these collocations constitute core business language and they need to ensure they can use them. Check pronunciation of the compounds, highlighting difficult words like *campaign, budget* and *recruitment.* Get students to mark in the correct stress.

Discussion

5   Divide the class into small groups. Ensure that people from the same company work with colleagues from different departments. If students are in the same department, ask them to do the task with someone they do not work closely with on a daily basis. Ask students to complete the template, either using some of the collocations in exercise 4 or expressions linked with their own business. Encourage students to tell each other about the meetings they attend. As a follow-up activity, ask students to report back on their discussion and establish the most common topic for meetings in the group.

Making things clear

In this section, students practise the skill of paraphrasing through matching a set of indirect statements with their more direct equivalents. They listen to an extract from a meeting in order to check their answers and then practise responding to indirect statements in a more direct way. They listen to a series of short extracts from meetings which contain discrepancies and then do a fluency task to practise spotting discrepancies. The section ends with a series of short exercises on complex numbers and figures.

Paraphrasing

1   Write up these two sentences on the board: *We will be looking at the possibility of downsizing.* and *People may lose their jobs.* Ask what the sentences have in common (they both state that people may be made redundant, but the first is euphemistic and the second is more direct). Ask students which style of expression is preferred in the culture/company where they work and if they have experienced any difficulties in interpreting 'vague' language. Ask students to match the lists of statements.

2   **▭ 2.1** With weaker groups, check/pre-teach: *dismally, to overreact, innovative, redundancies.* Tell students they are going to listen to an extract of a meeting to check their answers in exercise 1. Play the recording through once, pausing after each example of paraphrasing if necessary.

    Play the recording again, pausing after each of the vague phrases and eliciting the more direct wording that follows. This will help prepare students for the next activity.

3   Write up the four expressions in the box on the board and ask the students to mark the main stress. Highlight the technique of echoing a word/phrase to show surprise/disgust e.g. *Not a complete success? What you mean is ... .* Divide the class into pairs and ask students to read and respond to the vague statements from exercise 1. Encourage students who are giving the more direct equivalents to cover exercise 1 and work from memory and/or use their own wording.

Spotting discrepancies

4   **▭ 2.2** Write the word *discrepancy* on the board and point out a frequent use in accountancy – *a discrepancy in figures.*

    Check/Pre-teach: *appraisal, to go on about, overspend, confidential.* Note that there is a short beep in each extract for you to pause the recording and give students time to discuss the discrepancy. With stronger groups, play the first extract, pausing at the beep, and elicit the discrepancy as a class example. Then play the rest of the recording, pausing at each beep, and have students complete the task. Check the answers with the class. With weaker groups, play the five extracts through once and ask students to list the main topic of each discussion but do not mention the discrepancy at this stage (1 appraisals, 2 salary increases, 3 project budget and schedule, 4 main markets, 5 bringing in an outside

consultant). Then play the recording again, pausing at each beep, and ask students to spot the discrepancies.

Refer students to the recording script on page 141 and ask them to focus on the structures in bold. Elicit which tense is used to question each discrepancy (Past Simple) and draw students' attention to the use of the negative question *Didn't you say ...?*

Fluency

5   Some students are quite reticent to point out discrepancies to other speakers, so review polite ways of doing this: *Sorry, I thought you said ..., Hold on a second, didn't you just say ...?, Wait a minute. You just said ..., didn't you?* Check pronunciation and highlight the need for contrastive stress by using some of the examples in recording script 2.2: *You said we pay twice as much, not three times.*

    Divide the class into AB pairs. Refer the A students to page 126 and the B students to page 128. Give students time to read their reports, giving help with vocabulary and pronunciation as necessary.

    Model the activity by asking one student to read the first few lines of their report and asking the class to highlight the discrepancies. Refer students to the useful language boxes in each role card.

    Monitor and take feedback notes. If students fail to spot all seven discrepancies, ask them to repeat the task. Give feedback on how well students handled the interruptions and on overall fluency before highlighting any important or common language errors.

Number crunching

6   **▭ 2.3** Get the students to work together and agree on how to say the numbers. Then play the recording to check. Be ready to give the students a quick drill to practise the stress and pronunciation on the longer phrases e.g. *twelve and a half billion dollars.*

7   Students in pairs work together to match the figures with the description. Check the answers with the class. Ask students to underline the expressions they are most likely to need to refer to numbers in their own job.

8   Ask students to write down some important figures in their job e.g. number of employees, annual turnover, percentage ratio of men to women in the company etc. With weaker students, elicit an example from a stronger student or use your own set of figures to model the task. Students work in pairs or small groups to explain the significance of their figures to a partner.

    As an optional follow-up task, ask students to look at the economic data page in *The Financial Times* or at the back of *The Economist* magazine and to give a brief oral summary of the key figures.

See page T12 for recording scripts 2.1, 2.2 and 2.3.

Making things clear

Paraphrasing

1 In meetings, people are sometimes reluctant to say exactly what they mean – especially if they have bad news! Match the vague statements to their blunter equivalents.

Vague	Blunt
a I'm sorry to report that the project has not been a complete success.	**1** Our assembly plant may be closed down too.
b Technically speaking, we have run into negative profit.	**2** Sales are falling.
c I think there's a general lack of consumer confidence.	**3** People are going to lose their jobs.
d You know we've always been a market-driven organisation.	**4** It's failed.
e Now is not the time to expand, but to consolidate.	**5** We'll have to hold another meeting!
f There will have to be some restructuring of the department.	**6** We've made a loss.
g We may also have to consider outsourcing production to cut costs.	**7** Let's do nothing.
h Of course, we won't be able to finalise anything today.	**8** We've never had an original idea.

2 ▣ 2.1 A computer games company has had problems with its latest product. Listen to an extract from their meeting and check your answers in 1.

3 Work with a partner. Take it in turns to read out the vague statements in 1 in random order. The other person should respond in a more direct way using the expressions below.

> You mean ...   What you (really) mean is ...
> In other words ...   So what you're (really) saying is ...

Spotting discrepancies

4 ▣ 2.2 Listen to short extracts from five meetings. Each contains one piece of information that doesn't make sense. After each extract, turn to a partner and decide what the discrepancy is. Then listen again and check.

Fluency

5 Work with a partner to practise pointing out discrepancies. Speaker A see page 126. Speaker B see page 128.

Number crunching

6 ▣ 2.3 How do you say the following numbers? Compare with a partner, then listen and check.

a 12^{1/2}$bn	**c** $^{2}/_{3}$	**e** 4:1	**g** 298m^3	**i** 400Gb
b €580,753	**d** $8,491	**f** 1.05km^2	**h** ¥52–58m	**j** 0.0012%

7 Which of the figures in 6 is:

a six-figure sum? [b]

a round figure? [i]

in excess of 12 billion? [a]

expressed as a ratio? [e]

somewhere in the region of 300? [g]

accurate to two decimal places? [f]

just under 8$^{1/2}$K? [d]

a fraction? [c]

a negligible proportion? [j]

a rough estimate/a ballpark figure? [h]

8 Write down some key figures in your job and explain their significance to a partner.

Queries and comments

1 Read the following extract from a meeting. A CEO is breaking some bad news to the board. Write in the board members' queries and comments using the notes in brackets to help you. The first one has been done for you.

A OK, everyone. It's bad news, I'm afraid. As you may have heard, the latest European sales figures are looking extremely disappointing.

B (say/fall short/projections again?) _Are you saying they've fallen short of projections again?_ (a)

A I'm afraid so. In fact, we may be 30% down. Now, this will be the third quarter in a row we've missed our targets and, frankly, unless things pick up considerably next quarter, we may have to rethink our whole pricing strategy.

C (suggest/introduce/price cuts?) _Are you suggesting we introduce price cuts?_ (b)

A If we still can, Anna. Certainly if we'd done that a year ago, it might have stimulated demand. But do it now and we may end up running at a loss. As you know, we're barely breaking even on some of our product lines as it is.

D (surely/not say/time/phase them out!) _Surely you're not saying it's time to phase them out!_ (c)

A No, no, of course not. At least, not yet. But what I am saying is that we need to keep production costs down somehow if we want to remain competitive.

B (this mean/should/invest more/new technology?) _Does this mean we should be investing more in new technology?_ (d)

A If only it was that simple, Erik. But right now we're not really in a position to invest in anything, even if we wanted to. No, I'm afraid the situation calls for more drastic action. It's clearly time for a major restructuring.

D (tell us/could be layoffs?) _Are you telling us there could be layoffs?_ (e)

A I don't see how we can avoid it, James – unless, of course, we can get some of our people to accept reduced hours.

C (mean some kind/job-share scheme?) _You mean some kind of job-share scheme?_ (f)

A Yes, either that or introduce a four-day week – providing the unions don't oppose it. Of course, it's not just a question of costs. It's also a question of product. The fact is, better products are coming onto the market all the time.

D (so/say/should/spend more/R&D) _So you're saying we should be spending more on R&D._ (g)

A As I've said, capital investment is no longer an option for us. Pour any more money into R&D and we'll simply slide further into debt. And then there are all the problems we've been having with our overseas distributors.

B (this mean/think/centralise distribution?) _Does this mean you're thinking of centralising distribution?_ (h)

A Well, that's one option, yes. But even if we decided to do that, and it's a big if, it would take time to implement – time we simply don't have. As you know, our share price has fallen to an all-time low of just 85 cents. And I wouldn't be surprised if, by our next meeting, it's fallen even further. The fact is, we're selling old product at inflated prices in a volatile market through inefficient distributors.

D (hope/not suggest/situation/hopeless) _I hope you're not suggesting the situation is hopeless._ (i)

A Well, let's put it this way: we've cancelled the Christmas party!

Queries and comments

In this section, students complete an extract from a meeting in which a CEO breaks bad news to the board. They build cues into complete sentences/questions which ask for further information. They listen to a recording of the meeting in order to check their answers. They then complete exercises on collocations and work on conditional forms.

Probing for further information

1   To lead in to the activity, ask students to brainstorm the type of news the CEO could be about to give e.g. possible redundancies, announcement of poor profits, a hostile takeover bid. With weaker classes, ask students to skim the extract and elicit examples of the bad news given by the CEO e.g. disappointing sales figures, high production costs, inefficient distributors.

With weaker groups, check/pre-teach: *projection, quarter* (three months), *in a row, to pick up, to break even, to phase out, drastic, layoff, to slide (into debt), to implement, a volatile market.* Focus attention on the key words and on the example and highlight the changes students need to make – tenses, question word order, adding prepositions. Point out that there are both questions and comments in the task and that students need to pay attention to the punctuation given with the key words. Have students continue building complete questions/comments.

Recording scripts for page T11

2.1

A: Right. That brings us on to our main business this morning – the new Quasar Online Gaming System. As you already know, the news is not particularly good. In spite of a considerable investment in design and marketing, **I'm sorry to report that the project has not been a complete success**.

B: Not a complete success? **What you mean is, it's failed** – dismally!

A: Now let's not overreact, Alan. Certainly, it's failed to meet our original expectations. And, yes, **technically speaking, we have run into negative profit** …

B: Negative profit! What do you mean negative profit? **You mean we've made a loss** – an enormous loss if these figures are anything to go by!

C: Can we come back to the figures later, Alan, if that's OK? First, let's consider why sales are so disappointing. Now, in my view, it's not the product, but the market. **I think there's a general lack of consumer confidence**.

B: **In other words, sales are falling**. Look, I'm sorry, Hannah, but you're just looking for excuses. It's obvious that Quasar is simply not sophisticated enough for today's market.

A: Alan, we leave sophistication to companies like Sony and Nintendo and Sega. What we do is copy the technology and do it cheaper.

C: Alan, **you know we've always been a market-driven organisation** …

B: Market-driven? **What you really mean is we've never had an original idea**. I say we need to be developing an innovative new product line …

A: What, when the market's so massively oversupplied? I don't think so. **Now is not the time to expand, but to consolidate**.

B: **So what you're saying is let's do nothing**.

A: No, I'm saying let's consolidate.

B: I see. And what will this 'consolidation' mean in terms of our staff? Redundancies, I suppose.

C: Well, obviously, **there will have to be some restructuring of the department**.

B: **You mean people are going to lose their jobs**.

C: It's a possibility, yes. And **we may also have to consider outsourcing production to cut costs**.

B: **In other words, our assembly plant may be closed down too**. I can't believe I'm hearing this!

A: **Of course, we won't be able to finalise anything today**.

B: **You mean we'll have to hold another meeting!** Huh! If we've all still got a job by then, that is.

A: Yes, well, I'm glad you raised that point, Alan.

B: What do you mean?

2.2

a

A: Right, I'm allowing an hour and a half for this meeting. Kate is going to fill us in on how the appraisals went. That'll take about a quarter of an hour or so. So that only gives us 45 minutes to deal with everything else. We'd better get started.

B: Sorry, **I thought we had an hour and a half**.

A: What? Oh, yeah, sorry. We've got 75 minutes, haven't we? Still, there's a lot to get through.

b

A: Look, it's no good going on about pay rises. We pay nearly twice what most of our competitors do. And I really don't see how people can expect another salary increase this year, when they're already earning three times the average rate.

B: Hang on a second. **You said we pay twice as much, not three times**.

A: Hm? Oh, all right, twice as much, then. It's still a lot more than everybody else.

c

A: You know as well as I do that this project was supposed to take sixteen weeks. And this isn't the first time we've run over budget, is it? I mean a 20% overspend is pretty serious. And surely three months was sufficient time to complete the project.

B: Just a minute. **I thought you said sixteen weeks, not three months**.

A: OK, OK, that's four months, then. But you've taken nearly six.

d

A: Frankly, with the Asian economic situation the way it is and the euro getting stronger, we're not doing well in the Far East. Southern Europe is where we should be concentrating our efforts. As a matter of fact, Spain is now our second biggest market after China.

B: Hold on. **Didn't you just say we're not doing well in the Far East?**

A: Well, I meant apart from China, obviously! China's always been a huge market for tobacco products.

e

A: I'm sorry, but I don't want us bringing in people from outside the company to sort this problem out. There's a lot of highly confidential information on our intranet. And we should really be able to deal with this ourselves. There's a guy I play golf with who runs his own consultancy. He's offered to help us out.

B: Wait a moment. **You just said you didn't want to bring in people from outside the company**.

A: Erm, well, what I mean is I don't want just anybody. This guy's different. I've known him for years.

2.3

a
Twelve and a half billion dollars.

b
Five hundred and eighty thousand, seven hundred and fifty-three euros.

c
Two-thirds.

d
Eight thousand, four hundred and ninety-one dollars.

e
Four to one.

f
One point zero five square kilometres.

g
Two hundred and ninety-eight cubic metres.

h
Fifty-two to fifty-eight million yen.

i
Four hundred gigabytes.

j
Point zero zero one two per cent.

2 📼 **2.4** Before playing the recording, ask students to compare their answers in pairs and highlight any differences in wording. Play the recording, pausing after each answer to allow students to compare their wording against the recording. Point out that there may be more than one way of using the key words to make correct queries/comments e.g. b could read *Are you suggesting we **should** introduce price cuts?* Accept any correct alternative wording and remind students that the key language is shown in bold in the recording script on pages 141–2.

Collocations

3 Give students one minute to re-read the extract and underline any collocations they can find. Write some of these on the board and draw students' attention to the common patterns in collocations e.g. *volatile market* (adjective–noun), *product lines* (noun–noun), *to centralise distribution* (verb–noun), *to run at a loss* ('fixed' expression). Students then choose six collocations which are relevant to them.

4 Select some of the collocations and tell the students how these relate to your work e.g. *Our school is reviewing its pricing strategy for next year.* Divide the class into pairs and have them explain their choice of phrases. If possible, get students from different departments/ companies to work together.

As a follow-up task, get the students to write a short summary of an aspect of their job or company using the collocations they have selected.

Conditionals

5 With weaker classes, do a short review of the forms used in each clause with present and past conditionals. Students often make mistakes with the use of *will* and *would (have)* e.g. *If the flight ~~will be~~ (is) delayed, you will have to cancel the meeting. /If we ~~would restructure~~ (restructured), we would cut our costs./If they ~~would have delivered~~ (had delivered) in time, we would have met our targets.* Students re-read the extract and answer the questions a–f. Ask students to compare their answers before checking with the whole class. If students query the answer 'twelve' in question a, point out that there are ten conditionals marked by the conjunctions *unless, if, and, even if* and *providing*, and a further two examples in which one speaker answers the previous speaker's question conditionally: *If we still can, Anna.* and *If only it was that simple, Erik.* Tell students there is more practice on types of conditional sentences in the Grammar link for this unit.

As a follow-up task ask students to write questions using the cues: *What would you do if…?* and *What would you have done if …?*

Direct students' attention to the Grammar link on page 102 for more information and practice on conditionals.

📼 **2.4**

A: OK, everyone. It's bad news, I'm afraid. As you may have heard, the latest European sales figures are looking extremely disappointing.

B: **Are you saying they've fallen short of projections again?**

A: I'm afraid so. In fact, we may be 30% down. Now, this will be the third quarter in a row we've missed our targets and, frankly, unless things pick up considerably next quarter, we may have to rethink our whole pricing strategy.

C: **Are you suggesting we introduce price cuts?**

A: If we still can, Anna. Certainly if we'd done that a year ago, it might have stimulated demand. But do it now and we may end up running at a loss. As you know, we're barely breaking even on some of our product lines as it is.

D: **Surely you're not saying it's time to phase them out!**

A: No, no, of course not. At least, not yet. But what I am saying is that we need to keep production costs down somehow if we want to remain competitive.

B: **Does this mean we should be investing more in new technology?**

A: If only it was that simple, Erik. But right now we're not really in a position to invest in anything, even if we wanted to. No, I'm afraid the situation calls for more drastic action. It's clearly time for a major restructuring.

D: **Are you telling us there could be layoffs?**

A: I don't see how we can avoid it, James – unless, of course, we can get some of our people to accept reduced hours.

C: **You mean some kind of job-share scheme?**

A: Yes, either that or introduce a four-day week – providing the unions don't oppose it. Of course, it's not just a question of costs. It's also a question of product. The fact is, better products are coming onto the market all the time.

D: **So you're saying we should be spending more on R&D.**

A: As I've said, capital investment is no longer an option for us. Pour any more money into R&D and we'll simply slide further into debt. And then there are all the problems we've been having with our overseas distributors.

B: **Does this mean you're thinking of centralising distribution?**

A: Well, that's one option, yes. But even if we decided to do that, and it's a big if, it would take time to implement – time we simply don't have. As you know, our share price has fallen to an all-time low of just 85 cents. And I wouldn't be surprised if, by our next meeting, it's fallen even further. The fact is, we're selling old product at inflated prices in a volatile market through inefficient distributors.

D: **I hope you're not suggesting the situation is hopeless.**

A: Well, let's put it this way: we've cancelled the Christmas party!

---

2 🔊 **2.4** Listen to the meeting in 1 and compare your answers.

Collocations **3** Underline at least six collocations in 1 you may want to use yourself e.g. *fall short of projections, miss targets, run at a loss, break even, slide into debt.*

4 Explain your choice of phrases in 3 to a partner. How do they relate to your own job?

Conditionals **5** Look back at the meeting in 1 and answer the following:

a How many examples of conditional sentences and expressions are there?
twelve

b Apart from *if,* which three words are used to link the conditional to the main clause?
unless , _and_ , _providing_

c Only one of the conditional sentences refers to the past. Which one?
If we'd done that a year ago, it might have stimulated demand.

d Why is the past tense used in the following example from the meeting?
*Even if we **decided** to do that, and it's a big if, it would take time to implement.*
It shows that the decision is unlikely.

e ***If only*** *it was that simple* (line 18) means:
I wish it was that simple. ☑   I doubt it's that simple. ☐

f *We're not really in a position to invest in anything,* ***even if*** *we wanted to* (lines 18–19) means:
We don't want to invest in anything. ☐
Wanting to invest would make no difference. ☑

Grammar link

for more on conditionals
see page 102

The language of meetings

Lexis link

for more on the language of meetings see page 103

1 ▭ 2.5 Complete the following extracts from meetings using the words in the box. Some of the expressions have already appeared in this unit. Then listen and check your answers.

point	question	answer	situation	fact	position	option	problem

a A scheduling meeting

A Right. Basically, the ___**position**___ is this: the contract is ours if we want it.

B But we're not in a ___ to take on another project right now, are we?

A I know. Jan, what's your ___ on this?

b An IT meeting

A Look, it's not just a ___**question**___ of software, Alessandro.

B Of course not. It's also a ___ of hardware. The entire system needs upgrading.

A But that's out of the ___ We can't afford that kind of capital outlay.

c A marketing meeting

A Sales are down. One ___**option**___ would obviously be to cut our prices.

B That's no longer an ___ for us. We're barely breaking even as it is.

A Well, then we've no ___ but to rethink our whole marketing strategy.

d An HR* meeting

A Well, there's no easy ___**answer**___ to this, but how about voluntary redundancy?

B I don't think that's the ___ but maybe we could reduce people's hours.

A That might have been the ___ if we didn't already have a strike on our hands!

e A strategy meeting

A Now, let's not make a ___**problem**___ out of this. What if we just pulled out of Sudan?

B Well, I've no ___ with that, but our partners won't be happy.

A No, but that's not our ___ is it? The political situation is just too unstable.

f A CRM** meeting

A I'll get straight to the ___**point**___ We're getting too many customer complaints.

B I agree with you. But the ___ is we don't have the staff to deal with them.

A That's beside the ___ We shouldn't be getting them in the first place!

g A crisis meeting

A I'm afraid the ___**situation**___ is serious. And if the press get hold of the story, …

B Look, we'll deal with that ___ if and when it arises. Let's not panic just yet.

A You're right. What this ___ calls for is calm and careful planning.

h A budget meeting

A The ___**fact**___ is, we're simply not spending enough on R&D.

B As a matter of ___ we've doubled our R&D budget this year.

C That may be so, but the ___ remains we're losing our technological lead.

* Human Resources
**Customer Relationship Management

The language of meetings

In this section, students listen to a recording of an extract from another meeting, focusing on the expressions used. They then practise the language in a dialogue-building activity.

1 🔊 **2.5** Before students start the exercise, write the word *meeting* on the board and ask students to brainstorm types of meeting e.g. *sales meeting, crisis meeting, marketing meeting* etc. Check how many examples students were able to predict from the meetings listed in exercise 1.

Students then complete the extracts a–h. Play the recording in order for students to check their answers.

Focus attention on the short introductory words *Look, …, Well, …, Right …, Now, …* and ask what effect they have (they can make what the speaker is saying more forceful or show that what follows is a serious point). Ask the students to read out the sentences that contain these words and try to sound convincing.

Direct students' attention to the Lexis link on page 103 for more practice on the language of meetings.

🔊 **2.5**

a
A: Right. Basically, the position is this: the contract is ours if we want it.
B: But we're not in a position to take on another project right now, are we?
A: I know. Jan, what's your position on this?

b
A: Look, it's not just a question of software, Alessandro.
B: Of course not. It's also a question of hardware. The entire system needs upgrading.
A: But that's out of the question. We can't afford that kind of capital outlay.

c
A: Sales are down. One option would obviously be to cut our prices.
B: That's no longer an option for us. We're barely breaking even as it is.
A: Well, then we've no option but to rethink our whole marketing strategy.

d
A: Well, there's no easy answer to this, but how about voluntary redundancy?
B: I don't think that's the answer, but maybe we could reduce people's hours.
A: That might have been the answer if we didn't already have a strike on our hands!

e
A: Now, let's not make a problem out of this. What if we just pulled out of Sudan?
B: Well, I've no problem with that, but our partners won't be happy.
A: No, but that's not our problem, is it? The political situation is just too unstable.

f
A: I'll get straight to the point. We're getting too many customer complaints.
B: I agree with you. But the point is we don't have the staff to deal with them.
A: That's beside the point. We shouldn't be getting them in the first place!

g
A: I'm afraid the situation is serious. And if the press get hold of the story, …
B: Look, we'll deal with that situation if and when it arises. Let's not panic just yet.
A: You're right. What this situation calls for is calm and careful planning.

h
A: The fact is, we're simply not spending enough on R&D.
B: As a matter of fact, we've doubled our R&D budget this year.
C: That may be so, but the fact remains we're losing our technological lead.

Dialogue-building

2 Divide the class into pairs and ask students to select one of the meeting types from exercise 1. With weaker students, ask the class to make a list of typical things that happen in the meeting they have chosen e.g. in a marketing meeting, there would be a presentation of sales figures, brainstorming of new opportunities etc.

Ask students to brainstorm the key issues in their meeting first and then to choose the expressions to use in their dialogue. With weaker groups, build a dialogue with the whole class as an example first. Students write their dialogues, working on an OHT or with word processors, if available. Monitor and help as necessary. Get each pair to read out their dialogue and get the rest of the class to add another line to the dialogue. With more creative groups, ask pairs to come out and 'perform' their dialogues to the group.

Breaking the bad news

In this last section, students take part in a fluency activity by roleplaying an interdepartmental meeting.

Fluency

1 Introduce the topic by asking students to define a 'hostile' takeover (one in which the company that is taken over is not happy about the acquisition). Give an example e.g. in 2003 the world's biggest hotel group, *Six Continents*, rejected a £5.6bn takeover bid by a corporate investor. Elicit further examples from the class. If appropriate, students can search the Internet for examples of hostile takeovers as a pre-lesson task and then report back to the class.

Set the scene by telling students that their company has been taken over by a competitor and everyone is waiting to find out what changes will be implemented by the new board. Tell students that they will be expected to support changes that the board would like to implement and present them in a positive way. Give students time to read the Executive Summary template but tell them they don't need to complete it until after the meeting.

2 Check/Pre-teach: *positive discrimination, alarmed, to outnumber, demotion, feng shui* (an ancient Chinese belief that the way a building is constructed and the way that you arrange objects affects your success, health and happiness), *rightsizing* (having the correct number of employees to run efficiently), *to lay off, scooter, reward, dismissal*.

Refer students to pages 126–7 and give them time to read the role cards and the proposals. Divide the class into groups and ask each one to choose one or more of the proposals. Remind students that they will need to present the proposals in a positive way and that they should discuss potential objections and decide how best to counter them. Give students time to discuss each aspect of the proposal(s). Encourage them to make notes on the key advantages of the proposal(s) and to decide who will give the presentation.

Explain that while each group presents their proposal(s), the rest of the class should take the part of the company staff and raise queries and objections. It is the job of the presenters to deal with these as positively as possible and also to note comments and suggestions for the follow-up report. Review useful language for breaking bad news e.g. *I've been asked to let you know that ..., I'm afraid that..., It seems that ..., The following options are being explored: ...* etc.

Set a 30-minute time limit for the meeting. Draw up an agenda, so that the students know the order of the proposals. Appoint one of the students as the chairperson. Monitor and take feedback notes.

After the meeting, give groups time to complete the summaries on page 15. Remind them to show the range of opinions given on the proposals during the meeting roleplay. As a follow-up task, students then give an oral presentation to summarise the reactions to their proposal, following the structure of the template on page 15. The rest of the class should take the role of the board and decide on which proposals to adopt. If appropriate, students fill in their template and present the reactions to the board in a subsequent lesson.

Give feedback on overall fluency and on how well students handled breaking bad news and then feed back on any important or common errors.

If you're short of time

Omit exercise 5 on page 10.

Omit exercise 7 on page 11.

Students can prepare for the final meeting (page 15, exercises 1 and 2) at home.

Dialogue-building   **2**   Work with a partner to write a short dialogue using at least five of the expressions in 1. Read it out to the rest of the class. Can they write the next line of your dialogue using another expression from 1?

Breaking the bad news

Fluency   **1**   Your company was recently acquired by a former competitor in a hostile takeover. The new board of directors has decided it's time for a serious shake-up. Each of you has been chosen to announce at a special interdepartmental meeting some of the changes they would like to see implemented. After the meeting, you will be expected to report back to the board on people's reactions to the proposal(s) you submitted. Read the template below before you hold the meeting.

Interdepartmental meeting:

Executive Summary

I am | delighted
pleased
sorry | to report that at the interdepartmental meeting held at _____

on _____ the proposed changes | got the full backing of everyone present.
were very well received by the majority of those present.
were broadly accepted, though with one or two reservations.
met with a certain amount of opposition.

1   The proposal that _____

was | particularly welcomed and the general feeling was that
eventually approved with the proviso that
considered impractical in view of
seriously questioned on the grounds that | _____

_____

Further
Alternative | suggestions included: **a**   _____
           b   _____
           c   _____

2   There was | also
however | some
considerable | support for the proposal that
doubt as to whether
disagreement with the thinking behind | _____

_____

Several other options were explored, including: **a**   _____
                                  b   _____
                                  c   _____

We, therefore, strongly recommend the board to _____

2   Work in groups and turn to pages 126–127 to see the board's proposals.

3 Material world

You can't have everything. Where would you put it? *Steven Wright, surrealist comedian*

Quiz **1** Work with a partner to see how much you know about the billionaire lifestyle.

Who wants to be a billionaire?

1 How many dollar millionaires are there in the world?
- a 720,000
- c 72 million
- **(b) 7.2 million**
- d 720 million

2 How many dollar billionaires are there?
- a 45
- c 4,500
- **(b) 450**
- d 45,000

3 What's the world's most expensive neighbourhood to live in?
- a Zürichberg, Zürich
- **(b) Eaton Square, London**
- c Fifth Avenue, New York
- d Motoazabu, Tokyo

4 Where can you find the highest concentration of multimillionaires per square metre?
- a Monte Carlo
- c Nassau
- **(b) Santa Barbara**
- d Geneva

5 With $25,000 to spend, what *couldn't* you afford?
- a your own Boeing 747 jumbo jet for an hour
- b one night in the world's most expensive hotel room – the Bridge Suite at the Atlantis Resort in the Bahamas
- **(c) a Harvard MBA**
- d 50 hours of helicopter flying lessons

6 With $2 million to spend, what would still be financially out of your reach?
- **(a) the world's most expensive watch by Chopard encrusted with over 200 carats of multicoloured diamonds**
- b the world's most expensive dress, embroidered with 2,000 diamonds, by Maria Grachvogel
- c a round of golf with the world's greatest golfer, Tiger Woods
- d the Fender Stratocaster Sunburst guitar that Jimi Hendrix famously set fire to on stage

7 Who sold the world's most expensive yacht *Katana* (valued at $68 million) to buy something a little bigger?
- **(a) CEO of Oracle, Larry Ellison**
- b Michael Jackson
- c the Royal Family of Qatar
- d Media mogul, Rupert Murdoch

8 Who *doesn't* own an island?
- a entrepreneur Richard Branson
- b actor Nicholas Cage
- **(c) ex-prime minister Margaret Thatcher**
- d the Barclays Bank brothers

9 Who *didn't* own a Rolls-Royce?
- a Vladimir Lenin
- b Ayatollah Khomeini
- c John Lennon
- **(d) Ronald Reagan**

10 Which classic car was voted the most desirable dream machine ever?
- a E-Type Jaguar
- **(b) Aston Martin DB5**
- c Ferrari Dino
- d Porsche 911

11 A case of Chateau Le Pin cost £400 in 1983. When ready to drink in 1999, how much was it worth?
- a nothing
- b £400
- c £12,000
- **(d) £36,000**

12 The most expensive painting ever sold at auction was bought by Japanese businessman Ryoei Saito for $82.5 million. Who was the painter?
- a Picasso
- b Cézanne
- **(c) Van Gogh**
- d Rubens

Check your answers on page 128

WN1384RA

Talking points 3 Material world

This is a unit on the theme of making money. It looks at billionaire lifestyles and the downfall of Barings Bank in 1995, which was brought about by individual greed.

Students start by doing a light-hearted quiz about billionaire lifestyles. They then discuss what success means for them and focus on the language of success and failure.

A recording of a documentary about the collapse of Barings Bank provides the stimulus for discussion and vocabulary work.

Finally, students discuss a short text on investing in 'politically incorrect' funds and then listen to a recording of speakers taking part in the same discussion.

In this section, students do a quiz in pairs to see how much they know about billionaire lifestyles. They discuss the concepts of personal success and happiness and then practise the language of success and failure. Finally, they apply this language to successes and failures in their own life.

Warm-up

Ask students to tell you if they are happy with what they own/have, or if they would like to be richer. Refer students to the amusing quotation from the comedian Steven Wright and elicit students' reactions. Ask if students know of anyone who thinks the opposite – that they *can* have everything.

Before starting the quiz, elicit the names of some world-famous millionaires, such as Bill Gates, Elton John etc. Elicit examples of their lifestyle e.g. several homes, luxury cars, off-shore investments, expensive hobbies etc.

1 Check/Pre-teach: *out of your reach, carats* from the quiz and *real estate, staggering* from the *Billionaire fact file* on page 128. Divide the students into pairs/small groups. If appropriate, set a time limit of about five minutes for the quiz.

When the students have finished and checked their answers on page 128, exploit the quiz and fact file further. Check any vocabulary which the students can deduce from context e.g. *encrusted, embroidered.* Ask students for their reactions to any of the questions in the quiz or to any of the points in the fact file. Ask follow-up questions e.g. *Is there anything in the quiz you consider a complete waste of money? Are famous paintings really worth such high prices?*

Discussion

2 Refer students to the quotation from Benjamin Franklin and elicit what Franklin means. Ask students if they agree that success does not necessarily bring happiness. Elicit examples of successful people who are not/were not necessarily happy e.g. Howard Hughes. Ask students to list what success means for them and then share their ideas with the rest of the class. Establish which three things mean success for the whole class.

The students complete the phrases, using the pairs of words in the boxes. Check the answers and then ask students to rank the aspects in order of importance. Students compare with a partner and discuss their priorities. Open the discussion to the whole group by asking students to compare their ranking.

Give further practice with some of the phrases by asking follow-up questions e.g. *What examples of 'doing your own thing' can you think of? What do the 'simple things in life' mean to you? In what ways can people 'make their mark' in the world?*

3 Give students a few minutes to think of the most successful person they know and the reason(s) why they think they became successful. Select a few students to tell the group who they chose and why.

The language of success and failure

4 Write up the letters S and F on the board and explain they stand for 'success' and 'failure'. Focus attention on sentences a–l and highlight strategies that students can use to categorise the sentences e.g. looking at the parts of the expressions they recognise, deciding if the sentences sound positive or negative. Focus on a few examples with the whole class:
fruitful – the idea of giving/producing 'fruit'
fell through – ideas of falling/going down = failure
smooth – sounds positive
a total flop – *flop* sounds negative

Ask the students to read through the sentences and mark them with the letter S or F. Students check the answers in pairs. Then check the answers with the whole class.

5 Divide the class into pairs. Students tell their partner about situations linked to the sentences in exercise 4. Hold a short feedback session and invite students to tell the class any interesting personal stories.

Alternatively, with less confident groups, assign each student a letter a–l and get them to jot down a sentence which puts the word into a personal business context e.g. *The last meeting I attended wasn't very fruitful because* … Students then read out their sentence to the class.

Discussion

2 According to Benjamin Franklin, 'Success is getting what you want; happiness is wanting what you get.' What does success mean for you? Complete the following using the pairs of words in the boxes. Then discuss their relative importance with a partner.

> making + money   being + thing   getting + career
> enjoying + life   spending + family   making + world

a _getting_ on in my _career_

b _enjoying_ the simple things in _life_

c _making_ loads of _money_

d _spending_ quality time with my _family_

e _making_ my mark in the _world_

f _being_ free to do my own _thing_

> running + business   achieving + goals   having + suntan   living + full
> being + retirement   making + place

g _living_ life to the _full_

h _achieving_ all my personal _goals_

i _running_ my own _business_

j _being_ able to take early _retirement_

k _having_ the dream house, the flash car and the year-round _suntan_

l _making_ the world a slightly better _place_

3 Who's the most successful person you know? How did they become so successful?

The language of success and failure

4 The following sentences refer to either success or failure. Mark them S or F.

a It was a very fruitful meeting. _S_

b The whole thing came to nothing. _F_

c The investment paid off in the end. _S_

d It all went smoothly. _S_

e It was a total flop. _F_

f The deal went through. _S_

g The deal fell through. _F_

h The whole idea was a non-starter. _F_

i We pulled it off. _S_

j It was a major publicity coup. _S_

k We've blown our chances. _F_

l We tried in vain to reach agreement. _F_

5 Tell a partner about a situation in your own life to which one of the sentences in 4 could apply.

from *Macmillan English Dictionary*

upwardly mobile
/ˌʌpwədli ˈməʊbaɪl/ adj
someone who is upwardly
mobile moves into a
higher social class by
becoming richer and more
successful

whizzkid /ˈwɪzˌkɪd/ noun
[C] *informal* a young
person who is very
intelligent or successful

yuppie /ˈjʌpi/ noun [C]
someone who is young,
earns a lot of money, and
lives in a city in a style
that is too expensive for
most people. This word
usually shows that you
dislike people like this.

Nick Leeson in prison

Upward mobility

1 Work with a partner and discuss the following questions.

   a What do you know about the upwardly mobile whizzkids and yuppies of the 1980s and 1990s? What was business like in your country then?

   b Were you (or would you have liked to be) working during that period?

   c What do you know about the collapse of Barings Bank in 1995? Who was at the centre of the scandal?

2 ▭ **3.1** Listen to the story of the collapse of Barings. Check your answers to **c** above.

3 What do the following figures in the story refer to?

   a $10 million <u>the yearly profit Leeson was making for Barings</u>

   b 10% <u>the percentage profit Leeson was making for Barings</u>

   c £50,000 <u>Leeson's salary</u>

   d £150,000 <u>Leeson's bonuses</u>

   e $1.3 billion <u>Leeson's total losses</u>

   f 6½ years <u>Leeson's prison sentence</u>

   g 233 years <u>how long Barings had been in business</u>

   h £1 <u>what ING bought Barings for</u>

4 Who do you think was to blame for the disaster? Has anything similar happened at a bank in your country?

5 Match the halves of the following expressions you heard in 2.

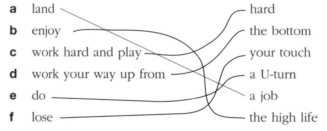

   a land   hard
   b enjoy   the bottom
   c work hard and play   your touch
   d work your way up from   a U-turn
   e do   a job
   f lose   the high life

   Which of the above mean:

   1 rise from the lowest level in a company? d

   2 completely change direction? e

   3 put a lot of effort into having fun as well as into your job? c

   4 partying, travelling, spending money on expensive things? b

   5 no longer have the special ability that made you successful? f

   6 get a job you really wanted? a

6 What noun can be preceded by these adjectives? Some of them were in 2.

   a mounting **b** crippling **c** outstanding **d** heavy <u>d e b t s</u>

   Which adjective means:

   unpaid? c   damaging? b   increasing? a   large? d

7 ▭ **3.2** Listen and find out what happened to Leeson after he got out of prison.

Upward mobility

In this section, students listen to a recording about the downfall of Barings Bank and check comprehension of the key numbers and figures in the story. They discuss the crisis, then practise some of the vocabulary taken from the recording.

1 Ask the students if they know the terms *upwardly mobile*, *whizzkid* and *yuppie*. Encourage them to guess the meanings and then check in the glossary. (*Yuppie* was the somewhat negative term which became associated with individual greed. It applied mainly to people working in banking and finance, especially those who traded stocks at high prices. The collapse of the Barings Bank is a remarkable story. An individual currency trader called Nick Leeson gambled with the bank's money and made huge losses which he then hid from his employers using a fictitious account. His rash behaviour brought down the bank in 1995.)

Divide the group into pairs to discuss the questions.
a   Check students understand what business life was like in the 1980s and 90s in the UK and USA (see above note on yuppies). Encourage students to compare this with life in their own country.
b   Students compare their recollections of working in the 1980s and 90s if they were employed, or reasons for wanting/not wanting to work then if they weren't.
c   Students brainstorm ideas and facts about the collapse of Barings Bank. Write relevant notes on the board including the symbol ? for anything students are not sure of. Tell them they can check their ideas in the recording in exercise 2.

2   **3.1** Check/Pre-teach: *speculative losses, obscure, to go on the run, to extradite, the futures markets, to stick by someone, humiliation, burdened.* Play the recording through once. Students check the predictions they made in exercise 1c. Establish the key facts of the case in a brief class check.

3 Ask students to read the figures and see if they remember any of them from the recording. Play the recording again, pausing if necessary to allow students to write their answers. Students check their answers with a partner and then check the answers with the whole class.

4 Ask students who they blame for the crisis: Leeson, Barings Bank for trusting one employee so much, or another factor such as the general climate of greed. Find out if they know of another banking disasters or misappropriation of funds e.g. the fall of the Bank of Credit and Commerce International (BCCI) in 1991 was, at the time, the largest fraud in banking history.

5 Students first match the two halves of the expressions and then match the expressions with the explanations. Check the answers and then give each student/pair a letter a–f at random and ask them to create a question for someone else in the group using the relevant expression e.g. *Name someone who worked their way up from the bottom.*

6 Elicit the answer and check the pronunciation of *debt*. Students then match the adjectives to the meanings. Check the answers and then elicit other phrases with the word *debt* e.g. *to be in debt, to pay off debts* etc.

7   **3.2** Check/Pre-teach: *to make ends meet, the lengths people will go to.* Elicit suggestions as to what happened to Leeson after being in prison and write them on the board. Play the recording and get students to check their predictions.

Ask students if they have seen the film about Nick Leeson or read the book *Rogue Trader*. Elicit students' reactions to the recording and ask follow-up questions e.g. *Is Leeson justified in blaming the international banking system for his actions? Do you think it's right that he has benefited from book/film royalties? Who should take responsibility in cases of fraud/misappropriation?*

3.1

A: Now, it's just coming up to 11 o'clock. Time for *Business Brief* with Malcolm McFadden. This week: the collapse of Barings.
B: The story of the collapse of Barings is not the biggest bank fraud of all time, but it is probably the most famous – not least because at the centre of the drama lies the colourful character of Nick Leeson.

Leeson was a typical working-class boy, a below-average student who failed his maths exams and left school with few qualifications. Nevertheless, he managed to land a job as a clerk at the royal bank Coutts in the City of London.

A succession of low-paid jobs at other banks eventually led in 1982 to his joining Barings, where he quickly made an impression and worked his way up from the very bottom to become its top currency trader at the Singapore office.

By 1993 Leeson was making his employers $10 million a year – 10% of Barings' total profits. His salary may have been a mere £50,000 but his bonuses were triple that. He and his devoted wife Lisa had a smart apartment in Singapore and spent their weekends partying or holidaying in exotic island resorts. Leeson worked hard and played hard, and fully enjoyed the high life.

But in 1994 the markets did a U-turn and Leeson seemed to lose his touch. The speculative losses built up. Amazingly, Barings had no idea of the scale of the problem, for Leeson had carefully hidden his mounting debts in an obscure account called Error Losses 88888. This enabled him to request further funds from the bank to carry on trading, even though by the autumn his losses stood at $300 million.

By the time he was discovered that figure had risen to $1.3 billion. Two days before his 28th birthday Leeson went missing. On his desk he'd left a hurried note. It simply said: 'I'm sorry.'

To avoid imprisonment, Leeson and his wife briefly went on the run, first to Borneo and then to Frankfurt, where Leeson was arrested, extradited to Singapore and finally jailed for six and a half years in 1995. When the news of his arrest reached the world's futures markets, there were loud cheers of celebration.

Lisa Leeson stuck by her husband until the news of his infidelity on business trips to Japan finally broke their marriage. Divorced and now suffering from cancer, Leeson still managed to write his amazing autobiography *Rogue Trader* while in prison.

Barings, which for 233 years had built up an excellent reputation in financial circles, now faced the final humiliation – bankruptcy. Burdened with crippling debts, it was eventually bought by the Dutch ING Bank for the sum of one pound.

3.2

B: But the story for Leeson doesn't quite end there. After the terrible ordeal of surgery and chemotherapy, Leeson's health improved. Though he returned to the UK to find himself homeless and without a job, he went on to study at university, whilst occasionally giving speeches at conferences to make ends meet. His book *Rogue Trader* made him an estimated £50,000. And when it was made into a film starring Ewan McGregor, Leeson apparently received a great deal more. The man who could make $10 million a year with other people's money may not be finished yet.

But whatever Leeson's future, *Rogue Trader* will stand as a lasting record of the lengths the whizzkids and yuppies of the 80s and 90s were willing to go to in the so-called 'age of greed'. In it Leeson blamed the international banking system for his spectacular failure. 'We were all driven to make profits, profits and more profits,' he said, 'and I was the rising star.'

8 Check/Pre-teach: *noble* and *nobility* and then ask students to guess what *downward nobility* means. Students read the extract from *Fast Company*, a magazine for business leaders. Ask students if they know anyone who is 'downwardly noble' and to describe their approach to life. Establish if students feel envious of such people or if they consider themselves to be 'downwardly noble'.

Making money

In this last section, students discuss a series of questions about ethical ways of doing business and read a text about investing in unethical companies. A recording provides the stimulus for the final discussion in this unit, giving three people's reactions to the idea of making unethical investments.

1 Ask students what they know about the well-known chain The Body Shop. Establish why people shop there e.g. they like the products, they agree with the principles on which The Body Shop is founded – that it is against testing on animals and it supports fair trade.

Students mark their cross on the scale and then compare in pairs/small groups. Ask follow-up questions to try to establish what constitutes 'moral' practice in business e.g. *An invitation to dinner is not usually seen as a 'bribe' to a potential customer, but what about a weekend away or a longer expenses-paid trip?*

Discussion

2 Students discuss the questions in pairs/small groups. Hold a short feedback session and elicit examples of 'unethical' companies e.g. arms manufacturing companies, tobacco companies and companies which are felt to unfairly treat or exploit their workforce.

3 Check/Pre-teach: *politically correct* and the abbreviation *PC*. Ask students how political correctness has affected language e.g. in English the use of gender-free terms like *chairperson* (not *chairman*) and neutral terms like *disabled* (not *handicapped*). Ask students if similar changes have affected their language and what is considered politically incorrect in their country.

Ask students to guess who Vice Fund are and what they invest in. Tell students to read the texts quickly and check. They should also list the four areas that Vice Fund invest in. Elicit students' reactions to Vice Fund. Ask if they would invest in such a company and why/why not.

Ask students to read the texts again and decide on the difference in tone and style (*When vice is capital* is tongue-in-cheek while the *Risk/Return Summary* is neutral/factual.) Ask students to highlight the parts of the first text that indicate it is tongue-in-check e.g. the use of exaggeration – *in the middle of a nervous breakdown*, informal language – *try your luck* etc.

4 📼 **3.3** Ask students to summarise their opinions of Vice Fund and write up some of the expressions on the board. This may help students with some of the language used in the recording.

Check/Pre-teach: *missile, to do harm, to do best* (perform), *to outperform, ethically sound, lobby*. Tell students they will hear three speakers talking about ethics and investments. Provide students with key headings for the main points e.g. *Examples of investments/products given, Overall opinion of ethical investments, Reason(s)* before you play the recording and be prepared to play it more than once. With weaker classes, listen to the first extract as a whole class activity.

Check the answers and elicit who students agree with most. (Speaker 1 is happy to invest in companies which sell alcohol and tobacco. Speaker 2 feels it is difficult to define ethics anyway, so you may as well invest as you wish. Speaker 3 prefers to exercise moral judgement.)

As an optional follow-up task, bring in copies of *The Financial Times* and have students work in groups and choose five companies they would/would not invest in, with reasons. Groups then report back to the class.

If you're short of time

Omit exercise 4 on page 17.

Omit exercises 8 and 1 on page 19.

📼 **3.3**
Speaker 1
Well, I don't have any problem investing in alcohol and tobacco products. Actually, I'm a smoker myself. Keep trying to give up but can't quite seem to manage it. Seems to me you can take this ethical investment idea a bit too far. I mean, who am I to say those businesses shouldn't be invested in? If they're good, profitable businesses, why not put your money into them? They're not doing anything illegal, are they? And anyway, if everybody stopped investing in cigarette companies, think of all the tobacco pickers and the cigarette factory workers who'd be out of a job. Gambling doesn't worry me too much either, not that I'm much of a gambler myself. I suppose I might be a bit worried about seeing my money going into manufacturing guns and missiles, though. But then again, someone's got to make them.

Speaker 2
What I want to know is: just what is an ethical investment these days? I mean, it's pretty hard to think of a company that doesn't do anybody or anything any harm in some way or another. Take books. To make books you have to cut down trees. Save the trees, books get more expensive, the poor can't afford them. Or how about shoes? To make leather shoes you have to kill animals. To make plastic shoes you have to pollute the environment. Or say you invest in a clothing company, then you've got to ask yourself who's making the clothes, where do they work and what are they getting paid for it? And what kind of clothes are they making? The latest fashions for the rich? Uniforms for the army? It's so complicated, you may as well just put your money where it's likely to do best and forget about the rights and wrongs of it.

Speaker 3
Whenever you make an important decision, you use your judgement and sense of right and wrong, don't you? So why should investment decisions be any different? As a matter of fact, a lot of 'green' investments have paid off very well in the last ten years, often outperforming less ethically sound stocks. I certainly wouldn't allow any of my hard-earned cash to go towards supporting companies that cause such misery, even though they're not actually illegal. And, anyway, who said cigarette companies were a good investment? What with all these court cases and the anti-smoking lobby, I don't think there's a great future there – at least, not in America. And arms? Well, in times of war I suppose that's a good business to be in, but the other day someone in the aviation industry actually told me that these days there's less money in making fighter aircraft than there is in making corporate jets. So, what does that tell you?

8   You've been talking about upward mobility. What do you think 'downward nobility' is? Read the magazine extract below. Do you agree?

> Want to show off? Walk into a room and say you're a happy person. Better yet, announce that you've been happily married for 25 years. Satisfaction and contentment are the status symbols of the future. That's downward nobility.

Watts Wacker in *Fast Company* magazine

Making money

1   Is there any connection at all between being moral and making money? Is it possible to do both? Look at the two opinions below. Where would you place yourself on the scale?

Being good is good for business.
Anita Roddick, founder of The Body Shop

⟵————————⟶

The surest way to remain poor is to be an honest man.
Napoleon Bonaparte, founder of the French Empire

Discussion

2   Work with a partner and discuss the following questions.

a   Do you think ethical investment in greener, environmentally friendlier, less exploitative businesses makes the world a better place?

b   Does it make sense financially for the individual investor?

c   Are there any kinds of company you wouldn't like to see your money being invested in for moral reasons, even if they were a sound investment?

3   Read about an investment fund which takes a different view of ethics and investment. Would you be interested in investing in their fund?

WHEN VICE is capital

'When it is good, it is very, very good, but when it is bad it is better.' This is the motto of the Vice Fund, the first investment fund not afraid to describe itself as 'politically incorrect'.

Imagine that you are one of that ever-increasing number of investors who have lost a fortune on the stock exchange. Feeling depressed, you decide to drown your sorrows in alcohol. Then in the middle of a nervous breakdown you start smoking again. You try your luck at gambling with the few savings you have left, but this also goes wrong. In sheer desperation, you consider the possibility of buying a gun.

Without realising it, the solution to your problems lies in your very miseries. Or, at least, that is what the managers of the Vice Fund claim – an investment fund which was born in the USA and invests in all those areas which pick up in times of recession – arms, alcohol, gambling and cigarettes.

Translated from *La Vanguardia*

VICEFUND Risk/Return Summary

The fund is not appropriate for investors that have short-term goals.

Principal investment strategies

1   First, we look for companies that derive a significant portion of their revenues from products often considered socially irresponsible, and

2   then we select companies from this group based on their financial soundness and potential for growth.

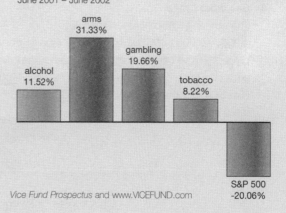

Percentage return in investments compared to S&P 500 index, June 2001 – June 2002

arms 31.33%
gambling 19.66%
alcohol 11.52%
tobacco 8.22%
S&P 500 -20.06%

Vice Fund Prospectus and www.VICEFUND.com

4   ▣ 3.3 Listen to three people discussing the question in 3. Who do you agree with most?

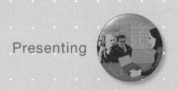

4 Voice and visuals

I do not object to people looking at their watches when I am speaking. But I strongly object when they start shaking them to make certain they are still going.
Lord Birkett, British judge

Quiz

1 When you stand up to speak in public, what keeps an audience interested in what you're saying? Expertise or enthusiasm? PowerPoint or natural presence? Work with a partner and underline the answers.

How to command attention

1 Am I boring you?
The attention span of the average audience member is
2 ½ seconds / <u>12 ½ seconds</u> /
2 ½ minutes / 12 ½ minutes.
(Clue: the attention span of a goldfish is about two seconds.)

2 Is anybody listening?
In a study carried out at UCLA, psychology professor Albert Mehrabian discovered that, of the total impression speakers make on an audience,
38% (55%) 7% is visual (how we look)
55% / 7% (38%) is vocal (how we sound)
(7%) 38% / 55% is verbal (what we say).

3 How low can you go?
Research shows that people generally prefer low voices to high-pitched ones. In a recent study at Wake University, North Carolina, which actor and actress were found to have the lowest and sexiest voices?
Bruce Willis / <u>Mel Gibson</u> / Michael Douglas /
Sean Connery
Gwyneth Paltrow / Michelle Pfeiffer
Nicole Kidman / <u>Julia Roberts</u>

4 See what I mean?
The human brain processes images
4,000 / 40,000 / <u>400,000</u> times faster than text and a presenter who uses visuals in their talk will improve audience recall on average by 100% / 200% / <u>400%</u>.
Use of colour makes visuals 25% / <u>85%</u> / 850% more memorable.

5 Not just a pretty face?
Although most people would deny it, we often judge others as much by their appearance as by their ability. Only one of the following statistics is false. Which one is it?

a A survey conducted by London Guildhall University claims unattractive Britons earn £3,000 less than better-looking colleagues.

(b) A UK report found that both male and female sales personnel earn at least 50% higher commission if they're good-looking.

c A study in America has shown that convicted criminals are twice as likely to avoid a jail sentence if they are attractive.

d Since 1900 the US presidency has been won by the taller (and usually better-looking) candidate in nearly 90% of the elections.

2 Check your answers on page 130. If these statistics are true, what are the implications? <u>your presentation has to be short; it's an advantage to look good and to have a low voice; use visuals (preferably in colour)</u>

Presenting

4 Voice and visuals

Giving competent and confident presentations is a vital skill for many business English students. There are three units on giving presentations and the language practised is useful for all students and for addressing both small and large audiences. This first unit has a specific focus on using voice techniques and visuals.

Students start by doing a quiz on surprising facts and figures about presentations. A reading text on the Nixon–Kennedy presidential debate shows the power of the visual in delivering a message. Students study the vocabulary used in the text and an extension activity provides practice on past modal forms. The students roleplay giving and receiving feedback on a presentation. This is followed by a recording of a manager giving feedback on the same presentation.

The students then discuss the range of visuals available for presentations and practise useful language for referring these to the audience. They draw a graph or chart and practise the language in a short presentation. The last section analyses and practises delivery techniques using famous speeches taken from films.

The grammatical focus is on modals verbs and the lexical focus is on the language of presentations.

In this first section, students do a quiz about presentations.

Warm-up

Read out the quotation from the British judge. Ask students to explain what the judge is trying to say (that if a presentation is boring, it may seem to drag on to the audience). Ask the students if they have ever attended a dull presentation and what they did to get through it.

Ask focus questions on giving presentations e.g. *Are you a nervous or confident speaker? How do you feel about presenting in a second language? Have you ever had a nerve-wracking experience when giving a presentation?* If your students do not need to give formal presentations, tell them that this unit will still be useful for attending business presentations and for overall language and fluency development.

Quiz

1 Focus attention on the title of the quiz and get students to brainstorm ways to command attention e.g. asking questions, using a prop, using your voice and language well.

Check/Pre-teach: *attention span, goldfish, high-pitched, recall* and check the word stress in *memorable*. Get students to do the quiz in pairs. Alternatively, create competition by getting students to work in teams and then score the answers to find a winner.

2 Tell students to check their answers on page 130. Elicit their reactions and find out which facts they found most surprising. Discuss the implications of the statistics with the class.

The television age

In this section, students read an intriguing text about the 1960 US presidential debate, which was televised for the first time, and discuss the power of image in politics. They do a vocabulary activity and a grammar exercise to practise past modal forms. Students roleplay a post-presentation feedback session between the presenter and his manager. Finally, they listen to a recording of feedback from a member of the audience, which throws a different light on the presentation.

1   Create interest in the theme by asking students what they remember about Kennedy and Nixon. (For Kennedy it may be the family dynasty, his colourful love life, or of course his assassination. For Nixon it will undoubtedly be the Watergate scandal.) Elicit examples of image-conscious politicians from the students' own country and on the international scene.

Focus students' attention on the glossary. Tell students that Kennedy came out the debate better and get them to predict what went wrong for Nixon. Students then skim the text to check their predictions. Ask students check questions: *Why did Kennedy perform better than Nixon?* (he appeared more confident and credible because of his body language and overall style*), What do you think was Nixon's greatest mistake?* (maybe simply under-estimating the power of the new medium of television, or agreeing to do a vital interview after a punishing round of speeches).

Elicit opinions on the role of image in the politics of the students' own country and other examples of image winning/losing an election/debate.

As a follow-up activity, ask students to scan the text again and note down five words or expressions which they wish to incorporate into their active vocabulary. Ask individual students which words they chose and why.

The television age

1 The televised debate between Richard Nixon and John F. Kennedy in the 1960 American presidential election was the classic case of verbal skills versus visual appeal. Read the full story below. Does image play as important a role in the politics of your country?

The Kennedy-Nixon debate

A milestone in television broadcasting came on September 26, 1960, with the first ever US presidential television debate between Richard Nixon and John F. Kennedy.

5 The polls had Nixon and Kennedy neck and neck: Nixon 47 per cent, Kennedy 47 per cent. Nine out of ten American families now owned a television set, and the viewing audience would be the largest ever assembled. The television

10 confrontation was expected to be decisive.

Nixon knew he had problems with television. His five o'clock shadow made him look grim and pallid, even after shaving. Nevertheless, Nixon believed he could rely on his verbal skills. In

15 face-to-face debates he hardly ever lost.

Kennedy prepared diligently, spending hours answering possible questions prepared by his staff. Nixon refused to practice; no one could tell him

20 what he needed to know.

The signs were ominous for Nixon from the time he arrived at the television studio. The gathered photographers flocked to

25 take pictures of the young, good-looking Kennedy. When the moderator introduced the

30 two candidates, Richard Nixon looked, according to author of

35 *Kennedy and Nixon* Christopher Matthews,

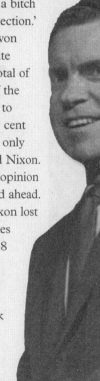

like an 'ill-at-ease, unshaven, middle-aged fellow

40 recovering from a serious illness. Jack Kennedy, by contrast, was elegant in a dark, well-tailored suit that set off his healthy tan.'

Verbally Nixon handled himself well. Americans who tuned in to their radios rather

45 than their television sets later rated Nixon the clear winner. But this was the age of television, and the images – the non-verbal body language – that were projected across millions of television screens had an impact. According to Matthews:

50 'Each time Kennedy spoke, Nixon's eyes darted toward him in an uncomfortable mix of fear and curiosity.' In stark contrast, Kennedy's body language projected strength and confidence.

Nixon's close adviser Henry Cabot Lodge, watching the last few minutes of the debate, remarked despondently:

'That son of a bitch just lost the election.'

Kennedy won the great debate decisively: a total of 43 per cent of the viewers gave it to Kennedy, 29 per cent called it even, and only 23 per cent favoured Nixon. In the all-important opinion polls Kennedy pulled ahead. On election day, Nixon lost by just 103,000 votes out of more than 68 million votes cast. For the rest of his life Nixon would refuse even to look at the tapes.

From *Artful Persuasion* by Harry Mills

2   The following words and phrases appeared in the text. Delete the incorrect definitions.

a   *A milestone* (line 1) is *a key stage/~~a terrible moment~~* in the development of something.

b   People who are *neck and neck* (line 5) are *equally placed/~~competing fiercely~~* in a race.

c   If you *prepare diligently* (line 16), you do it *with care and effort/~~because you have to~~*.

d   *Ominous* (line 21) means something *~~unexpected~~/bad* is going to happen.

e   People *flocked* (line 24) means they *~~fought each other~~/crowded round*.

f   If you are *ill-at-ease* (line 39), you are *not relaxed/~~not well~~*.

g   If you say something *despondently* (line 56) you feel *hopeless/~~angry~~* about it.

3   Read the extra information about the Nixon-Kennedy debate. Imagine you were Nixon's chief adviser Henry Cabot Lodge. What would you have said right after the debate? Complete the sentences below with your ideas.

> **Background to the story**
> Nixon had a lot of bad luck prior to his first debate with Kennedy. Exhausted after a tour of all 50 American states, he was suffering from a knee infection, had lost a lot of weight and was running a temperature. To add insult to injury, the TV studio had been painted an identical shade of grey to Nixon's suit, making him virtually invisible to the television audience!

a   What on earth were you thinking of? Do you realise you might have just …

b   If only you'd listened to me! I told you you should have …

c   Don't you think it might have been a good idea to …

Grammar link

for more on modal verbs
see page 104

d   I know there was nothing you could have done about …

e   And it probably wouldn't have made any difference even if you'd …

f   But surely you could at least have …

Giving feedback   4   Work with a partner to practise giving and receiving feedback on a presentation. Speaker A see page 130. Speaker B see page 129.

5   ▭ 4.1 Listen to the voice mail from your Taiwanese client following the presentation in 4. Discuss his reaction with a partner.

Visuals

1   When you give presentations, what visuals do you use?

overhead   handouts   PowerPoint   slides   flipchart   videos   websites

2   Read the book extract. Do you share the author's doubts?

> **Death by PowerPoint**
> Are you risking 'Death by PowerPoint'? This is when you inflict on your defenceless audience endless bullet-pointed slides, keywords and clipart that look pretty, yet cumulatively create a numbing effect and loss of impact. Beware of spending more time on the technology than on preparing yourself. Remember, you are the presentation.

Adapted from *The Ultimate Business Presentation Book* by Andrew Leigh

2 Tell students to refer back to the text to see the words in context. This will help them deduce the meaning. Ask students to compare their answers with a partner, then check with the whole class.

3 Ask students to read the extra information quickly and check comprehension of *prior to, to run a temperature, to add insult to injury*. Ask them to imagine what Nixon's frame of mind was before the debate. Elicit what students feel was bad luck and which things Nixon could have avoided.

Students need to be able to manipulate third conditional and past modals forms here, so, if necessary, do a quick remedial presentation using an example sentence and analysing the forms used in each clause e.g. *If the debate hadn't been televised, Nixon might have won the election.* Highlight the pronunciation of the contracted forms of *could have/should have/might have* in speaking and drill as necessary.

Tell students to complete the sentences as if they had been Nixon's adviser and then get them to compare answers in pairs. Elicit a range of possible answers.

Suggested answers

a	lost the election?
b	prepared your speech more carefully.
c	change your suit?
d	the colour of the studio.
e	not been ill.
f	had a shave.

Direct students' attention to the Grammar link on page 104 for more information and practice on modal verbs.

Giving feedback

4 Get students to brainstorm what can go wrong during a presentation e.g. the power fails, you lose the thread of your talk, people switch off etc. If appropriate, give a personal example from a lesson that went wrong and/or elicit examples from the class.

Check/Pre-teach: *to force a smile, insulted, to crack a joke, illegible, to handle, to break the ice, amplifier, to blame, rest assured*. Divide the students into AB pairs. Refer the A students to page 130 and the B students to page 129. Have students read the role cards and focus attention on the useful language boxes on students' respective pages. Elicit sample language to complete each phrase and check stress and intonation. Highlight the pronunciation of contracted forms in past modals.

Give students time to prepare for the roleplay, noting down key words/phrases. With weaker students, suggest that they note down the main points they want to make along with the key language. If appropriate, arrange the seating so that the B students need to go to A's 'office' for the meeting. Remind the A students they need to be direct but also make some suggestions for future presentations; B students should be clear about the reasons they had problems and also convince A that they won't happen again.

Monitor and take feedback notes. When students have finished, ask the A students how successful they think they were in delivering negative feedback and B if they were able to justify what happened. If giving feedback is important for your students, ask them to list techniques which make for effective feedback e.g. summarising the main points, sandwiching a negative message between two positive points.

5 📼 **4.1** Check/Pre-teach: *low-budget, unappreciative, at the expense of.* Ask students to predict what the client will say and then play the recording through once. Check students understand the client's reaction (he was very positive about the presentation). Divide the class into pairs and ask follow-up questions e.g. *Were you surprised at the voice mail message? Would you have changed your feedback to the manager if you had heard the voice mail earlier? Would you now tell the manager about the positive feedback?*

Visuals

In this section, students focus on the equipment and visuals involved in giving a presentation and discuss the possible pitfalls of using PowerPoint. They focus on the language of referring to visuals and finally practise this language by giving a short presentation themselves, using a graph or chart.

1 Students give examples of the visual aids they use. Encourage them to justify their choice, giving the pros and cons of using the various types of equipment e.g. PowerPoint/video have visual impact but can be affected by technical problems. If appropriate, elicit other relevant vocabulary e.g. OHP (*overhead projector*), OHT (*overhead transparencies*) etc.

2 Focus attention on the title and elicit the likely tone of the text. Students read the text quickly to check (the tone is humorous and irreverent). Check comprehension of: *to inflict, cumulatively, numbing, beware of* and then elicit other language which indicates the writer's tone e.g. *death, defenceless, endless*. Ask follow-up questions e.g. *Have you ever been bored in a PowerPoint presentation? How do you react to presentations which depend on technology?*

📼 **4.1**

Hello, this is Cheng Jing from Nanogen Taiwan. I just wanted to let you know that your presentation this morning was a tremendous success with everyone here. What a brilliant idea to do the whole thing in such a casual, low-budget and alternative way! Very clever. The board certainly got the message.

I hope we didn't seem unappreciative as an audience. Quite the contrary. You must understand that not all our vice-presidents have the benefit of my Harvard education. And some of them don't speak English very well. But they really liked your calm, quiet approach. So please pass on my congratulations to your excellent presenter.

Oh, by the way, the joke about Beijing was greatly enjoyed – even in translation. As you know, we Taiwanese always like a good laugh at the expense of our Chinese neighbours. So, see you at the next strategy meeting. Goodbye now.

3   Remind students that collocations form strong word 'units' e.g. *to put something in perspective*, and identifying these units will help them complete the phrases. When students have completed the task, check the answers and the pronunciation of each expression. Write up any problematic examples on the board and mark in the stress and intonation.

4   Elicit students' reaction to the cartoon. With weaker groups, get the students to brainstorm possible topics for their graph/chart e.g. the ratio of men to women in the company, recent sales and profits etc. If appropriate, students can use source material such as the visuals in their company brochure or sets of figures from their company website.

Give students time to produce their graph/chart. Encourage them to use any available equipment to display their graphs e.g. OHTs, a flip-chart. If you have sets of blank cards, ask students to transfer the expressions they would like to use from exercise 3 onto individual cards. Many students like using these cards as prompts and writing key words stops students from reading a presentation aloud.

Divide the students into groups to give their presentations. Monitor and take feedback notes and then give language feedback on important or common errors.

Direct students' attention to the Lexis link on page 104 for more practice on the language of presentations.

Voice

Students start by reading a short text on the power of the voice. They then listen to six extracts from presentations to decide if the speakers have a positive or negative delivery. They analyse the speakers' delivery and then practise saying sentences in a fluent and confident way. They listen to an extract from a radio programme on drama techniques used in presenting and then try to deliver a speech taken from a film, using their voice for dramatic effect. Finally, they compare their speech with recorded versions and then give a short presentation, again using voice techniques.

1   Ask students if there any powerful speeches they remember from films or by politicians. Elicit the aspects of delivery that made them so powerful and memorable e.g. repeating phrases, pauses at key moments etc.

Draw students' attention to the title of the book by Gerry Spence and remind them that he is a lawyer. Ask them to predict three things he is likely to say in the text. Students read the text quickly to confirm their predictions. Check comprehension of *blurred, to recede* and then elicit the three main points Spence makes (the voice tells you something about a person, silence and pauses are as important as words, and that feelings, not just words, communicate the truth). Ask students if they agree with Spence's ideas.

3 All the expressions below can be used to comment on a visual in a presentation. Complete them using the verbs in the box.

notice	give	point	learn	mention	have	put	draw
see	show						

Introduction   _Have_ a look at this. As you can _see_, ...

Highlights   One thing you'll immediately _notice_ is that ...

I'd particularly like to _draw_ your attention to ...

I'd also like to _point_ out ...

And perhaps I should _mention_ ...

Context   Just to _give_ you some of the background to this ...

To _put_ this into some kind of perspective ...

Conclusions   Clearly then, what these figures _show_ is ...

The lesson we can _learn_ from this is ...

Lexis link

for more on the language
of presentations see
page 104

4 Draw a simple graph or chart relating to an interesting aspect of the business you're in *or* the company you work for *or* your country's economy. Use some of the expressions in 3 to present it to the class.

PROFITS

"This is where things started getting really weird."

Voice

1 In a career spanning over 50 years, charismatic lawyer Gerry Spence has never lost a criminal case. Read what he has to say about the power of the human voice.

The sound and the fury

We speak with an instrument we call 'the voice'. Listen to the sounds people make when they speak – only the sounds – and you will discover something of the person who is playing the instrument.

I learned that the spaces between words were as important as the words themselves. A word could be emphasised and a thought underlined by silence, by space, whilst the rapid, close, unbroken delivery of words causes the ideas to become blurred and recede into noise.

The voice reveals who we are and how we are more than the words we choose. And the feelings communicated in the sounds of words are the only truth.

Adapted from *How to Argue and Win Every Time* by Gerry Spence

Delivery   2   🎙 4.2 Listen to three presenters speaking in different ways. Decide which presenter sounds **1** fluent and confident **2** fluent but boring **3** hesitant.

    a   There's a whole market in Eastern Europe just there for the taking. ☐ *1*

    b   Quite frankly, the results we've been getting are absolutely incredible. ☐ 2

    c   Now, I'm sure I don't need to tell you just how crucial this is. ☐ 3

    d   Net profits are up ninety-seven per cent – yes, ninety-seven per cent. ☐ *1*

    e   Would you believe that so far we've not been able to sell a single unit? ☐ 2

    f   Miss this deadline and we'll lose the biggest client this company's ever had. ☐ 3

3   Why does the boring presenter sound so monotonous?
He doesn't pause and fails to stress important words.

4   What exactly is the hesitant presenter doing wrong?
pausing and stressing in the wrong place

5   🎙 4.3 Work with a partner. Listen again to the fluent and confident versions. One of you should mark the pauses like this: | The other should underline the stressed words. Compare your results. What's the connection between where we pause and what we stress? _We tend to pause after stressed words._

6   🎙 4.4 Deliver all the sentences in 2 in a fluent and confident way. Experiment with longer pauses and stronger stresses. Then compare your version with the recording.

Discussion   7   🎙 4.5 According to Swedish businessman Jan Carlzon, 'All business is show business.' Listen to an extract from a radio programme on how several training companies have taken his opinion literally, and discuss the questions.

    a   Would William Freeman's advice help you face a business audience?

    b   What does Michael Lame think classically trained actors can teach business people? _how to speak effectively and relate to an audience_

    c   According to Richard Olivier, what makes someone a brilliant speaker?
       self-belief

    d   Which of the trainees' opinions would be closest to your own?

Fluency   8   Work with a partner. Choose one of the film speeches opposite and take turns to be the actor and director.

    •   The speeches are unpunctuated. Decide where you are going to pause – mark short pauses like this: | , longer pauses like this: | | and very long pauses like this: | | |

    •   Underline the words you are going to stress: usually nouns and verbs, but sometimes, for dramatic effect, you can stress pronouns and conjunctions.

    •   Highlight in different colours parts of the text you really want to project, even shout, and parts you want to say quietly or perhaps whisper.

    •   Try the speech a few times, the actor speaking, the director giving advice and feedback. When you are ready, perform it!

9   🎙 4.6 Listen to the speeches in 8. How does your performance compare with the recorded version? If you were competing, who'd get the Oscar?

10 Prepare a one-minute presentation on a topic which is relevant to your work. Make your voice as powerful and dramatic as you did in the film speech.

Delivery

2 **4.2** Ask students to read sentences a–f through quickly and deal with any vocabulary queries. Tell students they are going to hear the six sentences delivered in different ways and that they should write down the appropriate number 1–3 next to each one, depending on the speaker's delivery. Play the recording and get student to record their answers. Check the answers with the class.

3 Play sentences b and e again and elicit the answer.

4 Play sentences c and f again and check the answer. Emphasise the fact that pausing in the wrong place will make a speech sound stilted and give the impression that the speaker is lacking in confidence.

5 **4.3** Tell students that they will hear sentences a and d again. Divide the class into AB pairs – student A marks the pauses and student B underlines the stressed words. Play the sentences and get students to check their answers against the recording script on page 143. Play the recording again if necessary and elicit the connection between stresses and pauses (we tend to pause after stressed words). Point out that the more pauses a speaker uses, the more stressed syllables there will be and the more dramatic it will sound.

6 **4.4** With weaker classes, demonstrate a fluent and confident delivery of the sentences first. Get students to repeat the phrases in a quick drill if necessary. Ask students to read the sentences a–f out loud. Encourage them to have fun experimenting with the delivery but don't insist they 'perform' the sentences for the class at this stage. Play the recording to allow the students to compare their version.

Discussion

7 **4.5** Read out the quotation from Jan Carlzon and ask students to say what they think he means (that business involves an element of performance). Check/Pre-teach: *to make a debut, to take a deep breath, to act the part, classically trained actor, platform speaker, to pitch a client, to fake, paradoxically, to brush up*. Ask students to brainstorm the pros and cons of using drama techniques in business training e.g. it can improve confidence/help with delivery; people may not take it seriously/it may not be relevant etc. Tell students to see how many of their ideas are mentioned in the extract. Play the recording through once and check the answers.

Before playing the recording again, get students to read the questions a–d. Play the extract again, pausing after each speaker to let the students note down their answers.

Students discuss the questions in pairs/small groups. Hold a short class feedback session to check the answers and elicit students' opinions.

Fluency

8 Ask students which of the films on page 25 they have seen and elicit a brief summary. With weaker groups, check/pre-teach: *to fire shots, to lose track, punk, race, gender, PDA* (personal digital assistant), *consciousness, loathsome, repulsive, retarded, morally reprehensible, lousy* (US colloquial for 'awful'), *defiance, tyranny*.

Work on the first extract with the whole class to mark in the pauses, stressed words and parts of the text for special delivery. Work with a few confident students to get them to deliver the lines dramatically. Encourage the other students to 'direct' to achieve dramatic effect.

Divide the class into pairs and ask students to choose a film speech. Give students time to study the text, write in the pauses and stresses and highlight key parts. Remind students that speaking quietly can arouse audience interest and that pausing creates dramatic effect. Encourage students to practise the speeches more than once and get them to switch roles when they have finished. Monitor and help as necessary, but avoid directing the students yourself unless they find the task very difficult.

When the students have practised, get one or two students to come out and perform their speech. Allow students to have several 'takes' if they need them, and, if possible, create some kind of clapper board to set up each one. If your students prefer not to perform in front of the class, get them to make an audio recording and play these at the end of the lesson. Get the students to light-heartedly suggest a best actor award!

9 **4.6** Play the recording so students can compare their performance with the recorded versions. (Point out that the recordings are of actors speaking in the style of the original performers, not the film actors themselves.)

10 Students choose a title for a one-minute presentation e.g. *motivating people*. With weaker groups, provide a template to help structure the presentation e.g. Name/job/an opening 'hook' such as a rhetorical question/main point(s)/closing statement. Remind students to concentrate on getting their message across confidently and to try to use delivery techniques from this unit.

Keep to the one-minute time limit for each presentation. Ask the class to give constructive feedback on each student's performance.

See page T25 for recording scripts 4.2, 4.3, 4.4, 4.5 and 4.6.

If you're short of time

Set the text *The Kennedy-Nixon debate* on page 21 for homework.

Omit exercise 3 on page 22.

Omit exercise 1 on page 23.

Omit exercise 7 on page 24.

Recording scripts for page T24

4.2

a
There's a whole market in Eastern Europe just there for the taking.

b
Quite frankly, the results we've been getting are absolutely incredible.

c
Now, I'm sure I don't need to tell you just how crucial this is.

d
Net profits are up ninety-seven per cent – yes, ninety-seven per cent.

e
Would you believe that so far we've not been able to sell a single unit?

f
Miss this deadline and we'll lose the biggest client this company's ever had.

4.3

a
There's a whole <u>market</u> | in Eastern <u>Europe</u> | just <u>there</u> for the <u>taking</u>.

b
<u>Net profits</u> | are up <u>ninety-seven</u> per <u>cent</u> | – <u>yes</u>, | <u>ninety-</u> | <u>seven</u> | per <u>cent</u>.

4.4

a
There's a whole <u>market</u> | in Eastern <u>Europe</u> | just <u>there</u> for the <u>taking</u>.

b
Quite <u>frankly</u>, | the <u>results</u> we've been <u>getting</u> | are <u>absolutely</u> | <u>incredible</u>.

c
<u>Now</u>, I'm <u>sure</u> I don't need to <u>tell</u> you | just how <u>crucial</u> | this <u>is</u>.

d
<u>Net profits</u> | are up <u>ninety-seven</u> per <u>cent</u> | – <u>yes</u>, | <u>ninety-</u> | <u>seven</u> | per <u>cent</u>.

e
Would you <u>believe</u> | that <u>so</u> far | we've <u>not</u> been <u>able</u> to <u>sell</u> | a <u>single</u> <u>unit</u>?

f
<u>Miss</u> | <u>this</u> | <u>deadline</u> | and we'll <u>lose</u> the <u>biggest client</u> | this <u>company's</u> <u>ever</u> <u>had</u>.

4.5

A: Welcome back to CBN Business. To be or not to be? That is the question for an increasing number of companies putting their staff through drama courses, no less, in an attempt to turn them into better public speakers. Jon Heller meets a group of British managers making their theatrical debut.

B: 'Next time you are about to make a presentation, take a deep breath and imagine yourself walking on stage – about to give the performance of your life.' That's the advice of William Freeman of Cambridge Associates, one of a new breed of management trainers who believe that presenting is less about PowerPoint and more about acting the part.

At Prospero, a company with similar aims, Tina Packer and Michael Lame have taken the idea one step further and put Shakespeare on the program. Who better to teach managers how to speak effectively and relate to an audience, they ask, than classically trained actors? Whether you're a platform speaker at the annual conference, a salesperson pitching a client or just chairing your weekly staff meeting, actors have powerful communication techniques you can learn from. Prospero is certainly in demand, regularly running courses at Columbia Business School, Harvard and MIT.

So what is it that makes someone a brilliant speaker? Richard Olivier, Royal Shakespeare Company director, creative management consultant and son of acting legend Sir Laurence Olivier, thinks it's 'self-belief'. According to Olivier, 'Much of leadership is acting. Not faking it, but taking on a role. Paradoxically, the acting makes it real.'
But what do the trainees think? We questioned a few who'd taken a course in acting like leaders:

C: I thought my boss had gone quite mad at first. I mean, Shakespeare? No way, I thought! But, in fact, it's been really inspiring. And a lot of fun!

D: Frankly, I was terrified. Me, acting on stage? I don't think so. But I've learned a lot of stuff I never got on those boring presentation courses.

E: Well, the actors have been fun to work with. We've had a lot of laughs. I'm not sure how useful it all is, though – you know, in a business context. But, hey, it got us out of the office for a couple of days, so I'm not complaining.

F: Well, this really isn't my thing at all. I mean, public speaking just frightens the life out of me as it is, without getting up and acting in front of an audience. Frankly, it was hell. Never again!

G: Best course I've ever done – by far. Just totally brilliant. I never realised the true power of the voice and the confidence it gives you when you can make it work for you. I'd definitely recommend this kind of training.

B: So, there we have it. Time to shut down your laptop, brush up your Shakespeare and learn how to wow an audience with the professionals.

4.6

Take 1
I <u>know</u> what you're <u>thinking</u> | | did he <u>fire</u> <u>six</u> shots | | or only <u>five</u>? | | | <u>Well</u> | to <u>tell</u> you the <u>truth</u> | in all this <u>excitement</u> | | I've <u>kind</u> of lost <u>track</u> <u>myself</u> | | | but being as this is a <u>point</u> <u>four</u> <u>four</u> <u>Magnum</u> | | the most <u>powerful</u> <u>handgun</u> in the <u>world</u> | | and would <u>blow</u> your <u>head</u> <u>clean</u> <u>off</u> | | | I <u>guess</u> you've got to <u>ask</u> yourself one <u>question</u> | | | do <u>I</u> feel <u>lucky</u>? | | | <u>Well</u> | <u>do</u> you | <u>punk</u>?

Take 2
<u>What</u> we're <u>selling</u> here | | is <u>freedom</u> | | | <u>We</u> <u>offer</u> | through <u>technology</u> | | what <u>religion</u> | and <u>revolution</u> | have <u>promised</u> | | but <u>never</u> <u>delivered</u> | | | <u>Freedom</u> from the <u>physical</u> <u>body</u> | | <u>freedom</u> from <u>race</u> and <u>gender</u> | | from <u>nationality</u> | and <u>personality</u> | | from <u>place</u> | and <u>time</u> | | <u>Communicating</u> by <u>cellular</u> <u>phone</u> | and <u>hand-held</u> <u>computer</u> | <u>PDA</u> | and built-in <u>fax-modem</u> | | <u>we</u> can <u>relate</u> to each <u>other</u> | as <u>pure</u> | <u>consciousness</u>

Take 3
The <u>good</u> news is | you're <u>fired</u> | | | The <u>bad</u> news is | you've <u>got</u> | <u>all</u> you've <u>got</u> | is <u>one</u> <u>week</u> | to get your <u>jobs</u> <u>back</u> | | | Have I got your <u>attention</u> <u>now</u>? | | <u>Good</u> | Because we're <u>adding</u> a little <u>something</u> to <u>this</u> month's <u>sales</u> <u>competition</u> | | | <u>First</u> <u>prize</u> | as you <u>know</u> | is a <u>Cadillac</u> <u>Eldorado</u> | <u>Second</u> <u>prize</u> is a <u>set</u> of <u>steak</u> <u>knives</u> | | | <u>Third</u> <u>prize</u> <u>is</u> | you're <u>fired</u> | | <u>Do</u> you <u>get</u> the <u>picture</u>? | | <u>Are</u> you <u>laughing</u> <u>now</u>?

Take 4
I <u>think</u> | <u>No</u> | I am <u>positive</u> | that <u>you</u> <u>are</u> | the <u>most</u> <u>unattractive</u> <u>man</u> | I have <u>ever</u> <u>met</u> in my <u>entire</u> <u>life</u> | | | You <u>know</u> | in the <u>short</u> time we've been <u>together</u> | <u>you</u> have <u>demonstrated</u> | <u>every</u> loathsome <u>characteristic</u> | of the <u>male</u> <u>personality</u> | | and even <u>discovered</u> a few <u>new</u> <u>ones</u> | | | You are physically <u>repulsive</u> | intellectually <u>retarded</u> | you're morally <u>reprehensible</u> | <u>vulgar</u> | <u>insensitive</u> | <u>selfish</u> | <u>stupid</u> | | You have <u>no</u> <u>taste</u> | a <u>lousy</u> <u>sense</u> of <u>humour</u> | | and you <u>smell</u> | | | You're <u>not</u> even interesting enough to <u>make</u> me <u>sick</u> | | | <u>Goodbye</u> <u>Darryl</u> | | and <u>thank</u> you for a <u>lovely</u> <u>lunch</u>

Take 5
I | | | am <u>William</u> <u>Wallace</u> | | | And I <u>see</u> | a whole <u>army</u> of my <u>countrymen</u> | | <u>here</u> | in <u>defiance</u> | of <u>tyranny</u> | | | You have <u>come</u> to <u>fight</u> as <u>free</u> <u>men</u> | | and <u>free</u> <u>men</u> you <u>are</u> | | <u>What</u> will you <u>do</u> with that <u>freedom</u>? | | | <u>Will</u> you <u>fight</u>? | | | <u>Aye</u> | <u>fight</u> | and you may <u>die</u> | | <u>run</u> | and you'll <u>live</u> | | | at <u>least</u> a <u>while</u> | | And <u>dying</u> in your <u>beds</u> | many <u>years</u> from <u>now</u> | would <u>you</u> be <u>willing</u> | to <u>trade</u> | <u>all</u> the <u>days</u> | from <u>this</u> day to <u>that</u> | for <u>one</u> <u>chance</u> | | just <u>one</u> <u>chance</u> | | to <u>come</u> back <u>here</u> | and <u>tell</u> our <u>enemies</u> | | that they may <u>take</u> our <u>lives</u> | | but they'll <u>never</u> | | <u>take</u> our <u>freedom</u>!

Take 1: Clint Eastwood in *Dirty Harry*
A police detective tries to get a murder suspect to put down his gun after a shoot-out
I know what you're thinking did he fire six shots or only five well to tell you the truth in all this excitement I've kind of lost track myself but being as this is a point four four Magnum the most powerful handgun in the world and would blow your head clean off I guess you've got to ask yourself one question do I feel lucky well do you punk

Take 2: Demi Moore in *Disclosure*
The new boss in a software firm presents the company's latest product
What we're selling here is freedom we offer through technology what religion and revolution have promised but never delivered freedom from the physical body freedom from race and gender from nationality and personality from place and time communicating by cellular phone and hand-held computer PDA and built-in fax-modem we can relate to each other as pure consciousness

Take 3: Alec Baldwin in *Glengarry Glen Ross*
A sales manager is trying to motivate his team of sales staff to close more sales
The good news is you're fired the bad news is you've got all you've got is one week to get your jobs back have I got your attention now good because we're adding a little something to this month's sales competition first prize as you know is a Cadillac Eldorado second prize is a set of steak knives third prize is you're fired do you get the picture are you laughing now

Take 4: Cher in *The Witches of Eastwick*
A woman makes it clear she doesn't wish to see her lunch-date again
I think no I am positive that you are the most unattractive man I have ever met in my entire life you know in the short time we've been together you have demonstrated every loathsome characteristic of the male personality and even discovered a few new ones you are physically repulsive intellectually retarded you're morally reprehensible vulgar insensitive selfish stupid you have no taste a lousy sense of humour and you smell you're not even interesting enough to make me sick goodbye Darryl and thank you for a lovely lunch

Take 5: Mel Gibson in *Braveheart*
A Scottish rebel leader, outnumbered by an opposing English army, tries to motivate his men!
I am William Wallace and I see a whole army of my countrymen here in defiance of tyranny you have come to fight as free men and free men you are what will you do with that freedom will you fight aye fight and you may die run and you'll live at least a while and dying in your beds many years from now would you be willing to trade all the days from this day to that for one chance just one chance to come back here and tell our enemies that they may take our lives but they'll never take our freedom

5 Problems on the phone

No problem is so formidable that you can't walk away from it.

Charles M. Schulz, creator of the Peanuts cartoon

Discussion

1 It's been said that 'When the phone rings, there's usually a problem on the other end of it.' What problems do people phone you with at work?

2 How much of your working day do you spend on the phone? How much of that time is productive?

3 Complete the text below using the nouns and verbs in the boxes.

Glossary

chatterer person who can't stop talking about trivia

24/7 24 hours a day, 7 days a week

something	day	minute	point	line	thing	time
chatter	business	touch				

get	get	do	go	keep	say	listen	hear	continue	expect

HOW TO DISPOSE OF
CHATTERERS
ON THE PHONE

We are living in the age of telephony. One sixth of the planet now has a mobile. In Finland, where they have more mobiles per person than anywhere else on earth, 25% of the
5 country's exports are Nokia phones. Whenever we want, wherever we want, we can get in (a) **touch**.
But when we do, it seems we can never get to the (b) **point**. Up to two hours in every working day are wasted in idle (c) **chatter** on the phone. And
10 great skill and determination are needed to escape the deadly game of social chit-chat – 'How are you? ... Settling in to the new job? ... How's Ellen? ... And the kids? ... Hasn't your eldest just gone to college? ... How (d) **time** flies! ... Oh, I (e) **hear**
15 you're moving house as well. ... Did you have a nice holiday, by the way? ... I suppose you haven't heard the latest, then? ... Well, I'm not supposed to (f) **say**, but there's a rumour going about ...'
Of course, what you want to say in these
20 circumstances is 'Look, I haven't got all (g) **day**. Either state your (h) **business** or kindly get off the phone,' but professional courtesy forbids it. Here, then, is the definitive executive guide to 'chatterer disposal'.

Getting down to business The most tactful way of
25 bringing the conversation round to the subject of business is to ask in a slightly louder than normal voice

'What can I (i) **do** for you?' If you know the caller, you could try 'I (j) **expect** you're calling about ...' and then mention anything you can think of.
30 They, hopefully, will reply 'Er, no, actually, it's about something else.' Should this strategy fail, you may have to resort to a sterner 'Was there (k) **something** you wanted to talk to me about?'

Ending the conversation Phone call termination is
35 more difficult. The trick is not to seem too abrupt. 'Anyway, ...' – though a clear signal to most averagely perceptive people that you want to end the call – is much too subtle for chatterers. Try instead 'Well, I mustn't (l) **keep** you', 'I'll let you (m) **get**
40 on' or the more insistent 'I'll have to let you (n) **go** now.' If you feel that sounds a little too harsh, friendlier alternatives include 'Well, (o) **listen**, it's been great talking to you', 'We must (p) **get** together soon' or 'Oh, one last
45 (q) **thing** and then I really must go.' Of course, with a hardened chatterer this last alternative may be asking for trouble.

Drastic measures In genuine emergencies the following may be used: 'Ah, someone's just this
50 (r) **minute** stepped into the office. I'm afraid we'll have to (s) **continue** this conversation later. Bye.' Or 'Oh, I've got an international call just come in on the other (t) **line**. Can I call you back?' And, if all else fails, you can always try 'Hello? Hello? Are you
55 still there?' Of course the secret with this one is that when the caller says 'Yes, I'm still here,' resist the temptation to reply 'Well, I can't hear you!'

Desk work   5 Problems on the phone

Students fill in the missing words in a text about time-wasters on the phone. They listen to a recording of someone trying to get rid of an unwanted caller and then practise themselves through a roleplay. The students then focus on handling customer complaints and the appropriate language to use. They focus on the problem of angry/insulting e-mails, roleplay how to deal with them and rewrite two e-mails to make them more polite. (You can make photocopies of the e-mail template on page 184 for this task.)

The students do a series of activities based on recordings of telephone conversations between two people who are trying to solve a problem. They focus on idioms and useful expressions from the conversations. Fluency practice is provided by a final problem-solving exercise.

The grammatical focus is on complex question formation and the lexical focus is on phone, fax and e-mail.

In this first section, students discuss problems that other people phone them about and then think about how long they spend on the telephone in their jobs. They read a text about how to deal with chatterers on the phone and fill in the missing words. They listen to someone trying to end a phone conversation and then use key expressions in a phone roleplay.

Warm-up

As a lead-in to this unit, elicit pros and cons of using the phone e.g. it can save time/help in solving immediate problems/you can do other things while on the phone; there is no support from eye contact or body language/there can be technical and reception problems, especially on mobile phones. Ask students how they feel about using English on the phone.

Discussion

Read out the quotation from Charles M. Schultz and ask if students agree. Elicit how students prefer to deal with problems – by phone, letter or e-mail, or face to face – and get students to give reasons for their answers.

1   Divide students into groups and get them to list the problems they have to deal with by phone at work. Ask the students to categorise the problems e.g. internal with employees/management, external with clients etc. Ask a student from each group to feed back to the whole class.

2   Ask students to estimate the amount of time they spend on the telephone at work and then to say how much of that time is productive. Point out that time management training suggests people should 'block' phone calls i.e. only take calls at specific times of the day. Elicit other ideas to help deal with a high volume of calls e.g. set up specific slots for calls that happen on a regular basis.

3   Focus attention on the glossary to check/pre-teach: *chatterer* and *trivia*. Check students know how to say the term *twenty-four/seven*.

Write up the main and sub-headings from the text on the board and ask students to tell you what techniques they have used to 'dispose of chatterers'. Students skim the text to see if any of their ideas are included.

With weaker classes, check/pre-teach: *telephony, idle chatter, courtesy, tactful, stern, abrupt, subtle, harsh, hardened*. Ask students to read the text again and fill in the gaps. Call out the letters and elicit the answers as a whole class check. Check students understand the tone of the article (gently humorous). Ask them to give examples from the text which highlight this e.g. *deadly game, genuine emergency*.

Recording script for page T27

▭ 5.2

A: Hello. Thank you for calling the iDeals customer service line. All our customer service advisers are busy right now. Please hold and your enquiry will be dealt with shortly … This is the iDeals customer service line. Thank you for holding. All our customer service advisers are busy right now. Please hold and your enquiry will be dealt with shortly …

B: Oh, come on, come on!

C: Good morning. Lisa speaking. **How can I help you?**

B: Oh, hello. At last! I was just about to ring off.

C: I am sorry about that. The waiting system is a bit frustrating, isn't it? It's the only way we can offer our 24-hour service, you see.

B: Yeah, yeah. Look, it's about the computer I bought off you two weeks ago …

C: Yes? **What seems to be the problem?**

B: Well, I was transferring my files to it from my zip drive and it's lost the lot. Everything!

C: OK, now don't worry. I'm sure we can sort something out. First, can you give me a few details? The computer has lost all your data, you say?

B: Yes. But, you don't understand. It's wiped everything off the zip drive as well! My whole life, my whole life was in those files.

C: Oh, my goodness! Are you sure? Sounds like the problem's with your zip drive.

B: Of course I'm sure! And there's nothing wrong with my zip drive. I've had it years!

C: OK. **I can understand how upset you must be.** Now, I don't think we can deal with this on the phone, so I'm going to send a service engineer to see if they can retrieve your data. Can you give me your product reference number?

B: Hm? Er, yes. It's … here it is … it's SF11–003.

C: Thank you.

B: I'll be expecting a total refund *and* compensation if this can't be fixed!

C: **Unfortunately, we're not authorised to give refunds, but what I can do is send you a brand-new computer. How would that be?**

B: This is supposed to be a brand-new computer. You think I want another one of these, after what the last one did to my files?

C: Well, let's see what our engineer can do. Hopefully, it's not quite as bad as you think. Now, I've got your address here in your customer file. Oxford OX2 6BJ, right?

B: Yeah, right.

C: And it's Mr Harris, isn't it?

B: Yes.

C: Right, Mr Harris. We'll have an engineer with you this afternoon. And I'll ask him to bring a new hard disk with him. **Is that all OK for you?**

B: Er, well, I suppose …

C: Good. **Glad to be of assistance. Is there anything else I can help you with?**

B: Hm? Oh, no, no.

C: Well, best of luck this afternoon. I hope we can solve the problem for you.

B: Well, thanks. Erm, goodbye.

C: Goodbye, Mr Harris.

4 ▭ **5.1** Tell students they will hear a phone conversation between two men – Dan and George. Ask the students to note down who is the chatterer and who is trying to get rid of him and what is the purpose of the call. Play the recording through once and check the answers (Dan is trying to get rid of George. George eventually says he is coming to London and wants to meet.)

Play the recording again and ask students to underline the expressions they hear in the text in exercise 3. Pause the recording at intervals. Check the answers with the class or refer students to the recording script on page 144 where the expressions appear in bold.

Fluency

5 Ask the students to look at the recording scripts on page 144 and make a note of any key expressions they wish to use. If appropriate, get students to transfer the language onto cards to use as prompts during the roleplay. Check pronunciation and intonation of the key expressions.

Divide students in AB pairs. Refer the A students to page 130 and the B students to page 129. Have students read their role card and deal with any vocabulary queries. Check they know who is going to start the phone conversation. If possible, use internal telephones for the roleplay or ask students to sit back to back.

Monitor and take feedback notes. When the students have finished, ask one student from each pair to summarise the outcome of the conversation and to say if they did any business. Give feedback on overall fluency before highlighting any important or common errors.

Dealing with complaints

In this section, students discuss formal complaints they have made and then study a model of how to deal with customer complaints. They focus on the appropriate language to use when dealing with a phone complaint, comparing their choices with a recorded conversation. They read through two e-mails written in anger and then take part in a telephone roleplay with a partner to respond to the e-mails. They rewrite the angry e-mails to make them more polite and then repeat the follow-up phone roleplays to assess the difference.

Discussion

1 Give an example of a formal complaint that you made and then ask students to discuss the questions in pairs. Elicit a few examples from students and then ask follow-up questions: *What things helped produce a successful outcome? Did losing your temper help achieve the desired outcome, or did it have the opposite effect?*

2 Check/Pre-teach: *to reassure, to empathise*. After the students have ordered the stages, ask them to compare their answers with a partner. Then check the answers with the class.

3 When choosing the inappropriate expressions, encourage students to read the sentences aloud to highlight how they would come across to the person complaining. When the students have completed the task, check the answers and elicit what is wrong with the inappropriate expressions e.g. over-familiar, over-direct.

4 ▭ **5.2** Check/Pre-teach: *to ring off, frustrating, to sort out, to wipe (data) off, to retrieve, refund, compensation*. Ask students to listen to the conversation and note down: the problem, the outcome, the tone of the caller and of the customer services adviser. Play the recording through once and check the answers (the problem is with the hard drive and the caller has lost a lot of data; the company will send an engineer to sort out the problem or replace the faulty computer; the tone of the caller changes from anger to being pacified and the tone of the adviser is polite and helpful).

Play the recording again and get students to compare the phrases they chose in exercise 3 with what the customer services adviser said. Check which expressions she used: stage 1 a, stage 2 c, stage 3 c, stage 4 c, stage 5 a, stage 6 b. Find out if students chose the same options. Point out that both sets of options are equally valid.

See page T26 for recording script 5.2.

▭ **5.1**

B: Hello?
A: Dan?
B: Speaking.
A: It's George. George Chatterton.
B: Ah, George … How are you?
A: Couldn't be better, mate, couldn't be better! Someone happened to mention they'd bumped into you the other day. So I just thought I'd give you a call. See how you're doing.
B: Oh, right. … yes … er, George …
A: So how's it going, mate? Just been promoted, so I hear.
B: Er, yes, that's right.
A: Glad to see they've finally started appreciating you.
B: Er, yes, thanks. So, George, **what can I do for you?**
A: Bit more money too, I imagine.
B: Hm? Oh, a bit, yeah. Well, George, **I expect you're calling about** that …
A: And how's that lovely wife of yours?

B: Suzanne? Oh, she's fine.
A: Splendid, splendid. And the kids?
B: They're fine too. Look, George, I *am* rather busy right now. I've just got back from holiday, actually, and you know what it's like. **Was there something you wanted to talk to me about?**
A: Of course, how silly of me! You've just been on that safari you were planning last time we spoke, haven't you?
B: Yes, and what with the new job and everything, there's a bit of catching up …
A: Kenya, wasn't it?
B: What?
A: The holiday – Kenya.
B: Yes. Listen. George …
A: You know, I've always wanted to go to Kenya …

B: Well, now, George, **I mustn't keep you.**
A: What's that?
B: **I'll let you get on.** I'm sure you've got

things to do, busy guy like you. **It's been great talking to you**, though.
A: Yeah, likewise.
B: **We must get together soon**.
A: Yeah, yeah. As a matter of fact, I'm going to be in London for a few days next month.
B: Oh, god.
A: Sorry?
B: I said 'Oh, good.' Perhaps we can meet up for a beer.
A: Yeah, that'd be great.
B: But, erm, **I'll have to let you go now**, George. **Someone's just this minute stepped into the office**.
A: Oh, right, I see.
B: And it looks like **I've got an international call just come in on the other line** as well. Yes.
A: No worries. I'll call you back in half an hour, then. I haven't told you *my* good news yet. Wait till you hear it!
B: What? Er, no. Erm, George? George?

---

4 📼 5.1 Listen to someone trying unsuccessfully to get a caller off the phone. Underline the expressions they use in 3.

Fluency **5** Work with a partner to practise dealing with a chatterer. Speaker A see page 130. Speaker B see page 129.

Dealing with complaints

Discussion **1** When was the last time you made a formal complaint about something? Was it in person, in writing or on the phone? Were you satisfied with the way it was handled?

2 Put the following stages of handling a customer complaint into the most likely order:

- suggest possible solutions
- end on a positive note
- greet and reassure the caller
- get the details
- agree on a course of action
- listen and empathise

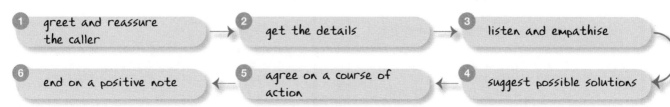

1 greet and reassure the caller → 2 get the details → 3 listen and empathise

6 end on a positive note ← 5 agree on a course of action ← 4 suggest possible solutions

3 Which of the following expressions would be most inappropriate at each of the stages in 2? Delete one from each set of three below. Then underline which of the remaining two you prefer.

Stage 1 **a** How can I help you?
b What can I do for you?
c ~~What's the matter, then?~~

Stage 2 **a** Can you tell me exactly what the problem is?
b ~~What exactly is your problem?~~
c What seems to be the problem?

Stage 3 **a** ~~Tell me about it! I know just how you feel.~~
b I can understand exactly how you feel.
c I can understand how upset you must be.

Stage 4 **a** ~~Well, I suppose I could always send you a new one, but I can't give you a refund. Sorry.~~
b I can't give you a refund, I'm afraid, but I can certainly send you a new one. How's that?
c Unfortunately, we're not authorised to give refunds, but what I can do is send you a brand-new one. How would that be?

Stage 5 **a** Is that all OK for you?
b ~~Are you satisfied now?~~
c Are you happy with that?

Stage 6 **a** I'm so pleased we've managed to sort this out. Was there anything else?
b Glad to be of assistance. Is there anything else I can help you with?
c ~~Good, well, that's that, then. Is there anything else or is that it?~~

4 📼 5.2 Listen to a customer services adviser at iDeals, a computer supplies retail chain, dealing with a complaint and compare what she says with your choices in 3.

5 A 'flame' is an angry or insulting e-mail. Have you ever received or been tempted to write one?

Fluency 6 Work with a partner. Read the flames you and your partner wrote below and take turns to hold the telephone conversations that might have followed. Caller, be as direct as you like. Receiver, calm the caller down and deal with their complaint.

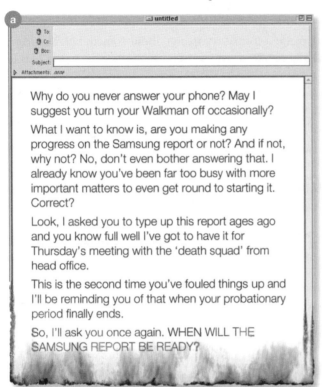

a

Why do you never answer your phone? May I suggest you turn your Walkman off occasionally?

What I want to know is, are you making any progress on the Samsung report or not? And if not, why not? No, don't even bother answering that. I already know you've been far too busy with more important matters to even get round to starting it. Correct?

Look, I asked you to type up this report ages ago and you know full well I've got to have it for Thursday's meeting with the 'death squad' from head office.

This is the second time you've fouled things up and I'll be reminding you of that when your probationary period finally ends.

So, I'll ask you once again. WHEN WILL THE SAMSUNG REPORT BE READY?

b

For the third time this week, WHERE IS OUR ORDER???

We ordered $15,000 of shirts from you three – yes, three – months ago and so far what have you sent us? That's right, nothing! Not even so much as an e-mail to explain why it's taking so long. This is an utter disgrace.

You call yourselves the world's leading promotional products company and you can't even manage to organise 6,000 polo shirts with a simple company logo on. Frankly, it's pathetic. I notice you had no problem debiting our account for the $15,000, though.

I'm sure it's too much to expect an apology, but if I don't see those shirts within the next 48 hours, I'll see you in court. GOT IT?

7 Rewrite the e-mail you sent in 6 to make it more polite but equally assertive. Use the prompts below to help you.

    a Unfortunately / unable / reach / phone

       Can / tell / managing / make / progress / Samsung report? // having / problems / please let / know / soon / possible // understand / been preoccupied / other matters / may not / even / made a start yet / although / hope / not / case

       did ask / some time ago / this report / as you know / do need / urgently / Thursday's meeting / people / head office

       not / first time / let me down / consequently / shall have / discuss / matter / when / probationary period ends

       really must know today how / longer / going / take

    b again writing / regard / order / ref no 099X

       records show / order / $15,000 / shirts / placed three months / but so far / received anything // Nor / sent / e-mail explaining / reason / delay // afraid / quite unacceptable

       You advertise / world's leading promotional products company // therefore / find / inability / take care / simple order like this both surprising / disappointing // notice / however / were more efficient / debiting / account / sum / $15,000

       should like / delivery / 48 hours / together / apology // Otherwise / no alternative / hand / matter over / legal department // hope / made myself clear

5 Discuss the question with the class and then ask students if they have ever received 'training' on using an appropriate tone in e-mails and if their company has a policy on handling 'flames'.

Fluency

6 Check/Pre-teach: *to bother, to get round to, to foul things up, disgrace, pathetic*. Divide the class into AB pairs and get students to read their e-mail quickly. Check the A students understand who the 'death squad' is referring to (difficult bosses). Ask students what make these e-mails inappropriate e.g. use of direct questions, blunt/sarcastic tone, direct threats, use of capitals/repeated punctuation.

Tell students that they will now act out the telephone conversations which might have taken place after sending the e-mails. If possible, use internal telephones for this exercise or ask students to sit back to back. Give students a few minutes to prepare their calls. Remind the caller to be direct and the receiver to calm him/her down and deal with the complaint as successfully as possible.

With weaker classes, model the roleplay with two stronger students first. Monitor and take feedback notes. Get students to swap roles when they have finished the first call. Hold a short feedback session and ask the students about the outcome of the calls and if they dealt with the complaint well. Feed back on overall fluency before highlighting important or common errors.

7 If appropriate, hand out copies of the e-mail template on page 184. Point out that the mark // indicates that students should start a new sentence. Ask the A and B students to rewrite their respective e-mails using the prompts. With weaker students, elicit a few opening lines of each e-mail with the whole class first. Check possible answers with the class, accepting any correct and appropriate alternatives.

Suggested answers

a Unfortunately I've been unable to reach you on the phone.

Can you tell me if you're managing to make any progress on the Samsung report? If you're having problems, please let me know as soon as possible. I understand you've been preoccupied with other matters and may not even have made a start yet, although I hope this is not the case.

I did ask you some time ago for this report and, as you know, I do need it urgently for Thursday's meeting with the people from head office.

This is not the first time you've let me down and consequently I shall have to discuss the matter with you when your probationary period ends.

I really must know today how much longer it's going to take.

b I am again writing to you with regard to our order, reference no 099X.

Our records show that our order of $15,000 of shirts was placed three months ago but so far we have not received anything. Nor have you sent us an e-mail explaining the reason for the delay. I am afraid this is quite unacceptable.

You advertise yourselves as the world's leading promotional products company. I therefore find your inability to take care of a simple order like this both surprising and disappointing. I did notice, however, that you were more efficient in debiting our account for the sum of $15,000.

I should like the delivery within 48 hours together with an apology. Otherwise I have no alternative but to hand the matter over to our legal department. I hope I have made myself clear.

Recording script for page T29

5.5

A: Hello?
B: Hello, Piotr.
A: Graham! You said an hour.
B: Sorry. I got held up.
A: What's happening, then?
B: Right. I've been on to the carriers and they're sending a new stand out on the next plane. You should have that by tomorrow morning.
A: Well, at least that's something.
B: **Can you get hold of the organisers** and tell them we'll set up tomorrow at 7?
A: Yeah, sure. **I don't suppose you remembered to put another CD player in** with the stand?
B: I've sent two – just in case.
A: Oh, right. Good. Thanks.
B: And **do you happen to have a phone number for the promotions people?**

Because if those CDs are defective, I'll get them to send more by courier.
A: I've got it somewhere. Graham, **is there any chance of sending someone else out here?** Kim, for instance.
B: Piotr, you know how short-staffed we are here right now.
A: What's this exhibition costing us, Graham? $18,000?
B: You're right. **I'll check with Liz and see if she can spare Kim for a few days**.
A: Thanks. It's murder here.
B: Well, **I'll see what I can do, but I can't promise anything**.
A: Hm. And **would you mind getting some brochures to me in Polish**, seeing as I'm in Poland?
B: Yes, we're having a few problems with that – seem to have run out. **Is there any point in sending the ones we've got in Russian?**

A: No, Graham, not a great idea. Send the German ones, if that's all we've got. But **are you absolutely sure we didn't order a reprint of the Polish ones?**
B: **I'll look into it the minute I get off the phone**.
A: OK, but **could I ask you to hurry that up a bit, please?** It *is* pretty important.
B: I know, I know. **Would it help if we got a local Polish interpreter in?** I know you speak Polish, but it might help you out a bit.
A: Well, I wouldn't have much time to brief them on the product, but yeah, anything's better than nothing.
B: OK, **I'll get on to that right away. Leave it to me**.
A: I did leave it to you and look what happened!
B: Yeah, well. You're doing a great job, Piotr. I owe you one!

Fluency

8 Students exchange and read their rewritten e-mails. Set up the same roleplay as in exercise 6, but this time tell the students to base the conversation on the rewritten e-mails. When the students have finished, ask them to compare the two sets of calls.

Direct students' attention to the Lexis link on page 107 for more practice on the language of phone, fax and e-mail.

Tackling problems

In this final section, the students listen to one side of a telephone conversation and guess the problem that is being discussed. They focus on idioms used in the conversation and then discuss how they would solve the problem described in the first recording. They go on to compare their solutions with those given in a second recording. Finally, they focus on useful expressions taken from the listening tasks and take part in a problem-solving exercise on the telephone.

Discussion

1 ▭ **5.3** Check/Pre-teach: *trade fair, stand* (at an exhibition*), carriers*. Tell students that they are going to hear one side of a telephone conversation and they need to take notes and then work out what the problem is. Play the recording through once. Elicit and write up key words as headings on the board i.e. *stand, CDs, CD player, carriers, brochures*. Have students write what they think the problem might be under each heading.

Focus attention on the phrases in the box and check pronunciation. Elicit the type of language which can follow each phrase. Divide the class into pairs and have them discuss what they think the problems are.

2 ▭ **5.4** Play the recording and get students to compare their guesses with what really happened.

See page T28 for recording script 5.5.

Idioms

3 Ask students to complete the gaps from memory and then check the answers.

4 Elicit from the class the five problems and write them on the board. Ask students what they would do in each of these situations.

5 ▭ **5.5** Play the recording through once and elicit the solutions Graham and Piotr come up with. Let students compare their own solutions with those on the recording.

Problem-solving on the phone

6 Students match the sentence halves. Ask them to read out the complete sentences as a whole class check.

Direct students' attention to the Grammar link on page 106 for more information and practice on complex question formation.

Fluency

7 Divide the class into AB pairs. Refer the A students to page 135 and the B students to page 133. Tell students to note down the missing information for each call and keep it to hand for use in the roleplay. Monitor and help with possible ideas and key language.

Use internal telephones for this exercise if possible, or ask students to sit back to back. Monitor and take feedback notes. Hold a short feedback session. Find out if the scoring made students change their approach in the conversations. Finally, feed back on overall fluency before highlighting any important or common language errors.

If you're short of time

Omit the *Dealing with complaints* section, on page 27.

Set exercise 7 on page 28 for homework.

▭ **5.3**
B: Hello?
A:
B: Yeah, speaking. Is that you, Piotr? Aren't you supposed to be at the Trade Fair in Krakow?
A:
B: What?
A:
B: You haven't got a stand? Well, how did that happen?
A:
B: Maybe it's the CD player you're using.
A:
B: Well, what happened to *our* CD player?
A:
B: Damn carriers. That's the last time we use *them*! I'll play hell with them when I speak to them.
A:
B: Where's Liesl?
A:
B: This just gets worse, doesn't it?
A:
B: What's gone wrong with the brochures?
A:
B: Portuguese! Oh, no …

A:
B: That may be because I forgot to phone Tony. You remember we were going to attend the Lisbon Trade Fair originally.
A:
B: It completely slipped my mind. Oh, I'm really sorry, Piotr.
A:
B: Well, we're snowed under at the moment trying to get things ready for the Midas launch, but, look, don't worry. I'll sort something out. Can I call you back in an hour?
A:

▭ **5.4**
B: Hello?
A: Graham?
B: Yeah, speaking. Is that you, Piotr? Aren't you supposed to be at the Trade Fair in Krakow?
A: I *am* at the Trade Fair in Krakow, Graham. I'm just about the only thing that arrived here in one piece!
B: What?
A: Well, the stand got badly damaged in transit, so I've basically just got a table here,

a few chairs and a couple of posters with nothing to attach them to! It's a complete disaster!
B: You haven't got a stand? Well, how did that happen?
A: Don't ask. Look, it's not just that. I've just tried out three of the promotional CDs and two were defective – wouldn't play at all. I don't know how many more are like that.
B: Maybe it's the CD player you're using.
A: Wouldn't surprise me. I had to borrow it from another exhibitor.
B: Well, what happened to *our* CD player?
A: I'll give you three guesses.
B: Damn carriers. That's the last time we use *them*! I'll play hell with them when I speak to them.
A: Yes, well, never mind that now. You've got to do something, Graham. **I'm working flat out** on my own here.
B: Where's Liesl?

A: She's come down with some sort of virus. I left her at the hotel.
B: This just gets worse, doesn't it?
A: Wait till you hear about the brochures …
B: What's gone wrong with the brochures?
A: The English ones are OK. The others are all in Portuguese.
B: Portuguese! Oh, no …
A: What?
B: That may be because I forgot to phone Tony. You remember we were going to attend the Lisbon Trade Fair originally.
A: And you didn't tell Tony about the change of plan?
B: **It completely slipped my mind**. Oh, I'm really sorry, Piotr.
A: Graham, you've got to get me out of this mess!
B: Well, **we're snowed under at the moment** trying to get things ready for the Midas launch, but, look, don't worry. I'll sort something out. Can I call you back in an hour?
A: OK, I'll be waiting to hear from you.

Fluency

8 Exchange rewritten e-mails with your partner and hold the two telephone conversations again. How do these calls compare with the ones you had in 6?

Lexis link

for more on phone, fax and e-mail see page 107

Tackling problems

Discussion

1 ▄▄ 5.3 Listen to an overheard telephone conversation. Take notes and, with a partner, try to work out what the problem is.

> It sounds like …
> It seems as though …
> There's been some kind of …, by the sound of it.
> I'm not (exactly) sure whether … or whether …
> It's definitely something to do with …

2 ▄▄ 5.4 Now listen to both sides of the conversation in 1 and check your ideas.

Idioms

3 You heard the following idiomatic expressions in 2. Can you remember the missing words? The first two letters are given. Use the definitions in brackets to help you.

  a I'm working fl_at_ out. (I'm working as quickly and as hard as possible.)

  b It completely sl_ipped_ my mind. (I completely forgot to do it.)

  c We're sn_owed_ under at the moment. (We've got too much work to deal with.)

4 What would you do in Graham and Piotr's situation?

5 ▄▄ 5.5 Listen to Graham and Piotr's second conversation and compare your solutions with theirs.

Problem-solving on the phone

6 Match the halves of the following sentences. You heard them all in 5.

  a Can you get hold   of sending someone else out here?

  b I don't suppose   to have a phone number for the promotions people?

  c Do you happen   getting some brochures to me in Polish?

  d Is there any chance   of the organisers?

  e I'll check   what I can do, but I can't promise anything.

  f I'll see   with Liz and see if she can spare Kim for a few days.

  g Would you mind   you remembered to put another CD player in?

  h Is there any point   the minute I get off the phone.

  i Are you absolutely   if we got a local Polish interpreter in?

  j I'll look into it   to me.

  k Could I ask you   in sending the ones we've got in Russian?

  l Would it help   to that right away.

  m I'll get on   to hurry that up a bit, please?

  n Leave it   sure we didn't order a reprint of the Polish ones?

Grammar link

for more on complex question formation see page 106

Fluency

7 Work with a partner to practise solving problems on the phone. Speaker A see page 135. Speaker B see page 133.

6 Leading meetings

Either lead, follow or get out of the way. Sign on the desk of Ted Turner, founder of CNN

1 How much influence do you have at the meetings you participate in? When it comes to meetings, would you rather lead, follow or simply get out of the way?

Discussion **2** Think about a regular meeting you attend and consider the following:

- Who is the most powerful person in the room? Does he/she actually lead the meeting?
- What are the seating arrangements – fixed or flexible?
- Does anyone tend to dominate the discussion? Is that ever a problem?
- Are there people who hardly speak at all? If so, why are they there?
- Who, if anyone, is the most 'dangerous' person in the room?

Explain to a partner how the meeting works. A simple diagram may help you.

Collocations **3** Combine one word from each box to make ten common problems encountered in meetings. Do you have similar problems in your meetings?

communication communication time point- hidden pulling inadequate late over group-	**+**	barriers wasting preparation breakdowns agendas rank scoring runs think starts

1. communication breakdowns
2. communication barriers
3. time wasting
4. point-scoring
5. hidden agendas
6. pulling rank
7. inadequate preparation
8. late starts
9. overruns
10. group-think

Which of the above mean:

misunderstandings? ☐1

failing to finish on time? ☐9

competition between colleagues? ☐4

the need to agree at all costs? ☐10

secret intentions or objectives? ☐5

using your status to get what you want? ☐6

things which make people reluctant to talk? ☐2

4 Read the suggestion below. Does it strike you as a good idea? Which of the problems in 3 might it help to solve? Which would it probably make worse?

> **The power table**
> Suppose you removed the table from your conference room and replaced the seats with armchairs. Suppose you turned it into a living room. How much would this affect your meetings?
> That's how much your meetings are about power, not communication.

David Weinberger, *The Cluetrain Manifesto*

Meetings

6 Leading meetings

This unit provides useful language both for participating in and chairing meetings. The business skills strategies and functional language covered will be especially useful for those students who need to chair meetings.

Students discuss features of meetings and focus on common problems encountered in meetings. They work on collocations for talking about these problems and look at some radical and surprising solutions. They focus on the skills involved in chairing meetings, at the specific language used and then study a text which presents an interesting alternative approach to running meetings.

Specific strategies for handling disagreement in meetings are studied and practised. A recording presents the language used to control a meeting, and finally, the students participate in three meeting simulations.

The grammatical focus is on linking and contrasting ideas, and the lexical focus is on the language of companies and capital.

In this first section, students discuss their own meetings, exchanging ideas on aspects like hierarchy and layout. They focus on useful collocations for describing typical problems in meetings and then read a suggestion for dealing with some of these problems. A recording provides examples of radical approaches to running meetings. Students discuss if any of these solutions could be applied in their own companies/ places of work.

Warm-up

Lead in to the topic by asking focus questions e.g. *Do the meetings you attend have a chairperson? Is it better to have a chairperson, do you think? Do different meetings require different approaches? Why/Why not?*

Focus attention on the quotation which Ted Turner, the founder of CNN, has on his desk. Ask students to tell you what they understand by it. (It suggests that people need clear roles and that if you don't fall in line with whoever is in charge, you shouldn't obstruct him/her; if you don't have a clear view, you shouldn't interfere.)

1　Get the students to assess how much influence they have in meetings and to describe how they see their own role: leader, follower, or general observer.

Discussion

2　If appropriate, give a brief description of a regular meeting that you attend e.g. a staff or teacher development meeting. Use a diagram to highlight the layout/hierarchy if possible. Give students a few moments to think about the questions and draw a simple diagram if possible.

Divide the class into pairs or small groups. If students work in the same company, ask them to regroup so that people in different departments are sitting together. Students explain how their meetings work referring to their diagram if appropriate. Hold a short feedback session, eliciting anything interesting which arose in the discussion. If students have drawn diagrams, get them to come up and draw them on the board so that students can discuss if there is an optimum layout/format.

Collocations

3　Write the word *communication* on the board and brainstorm words and phrases which can form collocations e.g. *communication breakdown, to break off communication* etc.

Divide the class into teams and set up the activity as a race with a time limit of two minutes. Check the answers. Get students to match seven of the collocations with their definitions and check the meanings with the class. Check pronunciation and get students to practise the language by asking questions across the class e.g. *What do you do when someone pulls rank? By how much do your meetings overrun? What caused a communication breakdown in a recent meeting?*

4　Ask students to read the short text and give their reactions. (The approach described in the text may help to alleviate communication breakdowns and overcome communication barriers. On the other hand, it would probably prolong meetings, as people may get too comfortable!)

5 Focus attention on the photograph at the top of page 31. Ask students if they think this type of informal gathering constitutes a meeting. Elicit the pros and cons of employees getting together in this way and list them on the board e.g. people can communicate freely and there may be a useful outcome; people may just be gossiping and so no effective decisions can be made. Ask students to relate this to their own workplace and elicit how much time they spend in 'unofficial' meetings.

Write the five types of meeting on the board: *non-stop, mobile, democratic, virtual* and *recreational*. Elicit a few common collocations or related terms e.g. *non-stop flight, mobile computing, democratic society, virtual space, recreational activity*. Get students to work in pairs and predict the key features of each type of meeting. Elicit some ideas for each example and write them on the board.

6 📼 **6.1** With weaker classes, check/pre-teach: *to take minutes, indispensable, to dispense with, ceremonial, irrespective, down-to-earth, hierarchy, to stick to, consensus*. Before playing the recording, check pronunciation of the company names. Play the recording through once and let students check their predictions from exercise 5. Then ask them to match the approaches to the companies, playing the recording again if necessary.

Tell students to listen to the recording again and note down the key features and any pros and cons mentioned for each approach. Play the recording, pausing after each example to give students time to take notes.

7 Divide the class into groups and get them to discuss each of the ideas, referring to their notes from the recording as necessary. Ask students to decide if any of the ideas would work in their own company. Hold a short class feedback session and elicit the students' reactions to each of the ideas. Ask them to vote for the one they think is most workable and then elicit other surprising or radical ways in which companies have approached the problem of ineffective meetings.

Refer students to the recording script on pages 145–6 and have students note down any useful vocabulary related to running meetings e.g. *to take minutes, to hold a meeting, chairing skills, to stick to the agenda* etc.

Chairing skills

In this section, students first discuss how to complete a phrase about chairing a meeting and then focus on collocations that express what the leader of a meeting might do. They read and discuss a text on the role of the chairperson in meetings and why meetings are often ineffective. They then focus on diplomatic disagreement strategies.

Discussion

1 Get students to complete the phrase within a two-minute time limit and then compare their ideas. Possible answers include: *a chicken without a head/a country without a leader/a company without a director*.

Collocations

2 Give students one minute to brainstorm typical things a chairperson does in meetings and write up a list on the board e.g. *welcome attendees, state aims* etc. Students complete the collocations, using the nouns/noun phrases. Check the answers with the class, highlighting the word stress on compound nouns e.g. *key issues*.

Students then categorise the skills as to whether they are managing content (C) or people (P). Check the answers and then give follow-up practice by asking questions using the collocations e.g. *Is it always possible to anticipate areas of conflict? How can a chairperson discipline troublemakers at a meeting? How important is it to stick to the agenda?* etc. Finally, ask the students to highlight three skills that they themselves demonstrate in meetings.

📼 **6.1**

A: Coming up on CBN Business: an interview with media king and head of News Corporation Rupert Murdoch, stock market report and Katy Alexander with the week's business news round-up. But first, suffering from boardroom blues? Tired of taking minutes at meetings that take hours? Tess Liebowitz may have the solution …

B: According to diplomat and economist JK Galbraith, 'Meetings are indispensable when you don't want to do anything.' Therefore, logically, if you really do want to do something, it's the meetings you must dispense with. But can you dispense with meetings altogether? And what would take their place? At several well-known companies they think they've found the answer.

At high-profile UK advertising agency St. Luke's, meetings are simply considered 'a ceremonial and rude interruption to

people's working day'. So they've introduced meetings-on-the-move. Any member of staff can hold a meeting anytime, anywhere – in the elevator, in a local café or just sitting cross-legged on the floor. Anywhere, that is, but in a boardroom!

At Internet company another.com they've gone one step further by building a 'park area' right in the middle of the building. Staff can go sit on the park bench amongst the flowers or even play on the swings while they hold meetings! They used to have real grass too, but watering it became a problem.

At media strategy company, Michaelides & Bednash they've come up with a different solution. All employees, irrespective of status, work around one enormous central table. Meetings become unnecessary when everyone in the company is sitting just across the table from you the whole time. The working day is a constant meeting!

At the Xerox Corporation a more down-to-earth approach has proved successful. All staff, from junior management upwards, are trained in chairing skills and get an equal opportunity to use them. This breaks up hierarchies in the workplace, creating democratised meetings, where everyone can practise their leadership skills.

Finally, at Federal Express, they've been experimenting with technology. Using specially designed software, people sit around a large U-shaped table at workstations connected over a local area network. Meetings stick strictly to the agenda, are highly focused and more or less silent. Items instantly appear on the participants' screens and people simply key in their views rather than voice them. The software allows you to attach further comments and to see graphically how your position differs from the consensus. The only problem is the price – $35,000 for the fully functional system!

5   Five alternative approaches successful companies have taken to the problem of meetings are listed below. What do you think they might involve?

   a the non-stop meeting   **d** the democratic meeting
   b the mobile meeting   **e** the virtual meeting
   c the recreational meeting

6   ▭ **6.1** Listen to an extract from a business news programme and match the approaches in 5 to the companies that have adopted them.

Federal Express e   another.com c   Xerox Corporation d

Michaelides & Bednash Media a   St. Luke's Advertising b

7   Could any of the ideas in 6 work in your company? Would any be thought ridiculous?

Chairing skills

Discussion

1   Complete the following and compare with the other members of your group.

A meeting without a chairperson is like (a) _____ without (a) _____ .

Collocations

2   Complete the collocations by writing the nouns and noun phrases in the right-hand boxes. They are all things the leader of a meeting might do.

| the agenda   points of view
the final decision   the main goals
the participants   the meeting | | areas of conflict   follow-up tasks
an action plan   the key issues
other speakers   troublemakers | |

open close	the meeting	P	bring in shut out	other speakers	P
welcome introduce	the participants	P	anticipate avoid	areas of conflict	P
set stick to	the agenda	C	identify discipline	troublemakers	P
ask for summarise	points of view	P	work out draw up	an action plan	C
establish define	the main goals	C	prioritise assign	follow-up tasks	C/P
deliberate over take	the final decision	C	explain focus on	the key issues	C

Which of the skills above are mostly about managing
• the content of the meeting? • the people present?
Write C or P.

3 What, in your opinion, is the single most important task of a chairperson? Read the article below. Does the author agree with you?

Adapted from *Fast Company* magazine, www.fastcompany.com

You have to start meeting like this!

We work, therefore we meet. But why do so few of our meetings meet our expectations?

Michael Begeman is a *leading authority* on one of the business world's most *universal rituals*: the meeting. An anthropologist and computer scientist by training, he is manager of the 3M
5 Meeting Network.

So what's the most effective meeting that Begeman has seen lately? He says that it didn't take place in a *high-rise* office building or at a *cutting-edge* chip factory. In fact, it took place in a
10 tepee – in a scene from 'Dances with Wolves', the Oscar-winning film featuring Kevin Costner. The scene takes place after a group of Native Americans discover Costner not far from their camp. Between 20 and 30 members of the tribe
15 gather around for a meeting. There's one big question on their agenda: what should they do with this mysterious white man?

What follows, claims Begeman, is a *masterclass* in
20 good meeting behaviour.

'People actually listen to one another,' he *marvels*. 'There are some genuine disagreements, but everyone recognises *merit* in everyone else's
25 position and tries to *incorporate* it into his thinking. The chief spends most of his time listening. When the time comes to make a decision, he says something like 'It's hard to know what to do. We should talk about this some
30 more. That's all I have to say.' And the meeting ends! He is honest enough to admit that he's not ready to make a decision.'

How does Begeman compare that with what takes place inside most conference rooms today?
35 'Do you want to know the truth?' he asks. 'Here's my *mental image* of what happens at most business meetings: you could take the people out and replace them with radios *blaring* at each other, and you would not have changed very
40 much. That's what most meetings are like. People wait for the person who's speaking to *take a breath*, so they can jump into the empty space and talk. The quality of communication in most meetings is *roughly comparable to* the quality
45 of the arguments that you used to have with your ten-year-old brother.'

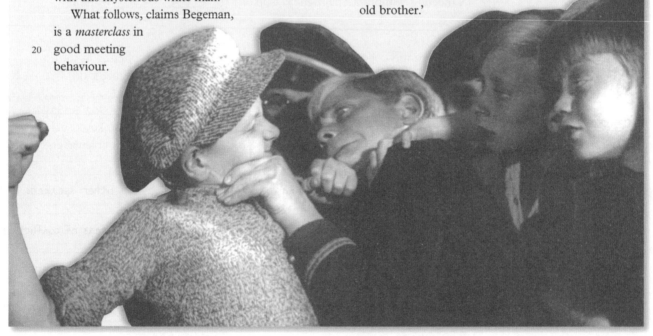

Glossary

tepee tent used by Native Americans

tribe ethnic or cultural group

4 How do you think Michael Begeman would describe the ideal meeting? You may want to refer to some of the terms in the box.

| listening | patience | decisions | consensus | diplomacy |
| disagreement | teamwork | respect | authority | |

5 With a partner, work out the meaning of the words and phrases in *italics*.

3   Ask students what they think is the most important task of a chairperson. Elicit possible answers and write them on the board e.g. *keeping to the agenda, dealing with troublemakers, ensuring that an effective action plan is produced.*

Check/Pre-teach: *anthropologist* and refer students to the glossary explanations of *tepee* and *tribe.* Explain the play on words in the title of the article. The usual expression is *We have to **stop** meeting like this!* and it is often used in films when two people are having an affair. Focus attention on the photo and ask students to predict why the title and photo have been used with the article. Students read the article quickly to check, not focusing on the words in italics at this stage. (The title is used to create interest in the example of an effective meeting; the photo is used to illustrate the quality of communication in the majority of meetings, according to the author.)

Students read the text again and compare their ideas on a chairperson's most important task with that of the author. (His view is that the most important task is to listen.) Elicit students' reaction to this view and to the description of the meeting from the film.

4   Divide students into groups and have them discuss what Begeman would consider the ideal meeting, referring back to the text as necessary to support their ideas. With weaker groups, elicit key language that students can use first and write it on the board e.g. *For Begeman the ideal meeting is … Everyone tries to be … and not to … The atmosphere promotes … and discourages …* etc. Check the answers with the class.

Suggested answer

> people listen to each other and have patience with each other, respect each other's views, try to reach a consensus before making decisions, they deal with disagreements diplomatically, people work as a team but respect each other's authority

As an optional follow-up activity, let students watch the meeting scene from the video/DVD *Dances with Wolves* and give their reactions.

5   Remind students of some key strategies for working out meaning: look at parts of the word e.g. *master + class;* use the context to help you: *radios blaring at each other* (radios produce sound and Begeman's view of meetings indicates that *blaring* is likely to refer to loud/unpleasant noise). With weaker classes, focus on the first two or three words/phrases with the whole class as examples. Students complete the task working in pairs. Check the answers with the class.

Answers

> *leading authority* – expert in a particular field
>
> *universal rituals* – things everyone does, perhaps for the sake of it
>
> *high-rise* – very tall, with many floors
>
> *cutting-edge* – the most modern/advanced
>
> *masterclass* – an excellent example of something
>
> *marvels* – is amazed by
>
> *merit* – something positive
>
> *incorporate* – include
>
> *mental image* – picture in your mind, generated by your imagination
>
> *blaring* – playing loudly
>
> *take a breath* – pause
>
> *roughly comparable to* – approximately the same as

Discussion

6 Check/Pre-teach: *to save face* (do/say something which will stop you feeling embarrassed or looking a fool). Focus attention on the questions and give students a minute to think about a time when they had to disagree strongly with someone without hurting their feelings. One piece of advice is to support the person, but 'attack' the problem i.e. disagree with the idea expressed, but at the same time say something conciliatory. Elicit some examples and ask students what helped them manage the situation. Elicit how important 'saving face' is in the students' own culture.

Diplomatic disagreement

7 Elicit ways of disagreeing diplomatically e.g. *I see what you mean, I hear what you are saying* etc. Have students read the list of disagreement strategies and match them to the examples a–j. Check the answers.

Point out that it is important to sound sincere when using these phrases. Check students' pronunciation and intonation, getting students to exaggerate their voice range if they sound rather 'flat'. Get students to practise the phrases by giving opinions on a range of topical subjects and eliciting appropriate disagreement e.g. business practices, current news stories etc. Students continue giving opinions and disagreeing diplomatically working in pairs/small groups.

8 Get the students to match the informal expressions with the strategies in exercise 7. Ask students which groups of phrases they would use with: longstanding colleagues, their boss, a potential new client, a new member of staff, a student doing work experience etc.

Direct students' attention to the Grammar link on page 108 for more information and practice on linking and contrasting ideas.

Managing meetings

In this section, three recordings of a chairperson managing people in a meeting provide listening practice. Students then focus on the language used in the recordings.

Direct students' attention to the Lexis link on page 108 for practice on the language of companies and capital.

1 ▄▄ **6.2** Check/Pre-teach the usual meaning of *timeshare* (holiday accommodation bought between a group of people so that they can each spend a period of time there). Tell students that the start-up company referred to in the recording has a different idea for timeshares. Play extract 1 and ask students to say what this idea is and what examples are given (to let people buy the use of a luxury item for a short time e.g. a Ferrari sportscar, a Rolex watch or an item of clothing by top fashion designer Jean-Paul Gaultier). Ask students to brainstorm the pros and cons of the company's idea and write their ideas on the board.

Check/Pre-teach: *to buy something outright, seed capital, to get side-tracked, procurement and delivery system, prohibitive.* Give students the names of the speakers in the recording: Luis, Ross, Jack, Tania and Lance. Ask students to listen to all three extracts and compare the pros and cons mentioned in the recording with the students' lists on the board. Play the recording and elicit further examples.

Ask students to read through the questions a–g and answer any that they can. Play the recording again and get students to complete their answers. Check the answers with the whole class.

Elicit students' opinions on questions f and g and then ask whether or not they would invest in dot.com companies.

▄▄ **6.2**
Extract 1
A: OK, **thanks for coming, everybody**. Erm, has anybody seen Lance, by the way? He was supposed to be here.
B: Oh, yeah, he phoned to say his flight in from Chicago had a two-hour delay. He said to go ahead and start without him.
A: Oh, I wanted his input on this one. OK, never mind, **let's get started, then, shall we?** Erm, so, **as I said in my e-mail, the purpose of this meeting is to** review last week's talks with the people from timeofyourlife.com and, secondly, to decide if we're interested in taking things further. **Luis is going to fill us in on the background. Luis?**
C: Yeah, thanks, Ross. Well, now, timeofyourlife is a really exciting business proposition. Basically, the idea is that ordinary people can buy a kind of timeshare in various luxury goods that they could never afford to buy outright. What happens is you buy points online at the timeofyourlife website and you can use these points to buy, like, a Ferrari for a day, a Rolex Oyster for a weekend or a Jean-Paul Gaultier original for an evening! Neat, huh? I just love this proposal …
D: Er, sorry to interrupt, but is this going to take long, Luis? Only I have an appointment at eleven and we *have* all read the summary on this company already.
A: **Jack, could Luis just finish what he was saying?** We're looking at twenty million dollars in seed capital here. I don't

want us rushing into anything. But **perhaps we could speed things up a little**, Luis. We *are* short of time and **by the end of this meeting I'd like some kind of decision on this**.

Extract 2
C: So, as you can see, the advance publicity alone is attracting half a million visitors to the timeofyourlife website every day.
A: Sorry, Luis, but **we seem to be getting side-tracked here**. This is all very interesting, but **can we go back to what we were discussing earlier?**
C: Oh, OK. Sure.
A: **Perhaps we can come back to this later**. Tell us about their logistics.
D: Can I just say something here?
A: **Hold on a minute, Jack – you'll get your chance in a moment**.
D: It's just that I thought we'd agreed we weren't investing in any more dot.coms.
B: No, Jack. That's what *you* wanted. But nobody actually agreed.
D: Tania, we've been through this. E-commerce is dead. We learned that the hard way.
B: Wait a minute. Who was it that said …?
A: **OK, OK! Let's all just calm down, shall we?** We're here to talk about this proposal we have on the table. **Tania, what's your position on this?**
B: Well, I agree with Luis that it's a great business plan. Like you, I'm a little concerned about the logistics, though. The procurement and delivery system for a business like this would be extremely

complex. And the insurance costs could be prohibitive.
C: Now, hold on a second! This is all covered in the proposal, Tania. What are you saying? I thought that you were with me on this one.
A: **Luis, I think what Tania is trying to say is** she likes the idea but the figures don't quite add up.
B: Exactly.
A: OK, **maybe we should take a short break at this point**, grab a coffee and meet back here in fifteen minutes.

Extract 3
A: **OK, so just to summarise what we've said so far**. Basically, we like the timeofyourlife idea.
D: (groans)
A: At least most of us do. We're aware of the risks involved in a major investment in an e-business, but we think the concept has great potential. We need to make another appointment with these people because we have some doubts about their logistics. **Luis, can I leave that one with you?**
C: Sure. I'll get right on to it.
A: We're also a little concerned about the amount of insurance a business like this would need. **Tania, can you get back to me on that?**
B: No problem, Ross.
A: Great. **I think that's about as far as we can go at this stage**. Thanks, everybody. **I'm afraid we'll have to stop it there**.
E: Hi, guys. Sorry I'm late. Tania told you the story, right? Say, did I miss anything here?

Discussion

6 In the article, Begeman points out that although 'there are some genuine disagreements' in the meeting, 'Everyone recognises merit in everyone else's position and tries to incorporate it into his thinking.' How can you avoid upsetting people you disagree with? How important is it in your culture for people to 'save face'?

Diplomatic disagreement

7 Match the examples on the right to the disagreement strategies they exemplify.

1 [e] and [i]   2 [a] and [g]   3 [c] and [h]   4 [d] and [j]   5 [b] and [f]

Disagreement strategies	**Examples**
1 Show support before you disagree	a I think I'm going to go with Janine's idea, **but tell me more about your idea first.**
2 Disagree but ask for more detail	b That's not quite how I see it, **but how about looking at this a different way?**
3 Check you've understood correctly	c I'm not so sure, **but maybe I'm missing something here. Run me through it again.**
4 Be specific about your disagreement	d I'm not against your whole idea, **just the part about** pricing.
5 Disagree but offer an alternative	e **While I agree with a lot of what you say,** I think you may be exaggerating the problem.
	f I don't quite agree with you there. **However, you've given me another idea.**
	g I'm not so sure I'm going to agree with this. **I'd like to hear more about it, though.**
	h Before I answer that, **let me just check I understand what you're saying.**
	i **I can understand exactly how you feel,** but at the moment it's just not an option.
	j **It's not so much** your actual plan **I have a problem with as** how you intend to implement it.

8 In informal meetings with people you know well, you can use simpler expressions to show you disagree, but if there are problems it is usually better to be more formal and explicit. Match the informal expressions below to the strategies in 7.

Go on. I'm listening. [2]   Yeah, but … [1]

Hm, well, how about this instead? [5]   I'm not with you. [3]

OK, but just one thing. [4]

Grammar link

for more on linking & contrasting ideas see page 108

Managing meetings

1 🔲 6.2 A venture capital firm is discussing the start-up company it had talks with last week. Listen to three extracts from their meeting and answer the questions.

a Who's absent from the meeting and why?
   Lance. His flight back from Chicago is delayed.

b What are the main goals of the meeting?
   to review last week's talks; to decide whether to take the proposal further

c What's the main area of conflict in the meeting?
   the commercial viability of the dot.coms

d Who do you think the main troublemaker is?
   Jack

Lexis link

for the language of companies & capital see page 108

e What follow-up tasks are assigned?
   Luis to investigate logistics; Tania to find out about insurance

f Does timeofyourlife.com's business plan sound good to you?

g In your opinion, how effective was the chairman of the meeting?

Chairing language

2 The following expressions are all useful in chairing meetings. Complete them by filling in the missing letters.

Opening the meeting

a OK, let's get started, then, shall we?

b Thanks for coming, everybody.

Setting the agenda

c As I said in my e-mail, the purpose of this meeting is to …

d By the end of this meeting I'd like some kind of decision on this.

Managing the discussion

e Perhaps we can come back to this later.

f Let's move on to the next item on the agenda.

g We seem to be getting side-tracked here.

h Can we go back to what we were discussing earlier?

i Perhaps we could speed things up a little.

j OK, so just to summarise what we've said so far.

k Maybe we should take a short break at this point.

Managing other speakers

l Luis is going to fill us in on the background. Luis?

m Jack, could Luis just finish what he was saying?

n Hold on a minute, Jack – you'll get your chance in a moment.

o OK, OK! Let's all just calm down, shall we?

p Does anybody have anything they'd like to add?

q Tania, what's your position on this?

r Luis, I think what Tania is trying to say is …

Assigning follow-up tasks

s Luis, can I leave that one with you?

t Tania, can you get back to me on that?

Closing the meeting

u I think that's about as far as we can go at this stage.

v I'm afraid we'll have to stop it there.

3 Listen to the meeting in 1 again and tick the expressions as you hear them. Which two are not used? <u>f and p</u>

In the chair

Fluency

1 Work in groups of three. Take it in turns to lead three short meetings. Prepare for each meeting separately by reading the information at the back of the book and the related article below. Speaker A see page 131. Speaker B see page 132. Speaker C see page 134.

Meeting 1
Should genetic tests decide job prospects?

What if you were faced, at a job interview, with a test that would tell whether you could expect to develop Alzheimer's or Parkinson's disease? What if you were turned down because of that tiny bit
5 of your DNA?

This scary scenario is coming closer to reality with the development of a technology that will allow employers to carry out genetic tests and get the results in the time it takes to stroll to the
10 canteen and have a cup of coffee.

Would it be ethical? Would it be legal? Would it be acceptable to recruiters, let alone society at large? The moral debate lags behind the scientific advances. A technology that will identify DNA
15 electronically has been developed by Dr John Clarkson and his colleagues at the company Molecular Sensing. They plan to miniaturise it and build a hand-held device that will produce results in less than 30 minutes.

20 Simon Barrow, chairman of The Recruitment Society, opposes such genetic screening for illnesses, but would welcome tests for behaviour. And Professor Robin Plomin of the Maudsley Hospital's Institute of Psychology confirms that
25 genetic associations have been reported for reading disability, hyperactivity, personality and drug abuse.

Chairing language

2 Write the six categories for chairing language on the board. Elicit examples that students can recall from the recording without looking at the gapped expressions and write them on the board. Then ask students to work in pairs to complete the task.

Check the answers and students' pronunciation by asking them to read their answers aloud. Give initial practice by calling out different language functions and eliciting the correct expression(s) e.g. opening the meeting, moving the discussion on, coming back to the main point, asking someone to wait their turn etc.

3 Play the recording again and get students to tick off each expression as they hear them. With weaker classes, be prepared to pause the recording briefly as necessary. Elicit the two expressions which are not used.

As an optional follow-up task, refer students to the recording script on page 146 where the key language appears in bold. Ask the students to contrast the way of chairing the meeting and language used with their own meetings/language using focus questions e.g. *Are similar structures used? Does the chairing language used in English seem more/less direct than in your language?* etc.

In the chair

In this final section the students each have the opportunity to act as chairperson in a series of meeting roleplays.

Fluency

1 As a lead-in to the task, write the focus of each of the three meetings on the board and get students to brainstorm related issues and ideas. Check/Pre-teach relevant vocabulary (as shown in brackets below):

Meeting 1: Should genetic tests decide job prospects? (*psychometric tests, to undergo testing, vulnerability, stroke, to inherit, screening, (un)ethical, to discriminate against, DNA*)

Meeting 2: Employers spy on workers (*to check up on, CCTV, computer surveillance, gaming websites, covert, confidentiality, classified information, to encrypt, leaks, phone taps/tapping, security measures, tagging devices, implants, to track, invasion of privacy, to eavesdrop, to trace*)

Meeting 3: Creative ways to better management (*fad, weird, to build team spirit, stand-up comedy, to 'think outside the box', to put on a show, to think laterally*)

Divide the students into groups of three. With larger classes, or if you have an uneven number of students, ask two students to play the same role, but advise them to choose only *one* chairperson for each meeting. Refer the A students to page 131, B to page 132 and C to page 134. Give students time to read their role card and the relevant article for each meeting. Deal with any vocabulary queries as necessary.

Set a time limit of 15 minutes for each meeting. Before students start the roleplays, check they are clear about their stance on the issue and get them to make notes on the key argument for or against each proposal. With weaker classes, allow students with the same role to work together in preparing for the roleplay. Remind the student who is chairing each meeting to listen to the other students first, to keep the meeting to time and to try to reach a decision on what recommendations to make. Refer them to the useful language on page 34. Monitor each of the roleplays and take feedback notes.

Ask students to assess how well they chaired their meeting and to say what decisions were reached. Give students feedback on the skill of chairing and on their overall fluency. Then give feedback on any important or common errors.

If you're short of time

Omit exercises 2 and 4 on page 30.

Set the text *You have to start meeting like this* and exercises 3–5 on page 32 for homework.

Select just one of the meetings in the fluency task on pages 34–35. You can also hold the language feedback over until the next lesson.

Meeting 2
Employers spy on workers

Big Brother is watching. And it's increasingly likely to be your boss.

She might be recording the casual conversations between you and your co-worker, 5 or tracking e-mails on your company computer, or watching the goings-on in the staff lounge.

Sounds like an invasion of your privacy? Think again. Most employee monitoring in the workplace is perfectly legal, and it happens more 10 than most people realise.

Two-thirds of US businesses eavesdrop on their employees in some fashion – on the phone, via videotape and through e-mail and Internet files – according to a survey by the American 15 Management Association International.

In fact, employers can trace everything from deleted e-mails and voice mails to the exact computer keys a worker strikes. Special software can follow employees' paths across the Internet 20 and high tech employee badges even let bosses track their workers' movements within an office building. Wireless video cameras are small enough to fit in pagers.

Businesses have lots of good reasons to 25 monitor workers: to deter workplace crime, to protect business secrets and to make sure employees aren't calling Timbuktu! Those worried about the Internet sites that employees are surfing can buy software that watches employees' screens.

Adapted from Knight Ridder Newspapers

Meeting 3
Creative way to better management

From Chopin to Schubert and jazz to jive, music, along with theatre, film, drawing and painting, is now widely used in UK business schools to help executives improve their management skills.

5 It may all be great fun, but does it work? Opinion is divided. Strongly against is David Norburn, director of Imperial College Management School, London. He says that after a few drinks he could probably make a case for 10 any human activity having managerial relevance. 'Weber's clarinet concerto and emotion; jazz and chaos theory; sex and timing.'

His argument is that when executives and MBAs invest time in business school programmes 15 they want rigorous and relevant training.

But staff at many of the UK's leading business schools, such as Patricia Hodgins at the London Business School, disagree. 'The key to creativity is being relaxed and being able to think laterally. 20 Using arts, music and theatre helps us to find that.'

Gay Haskins, head of executive training at LBS, defends the techniques. 'We are highly geared towards capitalist values,' she says. 25 'Everyone in business needs to understand that there are other ways of seeing the world.'

Adapted from the Financial Times

7 Information age

There is nothing so deceptive as an obvious fact.

Sir Arthur Conan Doyle, The Adventures of Sherlock Holmes

Discussion

1 Work with a partner and discuss the following questions.

a Is it important in your job to have access to the most up-to-date information? Why (not)?

b Where do you get most of the information you need to do your job?

c Which of the following sources of information are the most reliable?

> the Internet newspapers magazines trade/academic journals
> TV news company reports specialist news agencies like Reuters
> opinion polls and surveys end-of-year accounts market research
> TV viewing figures government statistics scientific studies the grapevine

2 You are going to read an extract from *Great Myths of Business* by the journalist and self-made millionaire William Davis. First match the following words and expressions to what they mean.

a a mixed blessing   **d** have a vested interest in ...*ing*
b a spin doctor   **e** hearsay
c get the wrong end of the stick   **f** a myth

something believed by many but in fact untrue ☐f

completely misunderstand something ☐c

something that has disadvantages as well as advantages ☐a

something you've heard people say which may or may not be true ☐e

someone whose job is to make people or organisations look as good as possible ☐b

want things to happen in a particular way because it will benefit you ☐d

3 Now read the extract. How far do you go along with the argument it's presenting?

Information –
A mixed blessing

Many people seem to find it difficult to accept that the information they get may be unreliable. It does not come out of nowhere: someone, somewhere, has had to put it together. That someone
5 may have got the wrong end of the stick, or made use of hearsay, or deliberately set out to mislead.

Public relations people, for example, often put out press releases, which are little more than sales promotion. They can easily create a false impression.
10 Information is slanted, twisted, misrepresented. Achievements may be exaggerated and awkward facts may be suppressed. In politics, 'spin doctors' are experts in dissembling. In business too, there are many specialists who have a vested interest in
15 ensuring that everything a company does is presented in a favourable way.

My own profession is not without blame. Journalists frequently print stories which turn out to be inaccurate and TV programmes give a distorted
20 picture of what is happening in various parts of the world. It is dangerous to read newspapers casually. That's how the germ of a myth is planted. The next thing you know, it has grown into a fact. A glance at a headline, a swift scan of the introduction, a note of the
25 picture caption, and you are on your way to a firmly held misconception.

from Great Myths of Business by William Davis

7 Information age

This unit is about the overwhelming availability of information in society today, the so-called 'information age'. This has also been described as an age of 'spin', with politicians in particular trying to report all information in a positive way and the existence of disinformation designed to confuse.

Students discuss a range of sources of information and decide which they think are most reliable. They read a text which looks at the downside of the amount of information available today and then focus on the language of deception. A number of intriguing headlines provide a springboard for discussion. Students decide whether they are true, untrue or partially true, then listen to a recording which provides the surprising facts behind these headlines. Students then focus on the language of statistics.

Students read and discuss a text about the scandal surrounding the fall of the US energy company Enron. In the final section, they discuss problems related to the information economy. There is a second listening task, after which the students compare their own thoughts in this area with those of a number of business people.

In this first section, students discuss the importance of up-to-date information in their own jobs and compare a range of sources for obtaining reliable information in today's business world. They read a text called *Information – A mixed blessing* and discuss their reactions. They then focus on key vocabulary taken from the text.

Warm-up

Read out the quotation from Sir Arthur Conan Doyle and ask students what they think it means. Elicit examples of a business person or politician who has claimed one thing when the exact opposite has proven to be true. (The media attention on the British royal family provides a good example of how conflicting reports from the palace and from the media can convey different messages/interpretations of the truth.)

Discussion

1   Divide the students into pairs and focus attention on the questions a–c. Check/Pre-teach *the grapevine* from question c.
    a   If the group is short of ideas, write up a list of information that could be useful when trying to keep up-to-date e.g. details of competitors, market information, stock market prices etc.
    b   Elicit some examples before students discuss in pairs e.g. in-house briefings, the Internet etc.

c   Ask students to rank the sources of information according to reliability and then compare their order in pairs. Students then report their choices and reasons to the class. Help weaker students to get started by eliciting the pros and cons of different sources e.g. Reuters – generally considered a reputable and trustworthy news source; the Internet – anyone can write and upload text, so much of the information may be unsupported opinions, or simply untrue; the grapevine – may be based on rumours and hearsay.

2   Ask students if they have ever heard of William Davis or *Great Myths of Business*. (In this book he aims to show why it is important to challenge people who claim they have all the answers when they create myths and fashionable theories.) Students match the words and expressions to their meanings and then check in pairs. Check the answers with the whole class.

3   As a lead-in to the reading task, focus students' attention on the magazine pictures around the text. Give or elicit examples of how magazines portray news in a certain way e.g. a positive review of an awful film, features on the glamorous lifestyles of the rich and famous etc.

Ask students to read the text. Point out that other key words in the text are explained in exercise 4. Get students to explain the title *Information – A mixed blessing*. (The extract is saying that you cannot take what you read at face value and that it may be dangerous to read news in a casual way.) Students give their reactions to the writer's argument. If you have any students who work/have worked in public relations, elicit examples which support/refute the writer's views.

As a follow-up task, ask the students to give examples of the ideas presented in lines 13–16 (portraying a company in a favourable light) and 19–21 (an inaccurate TV programme) from their own experience.

The language of deception

4 Ask students to scan the article quickly and identify the words and expressions. Then check the answers.

As an optional follow-up task, ask students to work in pairs and produce a short text describing a business situation in which they use some of the expressions in exercises 2 and 4.

Headline news

In this section, students complete a series of surprising headlines. They then decide which they think are facts, half-truths and myths. They then listen to a recording which contains the news behind these headlines and discuss their reactions. Finally, students practise the language of statistics taken from the recording.

Discussion

1 Check/Pre-teach: CO_2 emissions, G7 (the world's seven richest countries), (to become) extinct, famine. Students work in pairs to complete the headlines, then check the answers. They then decide whether they believe the headlines and categorise them as facts, half-truths, or myths.

Allow students to compare briefly in pairs and then hold a class feedback session. Write up students' answers and reasons on the board as preparation for the listening task in exercise 2.

2 ▱ **7.1** Check/Pre-teach: to fluctuate, mergers and acquisitions, divestment (of stocks, for example),

demerger, to get by on, decline, to get a bad press, liberalisation.

Tell students they are going to hear eight short extracts which give the facts behind each headline. Play the recording through once, pausing at the end of each extract. Students check the answers they made in exercise 1 against the recording. Then check the answers with the whole class.

Answers

a	myth	e	myth
b	half-truth	f	myth
c	fact	g	half-truth (i.e. not known)
d	half-truth (i.e. not known)	h	fact

Focus attention on the phrases in the box. Check the word stress in astonished, debatable and scandalous and elicit a few examples of the expressions in context in order to highlight voice range and intonation. If necessary, suggest students exaggerate the stress on the key words to emphasise their point.

Divide the students into small groups. Play the recording again, pausing at the end of each extract, and ask students to take notes of the key facts from each one. With weaker classes, write down the figures from each of the extracts on the board and get students to make notes on these. Students use their notes and the expressions in the box to discuss their reactions to the facts.

▱ **7.1**

a
Contrary to popular opinion the planet is not getting significantly warmer. **Nor is there any real evidence that** global warming is caused by heavy industry. Over the millennia the Earth's temperature has constantly fluctuated. Between 1850 and 1940, when there were almost no CO_2 emissions, it went up by one degree. But in spite of much higher levels of CO_2 emissions between 1940 and 1979, the rise in temperature was just 0.5 degrees. And since 1979 NASA satellites have in fact detected a slight global cooling of around 0.02 degrees.

b
It's impossible **to quote an exact figure** for the number of mergers that fail, **but there does seem to be some truth in** a recent study by KPMG, which puts the figure as high as 83%. **There is, however, disagreement as to** the precise failure rate. The Journal of European Industrial Training says 70% and the American Management Association 65. Certainly, in 1997 more than $1.6 trillion were spent on mergers and acquisitions, half of which, according to the Academy of Management Journal, eventually resulted in divestment or demerger.

c
It's a sobering thought that the world's seven richest countries do indeed earn 67% of global GDP. In fact, the richest 30% of the planet gets 90% of its income, leaving the

remaining 70% of the world's population to get by on just 10%. The gap between rich and poor is now such that the average income in a rich country like Switzerland is around 280 times higher than that in a poor one like Mozambique, and the world's top three billionaires are able to earn as much as 600 million people in the poorest parts of the world.

d
The figure of 120 million km² may or may not be accurate, but with systematic replanting of new trees, the real question is: how many trees do we still have left? **It's simply not the case that**, as some environmentalists claim, the number of trees in the world has halved in the last 50 years. The fact is that global forest cover increased very slightly by 0.85% between 1950 and 1994 and is expected to continue to do so at least until 2100.

e
This is simply untrue. While there was a rise between 1984 and 1992, since then there has been an overall decline, in some years by as much as 33%. Young people typically get a bad press, each generation apparently worse than the last. But in a study by journalist Mike Males, he reports that, **statistically speaking**, today's teenagers are committing fewer crimes, smoking and drinking less, less likely to get pregnant and generally far healthier than adults. In fact, **surveys show** that 90% of them are happy, self-confident individuals.

f
The truth of the matter is that IMF and World Bank loans have not helped the economy of a single country they have been given to. In the old government-controlled days of 1969 to 1980 Latin America's per capita income grew by 73% and Africa's by 34%. Since IMF intervention and the subsequent privatisation and liberalisation programmes Latin America's growth has dropped to just 6% and Africa's to minus 23!

g
This figure was first referred to back in 1979 in Norman Myers' book The Sinking Ark. Myers estimated that a million species would die out in the following 25 years, which works out at 110 a day. In reality, however, no one even knows how many species there are – **estimates vary widely between** 1.6 and 80 million – much less how many have become extinct.

h
The shocking truth is that, in spite of international aid, 40 million people die from hunger every year. **To put that in perspective**, it's the equivalent of the entire population of Spain disappearing or 300 jumbo jets crashing every day of the year with no survivors.

4 Look back at the text in 3 and find words or expressions meaning:

a make someone believe something which is untrue (paragraph 1) _mislead_

b embarrassing pieces of information (paragraph 2) _awkward_ _facts_

c hidden from the public (paragraph 2) _suppressed_

d present something inaccurately (paragraphs 2 and 3)

create a _false_ _impression_

give a _distorted_ _picture_

e a wrong belief or opinion (paragraph 3) _misconception_

Headline news

1 Work with a partner. Complete the headlines below using the words in the box. Do you believe them? Divide them into facts, half-truths and myths.

world	failure	countries	crime	warming	species
deforestation	toll				

a CO_2 emissions to blame for global _warming_

b It's official – 83% of company mergers end in _failure_

c G7 _countries_ account for 67% of global GDP

d Cost of _deforestation_ – 120 million km² of trees disappear every year

e Latest police figures show rise in violent _crime_ amongst under-25s

f Free market economics bring prosperity to developing _world_

g 110 _species_ become extinct every day

h Spread of famine – annual death _toll_ climbs to 40m

2 🔲 **7.1** Listen to the surprising facts behind the headlines. Take notes and discuss your reactions after listening to each one.

It's good news that …	It's reassuring to hear that …
I'm astonished that …	I had no idea that … It's debatable whether …
I can hardly believe that …	It's not what I've heard.
I'm appalled that …	I think it's scandalous that …

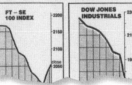

THE TIMES

No 62,904 TUESDAY OCTOBER 20 1987 (25p)

Dow Jones crashes 508 points: City wipes £50bn off shares

Wall Street's blackest hours

● Share prices on Wall Street plunged by nearly a quarter in one day, a far steeper drop than in the crash of 1929

● In London, the FT-SE 100 share index fell 250 points, cutting more than £50 billion from share values

● The dollar dropped sharply. Mr James Baker, US Treasury Secretary, went into urgent talks with the West German Finance Minister

● British Petroleum shares plunged 34p down at 316p, but the Government's offer price is 330p, but the Treasury said the sale would go ahead

By Kenneth Fleet

President Reagan, after "watching with great concern" Wall Street's blackest day, sought last night to reassure apprehensive and frightened Americans that "the underlying economy remained sound".

His words were echoed by other senior figures in Washington and New

In the foreign exchange markets the dollar wilted before the West German mark, while the pound remained firm but largely on the sidelines.

At the weekend the Germans seemed determined to raise their interest rates. This provoked a pained reaction from Mr James Baker, the US Secretary of the Treasury, who declared that this was "not in

Yuppies aghast at end of boom

From Charles Bremner
New York

Crowds of dazed young brokers milled around Wall Street yesterday evening trying to come to terms with the unthinkable – the roaring Eighties, the years of easy prosperity, could be over.

As Mr John Phelan, chair-

The language of statistics

3 Match the words and phrases below to summarise the information in 2. All the expressions were in the recording.

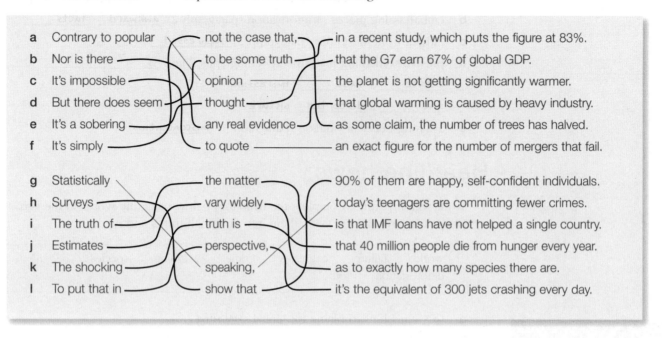

a Contrary to popular — not the case that, — in a recent study, which puts the figure at 83%.
b Nor is there — to be some truth — that the G7 earn 67% of global GDP.
c It's impossible — opinion — the planet is not getting significantly warmer.
d But there does seem — thought — that global warming is caused by heavy industry.
e It's a sobering — any real evidence — as some claim, the number of trees has halved.
f It's simply — to quote — an exact figure for the number of mergers that fail.

g Statistically — the matter — 90% of them are happy, self-confident individuals.
h Surveys — vary widely — today's teenagers are committing fewer crimes.
i The truth of — truth is — is that IMF loans have not helped a single country.
j Estimates — perspective, — that 40 million people die from hunger every year.
k The shocking — speaking, — as to exactly how many species there are.
l To put that in — show that — it's the equivalent of 300 jets crashing every day.

Lies, damned lies and statistics

Discussion

1 According to American writer Ray Stout, 'There are two kinds of statistics – the kind you look up and the kind you make up.' Which do you think makes up more statistics: companies or governments?

2 What do you understand by the term 'creative accounting'? Can you think of any companies who have been guilty of it in recent years? How common do you think it is?

3 Work with a partner. What do you know about Enron? You are going to read an article about the financial scandal that damaged the company in 2001. The following words and phrases are in the article. Use them to predict what it says.

> seventh-biggest corporation   steady growth   phenomenal share price
> huge debts   creative accounting   cash flow situation   tax losses
> shareholders   collapse

4 Now read the article on page 39 and check your ideas in 3. Do you think Enron really did anything wrong, other than get caught?

5 With a partner, work out the meaning of the words and phrases in *italics*.

6 To whom do you think a company is most accountable? Put the following in order of importance.

the government ☐
the general public ☐
the board of directors ☐
its employees ☐
its shareholders ☐
its customers ☐

38   7 Information age

The language of statistics

3 Students match the words and phrases and then check their answers in pairs. Ask the students to read their sentences aloud as a class check. Encourage students to use the expressions in the table to talk about their own experience/area of business. Elicit possible sentences e.g. *Contrary to popular rumour, the transport industry does not harm the environment. Statistically speaking, our industry has been the most productive in the last five years*, and then get students to continue in pairs/small groups.

Lies, damned lies and statistics

In this section, students discuss the idea that statistics can be made up and also identify what is meant by the term 'creative accounting'. They then read an article about the Enron scandal, and focus on some of the expressions in the text before discussing points arising from the article.

Discussion

Encourage weaker classes to search the Internet for information on the fall of Enron and/or to read the text on page 39 before the class.

1 Students read the quotation by the American writer Ray Stout and discuss the question. Encourage students to give examples and justify their opinions.

2 Ask students what they understand by the term 'creative accounting' (the act of changing business accounts to achieve the result you want). Elicit examples of accounting malpractice e.g. the fraud at Worldcom in 2002, Metallgesellschaft AG which announced that its 'Energy Group' was responsible for losses of approximately $1.5 billion.

3 Elicit what the students know about the Enron scandal. If appropriate, ask focus questions e.g. *What was Enron's business?* (energy and power plants*), When did the scandal hit the news?* (2001) *Which company did the auditing?* (Arthur Andersen). Check pronunciation of the words and phrases in the box, especially the silent letter in *debt*. Students predict the content of the article from the words in the box, working individually. They then summarise their predictions to a partner and compare.

4 Build two word fields on the board around the words *tax* and *flow*, eliciting relevant terms e.g. *tax loss, tax savings, cash flow, outflow, inflow*.

Students read the text and check the predictions they made in exercise 3. Establish which student(s) made the most accurate predictions. Ask students what they think should happen to each of the parties involved, including the company directors, employees, shareholders, pension fund members and the consultancy Arthur Andersen.

5 Divide the students into pairs and have them work out the meaning of the words in italics. Encourage them to use recognition of parts of the words/phrases and the overall context to help them. Check the answers with the class.

Answers

at its peak – at the highest point in the companies growth
the Internet boom – the time when investment was highest in the new Internet companies
wiped out – made to disappear completely
panic selling – selling of shares due to panic in the market
dot.com fever – the rush to buy shares in Internet companies
cooking the books – (informal) to falsify the accounts
bonuses – money paid on top of a salary
stock options – the possibility to buy shares
spelt disaster – created a huge problem
staggering – impressively high

6 Ask students to rank the groups of people in order of importance. Students compare their answers in pairs/small groups and give reasons for the order they have chosen. Point out that many companies in the private sector are answerable to their shareholders first and then elicit examples of who students thought most important. Elicit examples of companies which are particularly 'customer-driven'.

As an optional follow-up task, students working in accounting or financial fields could give a presentation on other examples of 'creative accounting'. Non-accountants could search the Internet and produce a time-line to show the key stages in a scandal such as Enron. Encourage students to recycle any of the vocabulary which they wish to use actively from this unit.

The information economy

In this section, students consider three issues: information overload, the idea that knowledge is power, and human error in working with computers. A recording presents the views of three business people discussing the same three problem areas. Students then discuss their reactions to the extracts and compare their views to those expressed in the recording.

Discussion

1   Write the following three phrases on the board: *information overload*, *knowledge is power* and *human error*. Elicit what the students understand by each term. Divide the class into three groups and ask students to discuss the three statements. Hold a whole class feedback session on the main points discussed and write up key language next to each phrase on the board.

2   **▭ 7.2** Check/Pre-teach: *the name of the game* (a very important factor), *maze*, *anxiety*, *syndrome*, *to benchmark*, *to outperform*, *to coach*, *to digitise*, *to outsource*, *bonds*. Also check students are familiar with *the FTSE 100 Index* (a number which expresses the value of the share prices of the one hundred most important British companies) and Salomon Brothers (a firm of stockbrokers). Tell students that they will hear the views of three business people: Stefan talking about information overload, Olga talking about 'knowledge is power' and Lee talking about human error. Ask the students to note down the following information and then play the recording through once. Check the answers (shown in brackets).

Extract 1: the name of the report; the name of the illness (*Dying for Information*; information anxiety syndrome)

Extract 2: who is benchmarked? What is KM? (all national divisions; knowledge management)

Extract 3: which two people made mistakes? What did they do? (a trader typed in an incorrect figure and the London FTSE 100 fell; someone at Salomon Brothers leant on his keyboard and accidentally sold some bonds)

Ask students to make notes of each speaker's main argument. With weaker students, provide key headings to help them with the note-taking e.g. *Name, Job, Main opinion(s), Reasons/Examples*. Play the recording again and pause between each extract. Check overall comprehension by asking students to summarise each speakers' main points from their notes.

Students then work in small groups to compare their views and experiences with the people on the recording. With weaker groups, ask specific focus questions e.g. *How reliable do you think the information is? Have you suffered from 'information anxiety syndrome'? Does your company benchmark? Can you give other examples of where pressure has caused an employee to lose money?*

As an optional follow-up task, students write a short report from their notes on information-sharing and knowledge management in their own company. Encourage them to include a recommendation for improving these aspects.

If you're short of time

Omit exercises 2–4 on pages 36–7.

Ask students to read the Enron text on page 39 for homework.

Omit exercises 1 and 2 on page 39.

▭ 7.2

1
A: Stefan, you work for a weekly business magazine in Frankfurt.
B: Uh huh.
A: So information really is the name of the game in your job, isn't it?
B: Yes, I suppose it is. But, erm, part of the problem today is that there's just too much information out there, and not all of it is reliable. It's, er, a complete maze of information, really.
A: You can get lost in it?
B: Exactly. Actually, Reuters produced a report on this very topic: information overload.
A: Oh, yes?
B: Yes, the report was called *Dying for Information*.
A: Very appropriate.
B: Yes. It was based on interviews with 1,300 managers in different countries, so it was very thorough. Anyway, what the report showed is that two thirds of managers suffer from stress and poor health, and one of the main causes is what they're calling 'information anxiety syndrome'.
A: Information anxiety syndrome?
B: Yes, caused mostly by the Internet. Apparently, managers are getting so frustrated knowing that the information they need is out there somewhere …
A: But it could take them the rest of their lives to find it!
B: Precisely. It's driving them crazy!

2
A: Olga, you work for the Russian subsidiary of a multinational mobile phone company.
B: Yes.
A: How well informed are you about what's going on in your sister companies around the world?
B: Well, pretty well informed, I think. In fact, we regularly benchmark all our company's national divisions against each other.
A: Benchmark?
B: Yes, compare them, according to different criteria, to see who's outperforming whom.
A: Oh, I see.
B: Yes, and then the top performers in each category coach the others on how to get the same results. Actually, we estimate that just one knowledge-sharing exercise like this boosted our sales revenue by $65 million.
A: Impressive.
B: Mm. It's all part of what we call 'knowledge management', or KM. We think our most important asset is the information our employees carry around in their heads: their intellectual capital. If you think about it, so much routine work can be automated, digitised or outsourced, your knowledge – your expertise – is all you've got, really. In fact, KM guru Thomas A. Stewart has calculated that whereas the cost of a product used to be about 80% materials and 20% know-how, now it's split 70:30 the other way. And there's a Swedish insurance firm, Skandia, which actually has its very own director of intellectual capital.

3
A: Lee, you work for a financial services company in the City of London.
B: That's right, yeah.
A: I imagine it's all much faster now in these days of computerised financial markets. Does it ever get too fast? Do people start making mistakes with all this information coming at them?
B: Oh, sure. There's quite a lot of room for error with computers, I can tell you. They're a disaster waiting to happen, really.
A: Can you give me an example?
B: Well, yeah, I mean losing a fortune can be as easy as pressing the wrong button!
A: Not as easy as that, surely?
B: Oh, yeah. A few years ago the whole London FTSE 100 Index actually fell by two per cent when some trader typed £300 million into his computer instead of 30 million.
A: You're joking!
B: No, it's absolutely true. Too much pressure, basically. And, er, oh, yeah, back in the late 90s, some guy at Salomon Brothers, I think it was, made an even bigger mistake. Sold 850 million pounds' worth of French government bonds – by accident!
A: By accident?
B: Completely by accident. He leaned on his computer keyboard and sold the lot!

THE FALL OF ENRON

FOR SALE
more information @
www.studio8.net

Enron was once the star of the new economy. As well as its traditional businesses, such as gas lines and power plants, it was also involved in Internet bandwidth operations and several obscure e-commerce ventures.
5 *At its peak* the company was worth $70 billion and was the USA's seventh-biggest corporation.

Of course, *the Internet boom* didn't last. On April 14th 2001 more than one trillion dollars in market capitalisation was *wiped out* in six and a half hours of *panic selling* on Wall
10 Street. *Dot.com fever* was over. But, miraculously, Enron survived. In fact, it seemed stronger than ever.

Enron's accounting system was always complex and obscure, but Wall Street trusted the company's steady record of growth and asked very few questions about just how it was
15 achieving it. The speculators loved Enron, especially when its share price reached a phenomenal $90. All the management gurus pointed to Enron as the model modern company.

But what the stock market investors didn't know was that the company had been *cooking the books*, inventing partner
20 companies that didn't really exist to hide huge debts and even huger losses. In 2000 Enron reported a net income of $979 million, even though it actually only earned $42 million. And by employing some of the most brilliant creative accounting ever, Enron managed to make $2 billion in tax savings, even
25 claiming some tax losses twice. In so doing, its cash flow situation was transformed from a $154 million outflow to a $3 billion inflow.

But by 2001 the authorities were closing in. Sensing disaster, in the weeks preceding its collapse, Enron's top 200
30 executives were paid $56.6 million in *bonuses*, $172.6 million in salaries and $1.1 billion in *stock options*, most of which were very swiftly sold. But for the company's many thousands of employees, shareholders and pension fund members, it was a different story.

35 In what has been called the greatest corporate failure of modern times, on December 2nd 2001 Enron was officially declared bankrupt. The court ruling also *spelt disaster* for the main accounting consultancy Enron had employed, the equally famous Arthur Andersen, which was fined a *staggering*
40 $500 million.

Both Enron and Arthur Andersen are still in business.

The information economy

Discussion   **1**   Work in groups to exchange opinions on the three issues below.

- Information overload: These days we are all suffering from having access to too much data.
- Knowledge is power: The intellectual capital of a company is more important than its financial capital.
- Human error: The weakest link in any computer network is the people who operate it.

2   ▣ **7.2** Listen to three business people discussing the issues in 1 and compare your views.

8 Promoting your ideas

We had snakes in Raiders of the Lost Ark and bugs in Indiana Jones and the Temple of Doom. But supposedly man's greatest fear is public speaking. That'll be in our next picture. *Steven Spielberg, film director*

Discussion 1 How important is it in your line of business to be able to present your ideas professionally? Do you enjoy giving presentations or generally try to avoid them?

2 ▭ 8.1 Listen to five experienced presenters talking about what still makes them nervous every time they give a presentation. Underline the speakers whose worries you share.

Speaker 1   Speaker 2   Speaker 3   Speaker 4   Speaker 5

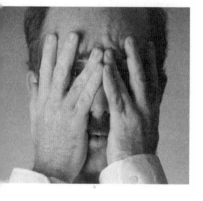

3 Complete the following expressions from the extracts in 2 using a single verb.

a	Your mind		blank.
b	Your mouth	*goes*	dry.
c	Your mike		funny.
d	The audience		quiet.
e	Everything		wrong.

4 Which of the expressions in 3 means:

you can't think of anything? [a]   your microphone doesn't work properly? [c]

Phrasal verbs 5 Complete the expressions from the extracts in 2.

up	up	up	down	down	out	about	over	of	to

a You dry _up___ completely.

b Your equipment breaks _down_.

c You run _run___ _out___ time.

d You run _over__ schedule.

e You pace _up___ and _down_.

f Your wave your arms _about_.

g Your heart speeds _up___.

h Your legs turn _to___ jelly.

6 Someone once observed: 'There is nothing wrong with having nothing to say – unless you insist on saying it.' Read the text. Can you think of any less extreme ways of achieving the same objective?

Keep it short and simple!

According to ancient custom, the elders of a remote African village have to stand on one leg while addressing their audience at council gatherings. As soon as their second foot touches the ground, they must stop speaking immediately.

Presenting

8 Promoting your ideas

This unit is about how best to promote your ideas, taking your own feelings, style and abilities into account, as well as those of your audience. It will be of particular interest to students involved in giving sales or product presentations.

Students discuss how important it is to present ideas professionally in their business. They listen to a recording of five business presenters talking about what makes them nervous and focus on useful language from the recording. As a final task in this section, they brainstorm ways to keep a presentation short and simple.

The students discuss cross-cultural aspects of giving presentations based on recordings about audience expectations in different countries. This is followed by a language focus on phrasal verbs and on idiomatic expressions. They read a short text on *intrapreneurs* – creative minds within an organisation – and study useful expressions from the text. A second recording of two managers presenting a new product idea provides a model for the students to prepare their own sales presentation in a final fluency activity.

The grammatical focus is on the passive and the lexical focus is on phrasal verbs.

In this first section, students focus on the importance of presenting ideas professionally and discuss how they themselves feel about giving presentations. They listen to a recording of five business presenters explaining why they get nervous. They then focus on useful expressions for saying what went wrong and practise phrasal verbs taken from the recording. A short text containing a radical idea for keeping presentations brief and clear provides stimulus for discussion.

Warm-up

Ask students if they have ever heard a speech which went wrong e.g. an after-dinner speech which went on too long, or if they have ever given a disastrous speech themselves.

Ask students to read the quotation from Steven Spielberg and ask if anyone shares the same fear of public speaking. Focus attention on the photograph and ask students to devise a suitable caption e.g. *I wish I didn't have to …, Why on earth did I …?*

Discussion

1   Ask students if they need to put forward ideas in formal presentations as part of their job. Do a quick show of hands on who is keen on giving presentations and who tries to avoid them. Elicit exactly what students enjoy/dislike about giving presentations.

2   🔲 8.1 Get students to brainstorm a list of what they think the speakers will mention, based on the students' own examples in exercise 1. Collate the ideas on the board. With weaker groups, check/pre-teach: *to sweat, nightmare, to stare at, not to have a clue, to ruin, to rush, distracting, tense.* Play the recording through once and get students to check their predictions. Then get students to summarise the problem for each speaker.

3   Students guess the word. Point out they can use any tense of the verb *go* to complete the expressions.

4   Give students a few seconds to identify the two phrases and elicit the answers. Get the students to practise the expressions by asking follow-up questions e.g. *Has your mind ever gone blank?*

Phrasal verbs

5   Students complete the task and then compare their answers with a partner. Call out each letter and get students to read out their answers as a whole class check.

6   Ask students to guess what the acronym K.I.S.S. stands for. (It is from training in writing skills and other areas and is the title of the short text in this exercise. It can also stand for 'Keep it simple, stupid!') Ask students to read the text and elicit their reaction. Students then brainstorm other ways of keeping a presentation short e.g. using a friend in the audience as a time-keeper.

🔲 8.1

1
Erm, well, to tell you the truth, there's a part of me that's still scared I might just **dry up completely**. I mean, you know, **your mind goes completely blank**? Makes me sweat just thinking about it. I have this nightmare where **the audience has gone deadly quiet**, and everybody in the room's just staring at me and I haven't got a clue what to say next! It's only ever happened to me once, thank god, but I still lose sleep over it in case it ever happens again.

2
Technology. Well, it's Sod's Law, isn't it? **If anything can go wrong it will**. About a year ago, I had not one, but two projectors **break down** on me. And then **my mike went funny** as well. I sounded like Darth

Vader out of *Star Wars* for about half an hour until they fixed it. Completely ruined my whole presentation, obviously. I went mad with the technicians afterwards. But what can you do?

3
I always seem to **run out of time** and then have to rush the end of the talk or, even worse, **run over schedule**. Audiences hate that. I've had people tell me I overprepare, but it doesn't seem to matter what I do, I always have at least twenty minutes too much material. So, for me, every talk's a race against the clock!

4
Well, some people, older people especially, have told me that I move around too much when I speak in public – you know, that I

pace up and down and **wave my arms about**. They say it's distracting. They can't concentrate on what I'm saying. But for me, as an Italian, you know, it's quite normal for us to jump around, be rather dramatic. So, now I worry about trying to stand still. And that just makes me feel tense and uncomfortable.

5
What was it Franklin D. Roosevelt said? The only thing to fear is fear itself? That's the thing I'm afraid of, still, after all these years in business – fear. Ridiculous, isn't it? But fear's an absolute killer in a presentation. **Your mouth goes dry**. **Your heart speeds up**. **Your legs turn to jelly**. In my experience, the first two minutes are usually the worst. Survive those and you're in with a chance.

Audience analysis

In this section, the students listen to a series of recordings on audience expectations in different countries and discuss cross-cultural aspects and stereotypes. Students then focus on phrasal verbs and idioms from the recordings.

1   ▣ **8.2** As a lead-in to the listening task, ask students if they have ever given a presentation to an audience from another country or culture. Ask focus questions e.g. *Did you change the content or the way you delivered the presentation to suit that audience? If so, how?* For example, including more technical data to justify their argument, omitting jokes they would have otherwise included.

Check/Pre-teach: *to offend, eloquent, the hard sell, assertive, slick, gimmick, humour, wisecrack, to overwhelm, harmony, compatibility, commitment, anecdote, (jokes) at your own expense, to build rapport, to wow.*

To prepare students for the listening task, elicit what expectations they think the countries have and what adjectives they associate with each nation.

Play the recording, pausing between each extract and give students time to record their answers. Play the recording again if necessary. Ask students to check the answers on page 132 and elicit their reactions. Check the key words students selected to justify their answers. Refer them to the recording script on page 148 to see the full context if appropriate.

2   Ask students how far they agree with the profiles given by the speakers and if they see globalisation as a way of eliminating stereotypes. Point out that while it may be useful to know common features about a cultural group, there is a negative side to stereotyping, which can be dangerous and harmful.

Phrasal verbs

3   After the students have matched the phrasal verbs, check the answers and the word stress.

4   Students match the phrasal verbs with the meanings. Check the answers with the class. As a follow-up, divide the class into groups and get students to write a set of six questions, using the phrasal verbs. Do an example with the whole class e.g. *How do Americans come across?* and then get students to ask and answer their questions.

5   Elicit ideas for giving effective presentations in different cultures and write them on the board e.g. *giving technical data, using technology, giving a handout, telling jokes/anecdotes* etc.

Divide the students into groups and ask them to write a list of tips for giving a presentation to an audience in their own country. Students present their ideas to the class, using an OHT if appropriate. With monolingual groups, students can compare their advice across groups; with multilingual groups, ask students if the advice fits with their own expectations about the nations discussed.

Direct students' attention to the Lexis link on page 111 for more practice on phrasal verbs.

Idioms

6   Ask students to complete the idioms from memory if possible. Refer students to the recording script on page 148 to check their answers.

7   After the students have decided which piece of advice is most important, ask them to compare in small groups.

▣ **8.2**

1
Er, well, I think the most important thing to remember is that people expect you to be an expert in your field of business. I mean a real expert. That means you should **have all the technical information at your fingertips**. Which is not to say they won't want to see it all in print after the presentation as well. And if you don't cover every detail in your pitch – costings, cash flow projections, everything – believe me, they won't be slow to interrupt you to ask for it. People here seem to like PowerPoint, the whole technology thing, you know. A word of warning, though: forget the jokes. If you try to be a comedian, they just won't take you seriously.

2
Erm, I think the main thing here is to **give your presentation the personal touch**. That's what they value above everything else. You see, they're judging *you* as much as, if not more than, what you're actually talking about. But, erm, I think too many presenters worry about offending the local culture and then they end up sounding much too conservative. Don't. Be loud, be lively, be eloquent. They love all that. It's true that attention spans do tend to be a bit short sometimes and you'll get loads of interruptions, but **just go with the flow**. In any case, people will probably want to talk to you about everything all over again later.

3
Well, it's almost a cliché, but the hard sell does actually work here. And, believe me,

you really can't be too assertive. In fact, they *want* you to impress them and expect you to work hard to maintain their interest. So, be fast, be slick, make sure you **have a few gimmicks up your sleeve**. They like all that stuff. And you can say as many nasty things about your competitors as you like – especially if they're funny. Humour's nearly always appreciated, and, er, you don't need to be too subtle with that. They don't want dark sarcasm, though – so nothing too negative. Wisecracks, clever remarks – that's what they tend to **go for**.

4
Erm, my main piece of advice here is: don't overwhelm them with your enthusiasm. Of course, they expect you to be highly competent and confident, but quietly confident. People'll probably have read through all the paperwork beforehand, but they'll want you to **go through** all the main points again. For the sake of formality and politeness, they'll want to hear it directly from you. But **don't get so carried away talking about your own ideas** that you forget to point out why it is their company you especially want to do business with. That's very important – creating a sense of harmony and compatibility between you and them. Oh, and a long-term commitment for them, by the way, is 20 to 25 years, not three to five, as it is in the States.

5
I suppose having a sense of humour's the main thing. In fact, you can't **do without** it really. Certainly, if you haven't made them

laugh even once within the first five minutes, you probably won't be very popular. People may even **switch off** altogether. Speakers are kind of expected to be fairly entertaining as well as knowledgeable about their product or service. You don't actually have to crack jokes the whole time, but anecdotes and amusing stories seem to **go down well**. Making jokes at your own expense, especially, seems to help build rapport with an audience that can otherwise seem a bit cold and unfriendly. And don't try to wow them too much with technology. Be too techno and people'll just think you're **showing off**.

6
Being stylish seems to be what matters here – both in terms of your personal appearance and how you actually **come across** as a person. It's true that you do have to **keep up** a certain formality and your talk should always be logical and well-organised, but within those constraints you can be as imaginative and innovative as you like. In fact, unless you are offering something pretty special, something 'sexy', something unique that they haven't seen before, you'll find them very difficult to persuade. Obviously, knowing exactly who you're presenting to is always important, but here it really is essential that you **do your homework**. And, er, don't be surprised if the questions you get asked seem quite hostile. Tough questioning is all part of the business culture here.

Audience analysis

1 📼 8.2 Listen to six business people comparing audience expectations of presentations in different countries. Which are they talking about? Give your reasons.

Country	Extract	
USA	③	assertiveness, gimmicks, competitiveness, humour
Germany	①	expertise, technical information, detail, PowerPoint, no jokes
Japan	④	quiet confidence, thoroughness, formality, sense of harmony, long-term commitment
UK	⑤	sense of humour, knowledge, storytelling, not too technological
France	⑥	style, formality, logical organisation, sexiness, preparation, ability to deal with tough questions
Kuwait	②	personal touch, eloquence, enthusiasm, liveliness

Check your answers on page 132.

2 In an increasingly global economy do certain national stereotypes still hold true?

Phrasal verbs 3 Match the phrasal verbs in these sentences. They were all in the extracts in 1.

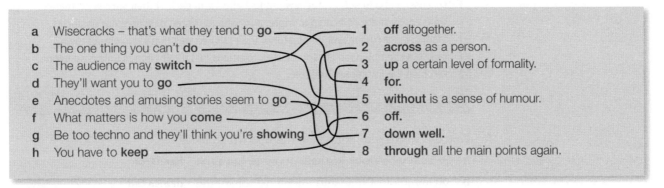

a	Wisecracks – that's what they tend to **go**	1	**off** altogether.
b	The one thing you can't **do**	2	**across** as a person.
c	The audience may **switch**	3	**up** a certain level of formality.
d	They'll want you to **go**	4	**for.**
e	Anecdotes and amusing stories seem to **go**	5	**without** is a sense of humour.
f	What matters is how you **come**	6	**off.**
g	Be too techno and they'll think you're **showing**	7	**down well.**
h	You have to **keep**	8	**through** all the main points again.

4 Match the phrasal verbs in 3 to the meanings below.

a present yourself _come across_   e like _go for_

b lose interest _switch off_   f repeat _go through_

c be appreciated _go down well_   g maintain _keep up_

d try to impress _show off_   h manage without _do without_

Lexis link

for more on phrasal verbs see page 111

5 In your experience, what sort of thing do audiences in your country tend to go for? What doesn't go down so well?

Idioms 6 You heard the following idiomatic expressions in 1. Complete them by filling in the missing letters. Use the words in brackets to help you.

a You should have all the technical information at your fi_ngertips_ (easily available)

b Give your presentation the personal to_uch_. (aim it directly at your audience's needs)

c You'll get loads of interruptions, but just go with the f_low_. (let things happen)

d Don't get too carried aw_ay_. (be overenthusiastic)

e Have a few gimmicks up your sl_eeve_. (plan some clever surprises to attract attention)

f It really is essential that you do your ho_mework_. (prepare very carefully)

7 Which piece of advice in 6 do you think is the most important?

Innovation

1 How much of your company's business depends on innovation? Give a few examples.

2 Look at the extract from a web page below. What do you think the title means? Now read the text. Does your company encourage this kind of initiative?

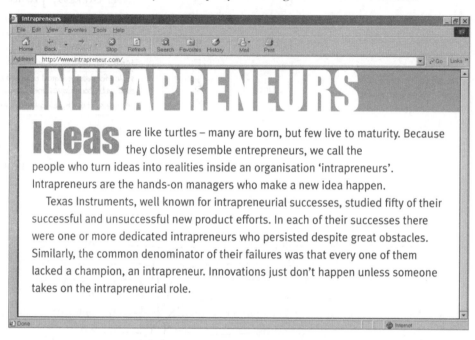

3 Find the words and phrases in the text which mean:

   a people who don't just talk about it, but do it __hands-on__

   b giving a lot of time and energy to something __dedicated__

   c kept on trying to do something __persisted__

   d things that make progress difficult __obstacles__

   e the only thing in common __common denominator__

   f someone who supports and fights for an idea __champion__

4 What new ideas within your company or department have you been closely involved with recently?

Innovation

In this section, students read a short text on 'intrapreneurs' (a term derived from *entrepreneur* used to describe people who are the driving force behind ideas in companies). They listen to a four-part recording of two managers presenting an idea for a new product to their board of directors. Finally, students devise a new product/service, and prepare and deliver a team presentation, using a template of language prompts.

1   Elicit examples of companies that need to keep ahead of competitors by bringing out innovative products/services e.g. Microsoft creates products which customers then realise they need, pharmaceutical companies which invest huge amounts in R&D (research and development). Ask students how important innovation is in their company and elicit some examples.

2   Write the word *intrapreneur* on the board and ask students to guess the meaning. Students then read the text to check. Ask students to discuss this type of initiative-taking in relation to their own company or other companies they know.

3   Ask students to read the text again and look for the words and phrases. Remind students to look for a word in the same form as the definition and also to use the context to help them. Check the answers with the class and then get students to record any of the new words they want to use in their active vocabulary. Expand on these by eliciting other forms of the words or useful collocations e.g. *persistence, to overcome an obstacle* etc.

4   Find out if students have been involved with the development of new ideas in their company and to give examples. If students haven't, ask if there is a R&D department which handles new ideas. Elicit ways in which the students' company keeps up with innovations in their industry e.g. by attending international conferences.

5 🔊 **8.3** Lead in to the recording by asking students how important the fitness industry is in their country. Ask students to estimate what percentage of people regularly attend a fitness centre/gym and what form of exercise they themselves take, if any.

Give students the names of the managers Rachel Weissmuller and Brad Kennedy. With weaker groups, check/pre-teach: *couch, disgraceful, findings, respondents, to stretch* (a brand), *to complement, prototype, sleek, to disassemble, childsplay, setting, bulky.*

Extract 1

Ask students to predict the order of the stages in task a first. Play the recording once and get students to check their answers.

Get students to read the remaining questions in b–d. With weaker classes, check students can read out the figures in task c. Play extract 1 again and have students complete their answers. Check the answers with the class, eliciting students' opinions for tasks b and d.

Extract 2

Working in pairs, ask students to discuss the questions in tasks a–d first and predict/guess as many answers as possible. Play the recording once and get students to check/complete their answers. Play the recording again if necessary. Check the answers. Elicit possible answers to e and write up ideas on the board.

Extract 3

Play the recording as far as *the ultimate go-anywhere exercise machine* to let students see if they predicted the product correctly.

Before playing the complete recording, check/review the vocabulary in the table in task d: *to fit into, to assemble, setting.* Ask students to read the questions a–f and play extract 3 through once. Play the extract again if necessary and then check the answers. Elicit possible answers to question f e.g. generating additional income while reinforcing the company's image.

🔊 **8.3**

Extract 1

A: Good morning, everybody. Thanks for coming. I'm Rachel Weissmuller, area manager for the north-west division, and this is Brad Kennedy, head of our physiological research unit.

B: Hi.

A: As some of you already know, Brad and I have been working on a project of our own for some time now – a project, which we think you're going to be as excited about as we are. Brad?

B: Thanks, Rachel. Well, now, as the USA's leading chain of health clubs with over 1,000 centres in 35 states, we pride ourselves on providing the best in fitness training programs, on getting nearly a quarter million Americans off the couch and into the gym. For us, staying in shape is not just a business. It's a way of life. There's just one problem – the majority of Americans don't seem to be getting the message. According to the National Center for Health Statistics, seven out of ten of us don't take regular exercise. Four out of ten are not physically active at all! Figures recently published by the Surgeon General show that 61% of Americans are now seriously overweight. That's 122 million people! A disgraceful statistic. But, you have to admit, one hell of a marketing opportunity! The question is, how do we reach that market with something totally new?

Extract 2

A: A recent report claims that a mere 13% of Americans are satisfied with their physical appearance. And a staggering 92% are dissatisfied with their current level of fitness. So, why aren't they doing something about it? We did a nationwide survey of people who had previously shown an interest in joining a MaxOut club and then changed their minds. Full details are in the report in front of you, but this chart highlights our main findings. As you can see, 15% of respondents said joining a gym was simply too expensive. Fifty-three per cent said they'd love to join if they weren't so busy. And, interestingly, 32%, almost a third, admitted they were just too embarrassed to join a health club in their present physical condition. They wanted to get fit first! So, what does all this mean? We think the implications are clear. There's obviously a huge market for an inexpensive alternative to going to the gym for people who are conscious of their appearance but short of time. And this represents a golden opportunity to stretch the MaxOut brand and develop a new product that perfectly complements our existing business.

Extract 3

B: OK. And now the moment you've all been waiting for! The MaxOut Micro-GYM! Forty per cent of our project budget went into constructing the prototype. And it's taken 18 months to get this far with the design. But does this look cool, or what? I'll pass it round in a moment. Ladies and gentlemen, what you're looking at is the world's smallest full-body workout system – ever. The ultimate go-anywhere exercise machine. And, we believe, a significant part of this company's future. With its sleek, lightweight design, the Micro-GYM weighs just over a pound, or 450 grammes. That's less than most quality cameras. Disassembled, it fits easily into a coat pocket. The assembly itself is childsplay. You can be ready to exercise in under 45 seconds. Now, I know what you're thinking. Can something so small possibly work? But let me reassure you. The Micro-GYM offers 35 different exercises for upper body, lower body and mid-section. It can be adjusted from the five-kilo setting for gentle exercise right up to the 18-kilo setting for a real workout. In fact, it can do just about anything that much bulkier and more expensive equipment can. When you can't get to the gym, the Micro-GYM comes to you. You can get fit at home, on holiday, at the office, even in-flight!

5 🔊 8.3 Two managers for MaxOut, an American chain of fitness centres, are presenting a new business idea to their board of directors. Listen to four extracts from their presentation and answer the questions.

Extract 1

a Put the stages of the first part of the presentation in chronological order.

quote statistics ⑥   build up expectations ③   pose a problem ⑤
introduce themselves ②   thank the audience ①   set a challenge ⑦
share corporate vision ④

b Are the presenters successful at arousing the curiosity of their audience? Why (not)?'   (suggested answer) Yes, because they built up anticipation before presenting the product.

c The following figures were quoted. What do they refer to?

1,000 _the number of MaxOut Health Clubs in the USA_

35 _the number of states the clubs are in_

250,000 _the number of Americans they are trying to get into the gym_

$^7/_{10}$ _the number of Americans that don't take regular exercise_

$^4/_{10}$ _the number of Americans that are not physically active_

61% (122m) _the number of Americans that are seriously overweight_

d On a scale of 1–5, how confident did the presenters sound? _5 (very confident)_ Would their presentation style be popular in your company?

Extract 2

a What do these figures refer to? Do you find them surprising?

a mere 13% _the number of Americans that are satisfied with their physical appearance_

a staggering 92% _the number of Americans that are dissatisfied with their level of fitness_

b What do you think 'mere' and 'staggering' mean? _mere = surprisingly low_ , _staggering = surprisingly high_

c Complete the following extract from the presentation.

We did a nationwide su_rvey_ of people who had previously shown an in_terest_ in joining a MaxOut club and then changed their mi_nds_. Full de_tails_ are in the re_port_ in front of you, but this chart hi_ghlights_ our main fi_ndings_.

d Complete the chart, which shows the results of the survey referred to in **c**.

Nationwide survey

Reasons given for not becoming a member of MaxOut Health Clubs

too busy = 53%

too embarrassed = 32%

too expensive = 15%

e What product do you think the speakers are about to present?

Extract 3

a What is the product? _a micro-gym_

b How much of the project budget was spent on making the prototype?
_40%_

c How long has it taken to develop?
18 months

d Complete the product features chart.

e What's the main selling point?
You can exercise anywhere.

f In what ways do you think the product would benefit MaxOut's main business?

Main product features

weighs just over _1lb/450g_

fits easily into _a coat pocket_

assembles in _under 45 seconds_

35 different _exercises_

settings _can be adjusted_

Extract 4　**a**　Complete the extract below using the verb phrases in the box. The first one has been done for you.

> might easily be sold　　are currently being considered　　has been suggested
> would probably be priced　　is included　　are all itemised
> ~~has been fully costed~~　　is still being carried out　　could be recorded

OK, to wrap things up. The Micro-GYM (1) **has been fully costed** – a complete breakdown (2) **is included** in the report. Estimated costs of manufacturing, packaging and advertising (3) **are all itemised**. Product testing (4) **is still being carried out**, but we would obviously need the go-ahead from you before we proceed much further with that. The Micro-GYM (5) **would probably be priced** at around $35: well within the reach of most people. It (6) **has been suggested** that exercise demonstrations (7) **could be recorded** on video and that the product (8) **might easily be sold** online. Both these suggestions would incur extra costs, but (9) **are currently being considered**.

Grammar Link

for more on the passive
see page 110

b　If you were on the board of MaxOut, would you give the new product idea the go-ahead? If not, what other information would you need before you were persuaded?

Fluency　**6**　Work with a partner to give a team presentation.

Step One: Brainstorm
Your job is to come up with an innovative idea for a product or service that could be developed by your company or a company you know. If you and your partner work for different companies, you could consider how the two firms could collaborate.

Step Two: Plan
Make sure the new product or service:
- is a new departure for your company or companies
- complements the products and services currently on offer
- meets a need not catered for at present.
Be as original and alternative as you like!

Step Three: Rehearse
Use the presenters' prompt cards opposite to help you structure your talk. Most of the key language on the cards was in the presentation you listened to. Create any visuals you need.

Step Four: Deliver
Give the presentation, handing over to your partner after each phase of the talk. Invite questions at the end.

Extract 4

Point out that all the phrases in the box are passive forms. Ask students to read and complete the extract. Play the extract through and let the students check/complete their answers. Elicit why the passive has been used in this part of the presentation (the focus is on the actions, not on the people who performed them).

Direct students' attention to the Grammar link on page 110 for more information and practice on the passive.

Divide the class into groups to discuss the questions in task b. Hold a short feedback session, eliciting what other information is needed e.g. more details on the exact timescale of the ROI *(return on investment)*, more market research etc.

Fluency

6   Tell students they are going to try out their creativity and presentation skills. Give students a few moments to read through steps one–four to set the scene. Divide the class into pairs. With larger groups, students can work in small groups.

Step One

If students work in very different sectors and collaboration is difficult, suggest that they invent a new company to develop their product/service. If students are short of ideas, brainstorm possible innovative ideas first e.g. an instantaneous electronic interpreter which makes learning a foreign language unnecessary, a pill which cures the common cold etc.

Step Two

Give students plenty of time to do the planning phase. Encourage them to be creative but also to check that the new product/service is viable. Write 'check' questions on the board to help students focus their ideas e.g. *How is it different? Has it been done before? How will it fit in with your current product/service range? What are the key USPs/selling points?* Make sure students make notes on the key points about their product/service. Monitor and help with vocabulary and pronunciation as necessary.

Extract 4

A: You'll have to excuse Brad. He gets a little carried away sometimes. But we do think the Micro-GYM could be an enormously successful sideline to our main business. OK, to wrap things up. The Micro-GYM has been fully costed – a complete breakdown is included in the report. Estimated costs of manufacturing, packaging and advertising are all itemised. Product testing is still being carried out, but we would obviously need the go-ahead from you before we proceed much further with that. The Micro-GYM would probably be priced at around $35: well within the reach of most people. It has been suggested that exercise demonstrations could be recorded on video and that the product might easily be sold online. Both these suggestions would incur extra costs, but are currently being considered. The prospects for Micro-GYM are exciting. What we hope you'll give us today is the authorisation to move on to the next stage. Thank you very much.

B: Thank you, Rachel. OK, we'd like to throw this session open now for questions and suggestions. But, no, sorry, you can't take the Micro-GYM home just yet. It's the only one we have at the moment!

Step Three

Ask students to read through the presentation template on page 45 and check comprehension of: *to pride yourself on, tremendous, untapped, to reassure.* Ask students to re-organise their notes to fit into the eight stages in the template. Get them to choose the option they want to use in the text in red to give detail to their talk. If appropriate, hand out blank cards and get students to write out the key expressions they want to use. Give students time to produce visuals such as graphs or charts, providing OHTs or a flip-chart if possible, and also to rehearse their talk. Get them to decide who will present each section and to make the handover between presenters as smooth as possible, using bridging expressions e.g. *Thanks, …/As … was saying, …/As … has already pointed out, …*

Step Four

Re-organise the seating if necessary to simulate a typical presentation – a semi-circle or rows may be preferable to standard classroom layout. Check that the audience can see the presenters and any visuals they want to use.

Students give their team presentations to the rest of the class. Join in as part of the audience but also take feedback notes for each team. Let students conduct the question-and-answer session after each presentation but set a time limit for each one.

At the start of the feedback session, ask students what they thought went well and what they would change or avoid doing if they gave the presentation again. Give students general feedback on fluency and on their presenting skills before feeding back on important or common errors.

If you're short of time

Omit the *Innovation* section, exercises 1–4 on page 42.

Ask students to prepare Steps One–Three of the fluency task on pages 44–5 for homework.

Open	Good morning, everybody, thanks for coming. I'm (*name*) and this is (*partner*). As some of you already know, (*partner*) and I have been working on this project for some time. By the end of this morning's/afternoon's presentation, we hope/think/feel confident you'll be as excited about this idea as we are.
Arouse interest	As the world's leading provider/a major player in the world of ..., we pride ourselves on ... For us, ... is not just a business – it's ... Figures recently published by ... show that ... That's a very worrying/somewhat alarming/quite staggering statistic. But it's also a tremendous marketing opportunity. The question is, how do we reach that market?
Refer to consumer research	A recent report claims that ... So we did a nationwide survey of/distributed questionnaires to/set up focus groups to find out ... Full details are in the report in front of you. But this chart highlights our main findings. As you can see, ...
Discuss potential	So, what does all this mean? We think the implications are clear. There's obviously a huge/substantial/growing/largely untapped market for ... And this represents a golden/an ideal opportunity to expand the company/stretch our brand and develop an exciting new product/service to complement our existing business.
Introduce product/ service	OK. And now the moment you've all been waiting for! Ladies and gentlemen, the new ... It's taken (*time*) to get this far with the concept/design/project. What you're looking at is the ultimate/world's first ... and, we believe, a significant part of this company's future.
Describe product/ service	The main features/benefits/selling points are ... And, as you'd expect ... Now, I know what you're thinking: how can ...? So, let me reassure you. We've really done our homework on this one. As far as the competition is concerned, our ... compares very favourably indeed.
Close	We really do believe the ... could be a bestselling product/first-class service and an excellent addition to our current range of .../enormously successful sideline to our main business. OK, to wrap things up. The ... has been fully costed. A complete breakdown is included in the report. What we need now is the go-ahead from you. Thank you very much.
Open Q&A session	Thank you, (*partner*). OK, we'd like to throw this session open now for questions and suggestions. As (*partner*) said, we need your authorisation to move on to the next stage. So, over to you!

9 Relationship-building

One of our ironclad rules is 'Never do business with anybody you don't like.' If you don't like somebody, there's a reason. *Henry Quadracci, CEO of Quad/Graphics*

Discussion 1 They say 'You never get a second chance to make a first impression.' Read the text and underline anything you disagree with. Then compare with a partner.

First **impressions**

Creating a positive first impression is essential in a competitive job market. Most of us recognise that when we meet people for the first time we make all sorts of judgements about them, consciously or subconsciously – how successful they are, how capable, how credible, how creative, how sharp, how professional, and so on.

In fact, studies in this area show that we judge people within five seconds of meeting them, and then add another 50% to that judgement in the subsequent five seconds. Staggeringly, it can then take another twenty experiences with that person to change our initial impression.

Adapted from The Guardian

Collocations 2 Match the nouns and noun phrases in the box to the adjectives below to make 30 things we usually notice about someone on first meeting them.

| voice | sense of humour | clothes | manner | handshake | laugh |

a firm/limp/aggressive _handshake_

b casual/shabby/smart/designer/expensive-looking _clothes_

c high-pitched/irritating/sexy/pleasant-sounding/soft/deep _voice_

d authoritative/confident/relaxed/cold/hostile/abrasive _manner_

e good/great/no/dry/weird _sense of humour_

f great/loud/infectious/annoying/nervous _laugh_

3 When you meet someone for the first time, which of the above do you find most:

a appealing?

b reassuring?

c off-putting?

What else do you tend to notice?

Discussion 4 Have you ever:

a felt an instant rapport with someone you've only just met?

b taken an immediate dislike to someone you've just been introduced to?

c misjudged someone by taking too much notice of the way they looked or sounded?

Questionnaire 5 How good are your networking skills? Complete the questionnaire opposite using the pairs of verbs in the boxes. Then circle your answers. Compare your answers with a partner and then read the analysis on page 129.

Networking

9 Relationship-building

This unit is about building successful client relationships.

Students read a short text on making first impressions, discuss their reactions and then focus on collocations connected with first meetings. They do a fun questionnaire on networking and then practise their networking skills in a fluency activity.

The central part of the unit is based on an article about the link between golf and doing business. The students listen to a recording of business people socialising before and after a round of golf. They practise multi-verb sentences taken from the listening task.

A second listening task set around a dinner invitation to a colleague continues the theme of socialising. There is a focus on the social language used during the evening. In the final section, the students act out a similar social situation of a guest visiting the home of a host.

The grammatical focus is on multi-verb sentences and the lexical focus is on social English.

In this first section, students read a short newspaper article on first impressions and then focus on adjective–noun collocations relating to what people tend to notice on first meeting. They do a light-hearted questionnaire about networking and discuss the results before practising their own networking skills in a fluency activity.

Warm-up

Ask students how important building up and establishing personal relationships is for the growth of their own company/business sector. Let the students read the quotation by Henry Quadracci. Encourage students to work out the meaning of *ironclad* from the root *iron* and the context (unbreakable). Ask if they agree with Quadracci's sentiment and how far they can follow his rule in their business life.

Discussion

1   To generate interest in the text, write the following gapped sentences on the board and ask students to predict the answers: *First impressions formed in … second(s)/minute(s) of meeting a person. First impressions changed after … meetings.* Students scan paragraph 2 of the text for the correct answers (5 seconds/20 meetings). Ask them to give their initial reactions to these figures. Students then read the whole text and highlight where they disagree. Divide the class into pairs and get them to compare their ideas. Ask some of the students to report back on their discussion.

Ask students to think about the implications of the text for interviewing people e.g. *How can people make a good first impression at interview?* Encourage students to give examples from their own experience of being interviewed.

Collocations

2   Ask students to read through the adjectives and underline any new ones, then check the meaning with a partner. Do a whole class check of any further unknown adjectives, getting students to say if they are positive or negative in meaning.

Ask students to do the matching task and then check the answers. Check pronunciation of the following adjectives, highlighting the word stress: *casual, expensive-looking, pleasant-sounding, authoritative, abrasive, weird, infectious.*

As a follow-up task, divide the class into small groups and have students create a set of five questions for other groups, using any new adjectives which they want to remember.

3   Elicit examples of cities where dress sense is especially important e.g. Milan, and jobs for which a dress code is important e.g. sales, management. Give students a few moments to think about their answers before discussing the questions with the whole class. With large classes, divide students into small groups. Elicit examples of what students find most appealing/reassuring/off-putting and what they notice when first meeting someone e.g. clothes/accessories, haircuts/styles, mannerisms/gestures etc. Ask students if they think they focus on different aspects when meeting a woman compared with a man.

Discussion

4   Students work in pairs to discuss the questions before reporting back with interesting examples/anecdotes. Draw students' attention to the expressions used in the questions: *to feel an instant rapport with, to take an immediate dislike to, to take too much notice of.* Encourage them to notice and record longer 'chunks' like these to help develop their own fluency.

Questionnaire

5   Find out who thinks of themselves as a good networker and tell students they are going to do a questionnaire to find out who is most effective in this area. With weaker groups, check/pre-teach: *to hover, to break the ice, to talk shop* (to talk about your own job/profession), *to bitch about someone, to let your hair down, to mingle, to persevere, to slip away, to give someone a nod.*

Elicit the answer to gap 1a in the questionnaire as an example. Point out to students that identifying the fixed expressions/collocations, i.e. *look them in the eye, say hello,* will help them complete the exercise. Students work individually to complete the questionnaire. Check the answers with the class.

Students then circle one answer for each question in the questionnaire. Refer students to page 129 to read the analysis of their answers. Ask if anyone chose all the 'correct' answers and if they agree with the analysis. If appropriate, give students time to record any vocabulary which they would like to use in the future.

Fluency

6   Ask students to give examples of positive experiences when networking and create a list of 'top tips'. Explain that students are going to do a roleplay which will allow them to try out their networking skills.

Divide the students into AB pairs. Speaker A, a sales director, reads page 135. Speaker B, a purchasing manager, reads page 133. Give students enough time to read and memorise the key information on their role cards and to prepare their approach to networking with their new contact. Focus attention on the useful language in each role card.

Get students to decide where they meet at the beginning of the roleplay and arrange the furniture in the classroom accordingly. While students act out the roles, monitor and take feedback notes. When they have finished, ask each pair of students to report back on the outcome. Ask what went well and what they would do better/ differently next time. Give feedback on overall fluency before highlighting any important or common errors.

As an optional follow-up activity, ask students to write an e-mail to their partner to summarise the outcome of the meeting and to organise the next stage.

Are you an effective networker?

talk + catch   relax + let   look + say   hover + wait   moan + bitch   crack + break

1 You meet a group of business people for the first time. Do you:

  a _look_ them in the eye, smile and _say_ hello?

  b _hover_ in the background and _wait_ to be introduced?

  c _crack_ a joke to _break_ the ice?

2 You meet up with some colleagues after work. Do you:

  a _talk_ shop and _catch_ up on all the latest gossip?

  b _moan_ about work and _bitch_ about the boss?

  c _relax_ and _let_ your hair down?

introduce + slip   feel + mingle   make + escape   try + draw   persevere + find   stick + ignore

3 You meet a fascinating person at a cocktail party. Do you:

  a _stick_ to them like glue and _ignore_ everyone else?

  b _try_ and _draw_ other people into the conversation?

  c _feel_ obliged to go and _mingle_ with other people?

4 You're stuck with a bore at a conference. Do you:

  a _persevere_ in the hope you'll _find_ something in common?

  b _make_ some kind of excuse and _escape_ ?

  c _introduce_ them to someone else and _slip_ away?

exchange + get   get + mention   go + make   cut + get   give + keep   look + pretend

5 You see someone you don't get on with at a function. Do you:

  a _look_ the other way and _pretend_ you haven't seen them?

  b _go_ over and _make_ the effort to speak to them?

  c _give_ them a polite nod, but _keep_ your distance?

6 You're introduced to a potential client. Time is short. Do you:

  a _cut_ the preliminaries and _get_ straight to the point?

  b _get_ to know them a bit before you _mention_ business?

  c _exchange_ business cards and say you'll _get_ back to them?

Fluency   **6**   Work with a partner to practise your networking skills. Speaker A see page 135. Speaker B see page 133.

Getting out of the office

1 Is the golf course or tennis court a good place to do business? Read the article and think about the questions on the right. Then discuss them with a partner.

Adapted from *Business Week Online*

Golf and business
A PERFECT COUPLE

What better way to get to know somebody, commune with nature, work a deal and improve your swing – all at the same time. US president Calvin Coolidge once remarked that 'The business of America is business.' He didn't quite get it right. As any CEO will tell you, the business of America is golf.

Golf and business have been *inextricably linked* for more than a century, and most executives seem to be as comfortable conducting business against the *serene backdrop* of a rolling emerald fairway as they are within the controlled confines of the office. Not everyone can play tennis, but everyone thinks they can play golf. In an age of health and *enlightenment*, golf has replaced the three-martini lunch as the preferred vehicle for *sealing deals*. The ability to play golf, understand its *etiquette*, and respect its traditions can *boost a career*.

John D. Rockefeller played every day of his life until his mid-90s. Today, the *titans* of high tech are no less enthusiastic. Sun Microsystems CEO Scott McNealy is a scratch golfer and Bill Gates is devoted to the game. Then there's Tiger Woods, readily identified with some of the biggest brands in business – American Express, Nike and Buick.

So why is golf the preferred sport of business? In a word, relationships. No other sport lends itself to developing *lasting professional bonds* like golf does. 'How else can one get outside for four hours in such a relaxed, quiet and beautiful setting?' asks Jim Henry, a business development executive with Deloitte Consulting. 'There is *ample time* to build or renew relationships.'

That is a key differentiator between golf and other sports. 'Four to five hours on the golf course, and you get to know the *character traits* of your golfing partners – honesty, humility, ability to handle success and failure, approach to risk, desire to have fun, etc.,' says Miller Bonner, a public relations veteran. 'That translates into a successful business relationship.'

Marketing director Derek Van Bronkhorst has his own test of character on the links. 'Do they cheat?' he asks. 'If they cheat in golf, would you want to do business with them?'

Golf glossary
swing the movement you make with your arms when you hit the ball
fairway the long part of a golf course that leads to the green
scratch golfer a player without a handicap
links a golf course by the sea

a Are you a golf fan? Or do you agree with the writer Mark Twain that 'golf is a good walk spoiled'?

b Why is golf so popular with the business community?

c Do you wish you could get out of the office more?

d What's the best way to get on in your company?

e Tiger Woods's contract with Nike alone is worth $100m. Can that sort of money really be justified?

f What are the risks of playing sport against the people you do business with?

g What might your opponent do in a game of golf that would tell you something about their personality?

h Are you a good loser?

2 With a partner, work out the meaning of the words and phrases in *italics*.

Getting out of the office

In this section, the students read an article about the link between golf and doing business. They discuss issues raised by the text and then focus on the meaning of some of the expressions used. The students listen to a group of business people socialising before and during a game of golf, and then practise some of the multi-verb phrases used in the recording.

1 Tell students they are going to read an article on the link between golf and business. Elicit examples of famous people in the business and entertainment worlds who play golf. Ask students to scan the text for more examples (John D. Rockefeller, Scott McNealy, Bill Gates, Tiger Woods). Also ask students to scan the text for a list of characteristics the writer thinks can be seen in a person who plays golf (honesty, humility, ability to handle success and failure, approach to risk, desire to have fun). Ask the students if they agree.

Ask students to read the article through, explaining that they will focus on the words in italics in the following exercise. Draw students' attention to the glossary at the bottom of the article. Give students a few moments to think about questions a–h. Divide the class into pairs and have them discuss the questions. With larger classes, divide the students into groups.

Elicit summaries of any interesting points which came up in the discussion. Feed in the following points/questions as appropriate:

b Golf can be an expensive sport, so it provides an image of wealth and exclusivity. It is played a lot by senior management and can be seen as a way of networking and furthering your career.

d Ask students if they think playing golf can encourage favouritism or even nepotism.

f Risks may include undermining someone senior, creating tension/jealousy by beating someone, becoming too familiar/competitive, confusing healthy competition in sport with the desire to 'win' in business. Ask students if they have experienced any positive/negative outcomes from mixing sport and business.

g Positive examples include being gracious in defeat, congratulating the winner/a good player, not taking competition too seriously; negative examples include causing another player to miss a shot, not accepting defeat, only playing against people who don't play as well as you.

2 Remind students of the range of strategies they can use in order to work out the meaning of the words – using the root of the word as in *enlightenment*, deducing the meaning from context as with *ample*, using general knowledge to help understand metaphorical language as in *titans* (Greek gods; derivatives include *titanic*). Get students to work in pairs to do the rest of the task. Then elicit answers from the whole class.

Answers

> *inextricably linked* – very closely connected
>
> *serene backdrop* – calm background
>
> *enlightenment* – a more informed view
>
> *sealing deals* – completing business deals (Note the rhyme, which is there for effect.)
>
> *etiquette* – social rules
>
> *boost a career* – help someone get promoted
>
> *titans* – important and powerful people
>
> *lasting professional bonds* – long-term business relationships
>
> *ample time* – more than enough time
>
> *character traits* – features of someone's personality

Ask students if they do any other sports/activities which could be beneficial to doing business e.g. squash, tennis, organised skiing trips, bowling evenings etc.

3 📼 **9.1** Tell students that the recording is divided into two extracts and there are four names to listen out for: Stella, Max, Craig and Karen. Check/Pre-teach: *to partner, to team up with, disposal operation, to dispose of, toxic substance, competitive spirit*. Ask students the following gist question and play the recording through once to check: *What are the characters talking about and what is the tone of their conversation?* (extract 1 – who will team up with who and the plans for the morning; friendly; extract 2 – how well they're playing; the disposal operation for some toxic waste; the candidates for an important job; more businesslike and slightly strained between Craig and Stella).

Ask students to read the questions for extracts 1 and 2. Play the recording again and let students complete their answers. If necessary, play the recording a third time to allow students to listen out for anything they missed. Check the answers with the whole class.

Ask students to give their reaction to each of the characters and how they handled the situation.

Multi-verb sentences

4 Point out that multi-verb sentences are complex because of the word order and range of structures that can follow different verbs e.g. *-ing* form, infinitive with or without *to*, a preposition. Ask student to reorder the words in bold to make correct sentences. Refer students to the recording script on page 149, where the answers are given in bold.

Write stems from the multi-verb sentences on the board e.g. *We should probably be thinking of …. We can't count on X doing Y, I've arranged for X to …, I've been meaning to …* etc. and elicit examples relevant to the students' own experience. Ask students to note down the most useful verb patterns and to try to integrate them into their active vocabulary.

Direct students' attention to the Grammar link on page 112 for more information and practice on multi-verb sentences.

📼 **9.1**
Extract 1
A: Stella! Max! You're just in time to join us in a little pre-match drink.
B: Hi, Craig. Hi, Karen. Oh, is that malt whisky? I don't know if I should. I mean, I just had breakfast!
A: Nonsense! It's just the thing to warm us up. Max, you'll have one, won't you?
C: Of course, thank you.
A: There you go. Stella?
B: Well, OK, just a drop. It *is* a little chilly this morning. Beautiful day, though.
A: Isn't it? Well, now, **we should probably be thinking of making a move quite soon**. Unfortunately, **we can't count on the weather staying fine at this time of year**. Max, you're partnering Karen. And Stella, you're stuck with me, I'm afraid. Now, **I've arranged for us to have lunch at the clubhouse** – they've got an excellent restaurant there. So I thought we'd start at the tenth and just play the last nine holes, if that's OK with you. That way **we should be able to get round the course in a couple of hours or so**.
C: Sounds perfect.

A: And, Max, I think you'll find my game's improved a little since we last played.
C: Splendid! I always like a challenge, Craig. You know that …

Extract 2
A: Damn! I don't know what's the matter with my game today. I just can't seem to keep the ball straight. Sorry, Stella. **You must be wishing you'd been teamed up with Max**.
B: Well, you have been in two sand-traps and a lake, Craig! And this is only our third hole!
A: I know, I know. Your shot, Max …
B: Craig, **I've been meaning to have a word with you about this disposal operation** of ours.
A: Ah, **I was wondering when you'd get round to mentioning that**. Look, Stella, you know my position on that …
B: Now, Craig, listen to me. You know I want that oil platform disposed of at sea. It's by far the most cost-effective method.
C: (*coughs for silence*)
B: Oh, sorry, Max. Not trying to put you off your game. Oh, great shot! Wow, that's almost all the way to the flag! Craig, you

didn't tell me Max was such a fantastic player.
A: No, I, er, look, Stella, this oil platform – disposing of it at sea. Don't you think that's a bit risky? I know it's technically possible. But there must be 130 tonnes of highly toxic and radioactive substances on that platform!
B: Craig, you're starting to sound like a Greenpeace activist, for goodness' sake! … By the way, I understand you've applied for the top job here in Scotland.
A: Yeah, so?
B: So's Max.
A: What?
B: Yeah. And the way it's looking he may well get it. Seems the board like his competitive spirit.
A: I see.
B: Of course, I could probably put in a word for you. Let's talk later. For the time being, I'd like you to concentrate on your game! I'm not a good loser, Craig!

3 📼 **9.1** Listen to a group of oil company executives chatting during a game of golf and answer the questions.

Extract 1

a Why doesn't Stella immediately accept Craig's offer? _She thinks it's too early for a drink._

b Why are they only playing nine holes? _They only want to play for a couple of hours, and they've booked a table for lunch._

c How would you describe the men's attitude to the game? _competitive_

Extract 2

a How's Craig playing today? _badly_

b What do Craig and Stella disagree on? _the location of the oil platform disposal_

c What do you think Craig has to do if he wants the job? _be more competitive_

Multi-verb sentences

4 Reorganise the words in **bold** to make correct sentences. They were all in the conversations in 3.

a We **be should thinking making probably of** a move quite soon.
We should probably be thinking of making a move quite soon.

b We **count staying can't weather fine the on** at this time of year.
We can't count on the weather staying fine at this time of year.

c I **have have arranged lunch us to for** at the clubhouse.
I have arranged for us to have lunch at the clubhouse.

d We **be get should able to around** the course in a couple of hours or so.
We should be able to get around the course in a couple of hours or so.

e You **be teamed been had must wishing you with up** Max.
You must be wishing you had been teamed up with Max.

f I **have have meaning been word you a with to about** this disposal operation.
I have been meaning to have a word with you about this disposal operation.

Grammar Link

for more on multi-verb sentences see page 112

g I **get would was mentioning wondering you when round to** that.
I was wondering when you would get round to mentioning that.

Visiting someone's home

Discussion **1** What are the advantages and disadvantages of inviting a client or colleague to your home? Is it common practice in your country?

2 🔊 9.2 Listen to some people entertaining at home and answer the questions.

Extract 1   **a** Did Magda have a problem finding Anne's house? <u>Yes, she got</u> <u>a bit lost coming off the ring road.</u>

   b What do you think 'Martin's still **slaving away** in the kitchen' means? <u>He's been in the kitchen for a long time, working hard.</u>

   c What has Magda brought as a present? <u>a bottle of wine</u>

Extract 2   **a** What do you think 'The whole place was **an absolute wreck** when we moved in' means? <u>The house needed a lot of building work doing.</u>

   b What does Magda have in her drink? <u>ice and lemon</u>

   c What do you think Martin means by 'I had to **rescue** the starter'? <u>It was almost ruined but now it's OK.</u>

Extract 3   **a** What do you imagine Anne and Martin's apartment to be like?

elegant ☑ comfortable ☑ spacious ☑ light & airy ☐ old & tatty ☐ ultra-modern ☐ tastefully furnished ☐ full of antiques ☑ dark & gloomy ☐

   b When Magda sees the chairs, she says 'I **could do with** some of those for my place.' What does she mean? <u>Something similar would be ideal for her flat.</u>

Extract 4   **a** How does Magda describe the duck? crispy ☑ tasty ☐ tender ☐ juicy ☑

   b Who raises the subject of business? Why? <u>Anne. She wants to</u> <u>know what's going on in Poland.</u>

   c How does Martin excuse himself? <u>He says he'll go and see to the dessert.</u>

   d How many times does Magda signal she's going to leave soon? <u>two</u>

Social English **3** All the remarks below were in the conversation in 2. See who can remember the most in just three minutes!

Arrival
Let me take your coat. → You managed to find us OK, then? → Oh, I brought you this. → You shouldn't have. → Come on through. → Oh, what a fabulous apartment! → Now, what can I get you to drink? → I'll be right back. → Make yourself at home.

The apartment
I was just looking at some of your oil paintings. → You've got quite a collection, haven't you? → And I love the way you've done the fireplace. → Was that here when you moved in? → Look at that view!

The meal
Dinner's ready when you are. → Sit wherever you like. → I thought we'd have a nice Spanish red. → Now, there's more duck if you want it. → And help yourself to vegetables. → Mm, this is absolutely delicious! → I'm glad you like it. → You must let me have the recipe. → A little more wine? → I shouldn't really. I'm driving. → Oh, go on. You've only had one. → Just a drop, then.

Farewells
Well, I ought to be making a move soon. → You don't have to rush off just yet, do you? → How about some more coffee? → OK, just half a cup. → And then I really must be going. → Thank you both for a lovely evening. → Next time you must come to my place. → Take care now.

Lexis link

for more on social English see page 113

Visiting someone's home

In this section, students listen to a couple entertaining a colleague at home. They practise expressions that both host and guest could use in this situation.

Discussion

1   Ask students if it is common to invite business associates home. Elicit some of the advantages and disadvantages e.g. it is a more relaxing atmosphere than the office, it can deepen the relationship as you can talk about personal things/meet family members, you can build up trust and possibly learn about another culture etc.; you may unwittingly offend your host or guest, you may have to deal with cultural unknowns e.g. what present to bring, if any, you may be asked to eat unfamiliar food.

2   **9.2** First brainstorm typical gifts you could take to a business associate's home e.g. flowers, chocolates, wine. Elicit examples from students' own experience of gift-giving in different countries.

Tell students they are going to hear a dialogue in four parts set at a dinner at someone's home. Let the students read through the questions for extracts 1–4 and predict as many answers as possible. Play each of the extracts in turn and get students to complete their answers. Check the answers with the whole class.

Give a personal anecdote of being a host to or guest of someone from another culture, saying whether it was a positive or negative experience and why. Elicit similar examples from the class and establish the main benefits and problems students experienced.

Social English

3   This exercise reviews the social language in the recording. Set a time limit of three minutes and get students to work individually. Students then check their answers in pairs. If students have not been able to complete any of the phrases, play the recording again and tell them to indicate where to pause. Then check the answers with the whole class. Students can refer to the target language in bold in the recording script on pages 149–150.

Activate some of the language by describing what happens in the dialogue and eliciting the key expressions e.g. Anne asks if Magda had any problems finding the flat – *You managed to find us OK, then?* Magda indicates she wants to leave – *I ought to be making a move soon* etc. Check student's intonation, pointing out that it is important to sound sincere and interested in the other person. Model the pronunciation as necessary.

Direct students' attention to the Lexis link on page 113 for more practice on social English.

9.2

Extract 1
A: Magda!
B: Hello, Anne. Brrr! It's a bit nasty out there tonight.
A: Horrible, isn't it? Come on in. **Let me take your coat. You managed to find us OK, then?**
B: Well, I got a bit lost coming off the ring road, as usual. Sorry I'm a bit late.
A: Oh, don't worry. Martin's still slaving away in the kitchen. Actually, he had a bit of a crisis with the starter just half an hour ago. You should have heard the language! Probably just as well you weren't here.
B: Oh, right. So Martin's cooking, is he?
A: Mm. He's quite an expert in the kitchen – fortunately for me. I can't boil an egg myself!
B: **Oh, I brought you this.** I wasn't sure what you liked, but apparently it's meant to be quite a good year.
A: Oh, thanks. **You shouldn't have.** Lovely. I'll put it in the fridge. **Come on through.**

Extract 2
B: **Oh, what a fabulous apartment!**
A: Thanks. We like it.
B: Have you been here long?
A: Um … about two years now. The whole place was an absolute wreck when we moved in. We had to do just about everything to it. **Now, what can I get you to drink?** How about a gin and tonic? That's what I'm having.
B: Yes, that'd be great.
A: Ice and lemon?
B: Please.
A: OK. **I'll be right back. Make yourself at home.**
(*pause*)
C: Hi, Magda. I'm Martin. I don't think we've met.

B: Hello, Martin. Pleased to meet you. You're the chef, I understand.
C: Oh, yes. Doing a good job of setting fire to the kitchen at the moment. I had to rescue the starter.
B: So I heard.
A: Ah, so you two have met. Good. There we are, Magda. Let me know if want more ice in that.
B: Thanks.
A: Are we nearly ready, then, darling?
C: Er, yes, I'm just waiting for the sauce. In fact, I'd better go and check on it. I don't trust that new cooker.
A: Oh, OK.

Extract 3
B: **I was just looking at some of your oil paintings**, Anne. **You've got quite a collection, haven't you?**
A: Mm, yes. Dutch mostly. Eighteenth century. They're Martin's, really.
B: **And I love the way you've done the fireplace. Was that here when you moved in?**
A: Yes, it's the original. We had to have it restored, obviously.
B: And what beautiful chairs. I could do with some of those for my place. French, aren't they?
A: Italian, actually. We bought them at an auction in Milan.
B: Oh, really? And, wow! **Look at that view!**
A: Good, isn't it?
B: You can see practically the whole city from here.
C: **Dinner's ready when you are.**
(*pause*)
C: Right, Magda, **sit wherever you like.** Now, we're having duck in a port sauce.
B: Mm, smells delicious!
C: So, **I thought we'd have a nice Spanish red**, something with a bit of body in it. Or do you prefer white?
B: No, red's fine, thanks.

Extract 4
C: **Now, there's more duck if you want it. And help yourself to vegetables.**
B: **Mm, this is absolutely delicious.**
A: It's one of Martin's specialities.
B: Mm, it's really good. The duck's all crispy on the outside and juicy on the inside.
C: **I'm glad you like it.**
B: **You must let me have the recipe.**
C: Oh, it's very simple, really. You just need the right ingredients.
A: **A little more wine**, Magda?
B: **I shouldn't really. I'm driving.**
A: **Oh, go on. You've only had one.**
B: Oh, all right, **just a drop, then.**
A: Magda, I've been meaning to talk to you about this business in Poland.
B: Oh, yes, that.
A: Do *you* know what's going on there? Because no one seems to be able to tell *me* anything.
C: Right, well, excuse me a moment. If you two are going to talk business, I'll go and see to the dessert.
(*pause*)
B: **Well, I ought to be making a move soon.** Early start tomorrow.
C: Oh, **you don't have to rush off just yet, do you? How about some more coffee?**
B: **OK, just half a cup. And then I really must be going.**
(*pause*)
B: Well, **thank you both for a lovely evening.** Martin, you're a brilliant cook.
C: I know. There's no point denying it.
B: **Next time you must come to my place**, although I can't promise you such a fabulous meal.
A: Bye, Magda. **Take care now.** See you tomorrow.

A dinner invitation

In this final section, students take part in a roleplay. One student plays the host and the other plays the guest, visiting the home of a colleague.

Fluency

1   As a lead-in to the roleplay, elicit what is expected of a 'good' host and a 'good' guest e.g. host – to put the guest at ease, to provide good food and drink, to make sure guests have what they need etc; guests – to turn up on time (at least in the UK), to show interest in the host and his/her home/family, to get on well with other people, not to outstay their welcome etc. Ask students if there is any special dynamic when the host is a guest's immediate boss e.g. the host may want to impress more than normal, he/she may want to 'test' the guest in some way; the guest may feel less relaxed than normal, he/she may feel they need to 'perform well' in order not to jeopardise his/her career.

Divide the students into 'guests' and 'hosts'. If you have an odd number of students, create a group of three with two students playing the role of guests. Ask each pair to decide on a name, location and business sector for their company and to specify their roles. Students also establish how business is going and specify current problems and opportunities. With students who are short of ideas, give them the following information as a framework, either on the board/an OHT or on role cards:

Company: Teleworld International

Sector: mobile phones

Location: headquarters in Paris

Business: fantastic current sales, but no-one can predict where the market is going and which will be next year's most successful product

Tell students that they both have an ulterior motive for the dinner. Refer the guests to page 135 and the hosts to page 133. Give students time to read the information and commit their role to memory. Check weaker students are clear as to their role and what they want from the evening. Ask if students need to amend any of the company information they chose in the light of the ulterior motive.

Focus attention on the photos and get students to brainstorm/review useful vocabulary e.g. *décor, fireplace, stylish; bay, marina, as far as the eye can see; local speciality/fish, prepared with/cooked in/served with* etc. Also refer students back to exercise 3 on page 50 for useful expressions.

Tell the students that you will signal when to move from step to step e.g. by clapping or tapping on the table. Remind them that they may have to work at keeping up the conversation, as happens in real life.

Monitor the roleplay, taking feedback notes. When students have finished, ask them how they think the evening went and how they handled their ulterior motive. Ask each pair to report back on what was decided about the guest's future. Feed back on students' overall fluency and performance in the roleplay before highlighting any important or common errors.

If you're short of time

Omit exercises 5–6 on pages 46–7.

Set the reading text *Golf and business* on page 48 for homework, ask students to prepare the discussion questions and do exercise 2.

A dinner invitation

Fluency 1 Work with a partner. Act out the situation of a business person (the guest)
visiting the home of a colleague (the host) from arrival to departure. The host is
the guest's immediate boss. Before you start, establish:

- what company you work for (name, location and main business activity)

- exactly what your roles are at work

- how business is doing and what problems or opportunities your company
currently has.

You both have an ulterior motive for the dinner. Guest see page 135. Host see
page 133.

Step 1 **This is the host's living room.**
Guest, make some positive comments, ask questions, show interest in the
answers and try to keep the conversation going. Host, make up any information
you like about your house to answer your guest's questions.

Step 2 **This is the view from the host's apartment.**
Guest, comment on what you see. Host, make up any information you have to.

Step 3 **This is the dinner.**
Guest, compliment your host on the meal. Host, explain what the food is.

Step 4 Guest, take your leave, thank your host. Host, say goodbye to your guest, thank
them for coming. Conclude any business you discussed during the evening or
arrange to meet to discuss it again.

10 Taking decisions

Standing in the middle of the road is very dangerous – you get knocked down by the traffic from both sides. *Margaret Thatcher*

Discussion

1 When was the last time you were faced with a difficult decision and were unable to make up your mind? How did you decide in the end, or was the decision made for you?

Glossary
curves unpleasant surprises

2 You may be a cool-headed decision maker in the office, but would you know what to do in a real life-and-death situation? Read the following extract from an unusual website and discuss the questions.

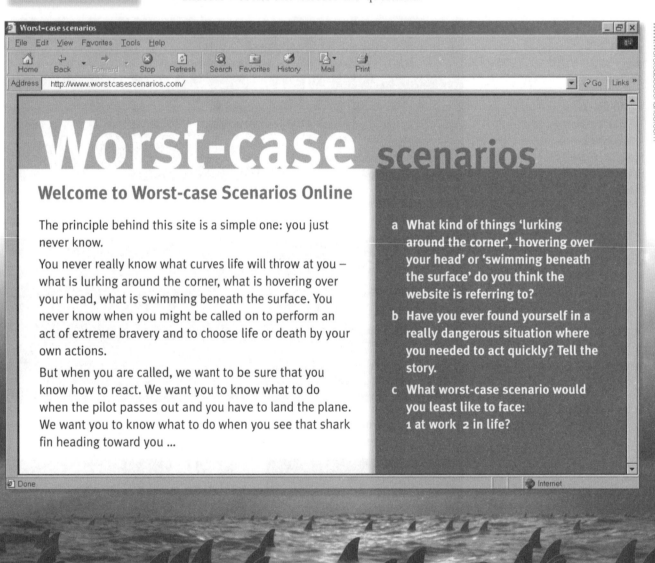

Worst-case scenarios

File Edit View Favorites Tools Help

Home Back Forward Stop Refresh Search Favorites History Mail Print

Address http://www.worstcasescenarios.com/   Go Links »

Worst-case scenarios

Welcome to Worst-case Scenarios Online

The principle behind this site is a simple one: you just never know.

You never really know what curves life will throw at you – what is lurking around the corner, what is hovering over your head, what is swimming beneath the surface. You never know when you might be called on to perform an act of extreme bravery and to choose life or death by your own actions.

But when you are called, we want to be sure that you know how to react. We want you to know what to do when the pilot passes out and you have to land the plane. We want you to know what to do when you see that shark fin heading toward you ...

a What kind of things 'lurking around the corner', 'hovering over your head' or 'swimming beneath the surface' do you think the website is referring to?

b Have you ever found yourself in a really dangerous situation where you needed to act quickly? Tell the story.

c What worst-case scenario would you least like to face:
1 at work 2 in life?

Done   Internet

www.worstcasescenarios.com

10 Taking decisions

Students start by discussing decision-making and what they would do in different life-and-death situations. They do a quiz on survival situations, and focus on the language of likelihood and giving advice. They then practise giving advice in a fluency-based task.

A recording offers insight into the decision-making process at three meetings. Students practise the language of decisions and study some of the idioms used in the recording.

Students discuss crisis management in the workplace, and read and summarise two recent accounts of crisis situations at McDonald's and Mercedes. They focus on the use of definite and indefinite articles and practise key collocations for dealing with crises.

The unit concludes with a recording of a case study – a crisis at Coca-Cola – and students roleplay crisis management consultants to the company.

The grammatical focus is on articles and the lexical focus is on marketing and legal English.

In this first section, students discuss decision-making before reading a short text from a website on worst-case scenarios. They do a quiz and discuss the choices they would make in eight life-and-death situations. A recording gives advice on how to survive the situations in the quiz and allows students to assess their survival skills. Students focus on the language of likelihood and complete an exercise on giving advice. Finally, they decide on the advice they would give in worst-case scenarios and workplace dilemmas.

Warm-up

Get students to brainstorm different ways of making decisions e.g. writing a list of pros and cons, tossing a coin, or drawing a diagram like a flow chart where you write in the possible outcome of each decision.

Ask students to read and explain the quotation by Margaret Thatcher (she argues against not saying which side of an argument you support). Ask students if they know anyone who is particularly bad at making decisions!

Discussion

1 Ask students to think about the questions for a few moments and then compare their answers in pairs or in small groups. Elicit interesting examples in a short feedback session.

2 Focus attention on the photograph and on the name of the website and ask students to predict the content of the text. With weaker groups, check/pre-teach: *to lurk, to hover, to pass out, shark fin*. Students read the text quickly and check their predictions.

Refer students to the glossary and point out that the meaning *unpleasant surprises* is relevant in the context of the text only. Ask students to read the text again and discuss the questions in pairs or small groups. Ask students to feed back on anything interesting arising from their discussion. Point out that there is also a worst-case scenarios book, which may have been translated into the students' own language.

As an optional follow-up activity, ask the students to write a short account of what they did in the dangerous situation referred to in question b.

Quiz

3 In order to generate interest in the quiz, elicit examples of life-and-death situations and ask students to assess their survivals skills on a scale of one to ten. Ask students to read the quiz quickly, encouraging them to guess any new words from context before answering vocabulary queries. With weaker groups, check/pre-teach: *to roll, cliff edge, crash barrier, to play dead, to flap, to drown, to leap, insulation, to somersault, obstruction, to skid, to plunge, to wind up/down, to trap, to free-fall, to snorkel, to punch, to collapse, to splash about, to touch down.*

Divide the class into pairs. Set a time limit and get students to do the quiz. When they have finished, ask them to give their choice of answers and justify it to the rest of the group. Record the range of answers and the students' initials on the board to create interest in hearing the 'correct' answers in the recording that follows.

4 🔊 **10.1** Check/Pre-teach: *to resist, fierce, futile, to crawl, water pressure, to grab, in distress, vulnerable, to overshoot, to triple.* Tell students they have a total of three lives and if they lose all three, they are out. Play the recording, pausing after each extract so that the students can check their answers. Compare the correct answers with the students' choices on the board and elicit their reactions. Find out who has the best survival skills.

🔊 **10.1**

1
Don't even think about jumping from a moving vehicle. At 70 miles per hour **the chances** of surviving **are remote**. And crashing into the mountainside at this speed will almost certainly send you straight through the windscreen. So, even though you may be scared of going over the cliff, your best chance of slowing the car down is to repeatedly run it against the crash barriers. After all, that's what they're there for.

2
Resist the temptation to run. You cannot outrun or outclimb a mountain lion. And **put any ideas of** playing dead **out of your mind**. Whilst it may work with grizzly bears, to a mountain lion you'll just look like a free lunch. **Your best bet is to** shout and flap your coat at the animal to make yourself look bigger and fiercer than you really are. Mountain lions are not proud. If you look like more trouble than you're worth, **there's a fifty-fifty chance** they'll back away.

3
Water transfers heat away from the body 25 times faster than air. So trying to keep warm is more or less futile. And while you're staying calm and conserving energy, the chances are you're dying. You have to get out. Turn in the direction you fell and use your elbows to lift yourself onto the edge of the ice. Reach forward as far as possible and kick your feet as if you were swimming. Once you are back on the ice, crawl to shore. **Do not in any circumstances** try to stand up.

4
The current world record for the long jump is just under nine metres, but most people can barely manage three or four. The chances are you can't either. To clear four and a half metres in conditions that are far from ideal you'd need a 20 to 30 metre run-up, perfect timing and a great deal of luck. Frankly, **your chances are slim**. The truck is a much better idea and it is quite possible to fall from the sixth floor and live. But don't jump out from the building unless there are balconies in the way. You'll be carried forward and miss the truck completely. Drop vertically and **take care to** land on your back to avoid breaking it.

5
The taxi could take anything from a few minutes to just a few seconds to sink. But **there's not much point trying to** force the door open because the water pressure will make this almost impossible. If the car does sink there'll be little or no air left anyway, so **forget about** trapping air inside. **By far the most sensible thing to do is** to open the window and actually let more water in. Even if you can't escape through the window, once the water pressure inside and outside the car are equalised, **there's a fair chance** you'll be able to open the door and save yourself – and maybe the driver too!

6
It's very unusual for both parachutes to fail, so by struggling with the emergency chute **there's an outside chance** you'll get it to work. But don't bet on it. You may just be wasting precious time. If you can share one of your friends' parachutes, **you're in with a chance**, but just grabbing onto the nearest person **is not a smart move**. The G-force when the parachute opens will throw you apart. At 14,000 feet and falling at your terminal velocity of 120 miles per hour you've got about 75 seconds before your appointment with Mother Earth. So firmly attach yourself to the chest straps of another parachutist. **You don't stand a chance** unless you do.

7
You are 30 times more likely to be struck by lightning than to be attacked by a shark, but this is little comfort in your present position. Splashing around and making a noise will simply give the shark the idea you're in distress and easy meat. **It's a common mistake to** think the shark's nose is the best area to target. Punch it there and you are liable to lose a hand or arm – depending on the size of the shark. **You'd do much better to** strike at its eyes or gills since these are a shark's most vulnerable points.

8
When landing a light aircraft, **make sure** that the nose of the plane is six inches below the horizon. As you approach the runway the plane should be flying at an altitude of about 100 feet. If you're higher, you'll overshoot the runway completely. The optimum speed on landing is about 60 miles per hour. Go faster and you may take off again. Go slower and you'll drop like a stone. Upon landing, **it's a good idea to** brake as soon as you've gained control of the steering. By reducing your groundspeed by 50% you triple your chances of survival.

3   Work with a partner. Try to agree on what to do in the following survival situations. Make the wrong choice and you face almost certain death. Good luck!

Life-and-death decisions

1 On a driving holiday in the Pyrenees you lose control of your hire car travelling downhill at 70 miles per hour on a mountain road. You've no brakes and there's a 300 metre drop to the valley below. Do you:

a try to jump out of the car and roll to safety?

b steer away from the cliff edge and into the mountainside to stop the car?

c steer into the crash barriers on the cliff edge to slow down?

2 On a trek through the Chilean Andes you get cut off from the rest of your group and become hopelessly lost. Just as you begin to work out which direction to take, you are confronted by a hungry mountain lion. Do you:

a lie down and play dead?

b shout and flap your coat at the animal?

c run and hide (maybe find a tree to climb)?

3 Whilst walking over a frozen lake in Norway, which you were assured was perfectly safe, you fall through the ice and are in danger of drowning. Do you:

a attempt to pull yourself out?

b move about in the water to generate body heat?

c stay calm, conserve energy and call for help?

4 While on business in Paris, you wake up in the middle of the night to find your hotel is on fire. Your way down is blocked and you end up on the roof. Your only hope of escape is either to jump onto the roof of the next building – a distance of some four and a half metres – or to leap onto a truck carrying soft insulation material parked six floors directly below. Do you:

a take a long run-up and jump onto the next building?

b somersault straight down into the truck and land on your back?

c leap well away from the building to clear obstructions and land in the truck?

5 On a business trip to Amsterdam your taxi skids on a patch of oil and plunges off the road and into a canal. In seconds you are half-underwater. Do you:

a force open the door and swim to safety (taking the driver with you)?

b wind down the window fully to let the water in?

c wind the window up to trap air inside the car in case you sink?

6 You agree to do a parachute jump for charity with a group of friends. But as you free-fall from 14,000 feet at 120 miles per hour both your parachute and emergency chute fail to open. Do you:

a keep struggling with your emergency chute? It must work, damn it!

b grab hold of the nearest member of the group before they open their chute?

c take valuable time to attach yourself to the chest straps of another parachutist?

7 Whilst snorkelling off the Great Barrier Reef in North-Eastern Australia, you suddenly see a large shark swimming swiftly towards you from the depths. Do you:

a try to attack the shark's eyes?

b punch the shark on the nose?

c splash about and make a noise to frighten it away?

8 During a flight over the Grand Canyon in a single-engined private plane, your pilot collapses unconscious and you're forced to take over the controls. You manage to find the emergency radio channel, but lose contact just as you are about to land. Do you:

a keep the nose of the plane pointing above the horizon as you descend to the airfield?

b slow down to about 60 miles per hour as you touch down and then hit the brakes?

c keep the plane at a steady altitude of 500 feet as you approach the beginning of the runway?

4   [cassette] 10.1 Listen to some advice on how to survive the situations in 3. How many lives did you lose?

The language of likelihood

5 Put the following expressions on the scale below according to how likely they are. Most of them were in the advice in 4. The first one has been done for you.

a You've a good chance.
b You don't stand a chance.
c There's a 50-50 chance.
d Your chances are slim.
e You're in with a chance.
f The chances are remote.
g You've blown your chances.
h There's a fair chance.
i There's an outside chance.
j It's a million-to-one chance.
k You haven't got a cat in hell's chance.

a   h   e   c   i   d   f   j   b   g   k

←───┼──────────────────────────────────────→

more likely   possible   less likely

Giving advice

6 Complete the following expressions using the nouns and verbs in the boxes. They were all in the advice in 4.

| mistake | bet | idea | point | circumstances | thing | move |

| forget | think | make | take | put | resist | do |

a Don't even _think_ about jumping from a moving vehicle.
b _Resist_ the temptation to run from a mountain lion.
c _Put_ any ideas of playing dead out of your mind.
d Your best _bet_ is to shout and flap your coat at the animal.
e Do not in any _circumstances_ try to stand up on the ice.
f _Take_ care to land on your back to avoid breaking it.
g There's not much _point_ trying to force the door open.
h _Forget_ about trapping air inside a sinking car.
i By far the most sensible _thing_ to do is to open the car window.
j Just grabbing on to the nearest person with a parachute is not a smart _move_.
k It's a common _mistake_ to think the shark's nose is the best area to target.
l You'd _do_ much better to strike at the eyes or gills.
m _Make_ sure that the nose of the plane is six inches below the horizon.
n It's a good _idea_ to brake as soon as you've gained control of the steering.

Fluency

7 Work with a partner. Practise using some of the expressions in 5 and 6 by giving advice on how to handle *one* of the following situations. Don't worry if you can't give expert advice!

Worst-case scenarios
- on a round-the-world cruise the ocean liner you're on hits an iceberg and starts to sink
- during a bungee jump from the Golden Gate Bridge your cord snaps mid-jump
- a poisonous snake has crawled into your sleeping bag
- you've been abducted by aliens

Workplace dilemmas
- your boss is working you to death
- a colleague is taking the credit for all your ideas
- a computer virus is destroying your hard disk and you've had no time to back things up
- you've been passed over for promotion – again!
- there's a rumour your company is about to be downsized

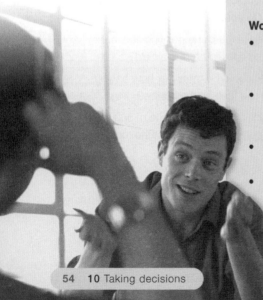

The language of likelihood

5 Play recording 10.1 again as a lead-in to this activity and let students follow the recording script on page 150. This allows them to see the expressions in this exercise in context. Point out how often the word *chance* is used and then get students to put the expressions on the appropriate part of the scale. Point out that some of the phrases will be at similar points. When students have finished, ask them to compare with a partner. Then check the answers with the whole class, accepting any reasonable variation.

To give students practice in using the expressions, divide the class into groups and ask students to brainstorm a further life-and-death scenario e.g. your plane is hijacked, you are caught in a bank robbery. Students present their situation to the other groups, who suggest possible courses of action, using some of the expressions from this exercise.

Giving advice

6 Tell students to read the words in the first box and note which are both verbs and nouns (*mistake, bet, point, move*). Tell them to see these words as nouns when completing expressions a–n.

Students complete the expressions. When they have finished, call out the letters and a student's name at random in order to check the answers. Model the pronunciation of any expressions which students found difficult and drill as necessary.

Ask students to look back at the expressions in exercises 5 and 6 and decide which ones are more informal/ spoken (exercise 5: b, e, g, k; exercise 6: a, d, h, j).

Fluency

7 Elicit examples of extreme situations from the recent news and examples of common workplace problems. Give further practice of the expressions in exercises 5 and 6 by eliciting possible pieces of advice for each situation/problem.

Check/Pre-teach: *iceberg, bungee jump, cord, to snap, to take the credit, to back up (data), to be passed over.* Divide the students into pairs and get students to take turns to present their problem and give advice. If appropriate, set the task up as a competition, with students scoring a point for each expression they use. Monitor the activity and take feedback notes.

Elicit examples of the best pieces of advice/solutions. Give feedback on the use of the key language and overall fluency before highlighting important or common errors.

The decision-making process

In this section, students read and comment on an anecdote about decisions made at meetings. A recording presents a number of business people involved in decision-making at three different meetings. Students then focus on the key language and idioms used in the recording.

1 Ask students to read the anecdote by John Adair about the head of General Motors and elicit the point being made. Ask students if they agree and elicit any other problems with group decisions e.g. people go along with the majority view rather than risk expressing their own opinion. Ask students to give examples of group decisions from their own experience and to say if they had a positive or negative outcome.

2 ▭ **10.2** Write up the three topics from the listening on the board: *an industrial dispute, political instabilities* and *a product recall.* Elicit examples of these from students' experience or from recent news e.g. in 2003 British Airways staff objected to clocking-in times, companies are often unwilling to invest in war-torn zones, Nestlé and Perrier have both had famous product recalls.

Check/Pre-teach: *to phase in, backlog of orders, to be plunged into (war), to be aware of, to overlook, drastic, to affect, I dread to think …, harm.* Tell students they are going to listen to three extracts from meetings and that you will play each extract twice. The first time, ask students to listen for the main topic on which the decision is being made. Play the recording through once and check the answers (1 what to do if the unions vote to go on strike, 2 whether or not to pull out of a production plant in Somalia due to possible civil war, 3 whether or not to recall all cars sold of a particular model on safety grounds).

Now ask students to read the questions in exercise 2. Play the recording again, pausing after each extract for students to complete the task. Check the answers with the whole class.

The language of decisions

3 Ask students to complete the sentences, using the words in the box. Be prepared to play the recording again if necessary. Check the answers and the pronunciation of any difficult items.

To get the students to practise the language of decisions, divide them into groups and ask them to devise three scenarios each involving a decision e.g. decide on a venue for the next Olympics from the following five cities: …; decide on a venue for new HQ; choose between high-, medium- and low-risk shares etc. Students give their scenarios to the other groups, who discuss them and try to reach a decision, using the language from exercise 3. Students report back on their decision, giving reasons for their choice.

Idioms

4 Ask students to work in pairs to complete the idioms and then check the answers. All four expressions are quite common in spoken English, so encourage students to use them as part of their active vocabulary, but not to over-use them.

As an optional follow-up activity, ask students in pairs to write three short dialogues each of which uses one of the idioms. Have students roleplay their dialogues for the rest of the class and give feedback on how naturally the students incorporated the idioms.

▭ **10.2**

1

A: Right, as you know, our last offer to the union was a three per cent pay rise and a two-hour reduction in the working week to be gradually phased in over the next 18 months. **The ball is** now firmly **in their court**. Ragnar, do you have any idea which way they'll vote?

B: The word is they'll turn it down. In fact, they might even be considering taking industrial action.

A: A strike?

B: I don't know, Dan. It's a possibility.

A: With the current backlog of orders a strike's the last thing we need!

C: Now, let's not **jump to conclusions**. They haven't announced the result of the vote yet.

B: My sources are usually accurate, Per.

A: **Look, time is short**. If the vote goes against us, I want us to be able to come straight back with an improved offer. **So let's put our heads together and see what we can come up with.**

2

A: **OK, we've weighed up the various pros and cons. Now it's time to reach a decision and stick to it.** Our latest information is that the political situation in Somalia is worsening. In fact, it may only

be a matter of days before the country is plunged into civil war. The proposal is that we should pull our people out of there immediately.

B: Now, wait a minute, Richard. **I don't want us rushing into anything. This whole issue requires long and careful consideration.** This is our biggest production plant in North Africa and we're talking about closing it down here.

A: I'm well aware of that, Hans. But **I take it we're all in agreement that our first priority is to safeguard the well-being of our personnel.**

B: Of course.

A: **Well, then, I don't see we have any option but to give this proposal our full backing.**

C: Aren't we overlooking something here? I mean it's all very well talking about flying our management team home and closing the plant, but what about our factory workers? They'll all be out of a job.

A: I'm afraid our responsibility to local workers is different, Andrea. **When it comes to the crunch**, we have to look after our European staff first …

3

A: OK, you've all seen the results of the road tests. It looks like the two-litre model has some kind of a steering problem and we

may have to authorise a total product recall while we conduct further tests.

B: Isn't that a bit drastic, Simon? I mean, it's only a slight steering problem, isn't it? And it doesn't seem to be affecting the smaller-engined models.

A: Well, that's what we're here to discuss, Matt. With a safety issue like this I don't think we should take any chances, but **I'd like your input on this before committing us to any definite course of action.** Laura?

C: Hm, **I'm in two minds about it.** I mean, I agree with you that the safety of our customers must come first. But if we take the whole series off the market, I dread to think what the newspapers will do with the story. **At this stage I think we should keep our options open.** And these test results aren't conclusive, are they?

A: Well, no, but I don't think we can just **sit on the fence** here. In the long run, failing to act quickly could do us a lot of harm.

B: So what do you suggest?

A: **Well, in the absence of more reliable data, I think I'm going to have to go with my gut instinct on this one.** I'm just not prepared to put our customers' lives at risk …

The decision-making process

1 Read the anecdote about Alfred P. Sloan, the man who built General Motors into the biggest company in the world. What point is being made about group decisions? _A quick agreement may not be the right decision._

2 🔲 **10.2** Listen to extracts from three different decision-making meetings and answer the questions.

1 An industrial dispute

   a Why is Dan so concerned about a strike? _There's a backlog of orders._

   b Who's the calmest person at the meeting? _C (Per)_

2 Political instabilities

   a What's Hans's objection to the proposal? _He objects to closing down the production plant in North Africa._

   b What's Andrea worried about? _local people losing their jobs_

3 A product recall

   a Whose side is Laura on? _neither Simon's nor Matt's_

   b Do you think Simon has already made up his mind? _yes_

The language of decisions

3 The following remarks were all in the meetings in 2. Complete them using the pairs of words in the box. Listen again, if necessary.

> agreement + priority   minds + options   anything + consideration
> option + backing   input + action   time + heads   cons + decision
> data + instinct

a Look, _time_ is short. So let's put our _heads_ together and see what we can come up with.

b OK, we've weighed up the various pros and _cons_. Now it's time to reach a _decision_ and stick to it.

c I don't want us rushing into _anything_. This whole issue requires long and careful _consideration_.

d I take it we're all in _agreement_ that our first _priority_ is to safeguard the well-being of our personnel.

e Well, then, I don't see we have any _option_ but to give this proposal our full _backing_.

f I'd like your _input_ on this before committing us to any definite course of _action_.

g I'm in two _minds_ about it. At this stage I think we should keep our _options_ open.

h Well, in the absence of more reliable _data_, I think I'm going to have to go with my gut _instinct_ on this one.

Idioms

4 You also heard the following idiomatic expressions in 2. Can you remember the missing words? The first two letters are given. The meaning of the idioms in brackets may help you.

a the ball is in their co_urt_ (we're waiting for someone else to make a decision)

b jump to co_nclusions_ (decide too quickly without considering all the facts)

c when it comes to the cr_unch_ (when a decision finally has to be made)

d sit on the fe_nce_ (refuse to support either side in an argument)

Crisis management

Discussion

1 What sort of crises can companies be faced with these days? Can you think of recent examples of any of the following?

> accusations of fraud   a lawsuit   a hostile takeover bid
> an environmental disaster   a product recall   a consumer boycott
> an anti-globalisation protest   mass redundancies   sabotage
> insider trading   an investigation by the monopolies commission

Articles

2 Work in two groups. Group A read about a crisis at McDonald's; Group B at Mercedes. Twenty-five articles (*a, an* and *the*) are missing from each text. Write them in. If you do the exercise correctly, both groups should have the same number of *a*'s, *an*'s and *the*'s.

McDonald's crying over spilled coffee

In 1994 Stella Liebeck, New Mexico grandmother, ordered coffee at McDonald's drive-through restaurant. Minutes later, sitting in her car in car park, she accidentally spilled coffee – heated, in response to customer preference, to scalding 180°F – and suffered severe burns requiring surgery. Crisis was about to unfold.

When McDonald's refused to take responsibility for paying woman's medical bills, she went to attorney and sued company. At trial jury found McDonald's liable and awarded $200,000 in compensatory damages (less $40,000 for negligence on Liebeck's part) and massive $2.7 million in punitive damages because of what they saw as McDonald's unacceptably dismissive attitude.

One might have expected bad publicity to ruin McDonald's, but instead newspapers leapt to company's defence, declaring what nonsense court's verdict was. 'America has victim complex,' announced *San Francisco Chronicle*. Punitive damages were later reduced by judge to $480,000 and, while awaiting appeal, parties made out-of-court settlement for undisclosed sum. But by then 'three million dollar coffee-spill' had already passed into corporate legend.

Mercedes on a roll

In automotive industry trend for many years has been towards smaller, more economical vehicle. So in autumn of 1997, Daimler-Benz introduced new economy model, Mercedes 'A Class'. It was car designed to compete with ever-popular Volkswagen Golf. But just before November launch, disaster struck.

Swedish auto magazine had conducted what they called 'elk test' on new car. Test is standard in Sweden to make sure cars can steer to avoid large deer crossing road. But at just 60kph 'A Class' overturned, injuring both test drivers. Storm immediately blew up in press and on TV, as buyers waiting to take delivery cancelled their orders. For Mercedes it was not only financial but image crisis too.

Daimler responded quickly, adding wider tyres, electronic stability mechanism and stronger anti-roll bars – all at no extra cost to customer. Highly successful advertising campaign and public support from Niki Lauda, ex-formula one racing champion, helped to restore consumer confidence in 'A Class' but at cost of hundreds of millions of dollars.

Lexis link

for more on marketing & legal English see page 114

Grammar link

for more on articles see page 114

Crisis management

In the final section, students discuss the kind of crises which companies can face. They do a jigsaw reading activity using short texts on a crisis at McDonald's and Mercedes and decide where the missing articles (*a, an* and *the*) should go in the texts. The unit ends with a case study of a crisis at the Coca-Cola company. Students listen to two recordings to get information about the case and then roleplay a strategy meeting. A final recording tells students what actually happened in the Coca-Cola case and allows them to compare their recommendations with the decision the company took.

Discussion

1 Check/Pre-teach: *fraud, lawsuit, boycott, sabotage, insider trading, the monopolies commission* (a body who investigates monopolies). Divide the class into groups and have them brainstorm recent examples e.g. the accountancy firm Arthur Andersen was involved in fraud, an oil slick hit the north-west coast of Spain creating an environmental disaster etc. If appropriate, students can search for examples on the Internet as a pre-lesson task.

Articles

2 Focus students' attention on the title of the texts. Check the literal meaning of *to spill* and highlight the play on words in the title – the original expression is *to cry over spilled milk* (to waste time worrying about a past mistake that can't be changed). Check the literal meaning of *to roll* and the meaning of the expression of *to be on a roll* (to be having a lot of success with what you are doing).

Divide the class into AB groups and assign the McDonald's text to group A, and the Mercedes text to group B. Tell students that *a, an* and *the* are missing from each text. Get students to predict what the crisis might be in their text from the title and then to read the text quickly to check, ignoring the lack of articles at this stage.

With weaker students, or with students whose first language means that articles are problematic, do a quick review of when we use *a/an/the* and when we use zero (no) article. Tell the groups to discuss where they think the articles go and remind them there are 25 missing articles in total. Ask students working on the same text to exchange books to check that the answers are the same. Check the answers with the class, by getting students to read out sections of the corrected text. Alternatively, write the complete text on an OHT with the articles in a different colour and get students to check their answers.

McDonald's crying over spilled coffee

In 1994 Stella Liebeck, **a** New Mexico grandmother, ordered **a** coffee at **a** McDonald's drive-through restaurant. Minutes later, sitting in her car in **a** car park, she accidentally spilled **the** coffee – heated, in response to customer preference, to **a** scalding 180ºF – and suffered severe burns requiring surgery. **A** crisis was about to unfold.

When McDonald's refused to take responsibility for paying **the** woman's medical bills, she went to **an** attorney and sued **the** company. At **the** trial **the** jury found McDonald's liable and awarded $200,000 in compensatory damages (less $40,000 for negligence on Liebeck's part) and **a** massive $2.7 million in punitive damages because of what they saw as McDonald's unacceptably dismissive attitude.

One might have expected **the** bad publicity to ruin McDonald's, but instead newspapers leapt to **the** company's defence, declaring what nonsense **the** court's verdict was. 'America has **a** victim complex,' announced **the** *San Francisco Chronicle*. **The** punitive damages were later reduced by **the** judge to $480,000 and, while awaiting **the** appeal, **the** parties made **an** out-of-court settlement for **an** undisclosed sum. But by then **the** 'three million dollar coffee-spill' had already passed into corporate legend.

a = 8, *an* = 3, *the* = 14; total = 25

Mercedes on a roll

In **the** automotive industry **the** trend for many years has been towards **a** smaller, more economical vehicle. So in **the** autumn of 1997, Daimler-Benz introduced **a** new economy model, **the** Mercedes 'A Class'. It was **a** car designed to compete with **the** ever-popular Volkswagen Golf. But just before **the** November launch, disaster struck.

A Swedish auto magazine had conducted what they called **an** 'elk test' on **the** new car. **The** test is standard in Sweden to make sure cars can steer to avoid large deer crossing **the** road. But at just 60kph **the** 'A Class' overturned, injuring both **the** test drivers. **A** storm immediately blew up in **the** press and on TV, as buyers waiting to take delivery cancelled their orders. For Mercedes it was not only **a** financial but **an** image crisis too.

Daimler responded quickly, adding wider tyres, **an** electronic stability mechanism and stronger anti-roll bars – all at no extra cost to **the** customer. **A** highly successful advertising campaign and public support from Niki Lauda, ex-formula one racing champion, helped to restore consumer confidence in **the** 'A Class' but at **a** cost of hundreds of millions of dollars.

a = 8, *an* = 3, *the* = 14; total = 25

Direct students' attention to the Grammar and Lexis links on pages 114–115 for more information and practice on articles, and for more practice on marketing and legal English.

Discussion

3 Ask students to make notes on the key points in their text as preparation for giving a summary of it and also to think of what lessons can be learnt from the crisis.

Ask students to cross-group so that the A students summarise their story for the Bs, and vice versa. Remind students to work from their notes, rather than read the information from the Student's Book page. Students then give examples of the lessons which can be learnt from these stories.

4 Students match the verbs with the words they collocate with. Check the answers with the class. Ask students to divide the actions into good and bad advice and then to compare their answers in pairs.

Case study

5 As a lead-in to the task, write some of the key words from the recording on the board and get students to predict what the crisis is: *global dominance, a loss of consumer confidence, contaminated, officially banned, consignments seized by officials*. Play the recording through once and get students to check their predictions.

Step 1

📼 **10.3** Ask student to read questions a–e and answer as many as they can. Play the recording again and get students to complete/check their answers. Check the answers with the whole class.

Step 2

📼 **10.4** Ask students what they think might have happened next, referring students back to the language in exercise 4 for possible ideas. Write students' predictions on the board. Check/Pre-teach: *bottling plants, toxicologist, psychosomatic, to deliberate, denial*. Play the recording through once and get students to check their predictions. Play the recording again and have students answer the questions a–e. Check the answers with the class.

Step 3

Elicit a summary of the crisis at Coca-Cola and write the key information on the board. Have students brainstorm the options the company has e.g. recall the product, start a damage limitation publicity campaign etc. Refer students to the brief for the strategy meeting and deal with any vocabulary queries.

Working individually, students focus on the options for the company in the strategy brief and also those brainstormed by the class and choose the ones they would recommend. Divide the class into groups and tell them to prepare an action plan for Coca-Cola.

Step 4

Set up the class for the presentation phase, allocating a space/desk for students to present from. Explain that they can give individual or team presentations and that they should set out reasons for their recommendations. Set a time limit of five minutes for each presentation and allow 15-20 minutes for the discussion and decision phase.

Monitor and take feedback notes during the presentations and discussions but don't give comments until after Step 5.

Step 5

📼 **10.5** Check/Pre-teach: *irreproachable, pesticide, mad cow disease, fungicide, to take measures, to withdraw, public relations coup*. Tell student they are going to find out what action Coca-Cola took. Play the recording and elicit students' reactions to what happened.

Give feedback on students' effectiveness in creating the action plan and on overall fluency before highlighting important or common errors.

If you're short of time

Omit exercise 7 on page 54 and exercise 1 on page 55. Set exercise 2 on page 56 for homework.

📼 **10.3**
The mighty Coca-Cola has been the world's number one brand for so long, it's hard to imagine anything threatening its position of global dominance. One of the company's own publicity brochures proudly declares: 'A billion hours ago human life appeared on Earth; a billion minutes ago Christianity emerged; a billion seconds ago the Beatles performed on the Ed Sullivan Show – a billion servings of Coca-Cola ago was yesterday morning.' Quite a claim. And one that makes a loss of consumer confidence unthinkable.

But take yourself back to May 1999. The unthinkable has just happened. Hundreds of people in Belgium and France have become ill after drinking what they claim is contaminated Coke. And when the cause of the problem cannot quickly be established, the famous soft drink is officially banned in both countries as well as Luxembourg and the Netherlands. The price you pay for being the brand leader is that customers expect quality, as Coca-Cola's CEO is the first to admit. 'For 113 years,' he says, 'our success has been based on the trust that consumers have in that quality.' Now that trust is shaken.

In fact, the four countries banning Coke only represent two per cent of the company's $18.8 billion in annual sales. But within a week consignments exported from Belgium to other countries as far apart as Germany and the Ivory Coast have also been seized by officials. Though no definite proof of contamination has yet been found, the panic is starting to spread …

📼 **10.4**
1999 is not a good year for soft drinks companies. Though the Dow is up 25%, both Coke and Pepsi, normally well ahead of the market, are down by around 13%. Coca-Cola is not going to rush into a highly expensive product recall.

In any case, early examinations of the Belgian bottling plants find nothing unusual and an official toxicologist's report concludes that the 200 cases of sickness are probably psychosomatic.

But while Coca-Cola is deliberating over what action to take, rivals Pepsi and Virgin Cola are quick to fill the gaps left on the supermarket shelves. And Coke's refusal to react until it has conducted a thorough investigation is starting to look like a denial of responsibility …

📼 **10.5**
This is how Coca-Cola actually handled the problem.

Initially, full-page advertisements were taken out in European newspapers to reassure the public that the quality of Coke was 'irreproachable'. This was not totally successful as the public at that time could still remember a similar contamination scare at Perrier some years before and all the talk was of pesticides on fruit and mad cow disease.

But, fortunately, the source of the Coke contamination was eventually traced to a strange fungicide on cans shipped from Dunkirk and poor carbon dioxide at Coca-Cola's bottling plant in Antwerp which makes the Coke taste a little different but does no real harm. It wasn't the Coke itself but the cans that were contaminated.

Coke took the necessary measures and, at enormous cost to the company, all 17 million cases of Coke were withdrawn. Finally, in a spectacular public relations coup, and as an apology to the Belgians who had been ill, Coca-Cola offered a free one-and-a-half litre bottle of Coke to each and every one of Belgium's ten million citizens! Coke was immediately back in the stores.

Discussion	3	Summarise the story you read in 2 to a member of the other group. What lessons can be learned from how the companies behaved?

4 What is the best thing a manager can do in a crisis? Match the following. Which do you think are good advice?

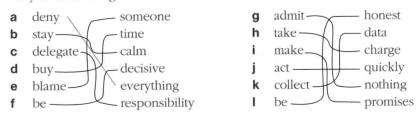

a deny   someone
b stay   time
c delegate   calm
d buy   decisive
e blame   everything
f be   responsibility

g admit   honest
h take   data
i make   charge
j act   quickly
k collect   nothing
l be   promises

Case study 5 Work in groups to act as crisis management consultants to the Coca-Cola Company. It is May 1999 and the world's most famous brand is in trouble …

Step 1 🔊 10.3 Listen to the first part of the case and answer the questions.

a How many Cokes are sold each day? _one billion_

b How would you describe Coca-Cola's advertising strategy? _aggressive, powerful_

c What has just happened? _People have become ill after drinking contaminated Coke._

d Which markets are directly involved in the crisis? _Belgium, France, Luxembourg, the Netherlands_

e Calculate how much those markets are worth in annual sales. _#376 M_
[2% of #18.8 billion]

Step 2 🔊 10.4 Listen to the second part of the case and answer the questions.

a What do the following figures refer to?

+25% _how much the Dow is up_   −13% _how much Coke and Pepsi are down_

b What is the significance of these figures? _Untypically, Coke and Pepsi were both behind the market._

c What have the inspectors at the Belgian bottling plant found? _nothing unusual_

d What is the toxicologist's verdict? _The 200 cases are probably psychosomatic._

e Who is benefiting from Coca-Cola's current problems? _rivals Pepsi + Virgin Cola_

Step 3 Hold a meeting to decide what recommendations to make to your client. As well as the information you have just heard, consider the following:

Strategy Meeting
Client: Coca-Cola Co.

- Should there be an immediate product recall in spite of the lack of solid evidence?
- In the absence of any proof of contamination, should Coca-Cola appeal to the four European governments to lift their ban? Or even threaten legal action against them?
- Should any decision be postponed until the final results of the tests become available? Or will this just give the competition time to increase its market share?
- How should the company persuade the public that there's no real threat?
- Should there be an official apology? Or would that look like an admission of guilt?
- Should Coca-Cola put the blame firmly on its Belgian bottling plant and their shippers, whilst exporting Coke directly to Europe from the USA?
- What kind of public relations exercise would restore confidence in the world's number one brand?

Step 4 Each group should present its recommendations to the class.

Step 5 🔊 10.5 Listen to the final part of the case and find out what really happened. How do your recommendations compare with the action Coca-Cola actually took?

11 Branded planet

I am irresistible, I say, as I put on my designer fragrance. I am handsome, I say, as I pull on my Levi's jeans. I am a merchant banker, I say, as I climb out of my BMW.
John Kay, British economist

1 How 'brand-aware' are you? Make a list of all the well-known brands you're wearing or carrying right now. Use the suggestions in the box if you like.

> clothes   shoes   mobile   palmtop/organiser   briefcase/handbag
> belt   cigarettes   lighter   watch   pen   tie/scarf   (sun)glasses
> perfume/aftershave/cologne

2 Compare with the rest of the class. Who are the most 'branded' people in the room?

3 Read the book extract and answer the questions.

The **surplus** society

This is the age of more. More choice. More consumption. More fun. More fear. More uncertainty. More competition. We have entered a world of excess, an age of superabundance. Shop till you drop.

Overcapacity is the norm in most businesses: 40% in automobiles, 100% in chemicals, 140% in computers.

Major label record companies launched 30,000 albums in the US in 1998 and the number of grocery product launches increased from 2,700 in 1981 to 20,000 in 1996. Disney's CEO Michael Eisner claims that the company develops a new product – a film, a comic book, a CD – every five minutes!

Funky Business, Jonas Ridderstråle and Kjell Nordström

a Do you agree with the authors that we are living in 'the age of more'? Is it just 'more of the same'?

b Find four words in the text which mean *more than is needed*.

<u>surplus</u> , <u>excess</u> , <u>superabundance, overcapacity</u>

c Is overcapacity the norm in *your* business? How can companies deal with the problem of supply exceeding demand? You may want to refer to some of the things below.

1 brand loyalty	4 price sensitivity	7 product positioning
2 market segmentation	5 product development	8 strategic alliances
3 stock control	6 customer service	9 advertising budgets

11 Branded planet

Talking points

This unit is about branding and the theme of globalisation. Branding makes it easier to recognise products and globalisation involves multi-national companies setting up factories abroad, and cross-border trading. Both areas are controversial and can therefore be a rich source of discussion. The theme of advertising affects us all, and the unit will be especially interesting and useful for students involved in marketing.

Students discuss the concept of branding. They read a short text which argues that we live in a society which over-produces. Students then focus on some of the lexis and look at the problem of overcapacity in relation to their own company and businesses in general.

A recording of a radio programme highlights the amount of money companies spend on advertising. The students then discuss a number of advertising ploys, deciding which really happened and which are fictitious. Students decide if they agree with an article which argues that branding is bad for developing countries, and focus on some of the vocabulary. They read an article written as a reply to the anti-branding argument and discuss their reactions to it.

A second recording presents a conversation between two people discussing the pros and cons of globalisation. The unit finishes with an activity, the *Name Game*, in which students choose the most appropriate brand names for the image of given companies.

In this first section, students do a light-hearted activity to check on how 'brand-aware' they are. They read and discuss a short text on consumer choice and over-production and then focus on useful collocations connected with supply and demand, and marketing.

Warm-up

Let students read the quotation from John Kay, the British economist. Elicit the point he is making (that 'you are what you wear/the brands you use'). Ask students why they think some people buy in to brands so strongly e.g. the power of marketing, needing to have the right image etc. Establish if this creates any problems e.g. elitism or over-pricing. Alternatively, refer students to the cartoon on page 59 as a general lead-in to this unit and to the topic of branding.

1 Tell students to make a note only of well-known brands/products they are wearing/carrying. Check/Pre-teach the term *designer* and words it can collocate with e.g. *clothes, watch, lifestyle* etc. Elicit related vocabulary e.g. *luxury, bespoke, top-end, exclusive* etc.

2 Before students compare their lists, stress that this is intended as a light-hearted activity and so shouldn't be taken too seriously. Have students compare and then find out who is the most brand-aware.

3 Focus attention on the photo and ask students what they think it says about today's society (that cars are seen as 'throw away' items that can be regularly replaced). Students brainstorm other industries which over-produce e.g. computers, mobile phones. If appropriate, also give the example of surpluses of products in trading areas such as the EU. Ask students to read the text and check which industries/products are mentioned (cars, chemicals, computers, record companies, grocery products, Disney films/comic books/CDs).

Students then answer questions a–c. Use the following notes to further exploit the ideas in this exercise.

a Ask students to re-read the text and decide if they agree with everything the author says. Ask follow-up questions e.g. *Do you feel that more should be done about the imbalance between the surpluses in the West and poverty in other countries? What do you think about trading rights for developing countries? Are they unfair?*

b After checking the answers, make sure students can place the stress on the words correctly.

c With weaker students, check comprehension and pronunciation of the terms in the list before students exchange ideas. (You could focus on section d of this exercise first if your students are unfamiliar with the terms.) If you teach students without a specific service or product, ask them to think about society in general e.g. supermarket products. Ask students to come up with solutions to problems such as agricultural surpluses e.g. sending the extra to help the third world, and access to health care e.g. making lower-priced pharmaceutical drugs available to developing countries.

d   When students have completed the activity, check their answers quickly. As a follow-up task, divide the students into two groups and refer them back to the list in c. Get them to evaluate their own company's marketing strategy and make recommendations, using as many of the terms as possible. Each group earns a point for each of the terms used.

Check/Pre-teach: *chunky*. Refer students to the cartoon and ask them to explain the joke. (It highlights that brand variety can be ridiculous if taken to extremes.) Ask students to think of other products that have a similar brand variety and their reaction to them e.g. mobile phones, hair products, trainers etc.

Branding

In this section, students discuss the affect of advertising on their lives as preparation for listening to a recording about the amount companies spend on advertising. They complete a comprehension exercise and discuss their reactions to the recording. Finally, they discuss a list of incredible advertising stunts, deciding which really happened and which are hoaxes.

1   ▭ 11.1 Get students to brainstorm examples of successful branding from their own country and elicit a range of examples. Alternatively, ask students if they have been to the USA and what they think about US TV advertising. Compare the length of commercials in different countries the students have visited. Ask how many times a film would be interrupted by commercial breaks, for example.

Ask students to discuss the three questions. Use the following notes to further exploit the questions in this exercise.

a   Get students to take themselves through the stages of a typical day when trying to calculate the number of advertisements. Remind them of less obvious examples like adverts on public transport, on the back of travel tickets, flyers given out when buying a product etc.

b   Ask students to rank the forms of advertising in order of effectiveness and then compare with a partner/the rest of the group. Elicit their reaction to 'junk mail' and 'spam'. Find out if they can be removed from mailing lists in their country and if they refuse to answer 'spam' (this is the recommended approach).

c   Check how many of the terms in the box students recognise. Tell them that *cool hunters* and *adbusters* will be explained in the recording. Ask students to mark the stress on each of the compound nouns and to practise saying the terms aloud.

Check/Pre-teach: *to bombard, billboard, to keep up with, to prowl, to blend, voracious*. Tell the students to listen out for what/who *cool hunters* and *adbusters* are during the first listening. Play the recording through once and check the answers (*cool hunters* are 'scouts' who look out for what is fashionable and popular in youth culture; *adbusters* is a magazine based in Vancouver which tries to work against consumerism. They tried to promote a 'Buy Nothing Day'.)

2   Students work in pairs to answer as many questions as possible. Then play the recording again to allow students to listen for any key information/answers they missed during the first listening. Check the answers with the whole class, eliciting students' reactions to the *Adbusters* and their campaign.

As a follow-up task, ask students to give examples of effective adverts from their own country and discuss the techniques the advertisers used. Ask further follow-up questions e.g. *Who is most likely to be used as celebrity endorsement in your country? What examples of product placement can you give?*

▭ 11.1

A: Next on CBN Business: *'Branded!'* Ruth Silbiger reports on the companies aiming to brand our lives and the 'adbusters' out to stop them.

B: The average American is bombarded with 274 advertisements a day – or seven million over a lifetime! On billboard and football shirt, TV screen and PC monitor, there's no escape from our branded planet.

The stakes are high. In 2002 PepsiCo spent nearly nine million dollars on a 90-second commercial featuring Britney Spears to be screened at the world's biggest sporting event, the American Superbowl. Sure enough, 75 million viewers watched the ad.

But were they paying attention? Celebrity endorsements like the Spears ad seem to make a big initial impact. But then what? These days, most of us channel hop during commercials, throw junk mail straight in the garbage and delete spam unread.

In the never-ending battle to keep our attention, the advertisers have tried everything. First they tried corporate sponsorship. But do we buy Vodaphone because it zooms past us at 180 miles per hour on the side of Michael Schumacher's Ferrari? Probably not.

Then they tried product placement. But when Tom Cruise walks into a GAP store in the film *Minority Report*, we barely notice. We're looking at Tom, not the clothes.

Now they're trying branded content – commercials so subtle, they look like straight entertainment; commercials so cool people *choose* to watch them. Nike's latest, a basketball skills film with a loud dance beat, was so popular MTV ran it as regular programming. The company was scarcely mentioned. But not a basketball player under the age of 20 didn't know who it was.

So how do the top brand names keep up with what's cool? In the youth market, by employing so-called cool hunters to prowl the streets, shopping malls, nightclubs and inner-city basketball courts. These cool hunters blend in with the rest of the teenagers and report back on what's in, what's out and what's going to be the next big thing.

But has all this wild consumer-spending gone too far? The Vancouver-based magazine *Adbusters* thinks so and went on CNN to propose an alternative in a controversial TV commercial that was subsequently turned down by ABC, NBC and CBS. This is what they said:

'The average American consumes five times more than a Mexican, ten times more than a Chinese person and thirty times more than a person from India. We are the most voracious consumers in the world – a world that could die because of the way we North Americans live. Give it a rest. November 29 is Buy Nothing Day.'

d Which six things in **c** involve:

collaborating with competitors? ⑧

customers sticking to the names they trust? ①

working out how much you can spend on promotion? ⑨

dividing up the market into sectors? ②

deciding whether your product is up- or downmarket? ⑦

customers shopping around for the cheapest option? ④

Calvin and Hobbes © 1995 Watterson. Reprinted with permission of Universal Press Syndicate. All Rights Reserved.

Branding

1 ▭ **11.1** You are going to listen to a radio news feature entitled *Branded!* First, discuss the questions below.

   a Roughly how many advertisements do you think you are exposed to in the press, on TV and the radio, in the street and on the Internet in a typical day? 20? 50? 100? More?

   b Which are the most effective forms of advertising: TV commercials, press ads, billboards, Internet ads, direct mail ('junk mail') or e-mail ('spam')? Which just annoy you?

   c Work with a partner. How many of the terms below are you familiar with?

> celebrity endorsements   corporate sponsorship   product placement
> branded content   cool hunters   adbusters

Now listen to the programme.

2 Listen again, if necessary, and answer the questions below.

   a In what context were the following people mentioned?

Britney Spears _the PepsiCo ad which was screened at the Superbowl_

Michael Schumacher _the Vodaphone ad on his Ferrari_

Tom Cruise _his entering Gap in 'Minority Report'_

   b What do the following figures refer to?

7 million _the number of ads the average American sees in a lifetime_

$9 million _the amount PepsiCo spent on a Britney Spears ad_

30 times _how much more an American consumes compared to an Indian_

November 29 _Buy Nothing Day_

   c Are you shocked by the statistics mentioned in the *Adbusters* commercial? Does 'Buy Nothing Day' sound like a good idea to you?

Discussion

3 There seem to be no limits to what the world's biggest companies will do to raise brand awareness. Five of the following are facts and three are hoaxes. Which are which? Mark them F or H.

a Swiss watchmaker Swatch has suggested replacing hours and minutes with their own global branded time system called 'Swatch beats'. **F**

b McDonald's is negotiating with the city of New York to replace the Statue of Liberty with a similar-sized statue of Ronald McDonald for 18 weeks. **H**

c Taking the idea from the Batman comics, Pepsi-Cola is proposing to project its logo onto the surface of the moon. **F**

d Toy manufacturers Mattel celebrated 'Barbie Pink Month' by painting an entire street in the UK bright pink – houses, cars, trees, even dogs. **F**

e Nike has been given the go-ahead by the Greek government to place a neon sign of its famous 'swoosh' logo on top of the Acropolis in Athens. **H**

f In Kazakhstan a Russian rocket due to dock with the international space station was launched with the Pizza Hut logo displayed on its side. **F**

g Gordon's Gin fills selected British cinemas with the smell of juniper berries when its commercials are being screened to get the audience in the mood for a gin and tonic. **F**

h Calvin Klein is proposing to 'clothe' the twin Petronas Towers in Kuala Lumpur in a giant pair of CK jeans. **H**

Check your answers on page 129.

Globalisation

1 Naomi Klein is the author of the world's bestselling book on brands and globalisation *No Logo*. Read the article about her. How would you counter some of the points made?

LOGOMANIA

From the age of six, Naomi Klein was obsessed with brand names and what she could buy. She used to stitch little fake alligators to her T-shirts so they would look like Lacoste, and her biggest fights with her
5 parents were over Barbie and the price of designer jeans.

But, aged 30, Klein wrote a book, *No Logo*, which has been called 'the *Das Kapital* of the growing anti-corporation movement'. The former teenager
10 fixated on brand names has become a campaigner against our overbranded world.

In *No Logo*, Klein shows how globalisation has hit the poor the most. She writes that Nike paid Michael Jordan more for endorsing its trainers ($20 million)
15 than the company paid its entire 30,000-strong Indonesian workforce for making them.

Klein's argument starts with what we all recognise. Logos, she says, are 'the closest thing we have to an international language'. Most of the world's six billion
20 people could identify the McDonald's sign or the Coca-Cola symbol – we are united by what we are being sold.

Furthermore, advertising today is not merely about selling products; it is about selling a brand, a dream, a
25 message. So Nike's aim is not to sell trainers but 'to enhance people's lives through sport and fitness'. IBM doesn't sell computers, it sells 'solutions'.

And while the corporations are busy doing what they think is important – branding a way of life –
30 someone, somewhere, has to make the stuff. Very often, it seems, it is produced under terrible conditions in free-trade zones in Indonesia, China, Mexico, Vietnam, the Philippines and elsewhere. In some of the sweatshops Klein visited they have rules
35 against talking and smiling. There is forced overtime, but no job security – it's 'no work, no pay' when the orders don't come in.

Anti-corporate activism is on the rise precisely because branding has worked so well, believes Klein.
40 Multinationals such as Nike, Microsoft and Starbucks have sought to become the chief communicators of all that is good in our culture: art, sport, community, connection, equality. But the more successful this project is, the more vulnerable the companies become.
45 When in the US a group of black 13-year-olds from the Bronx – Nike's target market and the one exploited by it to get a street-cool image – learned that the trainers they bought for $180 cost $5 to make, it led to a mass dumping of their old trainers
50 outside New York's Nike Town. One boy, reports Klein, looked straight into the TV news camera and said, 'Nike, we made you. We can break you.'

Adapted from *The Guardian*

Discussion

3 Check/Pre-teach: *hoax, be given the go-ahead, neon, to dock with, to screen.* Also highlight the stress shift in *project* (n) and *to project* (v). Ask students if they have ever received a hoax e-mail – they contain bogus warnings, often about computer viruses, intended to frighten or mislead.

Students read through the publicity stunts and decide which actually happened and which three are hoaxes. Get students to compare their ideas in pairs/groups. If there is disagreement, ask students to justify their choices and try to reach whole class consensus on the answers. Then ask students to turn to page 129 to check. Ask students if they were surprised by any of the answers and to say which of the true marketing stunts they thought were the most daring/clever. Elicit examples of amazing marketing ploys from the students' own country/industry.

Globalisation

In this section, students read an article about Naomi Klein, who, in her book *No Logo,* argued that branding is bad for developing countries. Students focus on vocabulary in the text and then read an extract from a reply to *No Logo* originally published in *The Economist.* A listening task presents two people discussing the pros and cons of globalisation and students then discuss the issues raised in the recording.

1 Ask students if they have heard of the writer, Naomi Klein, or read her book *No Logo.* If they have, ask students to pool the information they know about the writer and the book. If they haven't, give students some brief background details. (Naomi Klein is a campaigner against over-branding, arguing that globalisation has adversely affected poorer nations. In her book, she describes branding as a 'common language' throughout the world and argues that corporate power has been achieved through exploitation of developing countries.) Point out that the text has been adapted from a longer article and that the complete version can be location in *The Guardian* archive online.

With weaker groups, check/pre-teach: *to stitch, fake, fixated, to endorse, stuff, to seek* (past – *sought*), *activism.* Ask students to predict the names of the global brands that appear in the text. Then ask them to read the text through quickly to check their predictions and to say in what context the brands are referred to. (Lacoste, Barbie – Naomi's favourite brands as a child; Nike – paying huge amounts for celebrity endorsement but exploiting their workforce and customers; McDonald's and Coca-Cola – part of an international language of logos; Nike and IBM– selling a dream; Nike, Microsoft and Starbucks – aiming to become the main communicators of everything that is good).

Students then read the article again and decide how they would answer the points the writer makes. Elicit a range of answers from the class e.g. globalisation gives people in developing countries the opportunity of paid employment, it may encourage the development of entrepreneurial spirit etc.

2 Ask students to look back at the article and identify the words a–d. Remind students of useful strategies here e.g. look for a word of the same type, look for synonyms, use the context to help you.

3 Ask students to read the extract. Elicit their reactions and ask if they agree that life is better in developing countries which have accepted globalisation.

4 🔲 **11.2** Tell students that they will hear a recording of two people discussing the issue of globalisation. Check/Pre-teach: *disgrace, standard rate, warehousing, a bunch of anarchists, to make a nuisance of yourself, sustainable development, financial speculators, GDP* (gross domestic product), *per capita, protectionist, assets, to exceed.*

Before playing the recording, write out a list of headings (see bracketed text below) in random order on the board for students to sequence. Play the recording through once and have the students number the headings in the correct order (1 exploitation in Indonesia, 2 Nike workers in Vietnam, 3 the costs of running a business, 4 sustainable development, 5 McDonald's in France, 6 GDP in US vs India, 7 IMF and World Bank loans, 8 conditions on loans).

Ask students to write out the above headings in the correct order and use them when making notes about the issues discussed in the recording. Tell them they should focus on key arguments for and against globalisation, examples of countries and brands, and numbers and figures. Play the recording through a second time.

Ask students which speaker they agree with most, A or B.

5 Focus students' attention on the phrases in the box and elicit complete examples. Divide the class into small

groups and get them to discuss the points made in the recording, using their notes from exercise 4 and the expressions in the box. Monitor the discussions, helping as necessary. At the end of the discussions, ask a spokesperson for each group to summarise their opinions for the whole class.

The name game

In this final section, the students test their branding skills in an activity called the *Name Game*.

Fluency

1 Set up the *Name Game* by asking students for examples of brand names they think work well and ones they think give a negative impression. Point out that what works in one language may not 'travel' well to another country/culture. Divide the class into small groups and have them discuss each client and choose the best names.

2 Ask students to report their decisions to the class and then turn to page 134 for the answers. Establish how good they were at spotting the best names and then ask what names would work best in their market.

If you're short of time

Set the text *Logomania* on page 60 for homework.

Omit the *Name Game* on page 61, or return to it as a discrete fluency activity in another lesson.

🔲 **11.2**

A: … Well, it's the old exploitation argument, isn't it? Ten-year-old kids working for ten cents an hour in Indonesia to make overpriced sports shoes that sell for $180 in the West. We've heard it all before.

B: It's still a disgrace. Did you know that in the last 20 years the number of people living on less than a dollar a day has actually *increased?* So much for globalisation! Look at the profits those companies must be making.

A: That's not the point. They just pay the standard rate for the countries they're in. Did you know that in Vietnam a Nike worker gets paid more than some doctors?

B: No way!

A: It's true. And, anyway, there's a lot more to running a business than just the price of making stuff.

B: There is if you pay some adolescent pop star millions to promote it, yeah.

A: It's not just that. You've got design and development costs, warehousing, shipping, whole finance and marketing departments. These so-called anti-globalisationists – they just don't understand the first thing about how business works. Take these protesters in Seattle and London and just about everywhere else these days. They're just a bunch of anarchists.

B: Made the World Bank change its mind though, didn't they?

A: Did they? Just made a nuisance of themselves, if you ask me.

B: No, apparently, the World Bank's now finally accepting that economic growth is not enough to reduce poverty. You've got to have sustainable development as well.

A: Sustainable development!

B: It's true. The French are particularly in favour. They've got that tax now – what is it? … the Tobin tax – to stop financial speculators taking capital out of poorer countries.

A: Oh, well, the French, yes. But they're just anti-American, aren't they? Like that guy … what was his name? Smashed up a McDonald's restaurant in his tractor or something. Ridiculous!

B: He was simply saying France doesn't want any more junk food, thanks very much. Good luck to him, I say.

A: Well, that's a joke for a start. McDonald's is France's biggest restaurant chain.

B: No way! Where did you read that?

A: It was in *The Economist* the other day. They've got nearly a thousand McDonald's in France now.

B: Good god. Well, I mean that's just my point, isn't it? All these brands are taking over the world. Apparently, more people go to Ikea on Sundays than church these days.

A: Doesn't surprise me. According to this programme I watched, you can get married at Disney World and buried in a Harley Davidson coffin as well if you want to.

B: What's it all coming to, eh? You know the average American consumes thirty times more than an Indian?

A: Yeah, but that doesn't mean much. I mean, if you look at the GDP per capita, you'll find the average American *produces seventy* times more than an Indian.

B: Does he?

A: Roughly. Look, the thing is, world trade is good for jobs. And living standards. Capitalism works. Those World Bank

figures prove it. The more globalisation, the more growth.

B: Yeah, but it's not quite as simple as that, is it?

A: Isn't it?

B: Well, you know all those countries that have been getting these IMF and World Bank loans?

A: Like in Latin America and Africa, you mean?

B: Exactly. Well, did you know that they were actually better off before they got the loans?

A: What? Under all those military, socialist, protectionist governments? I don't think so.

B: No, it's true. You see, there are always conditions to these loans. Like Mexico joins NAFTA, right, gets a loan provided it accepts a load of toxic waste as well.

A: Ah, yeah, but that's different …

B: Or Ecuador gets a World Bank loan and is ordered to liberalise its markets – let capital flow in and out freely.

A: So what's wrong with that?

B: What's wrong is it flows freely all right – but only out. So they raise interest rates to 90%, sell off all their assets, anything to bring cash back into the country and it all goes to hell.

A: Well, yeah, but …

B: And look at Brazil. It owes about, what, $235 billion now?

A: Well, no one expects them to pay that back, do they?

B: They already have paid it back.

A: The whole amount? 235 billion?

B: Yeah – in interest!

A: What, you mean the interest is now as much as the loan?

B: No, now it exceeds the loan. You see, the thing is, in some places capitalism just doesn't work. Take Africa …

---

2 Find the words and phrases in the article you've just read which mean:

a always thinking about (paragraph 1) obsessed with

b improve (paragraph 5) enhance

c factories where people work hard in terrible conditions (paragraph 6)
   sweatshops

d easily harmed or damaged (paragraph 7) vulnerable

3 When *No Logo* was first published a long reply was published in *The Economist*. Read the extract. Are you convinced by what it says?

Pro Logo

Opponents of globalisation claim that poor countries are losers from global integration. A new report from the World Bank demolishes that claim with one simple statistic. If you divide poor countries into those that are 'more globalised' and those that are 'less globalised' – with globalisation measured simply as a rise in the ratio of trade to national income – you find that more globalised poor countries have grown faster than rich countries, while less globalised countries have seen income per person fall.

4 11.2 Listen to two people discussing the articles in 1 and 3, and the whole issue of globalisation. Take notes. Who do you agree with more?

5 Discuss your reactions to the discussion in 4.

> I'd no idea that …   It doesn't surprise me in the least that …
> I'm not sure I believe that …   I totally agree with the idea that …
> I think I'd go along with the point that was made about …
> I think both speakers have missed the main point, which is …
> Frankly, the person who said … clearly doesn't know what they're talking about!

The name game

Fluency

1 In a highly competitive marketplace, thinking up distinctive names for new companies and their products is a specialist business. Lexicon Naming, who gave us 'Pentium' and 'Powerbook', designed the following Name Game to test people's branding skills.

Work in groups. You are Lexicon Naming. Hold a meeting to choose the brand name that best matches the image the four client companies below would like to project.

Client 1 This cutting-edge video game company targets young males with its fast, fun, action-packed titles.
a Zule **b** Zyex **c** Mimem **d** Lura

Client 2 This environmentally progressive cosmetics company manufactures comforting, healing and improving products for women aged 18–34.
a Tromos **b** Vaxlaz **c** Dartu **d** Ios

Client 3 This manufacturer specialises in miniature high tech gadgets like cellphones and PDAs. Their products are powerful, reliable, advanced, yet also lightweight and user-friendly.
a Parmeon **b** Semsa **c** Areon **d** Zytos

Client 4 This prescription pharmaceuticals firm develops and manufactures innovative precision drugs for the traditional marketplace and for biotech applications.
a Sylag **b** Tura **c** Zantis **d** Bagnum

See page 134 for suggested answers.

2 Report your decisions to the class.

12 E-mailing

The beautiful part of writing is that you don't have to get it right the first time, unlike, say, a brain surgeon. *Robert Cormier, author*

Discussion

1 Work with a partner and discuss the following questions.

a How important is e-mail in your job? If you did what this businessman did, do you think you might find the same thing?

> A friend of mine, a merchant banker, decided that for one month he would turn off his e-mails. When he switched back into gear he found that out of 753 e-mails, ten were really useful. Out of the ten, two were vital – so vital that the senders all took the precaution of ringing to confirm, just in case their e-mails were missed. *Business Life magazine*

b According to the Electronic Messaging Association, around seven trillion emails are sent annually. How many of them end up in *your* inbox? And how do you deal with the following problem?

> When everybody has e-mail and anybody can send you e-mail, how do you decide whose messages you're going to read and respond to first and whose you're going to send to the trash unread? Tom Peters in *Fast Company magazine*

c Is e-mail a time-saver or does it distract you from more important business? Does this company's idea sound like it could work?

> Signs are that the first rush of enthusiasm for e-mail may be waning. One big company in the computing industry is considering banning e-mails in the afternoon. It found that its people had stopped talking to one another. *A Freethinker's A–Z of the New World of Business*

d The Institute of Management puts working with computers amongst 'The Top Ten Stress Factors at Work'. Have you ever resorted to the following?

> A survey by Mori reveals that three quarters of computer users shout and swear at their machines. A similar study by IT support company Sosmatic shows that 43% of them have slapped, smacked and even kicked their computer. The mouse is the most maltreated piece of equipment, coming in for 31.5% of the punishment, followed by the monitor, the printer, the hard drive and the keyboard. Over a year such outbursts of 'computer rage' can cost companies up to £25,000 in lost earnings and damaged hardware.

Writing e-mail

1 According to the novelist Ernest Hemingway, 'All good writing is rewriting.' Do you ever rewrite your e-mails? Do you attach the same importance to them you would to a business letter or is the important thing just to fire them off as quickly as possible?

Desk work

12 E-mailing

The growth of e-mail has radically changed the nature of business communication and has affected nearly everyone. This unit looks at appropriate e-mail style and gives students practice in composing and replying to e-mails.

Students discuss their reaction to various short extracts about e-mailing. They read a text about the dynamics of e-mailing and then analyse two e-mails in the light of the text, correcting the mistakes in one of them and rewriting the other to make it more appropriate.

They focus on e-mail style, selecting the best expressions to use in a model message and then writing a reply. (You can make photocopies of the e-mail template on page 184 for this task.) They also focus on useful expressions in e-mailing. A recording about the biggest e-mail blunders ever made provides listening practice and a springboard for discussion. Finally, the students take part in a written fluency task and exchange e-mails. (You can also make photocopies of the e-mail template on page 184 for this task.)

The grammatical focus is on future forms and the lexical focus is on prepositional phrases.

In this first section, students read four short texts from the business press about e-mails and using computers, and discuss their reactions.

Warm-up

Ask the students how many e-mails they receive a day and if they think they could now live without e-mail at work. Read the quotation from the author, Robert Cormier. Check that the students can explain the humour in the quotation and elicit examples of other tasks which need to be done right first time e.g. air-traffic control. Point out that, traditionally in business writing, time should be built in for checking and re-drafting. The same is true of e-mails, but of course many are written and sent in haste.

Discussion

1 Focus attention on the photo and ask students what might have provoked such a reaction e.g. a computer problem, an angry or abrupt e-mail. Check/Pre-teach: *to switch into gear, vital, to take the precaution, trash, to wane, to slap, to smack, to maltreat, outburst.*

Divide the students into groups of four and assign a text a–d to each student. Each student reads their text and notes down the key information. Ask students to summarise their text for the others and find out their reactions. Hold a short feedback session and encourage students to discuss any particularly interesting points which arose.

With weaker groups, write specific prompt questions on the board and ask students to exchange the key information e.g.
a What percentage of e-mails that you receive are useless?
b Do you use the 'Urgent' label to highlight important e-mails?
c Would banning e-mails be effective in your company?
d Have you ever shouted at or hit your computer?

Writing e-mail

In this section, students discuss how they approach writing e-mails and then read a surprising text which suggests that the sloppier the mail, the more likely the writer is to be successful. The students discuss the article and study some of the vocabulary. They focus on two e-mails, correcting the grammar, spelling and punctuation mistakes in one and deleting unnecessary words in the other.

1 Elicit the students' reactions to the quotation from Hemingway. Ask students if they think that good writing can be composed quickly e.g. some poetry and novels are written in this way. Ask students if they ever rewrite e-mails or if they just draft them and hit 'send'.

2   Ask students to list the pros and cons of rewriting an e-mail e.g. accuracy reduces the possibility of misinterpretation, rewriting can improve the tone and so avoid causing offence; loss of speed, accuracy may be unnecessary, people see e-mail as 'speech-writing'.

Check/Pre-teach: *to bother to do something, tendency, to resort, to blind cc someone* (to copy in someone on a message without the other recipients being aware), *emoticon* (*emotion* + *icon*). Focus attention on the title of the article and get students to explain what they think it means. Give them two minutes to skim the text before eliciting the answer. With weaker groups, ask them to skim paragraphs 2–3 only.

Ask students to read the text a second time and think about their answers to the questions a–i. Divide the class into pairs/small groups and ask the students to discuss the questions. Hold a short class feedback session, eliciting any interesting points which came up in the discussions.

3   Students work individually to replace the italicised text with the expressions. Do a quick class check by calling out the numbers and have students read out their alternative phrase.

As a follow-up activity, ask students to select three vocabulary items from the text and write three questions for the other students in the group e.g. *What's the surest way of reaching the top of the corporate ladder?*

Adapted from the *London Evening Standard*

2 Read the article and discuss the questions with a partner.

Bad spelling is the key to success

Forget how to spell, never bother to check your grammar, and within a few short years you will have e-mailed your way to *the top of the corporate ladder* (1).

According to a new study into the dynamics of e-mailing by David
5 Owens, Associate Professor of Management at Vanderbilt University in Nashville, someone who sends messages that could have been written by a small child probably *has all the makings of* (2) a chief executive.

'High-status people in a company send short, *curt* (3) messages and they have the worst grammar and spelling in the firm,' he said. 'This
10 isn't because they are the least educated; they're probably the best educated, but they just don't have time to waste on *the small stuff* (4).'

Part of the reason top employees in a firm take so little care over e-mails is that they actually get their own way by 'face-mail': meetings with *underlings* (5) and clients. The *classic* (6) signs of a worker who
15 will go no further than middle management are a tendency to write long, overcomplicated messages, and send e-mails instead of talking to someone in person.

People who *aren't cut out for* (7) the top are more likely to resort to *sneaky* (8) tactics such as carbon copying (cc-ing) and even blind
20 cc-ing their bosses on correspondence with other workers. In contrast, confident power e-mailers rarely cc anyone on their e-mails because they want to give the impression they are giving the recipient their undivided attention.

Anyone who uses office e-mail to forward jokes or electronic
25 greetings cards, or uses happy symbols like ☺ is *destined* (9) never to see the inside of the executive dining room, warns the study. According to Professor Owens, company jokers *play an important role as social glue* (10), but if staff even have to ask whether forwarding 'amusing' e-mails is a bad move then their
30 career *is a lost cause* (11).

The professor advises keeping e-mails brief but *pouring every ounce of charm and intelligence you have into them* (12). Before you press the send button make sure you'd be happy to see what you've written stuck on
35 the company noticeboard or appear in the newsletter.

a Do you use grammar- and spell-checks on your e-mails?

b If Owens is right, are you writing the kind of e-mails that will get you promoted?

c Is your English better than your boss's?

d Isn't more business conducted by e-mail than 'face-mail' these days?

e Who sends you the longest e-mails?

f Have you ever blind cc-ed your boss on an e-mail? Did you have a good reason?

g Have you committed 'professional suicide' in any of these ways (lines 24-30)?

h Is there a joker in your office?

i How can you inject your personality into an e-mail?

3 Which of the words and phrases in *italics* in the article could be replaced by these alternatives without changing the meaning too much?

typical ⑥   certain ⑨   the highest level in the company ⑴   abrupt ③

has all the necessary qualities to become ②   low-ranking employees ⑤

unfair ⑧   will never succeed ⑾   giving them a real personal touch ⑿

do not have the necessary qualities to reach ⑦   unimportant matters ④

are good at holding a group together ⑽

from *Macmillan English Dictionary*

asap /ˌeɪ es eɪ ˈpiː/ as soon as possible

BTW abbrev by the way: used in e-mails and text messages for adding additional information

FYI abbrev for your information: used in e-mails and text messages as a way of introducing a useful piece of information

4 Look at the two e-mails below. From what Owens said in the article in 2, which do you think was written by a junior manager? <u>the second one</u>

5 Correct the grammar, spelling and punctuation mistakes in the first e-mail. There are 18. Break up the text into short paragraphs and add a suitable subject line.

6 Were the mistakes in the first e-mail mainly language errors or mainly typos? <u>mainly typos</u> Do e-mails like this create a bad impression or doesn't it matter as long as the message is clear and the tone friendly?

To: stephen.steele@cellmax.co.uk
Cc:
Bcc:
Subject:
Attachments: *issue*

Steve

Can you udpate me on where you are with hte Rome Expo arrangements I was unable to open the attatchment you sent me, so i dont have a copy of the programme. As for as the Copenhagen conference is concerned I don't just have time for dealing with it myself. So please can you sort this out with the Danes asap? You'll need probably to contact Margrethe Rasmussen at there headquarters in helsingborg. Copy me in on any correspondance.

Thanks alot. Your a star!

Maxine

(BTW any news on Garys feasability study???)

To: stephen.steele@cellmax.co.uk
Cc: fiona.kennedy@cellmax.co.uk michael.hadleigh@cellmax.co.uk
Bcc: maxine.demourges@cellmax.com
Subject: Approval of ComTech feasibility study; Copenhagen meeting
Attachments: ComTech feasibility study report (first draft)

Dear Stephen

I ~~do~~ realise ~~that~~ you must be ~~very~~ busy ~~at the moment~~ with ~~all~~ the arrangements for ~~our exhibition stand at~~ the ~~Rome~~ Expo ~~in two weeks' time~~, but, ~~if you have a spare moment sometime over the next few days~~, could you ~~possibly just~~ have a quick look at ~~the first draft of~~ my report on the ComTech feasibility study, ~~which I've been working very hard on since we last spoke~~? ~~As I'm sure~~ Maxine ~~has already told you, it was actually due last week and I know that she~~ needs it quite urgently, but there are ~~just~~ a couple of points I need to check with you, ~~if that's OK~~, before I submit the final report – see attachment.

~~FYI, I don't know if anyone has spoken to you about it yet, but~~ it looks like I'm ~~probably going to be~~ coming to Copenhagen with you, ~~Fiona and Michael~~ in September after all. ~~You'll remember from my CV when you interviewed me for this position that I studied German and Danish at university and, as a matter of fact,~~ I still speak pretty good Danish, which might ~~just~~ come in handy in ~~some of~~ the bars ;-) ~~although I'm quite sure most of the Danes we'll be meeting at the conference will have no problem whatsoever with English!~~

Many thanks, Gary

4 Focus attention on the words in the glossary. Elicit other examples of common abbreviations used in e-mails e.g. *atb* (*all the best*) and ask students if they use abbreviations in the same way when e-mailing in their own language.

Ask students to quickly read the two e-mails and say which was probably written by a junior manager. Ask the students to justify their choice based on the article in exercise 2 (the message in the second e-mail is accurate but overly long and complicated; it uses an emoticon; the writer has used the blind cc function; he could have said everything in the message in a quick call or face to face).

5 Elicit the first two mistakes in the e-mail (see below). Students correct the remaining mistakes. Remind them to mark the paragraph breaks and add in a subject line. Ask students to compare their answers with a partner and then check the answers with the whole class.

Suggested answer

> Steve
>
> Can you **update** me on where you are with **the** Rome Expo arrangements**?** I was unable to open the **attachment** you sent me, so **I don't** have a copy of the programme.
>
> As **far** as the Copenhagen **conference** is concerned I **just** don't ~~just~~ have time **to deal** with it myself. So please can you sort this out with the Danes asap? You'll **probably** need ~~probably~~ to contact Margrethe Rasmussen at **their** headquarters in **H**elsingborg.
>
> Copy me in on any **correspondence**.
>
> Thanks **a lot**. **You're** a star!
>
> Maxine
>
> (BTW any news on **Gary's feasibility** study???)

Refer to the answer key above to check where the paragraph breaks should go and elicit possible subject lines e.g. *Rome Expo/Copenhagen conference.*

6 Check comprehension of *typos* (typographic errors) and ask students to analyse the mistakes in the message. Point out that the presence of a lot of typos didn't make the overall message impossible to understand. Elicit students' opinions on the importance of accuracy. Ask them how important it is to be accurate when e-mailing different people e.g. clients, colleagues, your boss.

7 Students delete as many words as they can from the second e-mail, while retaining the basic meaning, and then compare with a partner. Alternatively, students work in pairs/small groups to produce the shortened version. If appropriate, ask students to write their versions on an OHT to compare with the rest of the class. Check the answers with the class, accepting any reasonable variation.

8 Ask students to add a sentence or two to personalise the e-mail then elicit possible answers.

Suggested answers

> (BTW) Congratulations on becoming a father!
>
> (BTW) I heard you applied for that job – good luck!
>
> (BTW) I know you are under a bit of pressure at the moment so let me know if I can do anything to help.
>
> (BTW) I know Denmark quite well if you need any help organising the visit.
>
> (BTW) If you fancy a game of squash one evening, just let me know.

E-mail style

In this section, students read another e-mail and select the best expressions to use in terms of style. They then write a reply to the same e-mail, working from prompts. Finally, students focus on useful expressions to use in e-mails.

1 Ask students who they write e-mails to and if they consciously change the style of writing depending on the recipient.

Check/Pre-teach: *Yo!* (an informal greeting between people who know each other well), *to blow someone away, (the packaging) sucks* (slang for 'is really awful'), *to scrap, to chew over, to give someone a buzz* (to telephone). Remind students that a friendly, neutral style works best in e-mail. Get them to read the message and underline the most appropriate expressions. Check the answers and get students to say why the others are not suitable (some expressions are too colloquial or over-direct, others are too formal for an e-mail).

2 If appropriate, hand out copies of the e-mail template on page 184. Tell students to read through the prompts and point out that the mark // indicates students should start a new sentence. With weaker classes, elicit the first two sentences with the whole class. Set a time limit to encourage students to focus on fluency. If students have access to computers, encourage them to type and print out their answers. Students can exchange their e-mails and check them for corrections. Then check possible wording with the whole class.

Suggested answer

> Hi Simon
>
> I'm glad you enjoyed the presentation and I'm also pleased about the response to the product demo. I was disappointed to hear you are not keen on the design. I thought it was quite stylish. Let me know when you are free to discuss alternatives. I'm around most of next week.
>
> I'm happy to go through the report. The costing will be ready within a few days. I may need to check a few things with Sandra. Do you happen to know her extension number?
>
> Thanks a lot
>
> [*your name*]

7 Make the second e-mail shorter and simpler by deleting as many words as you can without changing the basic message or sounding too direct.

8 Now make the shortened second e-mail friendlier by adding a few personal touches. Use some or all of the following information to personalise it in your own way.

Stephen Steele
- has just become a father for the first time
- has put in for a promotion
- is under a lot of pressure because three people in his department are off sick
- has never been to Denmark (Gary knows it well)
- is a keen squash player (so is Gary).

E-mail style

1 How you write an e-mail largely depends on who you are writing to, but, in general, a friendly, neutral style will work best – neither too formal nor too familiar. Avoid unnecessary acronyms, abbreviations and slang which may confuse, date or sound silly. Underline the best option in each section of the e-mail below.

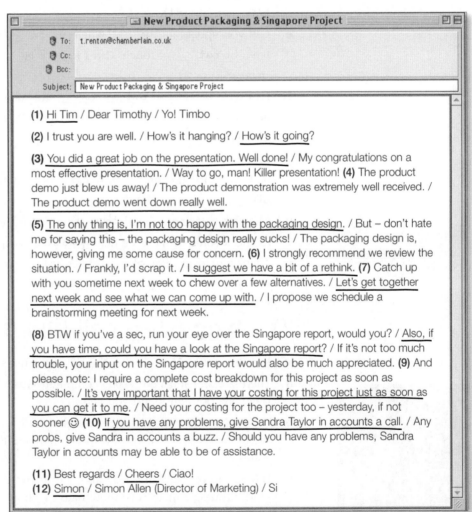

2 Write a short e-mail in reply to the one above using the prompts below.

glad / enjoyed / presentation / also pleased / response / product demo // disappointed / hear / not keen / design // thought / quite stylish // let / know / free / discuss / alternatives // around / most / next week // happy / go through / report // costing / ready / within / few days // may need / check / few things / Sandra // happen / have / extension number? / thanks

E-mail expressions 3 The following expressions are all useful in e-mails. Complete them using the prepositions in the boxes. Some of them have already appeared in this unit.

at	against	out	of	to	down	through	in	back
off	off	up	up	on	on	on	with	with	with
with	with	with	with

| back + to | through + to | up + on | in + on | up + to |
| out + with | on + to | out + on |

a Have a quick look _at_ these figures and get _back_ _to_ me asap.

b Let me know if you need any help _with_ the Koreans. And copy me _in_ _on_ any correspondence _with_ them.

c Could you get _on_ _to_ our suppliers and sort something _out_ _with_ them? I'll leave the details _to_ you, but keep me _in_ the loop.

d BTW, you did a great job _on_ the presentation. It went _down_ really well _with_ the Belgians. We'll just have to wait and see what they come _back_ to us _with_.

e Can you update me _on_ where we are _with_ the Expo arrangements? I'm a bit _out_ of touch. Can I leave it _up_ _to_ you to contact the speakers?

f I'd like to sound you _out_ _on_ this new packaging idea. Let's meet _up_ to discuss it sometime next week. BTW, I still can't seem to get _through_ _to_ Monica.

g I know you're _up_ to your neck in work at the moment and probably don't want to take _on_ any more, but could you take this Milan thing _off_ my hands? THNQ

h I haven't had time to read _through_ the whole report and I'll probably need to check some of these figures _against_ the computer, but leave it _with_ me.

i Thanks for your offer _of_ a beer. If I can finish this report _off_ by 7, I may just take you _up_ _on_ it! I could certainly do _with_ one!

Lexis link

for more on prepositional phrases see page 117

The biggest e-mail blunders ever made

Discussion 1 Work with a partner and discuss the following questions.

a There are an estimated 50,000 computer viruses out there in cyberspace. Have any of them found you yet?

b What kind of things do people use their office computers for which are not strictly business? Have you ever been tempted to do any of these things yourself?

c Have you ever sent an e-mail and later regretted it? How dangerous is it to send business e-mails (even internally) without considering the possible implications?

2 🔊 12.1 Listen to the story of some of the biggest e-mail blunders ever made and number the following in the order they are mentioned.

Netscape ⑨ Merrill Lynch ⑦ Dow Chemical ⑤ Cerner ⑥
the Love Bug ① Western Provident ③ AOL ⑩ Norwich Union ②
Microsoft ⑧ Norton Rose ④

The 'I Love You' e-mail virus known as the 'Love Bug'

E-mail expressions

3 Check students understand the abbreviation THNQ (*thank you*). Ask students to work in pairs to complete the sentences. Then check the answers with the class.

Ask students to choose the most useful expressions from this exercise and create a template to refer back to. If appropriate, get them to save the phrases onto computer so that they can copy and paste them into their e-mails of a similar type.

Direct students' attention to the Lexis link on page 117 for more practice on prepositional phrases.

The biggest e-mail blunders ever made

In this section, students discuss aspects of computer use and e-mailing, such as the spread of viruses and the sending of inappropriate or angry e-mails (flaming). This leads into a listening task on the biggest e-mail blunders ever made.

Discussion

1 Check/Review the verb *to flame* and the noun *a flame* as another way of saying 'to fire off an angry e-mail'. Ask students to discuss the questions in pairs. Use the following points as prompt or follow-up questions:

a *Does your computer have anti-virus software installed? How often it is updated? Does your company have a firewall to protect the network against viruses?*

b *How tolerant is your company of the personal use of computers? Is it considered a perk? Some companies allow workers some personal use each day – is this a good solution to the problem?*

c *What other inappropriate material could be circulated via e-mail?* (company gossip, intimate messages between people who are in a relationship and who are also colleagues etc.)

2 🔲 **12.1** Check/Pre-teach: *blunder, to spread a rumour, to sue, sexually explicit, X-rated, to suspend, to reprimand, crap* (slang for 'rubbish'), *antitrust trials, to screw* (slang for 'to cheat/deceive'). Also give students the proper name Claire Swire.

Play the recording once and get students to number the items in the correct order. Check the answers.

🔲 **12.1**

A: This week on CyberReport Terry Lancaster takes a look at some of the biggest e-mail blunders ever made.

B: In April 2000 millions of computer users received an unexpected e-mail. The subject line was intriguing. It said: 'I love you.' Those whose curiosity got the better of them opened the message and unleashed what later became known as the Love Bug – a virus so lethal it has so far infected 45 million PCs and caused 8.7 billion dollars' worth of damage to computer networks worldwide.

Computer viruses like the Love Bug sound like every company's worst nightmare. But the real danger these days is not so much what can get *into* your e-mail system as what can get *out*. You just never know where that e-mail you now regret sending may end up.

The first high-profile blunder occurred in 1997 when employees at the Norwich Union insurance company started spreading a rumour about a competitor on their internal e-mail system. Western Provident, they said, was about to go bankrupt. Western Provident was *not* about to go bankrupt, and when the e-mails suggesting it was came into their possession, it sued. The case was eventually settled out of court for a cool £450,000.

Three years later, Londoner Claire Swire briefly became a celebrity when sexually explicit e-mails she sent to her boyfriend were forwarded to mailboxes right across the world. It might not have been so bad, had Swire's boyfriend not worked for Norton Rose, a company which gives specialist advice to businesses on effective electronic communications.

Understandably, then, when Dow Chemical discovered hundreds of X-rated e-mails being exchanged between members of staff, the company took no chances. It fired 74 employees and suspended a further 435.

But disciplining your staff electronically isn't always a good idea, as the CEO of Cerner, Neal Patterson, found out to his cost. When Patterson reprimanded 400 managers by e-mail, his criticisms somehow found their way onto the Yahoo! website – for all the world to see. Cerner stock fell by 28% within the week.

And at Merrill Lynch in 2002, the company ended up paying out $100 million when Henry Blodget, an Internet stock analyst, strongly recommended buying stock in a company he had previously described, in what he thought was a private e-mail, as 'a piece of crap'.

But perhaps the most famous business e-mails in history came to light during the Microsoft antitrust trials. Netscape CEO Jim Barksdale claimed his company never wanted to collaborate with Microsoft in the Internet browser market – until, that is, Microsoft lawyers unearthed an e-mail from Netscape president Jim Clark to a senior executive at Microsoft stating clearly: 'We do not want to compete with you.' And Microsoft, for its part, denied any attempt to push Netscape out of the market – until an e-mail from Bill Gates to AOL executives was submitted as evidence. The e-mail read: 'How much do we need to pay you to screw Netscape?' Oh, dear!

So the message is clear. With e-mail, honesty is not always the best policy. And if you must tell the truth, think twice before clicking that send button.

A: That was Terry Lancaster talking about the biggest e-mail blunders ever made. And now a sneak preview of the latest in wireless technology …

3 Divide the class into pairs. Ask students to work together to see if they can remember any of the key information. Play the recording again to let students complete/check their answers.

With weaker groups, write up all the figures from the recording and ask students if they can remember what they represent: 2,000 million, 45 million, $8.7 billion, £450,000, 74, 435, 400, 28%, $100 million. Get students to choose the correct figures to answer a, b, d and f. Play the recording again and let students check their answers.

Elicit students' reactions to the blunders. Ask follow-up questions e.g. *Has your company suffered from the Love Bug virus? What do you think about Claire Swire's actions? What would happen if someone in your company made any of the blunders described in the recording?*

Answering your e-mail

In the final section, the students take part in an e-mail exchange exercise and so practise fluency in writing. They also get the opportunity to give peer feedback.

Fluency

1 For this task, students with access to computers can key the text of their e-mails, and if they are on an internal network, they can write and send them to the appropriate address. If computers are not available, use photocopies of the e-mail template on page 184.

Stage 1

Check/Pre-teach: *short notice, to be a pain, up to your neck in work, do you fancy* (would you like to), *to be kept in the loop, to stand in for.* Ask students to skim all four templates and choose the one they wish to use. Remind them they need to write to a real colleague and that they can adapt/add to the prompts.

If appropriate, hand out copies of the e-mail template on page 184. Remind students of the need for a friendly but neutral tone and for clarity but not total accuracy. Set a strict time limit so that students exchange e-mails at a set time. Get students to write their e-mail.

Stage 2

Divide the class into pairs and ask students to read stage 2. Tell students that they should reply as the employee

standing in for the colleague. Again, get students to keep to the same time limit as in stage 1. Students exchange e-mails and write their reply. If appropriate, place the e-mails in a central box for collection by the recipient, rather than just swap them between pairs of students. Be ready to deal with questions on staging/procedure but encourage students to address queries regarding the situation to the e-mail recipient and to use language from the unit as appropriate.

Stage 3

Check students understand that the correspondence will continue until the business in hand is brought to a conclusion but suggest a maximum of five e-mails in total and keep to the same time limit. Again, be ready to answer procedural questions, but don't offer too much help as this will interfere with the authenticity of the task.

Feedback

2 Ask students to review their partner's e-mails using a checklist of points to look for: tone and style, clarity, brevity, accuracy. If appropriate, set up a grading system of 1–5 for each point, where 5 is excellent. Students feed back on each other's writing, highlighting language mistakes that caused a problem for comprehension.

If accuracy in writing is important to your students, take in the e-mails and feed back on important errors.

Direct students' attention to the Grammar link on page 116 for more information and practice on future forms.

If you're short of time

Omit exercise 1 on page 62.

Set the text *Bad spelling is the key to success* on page 63 for homework and get students to prepare the discussion questions. Alternatively, set exercises 1–3 on pages 65–6 for homework.

Omit exercises 1–3 on pages 66–7.

The fluency task *Answering your e-mail* on page 67 can be done as a mini-project in the students' own time.

---

3   Work with a partner. Without listening again, can you remember:

a   how much the Love Bug cost businesses worldwide? _$8.7 billion_

b   how much the two insurance companies settled out of court for? _£450,000_

c   whose love life reflected badly on Norton Rose? _Clare Swire's_

d   how many people lost their jobs at Dow Chemical? _74_

e   whose stock fell by 28%? _Cerner's_

f   how much Merrill Lynch had to pay out because of Blodget's e-mail?
$100 million

g   who regretted sending e-mails in the Microsoft antitrust trial?
Jim Clark + Bill Gates

Answering your e-mail

Fluency   1   Work with a partner to practise exchanging e-mails.

Stage 1 Write an e-mail (maximum 150 words) to a real colleague on **one** of the subjects below. Use the suggested phrases to help you, but change and add anything you need to.

Subject: Change of plan

I was/we were originally hoping to ..., but I'm afraid that won't be possible now because ..., so what I'm/we're planning to do is ...

Sorry it's a bit short notice, but do you think you'll be able to ... or is that going to be a problem? I'll wait to hear from you.

Subject: Urgent request

I've got an important meeting/presentation coming up on ... and I'm going to need ... Can I leave it to you to ...? I expect I'll also be needing ...

I know you're probably up to your neck in work at the moment, but if you can get ... to me before next ..., it'll be a real help. Thanks.

Subject: Update please

Sorry to be a pain about this, but I'm still waiting for ... Can you let me know how much longer it's likely to be? Do you think you'll have it finished it by ... because ...?

If you anticipate any problems, let me know. I'll ... tomorrow to see how you're doing. Cheers!

Subject: Can you do me a favour?

I've had an e-mail/phone call from someone called ..., who wants ... Can I leave this one with you? I'm sure you'll know a lot more about it than I do. But keep me in the loop.

BTW a few of us may be ... on ... Are you going to be around? Fancy joining us? Should be fun.

Grammar link

for more on future forms see page 116

Stage 2 Exchange e-mails with your partner. You are standing in for the person they e-mailed while that person is off sick / on holiday / on maternity/paternity leave / away on a long business trip (you decide which). Write a reply (maximum 100 words) explaining the situation and asking for clarification or any details you need. Mention that you are new to the department.

Stage 3 Exchange replies and continue the correspondence as long as necessary to complete your business.

Feedback   2   Give your partner your impressions of the e-mails they wrote in 1.

• Do they sound friendly but businesslike?
• Is the style neutral?
• Have they kept their messages short and to-the-point?
• Have they made any important spelling, punctuation or grammar mistakes?

13 Making an impact

Speech is power: speech is to persuade, to convert, to compel.

Ralph Waldo Emerson, American writer, philosopher and orator

Opening

The opener to any business presentation is nearly always important, establishing the tone for the rest of the event. It's that vital moment when you take charge, gaining people's close attention.

People tend to remember openers more than any other part of a presentation, except perhaps for the closing remarks. You waste a wonderful opportunity if you resort to trivia like: 'Good evening, ladies and gentlemen, it's a great pleasure to be here today.'

Adapted from *The Ultimate Business Presentation Book* by Andrew Leigh

1 How important is it to make an impact right at the beginning of a presentation? Read the book extract on the left. Do you agree with the author?

2 With a partner, make a list of ways you can attract people's attention when you start a presentation. Could any of them be risky?

3 🔲 13.1 Listen to the openings of six business presentations. Do the speakers use any of the techniques you listed in 2? What other techniques do they employ? <u>1 quoting a statistic, 2 telling a joke, 3 thanking people, 4 quoting a famous person, 5 telling an anecdote, 6 making reference to a famous person</u>

4 How effective are the speakers in 3 at capturing your attention?

5 The openers below were all used in 3. Can you remember the first three words of each? Contractions (*I'd, I'm, it's,* etc.) count as **one** word.

a <u>Did</u> <u>you</u> <u>know</u> that of the world's one hundred biggest economies only 49 are actually countries?

b <u>One</u> <u>of</u> <u>my</u> favourite lawyer jokes is: this guy's having a quiet drink in a bar when a drunk starts shouting …

c <u>I'd</u> <u>like</u> <u>to</u> start off by thanking Dr Jensen, Dr Tan and Dr Martinez for inviting me to speak today.

d <u>I</u> <u>think</u> <u>it</u> was Thomas Edison who said: 'I have not failed. I've just found 10,000 ways that don't work.'

e <u>I</u> <u>was</u> <u>looking</u> through the appointments pages the other day and came across this unusual job advertisement.

f <u>Whenever</u> <u>I'm</u> <u>asked</u> about Total Quality, I think of the story of the American steel magnate, Andrew Carnegie.

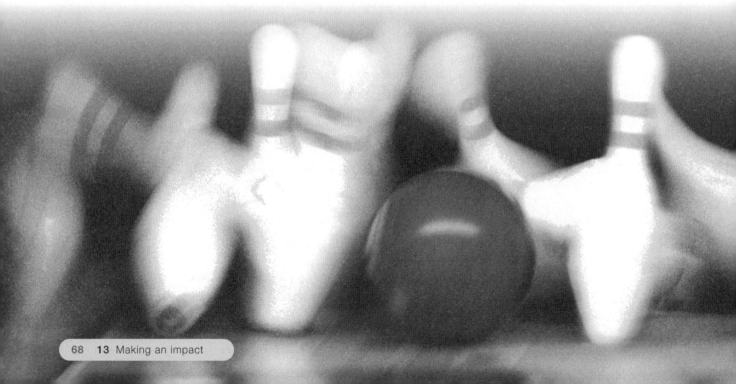

Presenting

13 Making an impact

This unit focuses on effective beginnings and endings of presentations, as well giving students the opportunity to use some rhetorical devices in English.

Students discuss the way presenters start their talks and listen to a recording of six openings of presentations in order to evaluate their effectiveness.

Students listen to a second recording of four famous political speeches, which all use rhetoric, and study the techniques used. They then listen to extracts from four presentations, rephrasing them to make them more effective and practising delivering them. Students then focus on techniques for closing presentations.

Finally, a fluency task in the form of a party political broadcast gives practice in preparing and delivering a speech and in using rhetorical techniques.

The grammatical focus is on rhetorical techniques and the lexical focus is on metaphor.

In this first section, students focus on the openings of presentations. They listen to and discuss the beginning of six presentations and focus on the language used.

Warm-up

Check/Pre-teach: *to convert, to compel, orator* and focus attention on the quotation by Ralph Waldo Emerson. Ask students if they agree with the sentiment expressed.

1　Ask students to think of the most memorable opening to a presentation they have ever heard and elicit examples from the group.

Ask the students why the opening to a presentation is important and then get them to read the book extract. Students compare their ideas with the author's (it establishes tone; it means the speaker can take charge; it should be memorable). Ask students how far they agree with the author, especially with his last sentence.

2　Point out that presentations often start with a 'hook' – something which involves the audience in some way e.g. asking a question, asking for a show of hands. Divide the class into pairs and get students to brainstorm techniques for getting people's attention. Ask them to decide which ones they think are risky.

3　▣ **13.1** With weaker groups, check/pre-teach: *G7 countries* (the major industrialised democracies), *scary, to outperform, to resent, corrupt, cybernetic* (use of technology to make copies of natural things), *on the right track, mean* (informal for 'cruel'), *Total Quality* (management philosophy which gives responsibility for quality to everyone in an organisation), *magnate.*

Play the recording and get students to check the techniques used against the list from exercise 2. Elicit which other techniques were used.

4　Ask students to rank the openers in exercise 3 in order of effectiveness. Students compare their order in pairs and then feed back to the class. Elicit which students thought were the most and least effective openers.

5　When students have completed the exercise, refer them to the recording script on page 153 to check their answers.

▣ 13.1

1
Did you know that of the world's one hundred biggest economies only 49 are actually countries? That's right, 49. The other 51 are companies! In fact, if companies were allowed to join the G7 group of the world's richest countries, Microsoft would take the place of Canada! I think it's getting a little scary, don't you, when a corporation can outperform a nation? And maybe it's time to stop and ask ourselves: should business really be that powerful?

2
You know, the joke books of the world are probably full of more lawyer jokes than just about anything else. **One of my favourite** lawyer **jokes is**: this guy's having a quiet drink in a bar when a drunk starts shouting 'All lawyers are dirty criminals!' The man jumps to his feet and cries 'I resent that remark!' 'Why?' says the drunk. 'Are you a lawyer?' 'No,' says the man, 'I'm a criminal!' But I'm here to tell you that not all lawyers are corrupt. It's just 99% of them who give the others a bad name.

3
Good morning. Erm, **I'd like to start off by thanking** Dr Jensen, Dr Tan and, er, Dr Martinez, of the faculty of cybernetic engineering for inviting me to speak today. Our company has a long history of collaboration with this university and it's always a great pleasure to address the robotics experts of the future. Erm, yes, before I begin, perhaps I could just take a moment or two to introduce you to the rest of my team, who are here with me this morning …

4
I think it was Thomas Edison **who said**: 'I have not failed. I've just found 10,000 ways that don't work.' Of course, Edison was an inventor, but he could just as easily have been talking about sales. In sales, our success rate is nowhere near as bad as one in 10,000. At least, it better not be! But we have to go through an awful lot of 'no sales' to make one sale. And the ability to deal with failure is the single most important characteristic of the successful sales professional. Could you just raise your hand if you failed to make a sale yesterday? … Just about everybody, right? Well, congratulations! You're obviously on the right track!

5
I was looking through the appointments pages **the other day** – don't we all? – **and came across this** unusual job advertisement. Here it is: 'Good hours, excellent pay, fun place to work, paid training, mean boss!' Oh, well, four out of five isn't bad. Wouldn't you like to be interviewed by that boss who admits he's mean? How powerful that little touch of honesty is. And that's exactly what I want to talk to you about this morning: honesty in advertising. And how you get people's attention when you simply tell the truth …

6
Whenever I'm asked about Total Quality, **I think of the story of** the American steel magnate, Andrew Carnegie. It seems Carnegie was doing a factory tour one day, when he stopped to speak to one of the machine operators – a grey-haired old guy obviously coming up to retirement. 'Wilson,' he said, reading the man's name badge, 'how many years exactly have you been working for me now?' 'Thirty-nine, sir,' Wilson replied with a proud smile. 'And may I add that in all those years I made only one very small mistake.' 'Good work,' mumbled Carnegie, 'but from now on, please try to be more careful.'

Presence and performance

Students start by discussing the meaning of *charisma* and then rank four extracts from famous political speeches according to how charismatic they sound. They complete gapped versions of the extracts, focus on the seven 'rules' of rhetoric and analyse the rhetorical techniques used in the speeches. They then re-word extracts from ineffective business presentations and practise delivering the improved versions with maximum impact. There is a further recording highlighting techniques for ending presentations, which students analyse before practising the delivery of the final part of their own presentation.

1   Have students read the definition of *charisma* in the glossary and elicit the adjective *charismatic*. Check pronunciation and make sure students produce the stress shift between the two words: *charisma, charismatic*. Ask students to think about the equivalent word in their language and then elicit examples of charismatic speakers internationally and from the students' own country.

Focus attention on the photograph. Ask what point it suggests about speeches (that they can really move people if the speaker and delivery have enough impact).

2   📼 **13.2** Ask students to cover the text in exercise 3. Tell students they are going to hear extracts from four speeches from the second half of the 20th century given by four former leaders. (Point out that the recordings are of actors speaking in the style of the original speakers, not the original orators themselves.) Ask them to guess

who the original speakers might be and which famous speech they deliver. Play the recording through once and get students to check their predictions and also rank the speeches according to how charismatic they sound. Check the speakers and elicit/check when/where the speeches were delivered.

Answers

1	John F Kennedy, 1961, from his inauguration speech as 35th president of the USA
2	Martin Luther King, 1963, from his address to the civil rights demonstrators who had marched on Washington
3	Margaret Thatcher, 1975, from her speech to the Conservative Party Conference in Blackpool
4	Nelson Mandela, 1994, from his inauguration statement as president of the Democratic Republic of South Africa

Play the recording again and get students to check/amend their ranking of the speeches. Then get students to compare their answers in pairs. Hold a short feedback session and establish which speech students thought most charismatic and why.

3   With weaker groups, check/pre-teach: *to shrink, faith, devotion, endeavour, glow, rooted, creed, brotherhood, sweltering, oppression, oasis, to beg, humbled, elevated, reconciliation, to fulfil*. Ask students to complete as much as possible of the extracts from memory, before playing the speeches again so that students can check/complete their answers.

📼 **13.2**

Extract 1
In the long history of the world, only a few generations have been granted the role of **defending freedom** in its hour of maximum danger. **I do not shrink from this responsibility – I welcome it. I do not** believe that **any** of us would exchange places with **any other** people or **any other** generation. **The energy, the faith, the devotion,** which we bring to this endeavour will **light** our country and all who serve it – **and the glow from that fire can truly light the world**. And so, **my fellow** Americans, **ask not what your country can do for you – ask what you can do for your country. My fellow** citizens of the world, **ask not what America will do for you – but what together we can do for the freedom of man.**
(John F. Kennedy, Washington DC, 20.1.61)

Extract 2
I say to you **today**, my friends … so even though we face the difficulties of **today and tomorrow, I still have a dream**. It is a **dream** deeply rooted in the American **dream. I have a dream that one day** this nation will rise up and live out the true meaning of its creed: 'We hold these truths to be self-evident; that all men are created equal.' **I have a dream that one day** on the red hills of Georgia **the sons of former**

slaves and the sons of former slave owners will be able to sit down together **at the table of brotherhood. I have a dream that one day** even the **state** of Mississippi, a **state sweltering with the heat of injustice, sweltering with the heat of oppression**, will be transformed into **an oasis of freedom and justice. I have a dream** that my four little children **will one day live in a nation where they will not be judged by the colour of their skin but by the content of their character. I have a dream today**.
(Martin Luther King, Washington DC, 28.8.63)

Extract 3
These are the two great challenges of our time – **the moral and political challenge, and the economic challenge. They have to** be faced together and we **have to** master them both. **What are our chances of success?** It depends **on what kind of people we are. What kind of people are we? We are the people that** in the past made Great Britain **the workshop of the world, the people who** persuaded others to buy British, not by begging them to do so, but because it was best. **We are a people who** have received **more Nobel prizes than any other nation** except America, and head for head we have done better than America, twice as well in fact.

We are the people who, among other things, **invented the computer, the refrigerator, the electric motor, the stethoscope, rayon, the steam turbine, stainless steel, the tank, television, penicillin, radar, the jet engine, hovercraft, float glass, carbon fibres, et cetera – and the best half of Concorde.**
(Margaret Thatcher, Blackpool, 10.10.75)

Extract 4
We are **both humbled and elevated** by the honour and privilege that you, the people of South Africa, have bestowed on us, as the first president of a united, democratic, **non-racial and non-sexist** South Africa, **to lead our country out of the valley of darkness**. We understand it still that **there is no easy road to freedom**. We know it well that none of us **acting alone** can achieve success. We must therefore **act together** as a united people, **for national reconciliation, for nation building, for the birth of a new world. Let there be** justice **for all. Let there be** peace **for all. Let there be** work, bread, water and salt **for all. Let each know that for each the body, the mind and the soul** have been **freed to fulfil** themselves. **Never, never and never again** shall it be that this beautiful land will **again** experience the oppression of one by another …
(Nelson Mandela, Pretoria, 10.5.94)

Presence and performance

1 For many people the magic ingredient great presenters have is charisma. What's the equivalent word in your language?

2 ▮ **13.2** Listen to extracts from four famous political speeches. Rank them in order of how charismatic they sound. Compare with a partner.

Extract 1 ☐   Extract 2 ☐   Extract 3 ☐   Extract 4 ☐

3 Can you remember the following extracts from the speeches?

Extract 1

a I d_o___ n_ot___ shrink from this responsibility – I wel _come___ it.

b I do not believe that a_ny___ of us would ex _change__ places with a_ny___ other people or a_ny___ other generation.

c The en_ergy___, the faith, the devotion, which we bring to this endeavour will li_ght___ our country and all who serve it.

d And so, my fellow Americans, a_sk___ n_ot___ what your co_untry___ can do for you – a_sk___ what you can do for your co_untry___.

Extract 2

a I st_ill___ have a dr_eam___. It is a dr_eam___ deeply rooted in the Am_erican___ dr_eam___.

b I have a dr_eam___ that one day on the red hills of Georgia the sons of form_er___ slaves and the sons of form_er___ slave owners will be able to sit down tog_ether___ at the table of bro_therhood_.

c I have a dr_eam___ that my four little ch_ildren___ will one day live in a na_tion___ where they will not be judged by the col_our___ of their skin but by the content of their char_acter___. I have a dream today.

Extract 3

a What are our chances of su_ccess___? It depends on what kind of pe_ople___ we are.

b What kind of pe_ople___ are we? We are the pe_ople___ that in the past made Great Br_itain__ the workshop of the wo_rld___.

c … the people who pers_uaded__ others to buy Br_itish___, not by begging them to do so, but because it was be_st___.

Copyright Margaret Thatcher. Reproduced with permission from the official website of the Margaret Thatcher Foundation, margaretthatcher.org

Extract 4

a We und_erstand_ it still that there is no easy road to fre_edom___. We know it well that none of us acting al_one___ can achi_eve___ success.

b Let ea_ch___ know that for ea_ch___ the body, the mi_nd___ and the soul___ have been fr_eed___ to fulfil themselves.

c Ne_ver___, ne_ver___ and ne_ver___ again shall it be that this bea_utiful__ land will again experience the opp_ression__ of one by another.

Rhetoric **4** The speakers in 2 used a number of rhetorical techniques. The main ones are listed below. Complete them using the words in the box.

> questions   language   words   threes   points   sounds   opposites

The **seven rules** of rhetoric

1 **Repeat** words
I still have a dream. It is a dream deeply rooted in the American dream.

2 **Repeat** sounds
We are the people ... who persuaded others to buy British, not by begging them to do so, but because it was best.

3 **Use contrasts and** opposites
Ask not what your country can do for you – ask what you can do for your country.

4 **Group key points in** threes
We must therefore act together as a united people, for national reconciliation, for nation building, for the birth of a new world.

5 **Ask rhetorical** questions
What are our chances of success? It depends on what kind of people we are.

6 **Accumulate supporting** points
We are the people who, amongst other things, invented the computer, the refrigerator, the electric motor, the stethoscope, rayon, the steam turbine, stainless steel, the tank ...

7 **Use metaphorical** language
To lead our country out of the valley of darkness.

Lexis link

for more on metaphor
see page 119

5 Look back at the extracts in 3 and find more examples of the rhetorical techniques listed in 4.

6 🔲 13.3 Look at the following extracts from ineffective business presentations and rephrase them to give them more impact. Then listen and check.

a Cash flow is the main problem we're facing.
What's the main problem we're facing? The main problem is cash flow.

b It's critical to our success, even though it's so risky and problematic.
It's so risky, so problematic, and yet so critical to our success.

c It's faster, cheaper, more reliable – that's the most important thing – and easier to use.
It's faster, cheaper and easier to use. But, above all, it's more reliable.

d We can still be the best, but we can't ever be the biggest again.
Even if we can never again be the biggest, we can still be the best.

e Fewer jobs are being fought over by more graduates, that's the point.
The point is, more and more graduates are fighting over fewer and fewer jobs.

Rhetoric

4 Check comprehension of the word *rhetoric* (language/ techniques used to create a powerful or dramatic effect). Elicit examples of rhetorical techniques students are familiar with e.g. repetition of sounds/words/phrases. Check/Pre-teach: to *accumulate, metaphorical*. Get students to complete the rules of rhetoric and then check the answers.

5 Refer students back to exercise 3 and get students to find more examples of rhetoric, working in pairs. Check the answers with the class.

Answers

> **Extract 1**
>
> a contrast; b repetition (words), group of three; c group of three, metaphor; d contrast, repetition (words), repetition (sounds)
>
> **Extract 2**
>
> a repetition (words), metaphor, repetition (sounds); b repetition (words), repetition (sounds), metaphor; c contrast, repetition (sounds)

> **Extract 3**
>
> a rhetorical question; b rhetorical question, repetition (words), repetition (sounds); c contrast, repetition (sounds)
>
> **Extract 4**
>
> a metaphor, repetition (sounds); b repetition (words), repetition (sounds), group of three; c repetition (words), group of three

As an optional follow-up task, refer students to the recording scripts on pages 153–4 where the rhetorical techniques are highlighted in bold. Get students to choose a speech and practise delivering it for dramatic effect.

Direct students' attention to the Lexis link on page 119 for more practice on metaphor.

6 🔊 **13.3** Get students to rephrase the extracts and then play the recording so they can check their answers.

🔊 **13.3**

a
What's the main problem we're facing? The main problem is cash flow.

b
It's so risky, so problematic, and yet so critical to our success.

c
It's faster, cheaper and easier to use. But, above all, it's more reliable.

d
Even if we can never again be the biggest, we can still be the best.

e
The point is, more and more graduates are fighting over fewer and fewer jobs.

f
Not only are we number one in Brazil. We're now number one in Latin America.

g
In this market, no company has outperformed us, not one – ever!

h
Not once, in over thirty years of business, have we ever had a complaint – not a single one!

7 Check students can define *clause* (a group of words with a subject and verb). Ask students to analyse the word order and then check the answer with the class. Ask students if this technique of switching word order can be used in their language.

8 With weaker classes, model one or two examples first, highlighting the stressed words and intonation. Divide the class into pairs/small groups and get students to deliver the extracts. If possible, record the students and play back the recording, getting students to assess the delivery and how to improve on it.

Direct students' attention to the Grammar link on page 118 for more information and practice on rhetorical techniques.

Closing

9 🔲 **13.4** As a lead-in, ask students which they remember most: the opening or closing of a presentation. Elicit examples of memorable closing remarks/techniques that they have seen or used themselves e.g. using a quotation.

With weaker groups, check/pre-teach: *on the brink of, nonsense, gene therapy, handout, reputation, to diminish, ironic, to sum up, to do something justice, masterpiece*. Play the recording and let students number the techniques in the order they hear them. Check the answers and elicit the key words/phrases that helped students decide on the order.

10 Tell students that they will now have a chance to practise closing a presentation. Refer students to the templates a–c and check comprehension of *threshold*. Then get them to select one and to think of how to apply it to a presentation they have given in the past, or may need to deliver in the future. If students are short of ideas, elicit examples e.g. a sales presentation on a product, a welcome speech to new employees, a merger announcement etc.

Give students time to prepare the closing remarks and to rehearse the delivery. Monitor and help as necessary. Students deliver their closing to the rest of the class. Hold a short feedback session, encouraging students to comment constructively on each other's delivery and impact.

🔲 **13.4**

1
Ladies and gentlemen, we are truly on the brink of a revolution in bio-technology. **I'm reminded of the words of** futurist and science fiction writer Arthur C. Clarke: 'People go through four stages,' he said, 'before any revolutionary development. Stage one: it's nonsense, don't waste my time. Stage two: it's interesting, but not important. Stage three: I always said it was a good idea. And stage four: I thought of it first.' In gene therapy we're about to enter stage four. **And I'd like this company to honestly be able to say** 'We thought of it first.' Thank you.

2
Uh-oh. Sorry. Looks like we've run out of time. Erm, so I'm going to have to cut it short. Er, yeah, I was hoping to show you some of the figures in our comparative study. But, erm, never mind. I think you'll find all the main points are covered in the handout. So I'll, er, I'll just leave copies here and you can pick one up on your way out. OK. So, sorry about that. That's it. Thanks.

3
Well, that just about brings me to the end of my presentation, except to say that the future of this company is now in your hands. For **if there's one central message I'd like to get across to you this morning it's this**: that this consultancy is no more and no less than the consultants who represent it. And whilst our reputation as a firm may have been damaged by the recent unfortunate events, our expertise as a team is in no way diminished. I want to see each and every one of you raising this company to new heights. I know you can. We built our reputation on crisis management, and it would be ironic indeed if we were unable to successfully manage this crisis of our own – and come out on top. Thank you very much.

4
So, how do you sum up the new Spearing Silhouette ocean cruiser? **I could tell you that** it has won just about every boat show in the USA and Europe this year, that the orders for it are coming in so fast we already have a five-year waiting list; that the first three names on that waiting list, though strictly confidential, include a famous Hollywood actor, a member of the Saudi Royal Family and one of the world's greatest sporting legends. **I could also mention that**, so impressed are they with our award-winning design, the directors of the Museum of Modern Art are actually proposing to place a full-size model on permanent exhibition. **But all that would fail to do it justice. For the fact is** that the Silhouette is in a class of its own. It is a masterpiece of marine engineering. **It is, quite simply**, the most stunningly beautiful boat ever built. Ladies and gentlemen, I give you … the Spearing Silhouette!

f We're number one in Latin America now, not just Brazil.

Not <u>only</u> <u>are</u> we number one in Brazil. We're <u>now</u> <u>number</u> <u>one</u> in Latin America.

g There isn't a company that's ever outperformed us in this market.

In this <u>market</u>, no <u>company</u> has <u>outperformed</u> us, not <u>one</u> – <u>ever</u>!

h We've had no complaints in over thirty years of business.

Not <u>once</u>, in over <u>thirty</u> <u>years</u> <u>of</u> <u>business</u>, have <u>we</u> <u>ever</u> had a complaint – not a <u>single</u> <u>one</u>!

7 Look carefully at word order and the order of clauses in the rephrased extracts in 6. What information tends to come last? <u>The most important words usually come at the end of clauses and the most important clause at the end of the sentence.</u>

Grammar link

for more on rhetorical techniques see page 118

8 Practise delivering the rephrased extracts to make as big an impact as possible.

Closing

9 🔲 13.4 The last few minutes of a presentation are your final chance to make a lasting impression. Listen to the closing remarks of four presentations and number the techniques in the order you hear them. Which is the most effective?

the sum up 4   the call to action 3   the famous quotation 1
the emergency stop 2

10 Choose one of the closes below and use it as the basis for closing a presentation you have given in the past or may give in the future.

a Ladies and gentlemen, we are on the brink/threshold of … I'm reminded of the words of …, who said … And I'd like this company/this department/us to be able to say …

b Well, that just about brings me to the end of my presentation, except to say … And if there's one central message I'd like to get across to you this morning/afternoon/evening, it's this …

c So, how do you sum up …? I could tell you that …, that … and that … I could also mention … But all that would fail to do it justice. For the fact is, that … It is, quite simply, …

The last paradise on earth?

1 If you wanted to escape from it all for a while, where would you go?

2 Read the article and information on Bhutan. Does it sound like your idea of paradise?

Gross national happiness

'Gross national happiness is more important than gross national product.' That's the official government policy of King Jigme Singye Wangchuck of Bhutan, ruler of what some have called 'the last paradise on earth'. Indeed, his programme of careful
5 economic development and gradual change has so far ensured that Bhutan, completely isolated from the rest of the world until 1961, has managed to balance the need to progress into the 21st century with the need to preserve its cultural heritage. But there's trouble in paradise.

Tiny Bhutan lies in the Himalayas, squeezed between the world's two
10 most densely populated countries, China and India. Roughly the same size as Switzerland, Bhutan is a country of dense forest and breathtaking mountain ranges – at 22,623 feet, Gangkhar Puensum is the highest unclimbed peak in the world. This haven of peace and natural beauty is home to a multitude of exotic wildlife, including the endangered red
15 panda and almost mythical snow leopard. Brightly coloured prayer flags fly from every hillside. The people here follow the Buddhist Middle Way, a philosophy based on pacifism, paternalism and egalitarianism. Time itself is measured differently in Bhutan – not in hours and minutes, but in *kalpas*, a unit of time equivalent to several million years.
20 At least, that's how it used to be. For now technology has finally come to this remote farming community. Foreign investment has helped build up the country's infrastructure, improve health and education and create a growing tourist industry. Cybercafés have opened in the capital, Thimphu, and the television aerials rising from the rooftops may soon outnumber
25 the prayer flags. But the traditional way of life, upon which so much of Bhutan's 'national happiness' has depended, is under threat.

In 1998 the king of Bhutan decentralised power and appointed a central cabinet. The country now has a seat at the UN. But the Bhutanese themselves seem divided over their country's future. Should they continue
30 to reap the many benefits progress has already brought or try to regulate the accelerating pace of change while there's still time?

- **Location** SE Asia
- **Area** 47,000 square km
- **Capital** Thimphu
- **Population** 657,000
- **Population density** 14.1 people per square km
- **Industry** farming, forestry, timber, limestone, food processing, chemicals, cement, hydroelectric power, tourism
- **GDP** US$2.1bn
- **GDP per capita** US$1,060
- **Inflation** 9%
- **Economic growth** 7%
- **National languages** Dzongkha (official), Nepali, English
- **Currency** ngultrum (Nu) of 100 chetrums, US$1 = Nu42.85

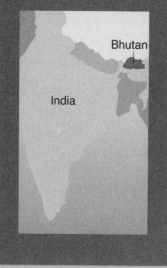

3 Work in two groups. Group A is the Bhutanese Preservation Party (BPP) and Group B the Progress Party of Bhutan (PPB). Read the introduction to your party's manifesto opposite.

The last paradise on earth?

In the last section of this unit, the students take part in a fluency task in which they prepare and deliver parts of a party political broadcast designed to win over potential voters to a cause. This task could be done as a team-teaching session, bringing two classes together.

1   As a lead-in to the task, ask students to write down where in the world they would go to escape from it all. Tell the students to stand up and mingle to find a partner or partners who want to go to the same destination. Accept close geographical areas as a pairing e.g. a trip to Australia and New Zealand. Get students to sit with their new partner(s). Elicit the chosen destinations from each pair/group.

2   Before students read the text, write *Bhutan* on the board and ask the class if they know exactly where it is. Get students to brainstorm what they know about the country, what they think they know, and what they would like to know. Write the information and questions in three columns on the board.

With weaker classes, check/pre-teach: *heritage, breathtaking, peak, haven, prayer flags, pacifism, paternalism, egalitarianism, endangered, infrastructure, to reap benefits, pace of change*. Get students to read the text quickly and check if the text answers their questions on the board. If not, remind students they can search the Internet and look for anything that remained unanswered. Find out which students think Bhutan sounds like paradise.

3   Divide the students into AB groups. Check pronunciation of the abbreviations of the names of the parties – BPP and PPB – in particular with students who have difficulty in distinguishing /p/ and /b/. Check/Pre-teach: *manifesto, steeped in, in harmony with, excess, to envy, to stand still, the reverse, priceless, prosperity*. Offer help with the pronunciation of some of the proper nouns in the text e.g. *Druk Yul, Jigme Singye Wangchuck.*

Fluency

4   Check/Pre-teach: *life expectancy, infant mortality, literacy, irreparably, flora and fauna, virgin forest, indigenous, sacred, to disturb, spirits, quota, worship, karma, malnourished, counter-productive, ecological.*

Refer group A to page 136 and group B to page 138 to read their specific brief. Students use the four headings in their brief to make notes on facts and key language for each section of their broadcast. With larger groups, suggest that students divide up to prepare one section each. Remind students they have ten minutes for their broadcast and so need to divide up the information across the time available. Get students to decide which rhetorical techniques they want to use for the key points in their speech. Refer students back to page 70 for the list of techniques, but remind them not to use too many and not to repeat the same one throughout the speech. Monitor and help as necessary throughout the preparation stage. If appropriate, get students to create posters and/or rosettes for their party.

Give students time to rehearse the delivery and timing of the speech. Have students choose a representative to deliver the speech and set up the room to allow students to address the audience. It is preferable to record the broadcasts on video for authenticity and to allow reviewing of students' performance. Alternatively, use audio to record the students. Monitor and take feedback notes.

As a follow-up, hold a discussion/debate on some of the points arising from the speeches. Select issues to vote on as a whole class and write up these on the board. Possible topics include: 'The forests and mountains of Bhutan should be open to tourists.' 'Internet access should be restricted.'

Ask students to decide which party gave the most persuasive performance and who people would be most likely to vote for. With a large enough group, set up a formal voting stage, where students can't vote for their own party. Reveal the votes one by one to create more suspense, rather than simply announce the final result. If possible, play the speeches to another group as a viewing/listening activity and get them to vote. Give feedback on students' use of rhetoric and on overall fluency before highlighting important or common errors.

If you're short of time

Omit exercises 3–5 on page 68.

Omit exercise 10 on page 71.

Get students to prepare for the fluency task on page 73 by doing exercises 1–3 on page 72 and reading the role cards from exercise 4 on page 73 at home.

Bhutanese Preservation Party

To the outside world we are Bhutan, a tiny Himalayan kingdom of scenic beauty and scientific interest, but little economic importance. But in our own ancient language we are Druk Yul, 'the Land of the Thunder Dragon', a land steeped in history and legend.

We in the BPP have never stood in the way of progress, so long as it is in harmony with the natural order and cultural traditions of our country. But we believe it is essential to protect the unique way of life we have enjoyed for over a thousand years from the worst excesses of the 21st century.

Will you join us in our campaign to preserve those qualities the rest of the world most envies about Bhutan – its simplicity, its tranquillity and the contentment of its people? Vote BPP.

Progress Party of Bhutan

For over a thousand years Bhutan has stood still. But the rest of the world has not. King Jigme Singye Wangchuck himself has said: 'Change is coming' and there is nothing in the teachings of the Buddha that tells us to resist change – rather the reverse. Change is not to be resisted, but to be embraced. It is time to end centuries of isolation and poverty.

The PPB has no wish to damage either our environment or our rich cultural traditions. Indeed, these priceless treasures are the basis on which we seek to build a better future for Bhutan.

Support our programme of culturally sensitive and environmentally aware development, and provide your children and your children's children with the opportunity and prosperity they deserve. Vote PPB.

Fluency   4   Work in your group to produce a ten-minute party political broadcast to the people of Bhutan. To help you prepare, Group A see page 136 and Group B see page 138. Use the rhetorical techniques you have studied to add impact to your speech. Your aim is to determine the future of what may well be 'the last paradise on earth'.

14 Out and about

Take a little of home with you, and leave a little of yourself at home.
Mark McCormack, founder of IMG sports agency

Discussion

1 When packing to go on a business trip, apart from your travel documents, what are the absolute essentials? A good book? Swimming things? A decent hairdryer? An air pillow? Compare with a partner.

2 In the film *The Accidental Tourist*, travel guidebook writer Macon Leary gives advice on how to pack for a trip. Read the extract and discuss the questions.

THE BUSINESS Traveller

From The Accidental Tourist

'The business traveller should bring only what fits in a carry-on bag. Checking your luggage is asking for trouble. Add several travel-size packets of detergent, so you won't fall into the hands of unfamiliar laundries. There are very few necessities in this world
5 which do not come in travel-size packets.

'One suit is plenty if you take along travel-size packets of spot remover. The suit should be medium-grey. Grey not only hides the dirt, but is handy for sudden funerals.

'Always bring a book as protection against strangers.
10 Magazines don't last and newspapers from elsewhere remind you you don't belong. But don't take more than one book. It is a common mistake to overestimate one's potential free time and consequently overpack. In travel, as in most of life, less is invariably more.

'And most importantly, never take along anything on your journey so valuable or dear that its loss would devastate you.'

a Do you tend to travel light or do you bring along everything but the kitchen sink?

b Have you ever had any bad experiences with lost luggage or hotel laundries?

c Is grey your colour? Are you a practical or power dresser?

d What's the best way of avoiding unwanted conversations with strangers?

e Is it important to allow yourself some free time on a business trip?

f Have you ever lost something valuable on a journey? Tell the story.

3 What kind of person is Macon Leary? Tick the correct answers. Would you want to sit next to him on a flight? *(author's suggestions)*

sociable ☐ outgoing ☐ lonely ☐ private ☑ sarcastic ☐
practical ☐ dull ☐ fussy ☑ witty ☑ gloomy ☑ bitter ☐
well organised ☑ antisocial ☑ overserious ☐ a bit paranoid ☑

Networking # 14 Out and about

This unit is about business travel. Students work on fluency and communication skills and practise telling anecdotes.

Two extracts from a film, *The Accidental Tourist*, set the scene for a discussion on travel. The students focus on ellipsis, the omission of certain words by native speakers, which frequently occurs in conversational English. They also focus on a range of expressions useful for striking up a conversation, and then roleplay conversations to practise using these techniques and expressions.

Students listen to a series of travellers' stories. They review narrative tenses and then go on to tell their own story or anecdote.

In the last section, two short texts provide a stimulus for discussion about business lunches. A recording of business people in a restaurant moving from one topic of conversation to another over dinner provides listening practice. Finally, the students take part in a roleplay set in a restaurant and discuss a variety of topics as they aim to keep a conversation going.

The grammatical focus is on narrative tenses and the lexical focus is on the language of storytelling.

In the first section, students decide which items are essential to take with them when travelling. An extract from the film, *The Accidental Tourist*, provides an introduction to the topic of business travel. Students identify difficult passenger types and then discuss a second extract from the same film. An exercise raises awareness of ellipsis, a key feature of native-speaker speech, which can be quite challenging for students. The students study different ways of starting up a conversation with a stranger, before roleplaying short conversations with fellow travellers on a plane.

Warm-up

Check which students make frequent business trips. Elicit students' general opinions of business travel and if there is a particularly popular destination. Ask students to read the quotation by Mark McCormack. Elicit possible interpretations e.g. you can beat homesickness by keeping home in mind.

Discussion

1 Divide the class into pairs and give students two minutes to brainstorm a list of essential travel items. Elicit examples and find out the strangest objects students take when travelling.

2 Lead in to the text by writing the following prompts on the board and asking students what they would pack for a five-day business trip: *number of travel bags, number of suits, number of books/magazines.*

Get students to read the text quickly and compare what they would pack with the advice given in the text. Check/Pre-teach: *detergent, laundry, spot remover, handy, devastate, everything but the kitchen sink.* Students read the text again and answer the questions a–f in pairs/small groups. Hold a short feedback session, eliciting interesting/funny anecdotes for questions b and f, and the best advice for question d.

Ask students to describe the tone and register of the text (humorous and ironic) and to give examples of how the writer achieves this e.g. *you won't fall into the hands of unfamiliar laundries, grey … is handy for sudden funerals, always bring a book as protection against strangers.*

3 Check/Pre-teach: *sarcastic, fussy, witty, bitter, paranoid.* Ask students to choose the relevant adjectives, giving reasons for their answers and referring back to the text where relevant. Ask if they would welcome Leary as a fellow passenger on a flight.

Discussion

4 Elicit examples of what irritates students most about their fellow passengers on flights. Focus attention on the example and ask students to match the rest of the passengers types and descriptions. Encourage them to deduce the meaning of any new words from context e.g. *to sprawl, to smooch, to giggle*. Get students to check their answers in pairs and then check the answers with the whole class. Hold a class vote for the two least popular types of passenger, then elicit if any of the class are guilty of similar behaviour.

5 Draw students' attention to the glossary entries. Tell students to read the text quickly in order to find the coincidence. Ask them to read the extract again and say what passenger type in exercise 4 Loomis corresponds to (the chatterer). Also elicit the difference in attitude and tone between the two men (Leary is characteristically non-committal, while Loomis is enthusiastic and complimentary).

6 Refer students back to the text and ask them to scan the conversation to find the correct expressions. Check the answers.

As an optional follow-up activity with groups that are keen on drama and roleplays, get pairs of students to act out the dialogue. First, check the pronunciation of the people and place names. Be ready to model the intonation and help students deliver the characters' lines to reflect their attitude to each other. If available, you could also play the relevant extracts from a video/DVD of *The Accidental Tourist*.

Conversational English

7 Focus on the first sentence as an example with the whole class. Elicit both the word that is missing (*The*) and the type of word (article). If appropriate, introduce *ellipsis* as the term for the omission of words such as subjects, auxiliaries and articles.

Discussion

4 Do any of following passenger types sound familiar? Match them to their typical behaviour. Which two would you least like to sit next to on a long-haul flight?

> **Space invaders ...**
>
> | | | | |
> |---|---|---|---|
> | **a** | the sprawler | **1** | wants to tell you their life story from the very beginning; may bring out family photos |
> | **b** | the bawler | | |
> | **c** | the discman | **2** | will smooch and giggle throughout the flight: two's company, three's a crowd |
> | **d** | the workaholic | | |
> | **e** | the chatterer | **3** | spends the entire journey glued to their laptop, spreadsheets scattered everywhere |
> | **f** | the sleeper | | |
> | **g** | the lovebirds | **4** | quiet at first, but may end up snoring like a bull elephant with their head on your shoulder |
> | | | **5** | under five years old, but can make a sound like a police siren for hours on end; may be sick |
> | | | **6** | bobs their head around to mindless music so loud that you can hear it through their headphones |
> | | | **7** | would be much happier on a sofa since they seem to need your seat as well as their own |

a	b	c	d	e	f	g
7	5	6	3	1	4	2

5 Read the following extract from *The Accidental Tourist*, where Macon Leary finds himself sitting next to an overweight man on a plane. What coincidence links the two men? <u>Loomis has read and is a fan of Leary's book.</u>

From The Accidental Tourist

Traveller: I'm sorry I'm so fat. *Name's Lucas Loomis.*

Leary: Macon Leary.

Traveller: *You a Baltimore man?*

Leary: Yes.

Traveller: Me too. *Greatest city on the earth.* One of these seats is not really enough for me. And the stupid thing is, I travel for a living. I demonstrate software to computer stores. What do you do, Mr Leary?

Leary: I write travel guidebooks.

Traveller: Is that so? What kind?

Leary: Well, guides for businessmen – people just like you, I guess.

Traveller: 'Accidental Tourist'!

Leary: Why, yes.

Traveller: Really? Am I right? Well, what do you know? Look at this. Gray suit – just what you recommend, appropriate for all occasions. *See my luggage?* Carry-on. Change of underwear. Clean shirt. Packet of detergent powder.

Leary: Oh, good.

Traveller: You're my hero. You've improved my trips a hundred per cent. I tell my wife, going with The Accidental Tourist is like going in a cocoon.

Leary: Well, this is very nice to hear.

Traveller: *Times I've flown clear to Oregon and hardly knew I'd left Baltimore.*

Leary: Excellent.

Traveller: I see you have your book for protection there. *Didn't work with me, though, did it?*

Glossary

cocoon warm, safe place
You're my hero I really admire you/your work

6 Find expressions in the conversation which mean:

a That's interesting. <u>Is that so?</u>

b I suppose. <u>I guess.</u>

c How did you know that? <u>Why, yes.</u>

d What a coincidence! <u>Well, what do you know?</u>

Conversational English

7 In natural conversation certain words are sometimes omitted. Look at the sentences in *italics* in 5 and decide which three types of word are missing.

<u>pronouns</u>, <u>articles</u>, <u>auxiliary verbs/verb 'to be'</u>

8 The following things were said at different times during a business trip. Delete any unnecessary words to make them more conversational.

a A: ~~Is~~ everything OK with your meal, sir?

B: ~~It's~~ delicious. ~~It~~ couldn't be better.

b A: ~~Do you~~ need anything else, sir?

B: ~~I~~ don't think so, thanks.

c A: ~~I~~ like your laptop. ~~It's a~~ Sony, isn't it?

B: Yeah. ~~I~~ haven't quite got used to it yet.

d A: ~~Are you~~ ready to start?

B: Yeah, ~~I'm~~ just coming.

e A: ~~Do you~~ mind if I switch the reading light on?

B: ~~It~~ doesn't bother me. ~~I~~ think I'll get another coffee. ~~Do you~~ want one?

f A: ~~I~~ saw you earlier in the fitness centre. ~~Have you~~ been here long?

B: ~~No, I~~ just got here yesterday. ~~Are~~ you here on business too?

g A: ~~Have you~~ got a light?

B: Sorry, ~~I~~ don't smoke.

Striking up a conversation

9 What are the advantages of having someone to chat to on a long journey? Do you find it easy to start conversations with people you don't know?

10 The most common ways of starting a conversation with a stranger are:

a make an observation
b pay a compliment
c make a request
d ask for information
e offer assistance
f make an apology

Categorise the following conversation starters by writing **a**, **b**, **c**, **d**, **e** or **f** in the boxes.

You couldn't help me with my bag, **could you?** `c`

Do you mind swapping seats? `c`

Looks like we're in for a bit of turbulence, doesn't it? `a`

Sorry about my kids. **Let me know if** they're bothering you. `f`

I couldn't help noticing you speak Dutch. `a`

Do you think I could borrow your paper if you've finished with it? `c`

Is this row 17, **do you know?** `d`

I like your PalmPilot. **Is that one of the new ones?** `b`

Let me help you with that. `e`

I'll get someone to come and help you. `e`

I see you're flying on to Caracas. `a`

Nice camera. **I used to have one like that**. `b`

I'm sorry, is that getting in your way? `f`

Are you from Lima, **by any chance?** `d`

Fluency

11 Work with a partner to practise holding short conversations with fellow passengers on planes. Speaker A see page 136. Speaker B see page 138.

8 Students work individually to delete the unnecessary words in the dialogues before checking with a partner. Then check the answers with the whole class.

Striking up a conversation

9 Elicit any advantages of striking up a conversation with strangers e.g. it helps to pass the time, a fellow traveller may be able to provide practical and even business information about the destination etc. Ask students how they feel about starting up conversations with strangers.

10 Students work individually to categorise the sentences. Then check the answers. Point out that the useful language in the exercise is shown in bold. Practise the pronunciation of the sentences, getting students to underline the stressed words and mark in the intonation pattern with arrows.

Fluency

11 Check/Pre-teach: *hyperactive, the red-eye* (a plane that flies during the night), *bumpy, casting meeting, to skip dinner, there goes (your relaxing flight), turbulence*. Divide the class into AB pairs and refer the A students to page 136 and the B students to page 138. Give students time to read and take notes on their roles and prepare for each of the conversations in turn. Remind them to choose a suitable opener for each conversation from exercise 10.

Rearrange the chairs in the same position as airline seating. Tell students that they should try to keep each conversation going for a minute or two and that you will indicate when to move on by clapping your hands. With weaker classes, model one of the roleplays with a strong student first. Monitor and take feedback notes while students roleplay the conversations.

When students have finished, elicit feedback from each pair on the outcome of their conversations. Elicit from students how easy or difficult it was to get started and to keep the conversation going. Give feedback on how well students handled starting the conversation and on overall fluency, before highlighting important or common errors.

Travellers' tales

In this section, students listen to four travellers telling stories about strange events which happened on flights and then focus on the use of narrative tenses in telling stories/anecdotes. Students put storytelling expressions into a logical order and match active listening expressions to prepare them for telling their own story or anecdote.

1 ▣ **14.1** Elicit examples of strange/frightening experiences students have had when flying. Check/Pre-teach: *runway, hammering* (noise), *fuselage, lifejacket drill, to divert, to not have a clue about something, nuisance.*

Before students listen, get them to read questions a–f and predict the possible answers. Write up students' ideas on the board. Play the recording through once and get students to check their predictions. Establish how many of the events they predicted correctly.

Play the recording a second time, pausing between each speaker, in order for students to complete their answers. Check the answers with the class.

In order to exploit the recordings further, play the recording a third time and get students to make notes on some of the details e.g. where the speaker was flying from/to, how the speaker and other people felt, what the outcome of the story was etc. Divide the class into two or more groups and ask students to use their notes to write two further questions from each recording for the other group(s). Students then cross-group to ask and answer their questions.

Narrative tenses

2 Students work individually to complete the exercise and then check their answers in pairs. Encourage students to say why they chose each tense. Check the answers with

See page T78 for extract 4.

the whole class, either by playing the relevant extract from the recording or getting students to check the recording script on page 154.

3 Tell students only to count the correct answers in exercise 2. Check the number of uses of each tense and elicit examples from the recording (see Answers below). Ask students to explain the use of tenses and if necessary give a remedial presentation, referring students to the summary of narrative tenses in the Grammar link on page 120.

Answers

> past simple: said, went, opened, happened, got, didn't
>
> past continuous: were starting, was going
>
> past perfect simple: they'd locked
>
> past perfect continuous: we'd been sitting

Direct students' attention to the Grammar link on page 120 for more information and practice on narrative tenses.

Telling anecdotes

4 Tell students a business anecdote. (One, which is sometimes told on time management seminars, involves a workaholic who has a heart attack, but is alone in the office late at night, so cannot be helped. Point out that there is a moral to the type of story.) Give students a few moments to think of an anecdote from the business world and elicit examples. Then ask the students to read the quotation by David Weinberger and ask if they agree. Elicit how useful students think stories are in business and if they have to be true. Ask students for examples of people, privately or professionally, who are able to tell a good story and if they see themselves as good storytellers.

▣ **14.1**

1: Emma
A: So Emma, what's your worst flying experience?
B: Well, I think the worst one's probably flying back from Bangladesh to Heathrow. **It's quite a few years ago now, but I can still remember it.** We were at the gate, ready to taxi to the runway, and suddenly there was this terrible hammering noise from outside the plane.
A: A hammering noise?
B: Yeah, **and the strange thing was** that the cabin crew just seemed to be ignoring it. But all you could hear was this bang, bang, bang on the fuselage. After a while, some of the passengers were starting to get nervous, me included.
A: **I'm not surprised.**
B: Anyway, eventually, after we'd been sitting there for about ten minutes with no announcement and the plane still not moving, I said something to one of the stewards and they went and opened the door to see what was going on.
A: And what happened?
B: The pilot got in!
A: **You're joking!**
B: No, they'd locked him out. **Seems quite funny now, but it didn't at the time.**

2: Enrique
A: Enrique, what's the worst flight you've ever been on?
C: Definitely the time I was flying from Malaga to Stansted in the UK. **This was around the time of** the terrible attack on the World Trade Center in 2001 and people were still very nervous about flying.
A: Oh, yes, of course.
C: I was travelling on business, but most of the passengers were British tourists.
A: Uh huh.
C: Anyway, we were cruising at 30,000 feet and I looked out of the window and saw this French air force fighter plane flying alongside us.
A: What? **Oh, yes, I read about this.** Didn't they think the plane had been hijacked or something?
C: Well, apparently, air traffic control had lost radio contact with our plane, so they weren't sure what was going on and they weren't taking any chances. I mean this French jet was armed with missiles and everything.
A: **Sounds terrifying!**
C: It was.
A: **So, what happened?**
C: Well, the jet was there for about ten minutes checking us out. Fortunately, the captain of our plane managed to keep everybody calm. **And anyway, to cut a**

long story short, everything turned out OK. We even landed on schedule!
A: But I bet you were glad to be back on the ground, weren't you?
C: You can say that again!

3: Joe
A: Joe, have you had any bad experiences on planes?
D: Oh, yes, several. One flight I was on, I couldn't understand why they were making us go through the lifejacket drill for landing on water.
A: But don't they always do that?
D: What, on a domestic flight from Manchester to London?
A: Oh, right. **I see what you mean.**
D: I'm not sure which flight path they were planning to take but it goes nowhere near the sea. **But that's nothing compared to** one of my recent trips to Frankfurt.
A: What happened there, then?
D: Well, we didn't land in Frankfurt.
A: You were diverted?
D: No, no, the pilot just landed in completely the wrong country!
A: What, you mean he didn't know?
D: Hadn't got a clue. Just about everybody on the plane was looking out the windows and saying 'Er, look, I'm sorry to be a nuisance, but this isn't Frankfurt.'
A: So where *did* you land?
D: Luxembourg.
A: **Oh, my god! I don't believe it!**

Travellers' tales

1 ▣ **14.1** Listen to four business people talking about their worst flying experiences and answer the questions.

   a What was all the noise about on Emma's flight?

     <u>*The pilot was hammering on the fuselage to get in the plane.*</u>

   b How might Enrique's flight have ended in disaster?

     <u>*The air force jet might have shot them down.*</u>

   c What surprised Joe on his flight to London?

     <u>*They did the lifejacket drill even though they weren't flying over water.*</u>

   d Who got lost on Joe's flight to Frankfurt?

     <u>*the pilot*</u>

   e What was the strange request on Selina's flight in Asia?

     <u>*She was asked to sit in the toilet during take-off.*</u>

   f How did the Nigerian army solve the overbooking problem?

     <u>*They asked passengers to run round the aircraft twice: the fastest runners got seats on the flight.*</u>

Narrative tenses

2 Read this extract from the first conversation and underline the best grammatical choice.

   B: After a while, some of the passengers **were starting**/had been starting to get nervous, me included!

   A: I'm not surprised.

   B: Anyway, eventually, after were sitting/**we'd been sitting** there for about ten minutes with no announcement and the plane still not moving, **I said**/I'd said something to one of the stewards and they **went**/were going and **opened**/were opening the door to see what went/**was going** on.

   A: And what **happened**/had been happening?

   B: The pilot **got**/had got in!

   A: You're joking!

   B: No, **they'd locked**/they'd been locking him out. Seems quite funny now, but it **didn't**/wasn't doing at the time.

Grammar link

for more on narrative tenses see page 120

3 In the extract in 2 how many examples can you find of the:

   past simple? ⬚6   past perfect simple? ⬚1

   past continuous? ⬚2   past perfect continuous? ⬚1

Telling anecdotes

4 According to publisher David Weinberger, 'We live stories; we breathe stories; most of our best conversations are about stories.' How useful is it in business to be able to tell a good story? Do you agree that the best ones are usually true?

5 Listed below are the typical stages in a story or anecdote. Add the expressions in the box to the correct place in the list. They were all in the conversations in 1.

> And the strange thing was ...   I ended up ...
> And then, to top it all, ...   Did I ever tell you about the time I was ...?
> Way back in (*1985*) it was.   But that was nothing compared to ...
> Anyway, to cut a long story short, ...   This was around the time of ...
> Seems quite funny now, but it didn't at the time.

Opener   I'll never forget the time I was ...
  Did I ever tell you about the time I was ...?

Context   It's quite a few years ago now, but I can still remember it.
  Way back in (1985) it was.
  This was around the time of ...

Emphasis   You're not going to believe this, but ...   You should have heard/seen ...!
  And the strange thing was ...
  And then, to top it all, ...
  But that was nothing compared to ...

Close   Anyway, in the end ...
  I ended up ...
  Anyway, to cut a long story short, ...
  Seems quite funny now, but it didn't at the time. ✓

Lexis link

for more on the language of storytelling see page 120

6 Tick which one of the closes could also come straight after an opener.

Active listening   **7** Match the following to make ten things you might say while listening to someone telling a story. They were all in the conversations in 1.

a	You're	god!
b	I don't	earth for?
c	Oh, my	happened?
d	So, what	joking!
e	What on	believe it!

f	I'm not	terrifying!
g	I see	read about this.
h	Sounds	be serious!
i	Oh, yes, I	what you mean.
j	You can't	surprised.

Fluency   **8** Tell the story of your worst (or best) travel experience to the rest of the class.

The business lunch

Discussion   **1** What's the most expensive meal you've ever had? Was it worth the money? Who was paying? Was it on expenses? Tell a partner about it.

5 Write the four stages of a narrative on the board: *opener, context, emphasis, close.* Prepare students for the fluency activity by telling them a story of your own, using this narrative structure and some of the expressions in the box. After you have finished, ask the students if they remember which phrases you used at each stage.

Students categorise the expressions and then do a whole class check by asking individuals to read out the phrases. Highlight intonation and voice range, writing any problematic sentences on the board and marking in the intonation pattern.

6 Students choose the correct expression. Check the answer. (*It seems quite funny now, but it didn't at the time.*)

Direct students' attention to the Lexis link on page 120 for more practice on storytelling. Also remind students that the key expressions from exercise 1 are shown in bold in the tapescripts on pages 154–5.

Active listening

7 Ask students what 'active listeners' do. This includes nodding, making encouraging noises and reacting to what the speaker is saying. Ask students if these features are important in their language. Find out if silence is important when someone else is speaking and how people react to short interjections.

Tell students to look at the two halves of the phrases and match them. Call out a letter a–j and get individual students to give the answer. Check and model correct stress and intonation to help students sound natural.

With classes who need help with delivery and voice range, get the students to say the expressions in a number of different ways e.g. disbelief, surprise, shock, excitement. Encourage students to exaggerate if necessary.

Fluency

8 Give students a few minutes to think of an appropriate travel experience. Refer students back to the stages in exercise 5 and get them to note down key words and phrases as preparation for telling their story. Set a time limit of four or five minutes for the preparation stage. Ask a confident student to start the storytelling and try to make sure all students have an opportunity to tell their anecdote. With bigger classes, students can work in groups to tell their stories. Monitor and take feedback notes. Feed back on how well students told their stories and on overall fluency before highlighting important or common errors.

The business lunch

The students discuss the most expensive business meal they have had before reading about two surprising stories connected with dining out. They listen to a recording of a business meal in which the topic keeps changing and this gives practice in listening for gist. A final fluency activity gives the students a chance to roleplay keeping a conversation going in a restaurant.

Discussion

1 Tell students about the most expensive meal you have ever had and then get students to discuss the questions in pairs. Elicit any interesting examples from the class.

Recording script for page T77

4: Selina
A: Selina. You've flown all over the world. You must have some stories to tell.
E: Hm, quite a few. **I'll never forget the time I was** flying in Asia and the cabin crew asked me to sit on the toilet during take-off.
A: What?
E: Yeah, they wanted my seat next to the emergency exit.
A: Doesn't inspire much confidence in the airline, does it?
E: Not a lot, no. **And then, to top it all, I ended up** sitting next to a guy with a rattlesnake in a basket!

A: Good god!
E: Yes, that's what I said. Apparently, he just brought it on as hand luggage. But **erm, … did I ever tell you about the time I was** working in Nigeria?
A: No, I don't think so.
E: Well, er, **you're not going to believe this, but way back in 1985 it was**, I was on this internal flight, right? And it was three times overbooked!
A: Three times?
E: Oh, yeah, that was quite common in those days. But **you should have heard** the arguments at check in.
A: I can imagine.

E: **Anyway, in the end**, they brought the army in to sort it out.
A: The army?
E: Yeah. **And you'll never guess what they did …**
A: What?
E: They made everyone run round the aircraft twice.
A: **What on earth for?**
E: So they could give the seats to the fastest.
A: **You can't be serious!**
E: It's absolutely true.
A: And did you win a seat?
E: Certainly did. I came third. I was quite quick in those days!

2 Ask students how long a typical business dinner lasts with clients and how much business people usually pay for a meal at a local restaurant. Students then scan the texts to find how long one lunch lasted (five hours) and how much the most expensive business lunch cost (£44,000). Elicit students' reactions to the figures.

Students read the texts again and ask then discuss the questions. Elicit a range of opinions and then ask what would happen in the students' own company e.g. *Would an employee be sacked for taking such a long lunch?*

3 📼 **14.2** In order to set the scene, ask students to tell the group about their favourite restaurant and why they like it. Suggest one of the restaurants as the setting for the fluency task in exercise 5, especially if it is noisy and busy!

Tell the students that you will play each extract twice and that during the first listening they only have to identify the general topic. Encourage them not to worry about understanding every word.

Play the recording once and tell students to note down the topics. To create friendly competition, ask students to put up their hand immediately they know the topic. Pause the recording and write the prediction on the board. Play the rest of the extract so that students can check if they were correct.

4 Play the recording again and ask students to write down the key words. With weaker students, do the first extract with the whole class as an example. Students compare their words in pairs and then check against the recording script on page 155 where the key words are given in bold. Clarify the meaning of any new vocabulary and encourage students to note down any useful words and expressions.

Fluency

5 Tell students they are going to roleplay a conversation over a business lunch. Focus attention on the expressions in the box and elicit possible ways of continuing e.g. a gerund, a preposition, a noun/noun phrase, and elicit complete examples. Check pronunciation and model intonation as necessary. With weaker students, ask students to transfer the phrases in the box onto cards to use as prompts during the roleplay.

Before starting, ask the students to think of ideas for each of the topics in the boxes. Encourage them to write down key words as prompts. Then divide the class into groups and get them to sit at different tables. Bring in real menus if possible to help the authenticity of the roleplay. Check students understand that the aim of the fluency activity is to keep the conversation moving from topic to topic while not sounding abrupt. Allow about ten minutes for the roleplay. Monitor and take feedback notes.

When the students have completed the activity, elicit how they felt they performed in the roleplay and what they found difficult. Give students feedback on how they handled changing the subject and keeping the conversation moving, before highlighting important or common errors.

If you're short of time

Omit exercises 2–4 on pages 74–5. Alternatively, omit exercises 9–10 on page 76.

Students select one roleplay in exercise 11 on page 76.

Omit the final section *The business lunch* and return to it as a discrete fluency task in a subsequent lesson.

📼 **14.2**

a
A: Ugh, isn't it **dreadful**? And we'd got plans for the weekend as well. Thought we might have some friends round for a barbecue.
B: Well, it's always the same, isn't it? You plan anything, it **always lets you down**. And it was **so fabulous** yesterday.
C: Yes, wasn't it? Never would have thought it could **turn so nasty** in just 24 hours. But that's Britain for you, I suppose. **Heatwave** in the morning, a **downpour** in the afternoon and a **howling gale** by dinner time. Bloody weather!

b
B: I'm not sure this is quite right, is it?
A: Hm?
B: This. Is it supposed to be like that? Looks a bit **soggy** to me.
A: Hm, yes, it does a bit. It should be all **crisp** and **golden**, shouldn't it, the **pastry**? Not very **appetising** at all. And there's **not a lot of it**, is there?
B: No, I thought **it came with something else**. Like a **side salad** or something … Ugh! **The meat's as tough as old boots** as well!
A: Oh, dear. I'd **tell the waiter to take it back**, if I were you …

c
C: Line them up against a wall and shoot the lot of them, that's what I say.
A: We can always rely on you for a balanced and mature view, Roger.

C: Well, you know what I mean. Interfering in **policies** that have nothing to do with them. **Power-mad** they are. And who actually **voted** for them, that's what I want to know.
B: Well, I'm not sure I'd …
A: Actually, Roger has got a point there, even if he is being a bit **right-wing** about it, as usual. A lot of these **Eurocrats** are just **self-appointed**, aren't they? They've never had to go through any kind of **democratic election process**.
C: No, and that's how half of Europe has ended up being **governed** by a bunch of **unelected civil servants** in Brussels!

d
B: No, it's not my thing at all, I'm afraid.
A: Oh, but I thought it was marvellous! And **it was so well done**. Because it must have been a very difficult **adaptation**, don't you think? All those enormous books.
B: Hm, yeah. **It went on a bit**, though, didn't it? I mean, what was it, three and a half hours? Should have had an **intermission** really.
A: Well, I found the whole thing absolutely **compulsive viewing**. And **brilliantly directed**. And the **special effects** were incredible!
B: Yes, well, they *were* good, I'll admit, but they've all got those nowadays, haven't they? I mean it's all **digital animation**, like *Star Wars* …

e
B: I'd really appreciate it, because I'm just **snowed under** at the moment, what with all this **backlog** to deal with.
A: Yes, I'm sorry to have **dumped all that on you**. Couldn't think of anyone else I could trust. And with the **deadline** coming up so fast …
B: It's no problem, but if you *could* let me borrow Kim for a couple of hours, I'm sure that together we could **polish the whole thing off** that much faster.
C: You **overworking** this poor boy, Suzanne? That's how she lost her last **assistant manager**, you know, Ian.
A: Oh, ignore Roger. I'll speak to Kim about **giving you a hand** as soon as we get back to the **office**.
B: Thanks.

f
C: What on earth is this?
A: You don't like it? It's one of my favourites. Lovely **bouquet**. **Fresh** and **fruity**.
C: **Smells off to me**.
A: Nonsense! It's fine.
C: Like **something with a bit more body to it**, myself.
B: Hm, that's not at all bad.
A: See? Ian likes it.
C: Hm. All right for lunch, I suppose. But it's still **too young**, if you ask me. Could do with another couple of years in the bottle.
A: Oh, don't be such **a wine bore**, Roger. Get yourself **a glass of something** else if you don't like it.
C: Think I will …

2 Read the information below. Does it shock or amuse you?

Out to lunch

In 1997 a London banker made the headlines when he was sacked for taking a five-hour lunch break – from 11.30am to 4.30pm!

He won back his job after an industrial tribunal ruled that he had been unfairly dismissed. The court decided that five hours is not an excessive amount of time to conduct business over a meal.

Do you agree with the court ruling?

This one's on me

The world record for the most expensive business lunch ever is held by six Barclay's Bank employees, who in July 2001 ate at the Pétrus restaurant in London.

The three bottles of vintage claret alone which they consumed during the meal set them back a staggering £33,410 (charged to expenses, of course), bringing the total bill to just under £44,000!

How could so huge a bill be justified?

3 🔲 14.2 You are in a noisy restaurant with a group of colleagues and have to keep going outside to answer your mobile. Each time you come back in, the topic of conversation has changed. Listen and see how quickly you can guess what it is.

a   the weather _____
b   their meal _____
c   Members of the European Parliament
d   a film _____
e   their workload _____
f   the wine _____

4 Listen again and note down key words and phrases that helped you decide. Compare with a partner and then check in the recording on page 155.

Fluency **5** Work in groups. Use the chart below to practise chatting over lunch with business contacts. Start off by talking about what you've just ordered and then keep changing the subject as indicated until your meal arrives – it seems to be taking a long time! Try not to interrupt each other too abruptly, but keep the conversation moving.

> By the way, …   Incidentally, …   That reminds me …
> Before I forget, …   On the subject of …   Talking of …
> To change the subject for a moment …

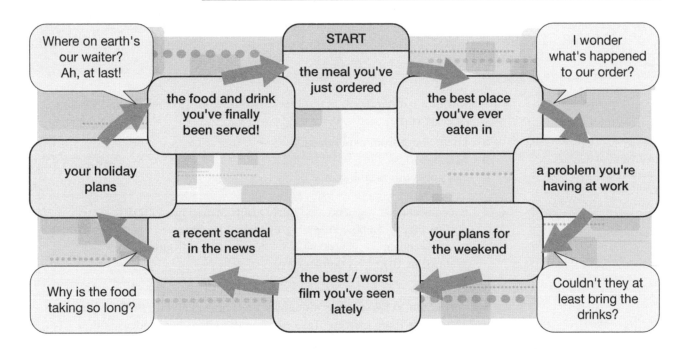

15 Big ideas

Why don't we just stop re-engineering and delayering and restructuring and decentralising and instead start thinking? *Henry Mintzberg, Canadian management thinker*

1 Read the article on business books and think about the questions on the right. Then discuss them with a partner.

A LICENCE TO
PRINT MONEY

Business and professional development books are the most lucrative area of publishing after fiction. At the last count, Amazon.com stocked 32,000 different titles – from meticulously researched case studies by Harvard academics to popular bestsellers like *The One Minute Manager* and *Who*
5 *Moved My Cheese?* Attention-grabbing titles assure us that *Everything is Negotiable* if we can just get used to *Thriving on Chaos* and learn how to *Awaken the Giant Within.*

 The big names like Tom Peters, Charles Handy and Peter Drucker sit alongside less well-known but equally hyped volumes by psychologists,
10 hypnotherapists, sports stars, out-of-work actors and retired naval officers. At almost every airport bookshop you'll find at least three metres of business literature drawn from the combined wisdom of management consultants, self-made millionaires, samurai warriors, Italian Renaissance courtiers and even Winnie the Pooh.

15 But by far the bestselling business books of all time are the *Dilbert* series by disenchanted MBA-holder Scott Adams, who spent 17 years working in 'cubicle hell' at Pacific Bell before his cartoons about office life won him 150 million fans in 65 different countries. Says Adams, 'I feel that being a micro-celebrity is the best of both worlds. I get enough
20 recognition to feel good, but I can go to stores and still be treated rudely by the sales staff.'

1 Do you ever buy books on business or management?

2 Have you ever read one from cover to cover?

3 Would any of the titles mentioned appeal to you?

4 What do you think 'hyped' means?

5 What's the silliest business book you've ever seen?

6 What do you think 'cubicle hell' means?

7 Are you a Dilbert fan? If so, try to convert someone who isn't.

Buzzwords

2 Work with a partner. Look at the business buzzwords in the box and discuss which ones you

a know about from experience
b have heard of
c can guess the meaning of.

buzzword /ˈbʌzˌwɜːd/
noun [C] a word that has become very popular, especially a word relating to a particular activity or subject: *The buzzword of the moment is 'accountability'.*

from *Macmillan English Dictionary*

re-engineering	synergy	Total Quality Management (TQM)
downsizing	empowerment	emotional intelligence	marketspace
the glass ceiling	glocalisation	co-opetition	outsourcing
Just-in-Time (JIT)	portfolio career

3 ▣ 15.1 Listen to two people discussing their understanding of the buzzwords in 2. There are three extracts. Take notes and compare your ideas with a partner.

Talking points # 15 Big ideas

Well-known business writers deliver talks and workshops worldwide offering solutions and ideas. Some business and professional development books also aim to provide revolutionary approaches, while others focus on new trends such as e-commerce. This unit is about new business trends and ideas.

Students read a text about the way some business gurus have tried to make money. They identify the meaning of business buzzwords, before listening to a recording of two people discussing what they understand by these words.

Students then read advice on how to become a business guru in preparation for creating their own new trend/idea. In the final section, they try to assess what famous leaders have in common. The students read short texts on six business leaders, then pool their information and discuss which leader they would prefer to head up their own business.

In the first section, students read a text about some business gurus and discuss a number of questions. They identify/guess the meanings of business buzzwords. A recording of two people discussing the same expressions provides listening practice and allows students to compare their definitions and guesses with those of the speakers.

Warm-up

Tell students about a business success story e.g. Friends Reunited – a website which charges users for a subscription to contact their old schoolfriends. This was a simple idea which led to the founders becoming multi-millionaires. Elicit further examples of successful business ideas.

Ask students to read the quotation from Henry Mintzberg. Elicit the point he is trying to make by using verbs such as *re-engineering, delayering* etc. (The implication is that many business/management ideas are based on complex jargon rather than clear thinking or innovation.)

1 Write the following examples of business books on the board and ask which is the best-selling: *Dilbert* (Scott Adams), *The One Minute Manager* (Spencer Johnson), *The 7 Habits of Highly Effective People* (Stephen Covey). Get students to guess the correct answer and then read the text through quickly to check (the *Dilbert* series).

Ask students to read the text a second time and then discuss the questions in pairs or small groups. Hold a whole class feedback session, eliciting useful points from the students' discussion and checking the answers to questions 4 and 6 (*hyped* – given a lot of publicity/ media attention, sometimes to make something appear better than it really is; *cubicle hell* – working in an office and feeling an insignificant part of the company).

Ask students what tone the writer of the text has used – serious and factual or tongue-in-cheek – and to give examples from the text to support their answer. (There are some straight facts in the text but much of the tone is tongue-in-cheek e.g. *Attention-grabbing titles … Awaken the Giant Within; at least three metres … the combined*

wisdom of management consultants etc.) Check students understand the writer's overall purpose (to show that you can make a lot of money out of business books but that some of the material available is rather silly).

Buzzwords

2 Direct students' attention to the glossary extract and elicit examples of any buzzwords students know, giving examples if necessary e.g. *restructuring*.

Focus students' attention on the words in the box. Do not explain any of the terms at this stage, as the students will hear the definitions in the recording in exercise 3. Check pronunciation of the more difficult words e.g. *synergy, co-opetition,* getting students to mark the stress on the words and phrases. Divide the class into pairs and get them to discuss the buzzwords. Elicit possible answers and write them on the board.

3 🔲 **15.1** Check/Pre-teach: *efficiency, performance, to sack, to come down to the same thing, to fire, mission statement, autonomy, non-existent, inventory, logistcs, equality, to get fed up, alliance.* With weaker classes, write the buzzwords on the board in the order they appear in the recording to help students focus their listening.

Play the first half of extract 1 and do the note-taking with the whole class to set up the task. Play the rest of the recording, pausing at the end of each extract to allow students to take notes.

Give students a few minutes to compare their notes and then do a whole class check.

Answers

re-engineering – making people redundant (synonym for 'downsizing')
synergy – energy created when two people combine their energy and ideas
Total Quality Management (TQM) – a quality control philosophy started in Japan
downsizing – making people redundant
empowerment – giving more autonomy to the workforce
emotional intelligence – people skills, the ability to communicate/deal with others
marketspace – part of the available market
the glass ceiling – an invisible barrier preventing women from reaching higher positions
glocalisation – global + local = a combination of thinking local and acting global
co-opetition – co-operation + competition = collaborating with the competition
outsourcing – contracting work out to freelancers
Just-in-Time (JIT) – manufacturing things just in time to meet demand and keeping only necessary levels of stock
portfolio career – having done a range of jobs/worked for a range of employers

See page T81 for recording script 15.1.

How to become a management guru

In this section, the students work through five steps to invent a new business trend and become management gurus.

Fluency

Focus attention on the quotation by Frank Capra and ask students for their reaction. Elicit a few examples of current trends e.g. *homeworking/teleworking*.

Step 1

As a lead-in the to text, ask students to brainstorm what they know about the Maharishi Mahesh Yogi. (He was the guru to the Beatles who started a trend of going to India and listening to words of wisdom. Although his followers gave up materialist lifestyles, the Yogi had several Rolls-Royces!)

Check/Pre-teach: *remote, mind-enhancing, dealership, catchphrase, ghost writer, to demean, lucrative*. Get students to read the text and list the main steps on how to become a guru. Check the answers (choose a catchphrase, write a book, market the book to make it a bestseller, travel giving seminars which repeat the content of the book, deny you are a guru).

Ask students to read the text again and focus on the tone of the article and the writer's purpose. (The text pokes fun at the concept of management gurus; there is the suggestion that they couldn't write a bestseller themselves, that they recycle material in different formats, that they are interested in appearing 'intellectually pure' and that their main aim is to make money.)

Step 2

Divide students into small groups to brainstorm ideas and a catchphrase. Encourage students to decide their core idea first and then focus on the type of image they want to create. This will help them devise a suitable catchword or phrase. If available, let students refer to dictionaries/the Internet during this stage, but also be ready to feed in words/prefixes often used in buzzwords e.g. *enviro-, multi-, e-, re-, de-* etc.

Step 3

Focus attention on the ideas for book titles in the box. Elicit a few examples from the class first e.g. *The 7 Secrets of Motivation, Beyond Training*. Ask students what they think of the more creative titles like the example given in Step 3. Allow students time to work on their book title. Monitor and help, checking students can pronounce their title in a convincing way.

Step 4

Provide students with the following template to help them structure their ideas:

- Our catchphrase/-word is:
- Our idea is to:
- This new concept appears in our book:
- You cannot live without this idea because:
- It's been supported by (+ imaginary quotation):
- Our statistics show:

Step 5

Give students a few minutes to add any final details to their idea and to choose who is going give the presentation (either individual or team). Set up this presentation phase as an 'award' ceremony, rearranging the classroom layout as appropriate. Invite each group to present their idea in turn and take feedback notes during each presentation. Then have a light-hearted voting session to decide on the winner. Feed back on the creativity of the ideas and effectiveness of the talks, and on overall fluency, before highlighting important or common errors.

Recording script for page T80

🔊 15.1

Extract 1

A: **Synergy** – well, that's just the old combining your efforts idea, isn't it? We're all more effective if we work together as a team.

B: Hm, depends on the team, but, yeah.

A: And **re-engineering** – that was the big thing in the 90s, wasn't it? Improving efficiency and performance …

B: … by sacking half your staff!

A: Well, I think there was bit more to it than that, but, basically, yeah.

B: Same as **downsizing**, really. Cutting costs by making people redundant.

A: More or less … delayering, restructuring … all comes down to the same thing in the end, doesn't it?

B: Job losses.

A: Exactly.

B: First, you fire people. Then you write a new mission statement saying 'Our people are our greatest asset' and promise to give everybody more autonomy.

A: **Empowerment**.

B: Oh, yeah, empowerment. That's what they all talk about nowadays, isn't it? We're all supposed to have more control over what we do. I must say I don't feel very empowered where I work.

A: No, me neither. The boss sticks his nose into everything I do.

B: Yes, I've met your boss. Not a nice person. No **emotional intelligence**.

A: None whatsoever. In fact, his people skills are practically non-existent. He's just got the one strategy really for dealing with people.

B: What's that, then?

A: He shouts at them.

Extract 2

A: Erm, **TQM**, well, that's total quality management, isn't it? Quality circles. Getting your production and inventory and logistics right, and so on.

B: Yeah, yeah, pretty standard stuff nowadays … like **JIT**. Manufacturing things just in time to meet customer demand. Makes perfect sense.

A: Yeah. Easier said than done, though. Now, **the glass ceiling**. Well, we've certainly got one of those where I work. There's hardly a woman who gets promoted beyond unit manager.

B: Did you know there are even fewer women in top jobs now than there were ten years ago? Apparently, at the current rate of change women won't achieve equality with men until 2270!

A: Huh! That's probably why a lot of women have got fed up waiting for promotion and started their own businesses instead.

B: Can't say I blame them. But nobody's job is really safe these days, is it? I mean more and more work gets outsourced to freelancers.

A: **Outsourcing**, yeah. What we all have to do is keep changing direction in our careers about every seven years.

B: Well, this is the so-called **portfolio career**, isn't it? Keep changing jobs. Nice idea, but, frankly, I have enough trouble doing the job I've got, thanks.

Extract 3

A: What's this **co-opetition**, then? I've never heard of it.

B: Hm? Oh, yeah, that's co-operating with the competition. You know, you collaborate with your competitors on some things … erm … whilst continuing to compete on others.

A: Sounds a bit risky to me.

B: Hm, me too. But **marketspace** – this is really interesting, actually, because the idea is that, in the end, it's pointless trying to fight the competition for the same bit of market.

A: Tell me about it. We're all making pretty much the same product for pretty much the same customers.

B: Right. And what we've got to do is stop winning a bit of market share here, losing a bit there and actually break free of the competition altogether. Create our own marketspace.

A: Innovate.

B: Not just innovate. We've got to look at opportunities *between* different industries. I've got a book on it, actually.

A: I guessed! … **Glocalisation** … I know, this is like 'think local, act global', isn't it? The world's breaking up into smaller and smaller countries. But at the same time you've got these big economic alliances developing – like the EU. With improved telecommunications, you can keep your business small and local, but the whole world's your market.

B: Yeah, that's what everyone keeps saying: 'The whole world's your market.' If only it was that simple.

How to become a management guru

Fluency   The film director Frank Capra said, 'Don't follow trends. Start trends.' Work with a partner to start a trend and turn yourselves into instant management gurus!

Step 1   Read business journalist Stuart Crainer's advice on how to become a guru.

'**g**urus once inhabited remote corners of the Indian subcontinent within easy reach of a plentiful supply of mind-enhancing stimulants and a Rolls-Royce dealership. Today's gurus are rather less colourful. Indeed, they are usually management consultants or business school academics. The route to guru status is to come up with a catchphrase (English purists need not apply), write a book (or employ a ghost writer), market it until it reaches the bestseller lists (this may involve buying a lot of copies), and then travel the world giving seminars which repeat the contents of the book. Along the way you have to strenuously deny you are a guru – it demeans the quality of your research and intellectual purity. If you are lucky, you can mine the lucrative world of management guru-dom for two years before your ideas are displaced.

The Ultimate Book of Business Quotations by Stuart Crainer

Step 2   Come up with a memorable catchphrase or catchword – something that sums up your new idea. Like many gurus, you may find it helpful to invent a completely new word by combining two others, for example,
co-operation + competition = coopetition; global + local = glocal.

Step 3   Think of a good title for the bestseller you're going to co-author. Here are some ideas to get you started:

> The 3/5/7 Secrets of …   Instant …   How to …   Beyond …
> Stop *-ing* and Start *-ing*   The Age of …   The Art of …   Rethinking …
> Reinventing …   101/1001 Ways to …   The Idiot's Guide to …
> The Rise and Fall of …   … for the 21st Century   The Ultimate …   Managing …
> Everything You Ever Wanted to Know about … (but were Afraid to Ask)

Alternatively, go for a more creative title but make sure you explain what it means in the subtitle. For example, *The Rhinoceros and the Butterfly*: Hard and Soft Negotiation Tactics

Step 4   Work out the basic concept behind your idea. Don't worry about details: concentrate on the big picture. Quote somebody famous. Make up any statistics you need.

Step 5   When you're ready, present your brilliant idea to the class. Decide who are the 'Management Gurus of the Year'.

Business leaders

Quiz

1 It's the biggest question in management literature: what's the secret of leadership? Look at the following real and fictitious leaders from the past and present. They all have one vital thing in common. What is it?

Julius Caesar	Mahatma Gandhi	Winston Churchill	Mao Tse-Tung
Bill Gates	John F. Kennedy	Saddam Hussein	the Buddha
Jeff Bezos	Alexander the Great	Margaret Thatcher	Ghengis Khan
Carly Fiorina	Cpt. James T. Kirk	Socrates Akio Morita	Joan of Arc
Vaclav Havel	Osama bin Laden	Queen Elizabeth I	Darth Vader
Richard Branson	Montezuma	Martin Luther King	The Lion King

2 ▣ **15.2** Listen and compare your ideas in 1 with the answer.
They all have (or had) followers.

3 Is there a particular leader you admire? Tell a partner about them.

4 Work in three groups to read the profiles of six of the world's greatest business leaders. Group 1 read profiles **a** and **b**, Group 2 profiles **c** and **d**, and Group 3 profiles **e** and **f**. Complete each profile using the verbs in the boxes.

a Jeff Bezos, Amazon

Since 1994 the founder of Amazon.com has seen his company grow from an office in a garage to become the number one virtual bookstore. A stream of acquisitions has permitted expansion into CDs and video, clothing, toys and medicines. In spite of the dot.com crash of 2001, Amazon has maintained its position as the world's largest retailer on the Internet.

The Bezos strategy

stay   diversify   establish   buck   pay

1 _establish_ a clear technological lead
2 _stay_ lean and efficient
3 _diversify_ into new businesses
4 _pay_ close attention to logistics
5 _buck_ the e-commerce trend

b Michael Dell, Dell Corporation

Dell is the founder and CEO of the Dell Corporation, the direct-sale computer business that has taken the PC world by storm. By bypassing retail stores and offering customers tailor-made systems at low prices, Dell has become the biggest in the business, and with its successful entry into the vast Chinese market, the company looks virtually unstoppable.

The Dell strategy

think   stick   cut   collaborate   put

1 _cut_ out the middleman
2 _put_ customers before product
3 _collaborate_ with suppliers
4 _stick_ to what you're good at
5 _think_ global

c Ricardo Semler, Semco S/A

The president of the Brazilian marine and food-processing machinery manufacturer Semco, environmental activist and author of the bestselling _Maverick!_ has created the world's most unusual workplace. At Semco it's the workers who choose and evaluate their bosses. Everyone has access to financial records and 30% of employees set their own salaries!

The Semler strategy

turn   ignore   eliminate   reward   involve

1 _involve_ employees in decisions
2 _eliminate_ hierarchies
3 _ignore_ conventional wisdom
4 _turn_ the company upside down
5 _reward_ talent

d Richard Branson, Virgin

Though head of the huge Virgin empire, Branson prefers to play the underdog. By competing with the likes of British Airways and Coca-Cola, he has earned a reputation for stealing business off complacent market leaders – and doing it in style. A skilled self-publicist, there seems to be almost nothing he wouldn't do to promote the vibrant Virgin brand.

The Branson strategy

generate   have   take   dare   stretch

1 _take_ on the market leaders
2 _generate_ publicity
3 _stretch_ your brand
4 _have_ fun
5 _dare_ to be different

Business leaders

In the final section, students decide on the one thing that famous leaders have in common. They read short texts on six business leaders, then share the information and discuss which leader they would prefer to be in charge of their own company.

Quiz

1 Elicit examples of real and fictitious leaders from the past. Then get students to check their examples against the names in the box.

Students work in pairs/small groups and discuss which leaders they know and what they have in common. Encourage students to pool information so that they find out about as many leaders as possible. Allow 3–4 minutes for this stage.

Ask students to call out the names of anyone they have not heard of, or are not sure of. Use the checklist below to provide brief answers.

Julius Caesar – Roman Emperor

Mahatma Ghandi – spiritual leader of India, overseeing independence

Winston Churchill – Prime Minister of Britain in the Second World War

Mao Tse-Tung – Chinese leader from last century

Bill Gates – Microsoft CEO

John F. Kennedy – former US President

Saddam Hussein – former Iraqi leader

the Buddha – religious leader, founder of Buddhism

Jeff Bezos – founder of Amazon.com

Alexander the Great – leader of the Ancient world

Margaret Thatcher – UK Prime Minister in the 1980s

Ghengis Khan – Mongol conqueror

Carly Fiorina – Business manager, Hewlett-Packard

Cpt. James T. Kirk – captain of the US Enterprise on the *Star Trek* TV series

Socrates – philosopher in Ancient Greece

Akio Morita – former chief of Sony

Joan of Arc – French military leader

Vaclev Havel – former Prime Minister of the Czech Republic

Osama bin Laden – terrorist leader

Queen Elizabeth I – Queen of England 1558–1603

Darth Vader – leader of rebel force in the *Star Wars* films

Richard Branson – head of the Virgin empire

Montezuma – leader of the Aztecs

Martin Luther King – leader of the US civil rights movement

The Lion King – the king of the jungle in a Disney cartoon

Elicit examples of what the leaders have in common and write students' ideas on the board e.g. self-belief, good communication skills, a clear 'message'.

2 🔲 **15.2** Play the recording to allow students to compare the answer with their own idea(s). Ask if they were surprised by the answer 'followers'. Ask follow-up questions e.g. *Do you think that there are natural leaders? What do you think about the idea that leaders are 'born, not made'?* If appropriate, relate the question to students' own situation and ask if they regard their own CEO as a natural leader.

3 Working in pairs, students discuss a leader they particularly admire. Elicit examples and write them on the board. Ask the class to shortlist the list to three and then cast a vote for a class number 1 leader. With some groups, you may need to check that the discussion does not get over-political or too argumentative by intervening and suggesting a quick vote to resolve the issue before moving on.

4 Check/Pre-teach: *tailor-made, to play the underdog, complacent, vibrant, a 'tough cookie'* (someone who strongly defends what they believe in), *dead-end, meteoric, merger, cut-throat.*

Divide the class into three groups and assign the profiles as follows: group 1: a and b, group 2: c and d, group 3: e and f. Ask students to complete the profiles. Monitor and give further help with vocabulary as necessary. Check the answers with each group when students have finished.

🔲 **15.2**

These leaders have nothing at all in common in terms of background, beliefs, achievements, management style or personal characteristics. So, ultimately, all attempts to define the qualities of leadership are a complete waste of time. The one thing the leaders do have in common is this: followers. Every one of them has, or had, people prepared to follow them in one way or another. A leader is not what you are, but what other people make you. And whether or not you yourself are a leader is not for you to decide.

Fluency

5 As a lead-in to the fluency task, ask students to brainstorm the ideal CEO for their company and his/her characteristics.

Regroup students so that each new group contains at least one student from groups 1/2/3. Explain that students have to pool information about the skills and management style of the leaders that they read about in exercise 4. List the key information that students need to give e.g. *name, company, achievements, core business philosophy* and get students make notes under these headings.

Students then discuss each leader in turn, exchanging the key information in their notes. Encourage students not to read from the profiles word for word. Give each group time to decide on the best leader. Monitor the discussion and take feedback notes. When each group has made their decision, ask a spokesperson from each one to tell the class who they have chosen and why. Feed back on overall fluency first before highlighting important or common errors.

As an optional follow-up task, get students to write a profile of another business leader who they admire, recycling as much of the key language in this section as possible. They can research this task for homework on the Internet and then deliver a short presentation to the rest of the class in a subsequent lesson.

If you're short of time

Set the text *A licence to print money* on page 80 for homework and get students to prepare the discussion questions.

Get students to complete their two texts from exercise 4 on page 82–3 at home.

e   Carly Fiorina, Hewlett-Packard

Fiorina has a reputation as one of the 'toughest cookies' in a tough business. After dropping out of law school, she had a number of dead-end jobs before rising meteorically to head one of Silicon Valley's heavyweights. Her no-nonsense style has antagonised some, but she silenced her critics by pushing through a highly successful merger with PC giant Compaq.

The Fiorina strategy

take	ride	lead	shake	grow

1 _lead_____ from the front
2 _shake_____ things up
3 _grow_____ by acquisition
4 _take_____ the flak
5 _ride_____ out the recession

f   Jorma Ollila, Nokia

Nokia has a long history going back to 1865. In those days it had diverse business interests in mining, rubber, paper and cable manufacture. Today, under the guiding hand of Ollila, it has overtaken Motorola and Ericsson to become the world's top mobile phone company – tightly focused and highly innovative in a notoriously cut-throat market.

The Ollila strategy

seize	sell	innovate	focus	stay

1 _focus_____ on your core business
2 _sell_____ off non-core operations
3 _seize_____ opportunities
4 _stay_____ one step ahead
5 _innovate___ or die

Fluency   **5**   Your CEO has left the company in mysterious circumstances and the six business leaders in 4 have all applied for the job! Who would you rather work for? And who would be best for the company? Team up with people from the other groups and hold an unofficial meeting to discuss the matter.

Teleconferencing is so rational, it will never succeed. *John Naisbitt, Megatrends*

1 Is business travel a perk or a pain? With today's sophisticated telecommunications, how much of it is really necessary?

2 Read the article below. Whose view do you share: George Mackintosh's or the airlines'?

Jet lag hater's
guide to business travel

George Mackintosh is not the airlines' best customer. In fact, he is working to keep other business people away from the executive lounge.

5 Mr Mackintosh runs Geoconference, which he describes as Europe's fastest-growing teleconferencing company. His clients are the same corporate folk the airlines want to go jetting across the globe to meetings with colleagues and customers. Mr Mackintosh is
10 trying to persuade them that they can be more productive by staying behind their desks.

Geoconference sells, leases and manages tele- and videoconferencing facilities for multinational firms. Instead of spending valuable
15 time and money travelling to meetings, its sales pitch goes, you can have the same discussions from your own office using a video phone. Hundreds of people can take part at a time, talking to colleagues in dozens of countries.

20 Today Geoconference boasts an impressive list of blue chip clients. IBM, NatWest, Merrill Lynch and Allied Domecq use the company's technology.

But for all the business's early success, Mr
25 Mackintosh admits it has one inescapable weakness. 'Videoconferencing is never going to eliminate the need for at least one face-to-face meeting,' he said. 'If you are doing business with someone for the first time, I don't dispute the fact
30 that you need to meet them, look them in the eye and shake their hand. After that it is likely you are going to be speaking to them on the phone or by e-mail. Videoconferencing allows you to have a more personalised relationship.'
35 The airlines, no doubt, would disagree.

Adapted from The Guardian

Discussion

3 Which of the following would you consider doing by phone rather than face to face? Discuss your reasons with a partner. Would a video facility make a difference?

- a project meeting
- a job interview
- a negotiation
- a crisis meeting
- a sales presentation

Glossary
jet lag tiredness caused by international travel
sales pitch what you say to persuade people to buy
blue chip financially very solid

Desk work

16 Teleconferencing

Teleconferencing uses telecommunications such as phones or video to link up people at two or more venues. There are two opposing views on teleconferencing – one is that it will change the way people do business across distances, the other is that they will always want to travel and meet face to face. This unit looks at business communication through teleconferencing.

Students discuss whether people really need to travel in order to do business. A text presents a number of arguments for tele- and videoconferencing and students discuss whether some business activities such as meetings or presentations can be done remotely.

Listening practice is provided by a recording about a business crisis and students study phrasal verbs and idioms from the recording. A continuation of the first recording presents an emergency teleconference and students complete the missing information in the minutes of this meeting, and do a puzzle with extracts from the recording.

In the final section, the students read another case study of a crisis at a company and roleplay a teleconference to devise an action plan.

The grammatical focus is on reporting and the lexical focus is on the vocabulary of personnel and production.

In this first section, students discuss the need for business travel, given the possibilities afforded by telecommunications. A text about a company called Geoconference puts the case for tele- and videoconferencing and students decide if they support the views of the founder. Students discuss a range of business activities and whether they are better done face to face or remotely.

Warm-up

Focus attention on the photo and ask students what is shown (an in-car communication system). Elicit more examples of technology used in business travel e.g. a global satellite positioning system; street or underground maps on a PDA (personal digital assistant), e-mail facility on a mobile phone. Find out what technology students use when travelling and which equipment they think most useful.

Focus attention on the quotation by John Naisbitt and ask students if they agree. Elicit why teleconferencing won't replace face to face communication e.g. people enjoy getting together, they enjoy going to different places.

1 Ask students to discuss the questions with a partner and then elicit a range of opinions.

2 Focus students' attention on the glossary of terms and check the stress on the compound words. As a lead-in to the text, find out the students' experiences of jet lag. Ask in which direction they prefer to travel for a business meeting – east or west – and to say why.

Check/Pre-teach: *to lease, to boast, inescapable, to eliminate, to dispute.* Ask students to scan the text to find the following information: the advantages of tele- and videoconferencing as described by Geoconference, their client list, one disadvantage of videoconferencing. Get students to read the text ands check the answers (you can save time and money, you can have the same discussions from your own office, you can unite hundreds of people from different countries; IBM, NatWest, Merrill Lynch, Allied Domecq; people need at least one face-to-face meeting).

Students read the text again if necessary. Ask them who they agree with most – George Mackintosh or the airlines. Ask follow-up questions e.g. *How often do you do business with people you have not met face to face? Will teleconferencing increase with the current threat of terrorism? Has business travel decreased in your company since the tragic events of 9/11?*

As an optional follow-up task, divide the class into AB groups: group A writes to their CEO to recommend a reduction in business travel by 50% and investment in Geoconference, and group B to protest against the intention to buy facilities from Geoconference. With weaker classes, get students to brainstorm arguments for and against teleconferencing before they draft their letter.

Discussion

3 Divide the class into pairs/small groups and ask the students to brainstorm the pros and cons of doing each of the activities by phone/with a video link or face to face. Hold a class feedback session and elicit a range of opinions. Establish which activity is the easiest to handle remotely and which is the most difficult.

Ask students which of the things in the list they have done via phone/video link and what their experiences were. Elicit advice they would give to ensure that such events run smoothly e.g. using a moderator to control who speaks, setting up technical checks.

Trouble at the plant

In this section, students listen to a conversation about a crisis at a fictitious company, Oriflamme. They answer comprehension questions, then focus on some of the phrasal verbs and idioms used by the speakers. They then listen to an emergency teleconference in which the management team consider solutions to the problem. The students do a comprehension check exercise and complete the minutes taken after the conference. Finally, they complete a puzzle containing some of the expressions used in the discussions.

1   **📼 16.1** Elicit what type of materials would be stored at the plant e.g. chemicals, perfumed oils, wax, and get students to brainstorm what kind of crises could occur e.g. machinery problems, an accident etc. Check/Pre-teach: *heat exchanger, leakage, oil heater* and get students to predict what has happened. Play the recording through once and elicit the answer to question a. Ask students to read questions b–d and then play the recording a second time. Check the answers with the class.

Phrasal verbs

2   Ask students to work in pairs to guess the words from the synonyms. Do a whole class check. Elicit other collocations with the verbs e.g. *to shut down machinery/ a business/a hospital/a school; to go up in smoke/flames; to have traffic/cars backed up.*

Idioms

3   Ask the students to work individually, then check their answers with a partner. To practise the phrasal verbs and idioms, get students to write three questions for a partner using the key language e.g. *Have you ever worked for a company where a plant has been shut down?*

4   Elicit ideas from the students, listing the implications of the crisis at the plant. Get students to think about the immediate implications and the wider business context e.g. safety issues at the plant, a loss in consumer confidence.

5   Check/Pre-teach *backlog, adverse, bottleneck, hazard*. Get students to match the columns. Check the answers with the class, making sure students have the stress in the correct place. Check how many of the expressions students included in their list in exercise 4.

Direct students' attention to the Lexis link on page 123 for more practice on the vocabulary of personnel and production.

Discussion

6   Ask students to write an action plan for Oriflamme, listing at least five points e.g. transferring stock from other parts of the company, offering clients some kind of incentive. Divide the class into pairs/small groups and get them to exchange ideas. Remind them their aim is to reduce the negative implications listed in exercise 5. Get students to agree on the three most important action points and the order of priority. Students then present their action plan to the whole class and compare the approach they think the company should take.

📼 16.1

A: Ugh! **Who on earth can that be?** Where's the ... the light switch! Ow! Er ... hello?
B: Pete, is that you?
A: Er, yes. Who is this?
B: It's Max.
A: Max! ... Max, it's ... it's two o'clock in the morning!
B: I'm sorry, Pete, but this is an emergency.
A: Well, it better be, I've got to be up in a few hours.
B: I think you'd better get up right now, Pete. **All hell's broken loose here**. We're going to have to **shut down** the Hamburg plant immediately.

A: What!
B: It's the heat exchanger. We've got a leakage between the hydrogenation section and the oil heater. There's nothing we can do but stop all production straightaway. Otherwise, the whole thing could **go up**!
A: But Max, do you have any idea what you're saying? If you authorise a plant shutdown, **everything grinds to a halt**. We'll have container lorries **backed up** from Hamburg to Lübeck!
B: Pete, do you think I don't know that?
A: Tell me this isn't happening. It cost us millions last time ... OK, look, I have no

idea how long it will take me and Monica to get a flight, but we're on our way.
B: I think that's best, Pete.
A: I'll phone you to fix up a teleconference once we're airborne. Contact Françoise and Otto right away, will you? **There's not a moment to lose ...**
A: Monica? It's Pete. Look, **I'm sorry to get you up at this unearthly hour**, but there's been a disaster at the Hamburg plant. Yeah. Better get dressed. I'll tell you about it on the way to the airport.

Trouble at the plant

1   ▭ **16.1** Peter Devlin is CEO of the European division of Oriflamme, a manufacturer of candles and home fragrance products. Currently on a business trip to Vancouver with his marketing director Monica Brookes, Peter was woken at 2am by an unexpected phone call from his plant manager in Hamburg. Listen and answer the questions.

   a   What has happened at the Hamburg plant?

   There's been a leakage and the plant's had to be shut down.

   b   Why didn't Max have any alternative?

   There was a risk of explosion.

   c   What happened last time there was a similar disaster?

   It cost the company millions.

   d   What does Peter suggest doing now?

   He and Monica are going to fly back to Germany.

Phrasal verbs   2   Complete the following sentences from 1 with the correct preposition. Use the synonyms in brackets to help you.

   a   We're going to have to shut _down_ the Hamburg plant immediately. (close)

   b   Otherwise, the whole thing could go _up_! (explode)

   c   We'll have container lorries backed _up_ from Hamburg to Lübeck. (queueing)

Idioms   3   You also heard the following idiomatic expressions in 1. Can you remember the missing words? The first two letters are given. Use the definitions in brackets to help you.

   a   Who on ea_rth_ can that be? (I have no idea who this is.)

   b   All he_ll_'s broken loose here. (Everything's in chaos here.)

   c   Everything grinds to a ha_lt_. (Everything comes to a complete stop.)

   d   There's not a mo_ment_ to lose. (We must act immediately.)

   e   I'm sorry to get you up at this unearthly ho_ur_. (I don't like to disturb you so late/early.)

4   Work with a partner. List the implications of a crisis like the one above.

5   Now match the following. Did you include them in your list in 4?

   a   a backlog of   bottleneck
   b   a production   hazard
   c   a safety   productivity
   d   a fall in   orders

   e   a damaged   manhours
   f   adverse   reputation
   g   lost   deliveries
   h   delayed   publicity

Lexis link

for more on the vocabulary of personnel & production see page 123

Discussion   6   Work with a partner to discuss what immediate action Oriflamme should take to avoid the implications in 5.

7 🔊 16.2 Listen to the emergency teleconference and answer the questions.

Extract 1 **a** Who hasn't been able to join the teleconference? _Otto_

b Where are Peter and Monica? _on the plane from Vancouver_

c How long will it take to fix the problem at the plant? _at least three days_

Extract 2 **a** What state is the plant in? _Pretty bad. The whole area has had to be cleared._

b Why can't the orders be met completely? _There's not enough stock in reserve._

c Describe Monica's response to Peter's suggestion that they buy product from their competitors to sell on to their customers 'to cover the shortfall'.

enthusiastic ☐ positive ☐ lukewarm ☐ cool ☐ negative ☐ hostile ☑

Extract 3 **a** Why may Handelsmann be prepared to help?
Oriflamme helped them in a similar situation.

b Is there still a safety hazard at the plant?
No, the area has been made secure.

c What arrangement does Peter make with Otto?
to keep him informed if the situation changes

8 The minutes below were taken by Françoise Fleurie directly after the teleconference. Complete them using the verbs in the boxes.

> **Points 1 and 2:**
> ~~confirmed~~ keep estimated assure informed ensure authorised

Grammar link

for more on reporting see page 122

> **Points 3 and 4:**
> mentioned pointed follow opposed get agreed reach proposed smooth OK'd

Hamburg Plant Shutdown: Minutes of the Teleconference		**Date:**
Participants: Peter Devlin, Monica Brookes, Max Schiller, Otto Mendel, Françoise Fleurie		Apologies: N/A
Next teleconference: 12pm ET		

Point	**Details**	**Action**
1 Situation report	PD _confirmed_ that a total shutdown of the H'burg plant has been officially _authorised_. OM _informed_ us that the site had been evacuated in order to conduct safety checks, but was later able to _assure_ us that the situation has now been brought under control.	OM to _keep_ PD up to date on any changes in the situation
2 Repairs estimate	MS _estimated_ that repairs will probably take three days to carry out. The main reason given for the delay was the amount of time needed to obtain a replacement heat exchanger (48hrs).	MS to oversee and _ensure_ completion of repairs within three days
3 Production plan	PD _proposed_ rewriting the production plan to give priority to key customers, but OM _pointed_ out that we hold insufficient reserve stocks to fully meet current orders. It was generally _agreed_ that our European plants are too overstretched to transfer goods to H'burg.	OM to _reach_ a compromise re main customers' orders and _get_ back to PD
4 Traded goods	PD's suggestion that traded goods be bought in from another supplier was initially _opposed_ by MB on the grounds that it would damage Oriflamme's reputation. FF _mentioned_ the possibility of Handelsmann being able to help us out. This was provisionally _OK'd_ by PD.	FF to _follow_ up the Handelsmann offer and _smooth_ things over with key customers

7 ▣ **16.2** Get students to recap on the situation at the Oriflamme plant and review the names of the people involved (Peter, Monica, Françoise, Max and Otto).

Extract 1

Check/Pre-teach: *to get through, rescue plan, up and running, replacement, to fit.* Tell the students to read questions a–c, then play extract 1. Check the answers with the whole class.

Extract 2

Check/Pre-teach: *to clear, in reserve, overstretched, shortfall, to build a reputation.* Tell students that in the next extract various actions/solutions are discussed. Write up the following in a random order on the board: *safety checks, rewriting production plans, discussing reserve stock, buying from a competitor.* Play the extract through once and get students to put the topics in the correct order as they hear them.

Before playing the extract again, ask students to read questions a–c. Elicit any answers they can give from memory and then play the recording again. Check the answers.

Extract 3

Ask students to read questions a–c and to guess who or what Handelsmann is and to predict possible answers to questions a and c. Play the recording through once and get students to check their predictions. Play the recording again if necessary and check the answers with the whole class.

As a follow-up task, write the following words on the board and ask students to brainstorm some verbs which collocate with them: *favour, conference call, secure, backlog, posted* e.g. *to do a favour, to make/book/organise a conference call.* Write the options on the board. Play extract 3, pausing if necessary and ask students to check which expressions were used (*make up a backlog, owe a favour, make secure, schedule a conference call, keep someone posted*).

Direct students' attention to the Grammar link on page 122 for more information and practice on reporting.

8 Before doing the exercise, check with students if they keep minutes of meetings and if they think it's a worthwhile task. Ask why it's particularly important to minute the Oriflamme teleconference (to deal with the crisis quickly and to make sure everyone knows what to do).

Tell the students to read the minutes of the videoconference. Draw attention to the convention of using initials. When the students have completed the gaps, tell them to check their answers with a partner before doing a whole class check.

With a larger group, divide the class into four and give one part of the report to each group. Then ask the students to regroup in order to exchange answers. When the students have finished, do a whole class check.

▣ **16.2**

Extract 1

A: **OK, so we're just waiting for Otto.** Françoise, you told him when to call in, right?

C: Yes, I did. Perhaps he's still at the plant or he may just be having problems getting through.

B: Pete, where are you and Monica?

A: Just left Vancouver about half an hour ago, Max. Should be back in 13 hours or so.

C: Pete, I think we should just start.

B: Yes, I think so too.

A: OK, we really need to talk to Otto, but **let's go ahead and get the meeting started** and hopefully he'll join us later on … Right, well, as you all know, we've had a serious mechanical failure at the Hamburg plant and, basically, we've had to shut it down. There'll be time for a proper analysis of what went wrong later. Right now we need a rescue plan. **Max, could you first of all just fill us in on what's going on?** When can we expect to get the plant up and running again?

B: **Well, Pete, it's difficult to say at the moment.** My technicians tell me they can't get a replacement heat exchanger for at least 48 hours. And then it'll have to be fitted, of course. We're probably looking at three days.

D: Three days!

A: It's worse than I thought. And is that your best estimate? Three days?

B: I'm afraid so, Pete.

A: Well, that's that, then. But I want us back in production no later than Thursday, Max. OK?

B: OK, Pete, **I'll see what I can do.**

Extract 2

E: Excuse me, Mr Mendel has joined.

A: Otto! Thank goodness you got through. Have you been to the plant yet? What's the situation there?

F: It's pretty bad Pete. We've had to clear the whole site for the fire service to run safety checks.

A: I see. Otto, is there any chance we can rewrite our production plan? I mean, can we make sure our key customers get priority on orders?

F: **I'm already working on that.** The problem is it doesn't look as though we'll be able to meet any of the orders completely.

A: What's the stock situation?

F: Not good.

A: Oh, great. Just what I needed to hear. Don't we keep any stock in reserve for this kind of thing?

F: What, for a complete plant shutdown? No, Pete, we don't.

A: OK, OK. Well, what about transferring stock from one of our other European plants?

F: It'd take too long. And, besides, they're already overstretched as it is.

A: Right … Monica, **is there any point in us buying in traded goods** from another supplier to cover the shortfall? **Just for the time being.**

D: You mean buy product from our competitors to keep the customers happy?

A: Just for the time being.

D: **Pete, you know how I feel about buying from the competition.** How are we supposed to build a reputation with our customers if we end up selling them other people's products instead of our own?

A: It's not as if we haven't done it before, Monica. And **what alternative do we have?**

Extract 3

A: OK, now, we've got to make up this backlog of orders somehow. How about Handelsmann?

C: Er, **can I come in on that?**

A: Go ahead, Françoise.

C: Well, **I've already been on to** Handelsmann. They owe us a favour, actually. We helped them out a few years ago when they were in a similar situation, if you remember. Anyway, it looks like they may be able to do something, but probably not until tomorrow morning.

A: Well, at least that's something, I suppose. **OK, get back to them and see if we can hurry things up a bit. And get somebody in after-sales to ring round all our biggest customers** and smooth things over with them.

C: **OK, I'll see to it now.**

A: Now, Max. Are you sure this thing can't just be fixed? I mean, if I gave your technical people, say, 24 hours … Max, you still there?

B: Still here. I've just been told the leakage area has now been made secure.

A: Well, thank god for that. Anyway, OK, that's it for now. We're going to try and get some sleep. I suggest we schedule another conference call for midnight European Time. But, Otto, **keep me posted if there's any change in the situation**, won't you?

F: Will do, Pete.

A: OK, thanks everyone …

Reporting

9 Ask students to evaluate the effectiveness of the photograph as an advertisement for mobile computers/ wireless telephony. Ask how many students have used a 'hot-spot' or wireless connection and how often they work away from the office. Elicit examples of unusual places they have contacted the office from. Ask if anyone feels that 'work is work' and is best done in an office environment.

Tell students to complete the words without referring to the extracts in exercise 7 if possible. This activity could be done as a race between teams. Award bonus points e.g. five for finishing first, four for finishing second etc. Refer students to the recording script on pages 156–157 to check their answers.

Give further practice in the grammar of this unit by asking students to report the extracts. Elicit a range of possible reporting verbs e.g. *suggest, admit, agree, inquire, urge* etc. and get students to report the extracts using a different verb each time.

9 Complete the puzzle using the extracts from the teleconference in 7 to help you.

a	OK, so we're just	w a i	t	i n g for Otto.
b	Let's go	a h	e	a d and get the meeting started.
c	Max, could you first of all just	f i	l	l us in on what's going on?
d	Well, Pete, it's difficult to say at the	m o m	e	n t.
e	I'll see what I		c	a n do.
f	I'm already	w	o	r k i n g on that.
g	Monica, is there any	p o i	n	t in us buying in traded goods?
h	Pete, you know how I		f	e e l about buying from the competition.
i	Just for the time	b	e	i n g.
j	What	a l t e	r	n a t i v e do we have?
k	Can I	c o m	e	in on that?
l	I've already	b e e	n	on to Handelsmann.
m	OK, get back to them and see if we		c	a n hurry things up a bit.
n	And get somebody in after-sales to	r	i	n g round all our biggest customers.
o	OK, I'll see to it		n	o w.
p	Otto, keep me posted if there's any	c h a n	g	e in the situation.

Desert island blues

Fluency The RJK Group is one of the world's leading advertising agencies with an impressive list of blue-chip clients. At the moment RJK (UK)'s top creatives are on location on the remote island of Oamu-Oamu in the South Pacific, filming a commercial for *Vivacity*, the new shower gel range from French cosmetics and toiletries giant Éternelle. But after eight days on the island, the film shoot is turning into a disaster.

Step 1 Work in groups of three. You are about to take part in a teleconference to decide what to do about the situation. First check your latest e-mail and make a note of any points you want to bring up.

Speaker A CEO of RJK (UK): You are currently attending an international conference in Milan. Read e-mails 1 and 2.

Speaker B Creative Director, RJK (UK): You are currently in the middle of a pitch for the €15m Heineken account. Read e-mails 3 and 4.

Speaker C Account Director, RJK (UK): You are currently on two weeks' holiday in Mauritius. Read e-mails 5 and 6.

Step 2 Hold the teleconference using the agenda below. The CEO should chair the meeting. Report what you have learned from your e-mail and try to commit to a definite course of action on which you all agree. The final decision, however, is the CEO's.

Agenda: Éternelle Account – *Vivacity* Shoot

1 Situation report: Clarification of the situation on location
2 Financial considerations: Éternelle account – budgetary constraints
3 Action plan:
  • Change of location? If so, where?
  • Switch to studio filming? Implications?
  • Change of actress? Contractual problems?
  • How to present change of plan to client?
  • Any other suggestions?

1

I'm becoming increasingly concerned about the costs we're running up on the Éternelle account. I think we're in serious danger of exceeding our budget.

As you know, the Éternelle marketing people were extremely unhappy when we came in €250,000 over budget last time, and it was for this reason that they insisted at the planning stage on a ceiling of €2.5m for the *Vivacity* campaign.

I've been looking at the figures and we're well past the €2m mark already. The main problem is this two-day film shoot on Oamu-Oamu which has already cost us €1m. The Hollywood actress the client insisted on using is costing us €100,000 a day! What on earth is going on there?

I estimate that with post-production costs, we could run €500,000–€700,000 over budget on this one.

We desperately need to talk.

Gavin Hartnell, Chief Financial Officer, RJK (UK)

2

I'm hearing rumours of a budget overrun on the *Vivacity* campaign. Please tell me I'm imagining things!

Had lunch with Éternelle's new head of marketing, Thierry DuPont, and he sounded pretty annoyed with what he called our 'endless production hold-ups'. He even said they may be forced to postpone the *Vivacity* launch.

I'm sure I don't need to remind you that Éternelle is by far this company's biggest European client (worth €10m annually) and that the loss of their account would have a drastic effect on both Group turnover and our reputation in the industry.

Your creative director must be in contact with our team on Oamu-Oamu. Are they still having weather problems or what?

I'm counting on you to sort this one out. Don't let me down.

Nathan T. Auerbach, RJK Group President

Desert island blues

In this final fluency activity, students roleplay directors of an advertising agency who have to deal with a crisis. They work in groups and read two of six e-mails in order to learn about the background to the problem, which has arisen while filming an advert in an exotic location. The students prepare for and hold a teleconference to decide on an action plan.

Fluency

As a lead-in to the topic, elicit examples of product endorsement by famous people e.g. sports personalities and trainers, actresses and beauty products etc. Ask if students believe that such endorsements help to sell products. Also elicit examples of students' favourite advertisement and why they like it.

Before step 1, set the scene by asking students to read the background information in the rubric. Ask check questions such as the name the company, the client, the location and the product.

Step 1

Check/Pre-teach: *to run up costs, post-production, to overrun, hold-up, drastic, in the can* (filmed and ready to be shown), *footage, secluded, to scout for, handler, lethal, through the grapevine, set building.* Divide the class into groups of three. Assign each student a letter, A, B or C. With larger groups, have students work together in pairs on the same role. Ask students to read their roles and their respective e-mails: A reads e-mails 1 and 2, B e-mails 3 and 4, C e-mails 5 and 6. Deal with vocabulary queries as necessary and check pronunciation of the proper nouns given in the scenario and e-mails. Write the following prompts on the board and give students time to make notes in preparation for the teleconference:

key points to update colleagues
important figures to quote
suggested action points and order of priority

Step 2

Ideally, use phones with a conferencing facility, or set up the seating for a teleconference, so participants sit in a group but don't look at each other. Remind the A students to act as CEO and chair the meeting. They also need to specify who speaks at any one time. Ask all students to read the agenda and set a time limit of thirty minutes for the teleconference. Monitor and take feedback notes.

When the activity has finished, give the students a few seconds to think about task, the outcome and their own performance. Then ask each group in turn to report back on what went well and what could have been improved. Give feedback on overall fluency before highlighting important or common errors.

If you're short of time

Set the text *Jet lag hater's guide to business travel* on page 84 for homework. Alternatively, leave out page 84 and start the unit with *Trouble at the plant* on page 85.

Set exercise 8 on page 86 and/or exercise 9 on page 87 for homework.

3

Well, we've had eight days of incessant rain, two cameras damaged in transit and now the electricity generator's broken down. Whose idea was it to use a real desert island for the shoot?

Flying Sandra in and out from Fiji every day is proving totally impractical. Didn't I say using a big Hollywood star was asking for trouble? She came down with some kind of tropical fever two days ago and hasn't come out of her hotel room since. So far we've only got about 15% of the commercial in the can.

To keep costs down the crew are staying on Oamu-Oamu until we're finished. Today is the first fine day, but there's still no sign of Sandra, so we're just getting some footage of the island.

I strongly suggest we either fly out a replacement or seriously consider filming the whole thing in a studio in Britain.

Ridley Hurst, Film Unit Director

4

No doubt you've already heard from Ridley. The good news is that Sandra's PA tells me she may be well enough for filming tomorrow. My suggestion is that we forget Oamu-Oamu and find a nice secluded spot here in Fiji. I'm sure that would suit Sandra much better if she's still not feeling too good. I've sent some of the team out scouting the beaches for possible locations.

The bad news is that the animal handler's gone missing. You remember that we wanted to use real animals on this shoot instead of adding them digitally later? Well, now I'm left here with 36 African parrots and a rather lethal-looking python.

Ridley seems to think we'd be better off doing the whole thing in a studio, but I think it would be a shame to pack up and leave now we're all here. Might be rather hard to explain the unnecessary expense to the client, too. Are we insured for this?

Amelia DeVine, Senior Account Manager, RJK (UK)

5

Sorry to bother you on holiday, but we're having major problems with the *Vivacity* shoot. As you've no doubt heard through the grapevine, we're running six days over schedule owing to bad weather, logistical problems and a leading lady with a fever …

I've been asked to look into alternatives and have come up with the following, which I thought I'd better copy you in on:

1 If we fly the film crew home to do the commercial in a studio, with set building, studio hire and post-production, we could be looking at an extra €750,000. Plus we'd be unlikely to finish on schedule.

2 Finding an A-list actress to replace Sandra at such short notice would be extremely difficult, although there is provision for her replacement, if unable to perform, in the terms of our contract. I did speak to someone at a lookalike agency who said he had 'Sandra's twin' and could let us have her for €5,000 a day.

Jason Roberts, Account Manager, RJK (UK)

6

I must say I am very disappointed with the number of delays on the *Vivacity* project. These problems with the film shoot are just the latest in a series of expensive mistakes. I trust the extra costs will not be coming out of our agreed budget.

Your Group President Nathan Auerbach tried to persuade me over lunch that everything was going well, but now I'm told we may have lost our actress for the commercial. I should emphasise that in France the use of celebrities to endorse products is a proven and powerful advertising technique. Sandra's appearance in the *Vivacity* commercial was part of the original brief to your agency and any replacement would have to be approved by my marketing department.

I might add that, as RJK's Account Director with overall responsibility for our account, I'm surprised to see you've found time to take a vacation in the middle of this crisis.

Thierry DuPont, Director of Marketing, Éternelle (Europe)

17 Negotiating deals

Don't ever slam a door. You might want to go back in. *Don Herold, US negotiator*

Fluency

1 a Are you a good negotiator? Work in groups of three to try out your negotiating skills. Speaker A see page 137. Speaker B see page 139. The third person in the group should observe and take notes on the kind of language the other two use.

b Speakers A and B, did you reach an agreement or did you get into an argument? What was the main problem you faced?

c Try the negotiation again, but this time read the extra information on page 131 first. The observer should again take notes.

d Was the negotiation easier this time? Did you manage to reach a compromise? Find out from the observer if the language used was different in the two negotiations.

2 ▣ **17.1** Listen to a management trainer giving feedback to some trainees who have just finished the negotiation in 1. Do you agree with the analysis?

Compound adjectives

3 Complete the collocations by matching the compound adjectives. Then match each adjective to its definition. You heard all the phrases in 2.

a a single-	sum game	one which is very direct
b a long-	win situation	one from which both sides feel they've gained
c a win-	issue negotiation	one that lasts
d a one-	term relationship	one where one side wins what the other side loses
e a zero-	on conflict	one that happens only once
f a head-	off deal	one where only one topic is being discussed

4 You also heard the following expressions in 2. Can you remember the missing words? The first few letters are given. The definitions in brackets may help you.

a There's little room for man_oeuvre_. (It's difficult to change your position.)

b win at all cos_ts_ (do whatever you have to do to win)

c It simply wasn't worth the hass_le_. (It was too much trouble.)

d The negotiation ended in dead_lock_. (Neither side was prepared to move.)

e resort to emotional black_mail_ (make people feel guilty to get what you want)

f reach some kind of comp_romise_ (an agreement that partially satisfies both sides)

Lexis link

for more on the language of negotiations see page 124

Meetings # 17 Negotiating deals

Everyone negotiates informally to some extent: with a partner, in a discussion with their boss and colleagues, or in a dispute. Many business English students also need to negotiate formally, and this unit looks at both the language and skills necessary to do this successfully.

Students test their skills as negotiators in a two-stage fluency task and then listen to feedback being given on the same negotiation. They focus on and practise compound adjectives.

Students then study different tactics in negotiating and discuss their effectiveness. They listen to extracts from negotiations to identify the strategies being used. The language work focuses on bargaining, showing disapproval and idioms, and further listening practice is given on negotiation strategies.

In the final section, the students discuss music and read an article on the music industry. This provides the background to a final fluency activity in which students roleplay a negotiation between a new rock band and a record company.

The grammatical focus is on the language of diplomacy and persuasion, and the lexical focus is on the language of negotiations.

In the first section, pairs of students practise negotiating in a short roleplay, while an observer takes notes on the language used. The roleplay is repeated, but with a change in the relationship and students discuss the differences between the two negotiations. A recording provides an analysis of this negotiation by a management trainer, and students then focus on some of the language used in the recording, including compound adjectives.

Warm-up

Find out which students need to negotiate formally in their work and if they find it easy or difficult. For those students who don't negotiate formally, ask them to think of a situation in which they needed negotiation skills e.g. asking for improvement to pay and/or work conditions, handling a dispute with a neighbour etc. Focus attention on the quotation from Don Herold and elicit what the implication is for negotiators (keep up good relations with people, as you may want to deal with them again in the future).

Fluency

1   Divide the class into groups of three – Student A, Student B and an observer. If the group does not divide into threes, assign the role of observer to two students or observe yourself.
   a   Check/Pre-teach: *to go mad for, a surge of panic, to slip your mind, to mumble, to grab*. Refer the A students to page 137 and the B students to page 139. Tell the observers that they will need to make notes on the stages/tone of the negotiation and on the

language used. With weaker students, give them examples of what to look for e.g. use of statements/ exclamations vs. questions; typical language e.g. *I need …, It's important for me to … because …* etc. Students roleplay the negotiation and the observers take notes. Monitor but don't offer help or interfere.
   b   Ask the negotiators to comment on whether agreement was reached and to highlight the main problems. Elicit comments from the observers on the key stages and whether the tone changed during the negotiation. Write up examples of key language on the board.
   c   Refer Students A and B from each group to page 131. Get them to try the negotiation again and remind the observers to note down the stages and key language, and any changes in body language, tone of voice etc.
   d   Elicit feedback on the second negotiation. Ask students if it was easier to reach a compromise and, if so, why. Ask the observers for their comments, eliciting any additional/different stages and how the key language changed. Establish if more 'social' language was used, if there were more questions than statements and if the tone was softer.

2   ▭ **17.1** Ask students to predict what the management trainer will say. Play the recording though once and get students to check their predictions.

Check/Pre-teach: *opponent, encounter, issue* (problem/point for discussion), *vice-versa, to pre-empt, deserving*. Tell students that they are going to hear the recording again and that they should take notes under the following headings:
What the activity demonstrates
1st negotiation: objective tactics

2nd negotiation: objective tactics

Play the recording again and get students to complete their notes. Check the answers and then ask students if they agree with the trainer's analysis.

Compound adjectives

3   Students form the collocations and then match them to the definitions. Get students to practise the compounds by asking follow-up questions e.g. *With which trading partners do you have a long-term relationship? How best can you avoid a head-on conflict in negotiations?*

4   Students complete the phrases, working individually or in pairs. Check the answers by playing the recording again or referring students to the recording script on page 157, where the key language is in bold. Check pronunciation of difficult words e.g. *manoeuvre, hassle* and then get students to practise the expressions by writing questions e.g. *Is it important to win at all costs? Can you give an example of emotional blackmail?* Students then work in pairs or small groups to ask and answer their questions.

Direct students' attention to the Lexis link on page 124 for more practice on the language of negotiations.

See page T91 for recording script 17.1.

Negotiating style

In this section, students match the names of high-pressure tactics in negotiations to their relevant descriptions and then discuss the tactics. They listen to a series of extracts from negotiations and they identify which tactics are being used. Students then complete exercises on the language of bargaining and on ways of showing disapproval. Listening practice is provided by a recording of a group of management trainers talking about negotiating strategy and the section ends with a focus on idioms used in the recording.

High-pressure tactics

1   Ask students if they have ever been on a negotiation skills training course. Get those who have to give examples of the techniques covered. With students with little or no experience of negotiating, name some of the techniques in exercise 1 e.g. the *good cop, bad cop approach, the take-it-or-leave-it challenge* and get students to guess how the tactics work.

Check/Pre-teach: *ploy, concession, unreasonable, to keep a straight face, to jeopardise, nasty.* Students work individually to match the tactics and descriptions. Then check the answers with the whole class. Ask students if they have ever used any high-pressure tactics and what the result was.

Discussion

2   Check if anyone in the group has been faced with high-pressure tactics and, if so, what strategies they used. Put the students into groups, if possible dividing the experienced negotiators in the class across different groups. Get students to brainstorm possible responses to each of the tactics in exercise 1. Hold a class feedback session and elicit possible answers e.g. *playing for time and asking for a break, calling the other person's bluff, asking for concessions* etc.

Ask students which tactics they think are high-risk and why. Also find out if students think any of the tactics are unethical. Students then select one tactic which they would like to try out and one which they think is beyond their negotiating skills.

3   **17.2** Check/Pre-teach: *volume, case, trial order, pack, margin, premium* (high-quality), *unique, unit, installation.* Tell students that they will hear each extract twice. Before students listen, give them the names of the characters in random order (see bracketed text below) and ask the following gist questions: *Who is negotiating? What product is under discussion?* Play the recording through once and check the answers (1 Ms Barrett/Mr Koivisto; a new brand of carbonated water; 2 Rob Hayes/Gavin and his negotiating partner; precision tools).

Tell students to now focus on the tactics used in each extract and on how successful they are. With weaker groups, give them a smaller range of tactics to select from by reducing the list of options to six or eight. Play the recording again and check the answers (in extract 1 neither tactic seems to work as Ms Barrett is close to walking away from the deal; in extract 2 the once-in-a-lifetime offer is not very successful as Gavin wants a bigger discount. The good cop, bad cop approach seems to work quite well, as Rob is keen to compromise.)

Recording script for page T90

17.1
The activity you just did is designed to demonstrate the critical importance in the negotiating process of relationship-building.

In your first negotiation you probably didn't think much about your opponent's interests. And why should you? After all, it was just a stranger who you'd never meet again. But by concentrating on only one objective, you reduced the whole encounter to a **single-issue negotiation** with **little room for manoeuvre**. This made it a simple **zero-sum game** – if I get what I want, you don't, and vice-versa.

In order to **win at all costs**, perhaps you became hostile and tried to pre-empt negotiation altogether by just grabbing the box off the other person. Or maybe you gave in completely, deciding **it simply wasn't worth the hassle**. Many professional negotiators act the same way if they think they are negotiating a **one-off deal**. As the negotiation **ended in deadlock**, perhaps you became desperate and **resorted to emotional blackmail**, inventing all sorts of reasons why your kid was more deserving than the other kid.

In the second negotiation, on the other hand, there was a **long-term relationship** you wanted to maintain. The circumstances were exactly the same, but the prospect of one of you 'losing' was no longer an option. By accepting the need to **reach some kind of compromise**, you were able to turn a **head-on conflict** into a problem-solving meeting. Now your main objective was to generate options in the hope that you could create a **win-win situation**, where you both got something you wanted.

See page T92 for recording script 17.2.

Negotiating style

1 Listed below are the ten most common high-pressure tactics negotiators use. Match each to its description. The first one has been done for you.

Tactics

1 The shock opener
2 The vinegar and honey technique
3 The strictly off-limits ploy
4 The take-it-or-leave-it challenge
5 The I'll-have-to-check-with-head-office ploy

6 The sorry-about-my-English ploy
7 The good cop, bad cop approach
8 The once-in-a-lifetime offer
9 The salami technique
10 The last-minute demand

Description

a Make it look as though you are ready to leave the negotiating table if your demands are not met, that you are not prepared to move an inch further.

b Point out at the start that, though you are prepared to negotiate A, B and C; X, Y and Z are definitely not negotiable.

c Having obtained a concession from your opponent, inform them that you need your boss's approval before you can do what they ask in return.

d Make unreasonable demands early on in the negotiation. When you later 'see reason' and modify your demands, they'll be all the more welcome.

e Make a ridiculous initial demand (or offer), but keep a straight face as you make it. This works particularly well on inexperienced opponents.

f Don't make all your demands right at the start. Make a small demand and get agreement on it before you make the next, and the next …

g Pretend not to understand any proposal you don't like the sound of. You'll make your opponent uncomfortable by forcing them to repeat it.

h Pressurise your opponent by suggesting that the offer you're making is only for a limited period and if they don't act quickly, they'll miss it.

i After the deal has been done, make one modest extra demand in the hope that your opponent will not want to jeopardise the agreement for one small detail.

j One of your team is friendly and flexible, the other unpleasant and unreasonable. Your opponent will want to please Mr/Ms Nice to avoid Mr/Ms Nasty.

1	2	3	4	5	6	7	8	9	10
e	d	b	a	c	g	j	h	f	i

Discussion

2 How might you respond to each of the tactics in 1? Can you see any risks in using them yourself?

3 🔲 17.2 Listen to extracts from two different negotiations. Which tactics in 1 are they trying to use? How successful are they?

Extract 1 ☐2☐ ☐4☐

Extract 2 ☐8☐ ☐7☐

The language of bargaining

4 Reconstruct the following sentences from the negotiation extracts in 3 by putting the words in **bold** in the correct order. Then listen again and check your answers.

a OK, so, do **take agreement we're in on I it** volume?

OK, so, do I take it we're in agreement on volume?

b Wouldn't it be a **idea before talk to good we prices go** any further?

Wouldn't it be a good idea to talk prices before we go any further?

c But in **happy principle taking about you're** forty cases, right?

But in principle you're happy about taking forty cases, right?

d Look, **price back getting to a for** moment.

Look, getting back to price for a moment.

e Can you give us some **what idea of of kind figure were you** thinking of?

Can you give us some idea of what kind of figure you were thinking of?

f There **seems slight a been have to** misunderstanding.

There seems to have been a slight misunderstanding.

g With **prices respect simply are your not** competitive.

With respect, your prices are simply not competitive.

h I'm afraid that **absolute really bottom our is** line.

I'm afraid that really is our absolute bottom line.

i Let's set the price **side moment the issue to one for**, shall we?

Let's set the price issue to one side for the moment, shall we?

j I'll throw **free service 12 parts and months' as in** well.

I'll throw in 12 months' free parts and service as well.

k Now, I **can't fairer that say than**, now can I?

Now, I can't say fairer than that, now can I?

l What we'd really like to **movement see is more on bit a** price.

What we'd really like to see is a bit more movement on price.

m A 6% discount **quite is had not what in we** mind.

A 6% discount is not quite what we had in mind.

n We were **closer hoping something for bit a** to 10%.

We were hoping for something a bit closer to 10%.

o I don't think **stretch far could I as as** that.

I don't think I could stretch as far as that.

p Surely **sort we something out can** here.

Surely we can sort something out here.

q Would **meet willing be you to** us halfway?

Would you be willing to meet us halfway?

r We might **position be a increase to in** our order.

We might be in a position to increase our order.

s We'd need to **bit on flexibility see a more** terms of payment.

We'd need to see a bit more flexibility on terms of payment.

t I suppose **manoeuvre room there be may some for** there.

I suppose there may be some room for manoeuvre there.

The language of bargaining

4 Ask students to do the task individually or, for variety, divide the class into groups and have students compete to finish the task first. Play the recording through again so that students can check their answers. Pause the recording after each phrase, to give students time to check. Alternatively, ask one of the students to come out to the front and operate the CD/cassette player and the rest of the class to indicate when to pause the recording.

Recording script for page T91

 17.2

Extract 1

A: OK, **so, do I take it we're in agreement on volume?**

B: Er, well, just a minute, **wouldn't it be a good idea to talk prices before we go any further?**

A: Yes, of course. **But in principle you're happy about taking forty cases, right?**

B: Er, well, in principle, yes, if the product's as good as you say it is …

A: Splendid, that's settled then.

B: … But, **look, getting back to price for a moment.** This would be just a trial order, you understand? Sale or return. Until we see how it sells. So, **can you give us some idea of what kind of figure you were thinking of?**

A: €50.

B: €50 per case.

A: Er, no. Per pack.

B: Per pack? **There seems to have been a slight misunderstanding.** A pack is just 12 bottles, right?

A: Yes, that's right.

B: Is this meant to be some kind of joke or something? €50 per pack? That's over €4 a bottle. By the time we've added a decent margin, you realise we're looking at a retail price of €7 minimum. How am I supposed to sell a one-litre bottle of water for €7, Mr Koivisto?

A: Ms Barrett, *O-Zone* is an innovative, premium product. A pure oxygen-enriched drink. We're not talking about a bottle of Perrier here.

B: Well, that's as may be, but €7!

A: *O-Zone* is an exciting opportunity to get in at the start of a new trend in luxury health drinks.

B: Well, there's no way on earth I'm paying you €4 for a bottle of oxygenated water, Mr Koivisto. **With respect, your prices are simply not competitive.**

A: Ms Barrett, there *are* no competitors in this market. *O-Zone* is a unique product and at €4 – well, **I'm afraid that really is our absolute bottom line**.

B: So you're saying it's take it or leave it?

A: I'm afraid so.

B: Well, then, I think I'll have to leave it …

A: Wha …? Now, just a minute. You said on the phone you might want 100 cases.

B: That was before I knew your water was more expensive than Chardonnay, Mr Koivisto. OK, look, **let's set the price issue to one side for the moment, shall we?** Tell me a bit more about the product …

Extract 2

A: OK, I tell you what I'll do. If you order 250 units today, I can offer you not our usual five but a six per cent discount, free delivery and **I'll throw in 12 months' free parts and service as well**. Now, **I can't say fairer than that, now can I?** Of course, that's only if you can give me the order today. Can't hold the offer, I'm afraid.

B: Well, erm, Robert, isn't it?

A: Rob. Call me Rob.

B: Well, now, Rob, we appreciate the free service and delivery, but to be honest with you, **what we'd really like to see is a bit more movement on price**. I'm afraid **a six per cent discount is not quite what we had in mind. We were hoping for something a bit closer to ten.**

A: Ten per cent? **I don't think I could stretch as far as that.** Not unless this was a substantially bigger order.

C: Oh, come on! You'll have to do a lot better than that, Mr Hayes. You're not the only precision tool manufacturer, you know.

B: Hold on, Gavin. Let's hear Rob out.

C: Well, frankly, I think we're wasting each other's time here. We've already been offered a much better deal by Magnusson's.

B: Now, wait a minute, wait a minute. **Surely we can sort something out here**. Rob, **would you be willing to meet us halfway?**

A: How do you mean?

B: Well, if you were to offer us an eight per cent discount, **we might be in a position to increase our order**, say, by fifty units. But **we'd need to see a bit more flexibility on terms of payment**. Maybe on installation costs too.

A: Erm, well, **I suppose there may be some room for manoeuvre there**. I'd need to check. Can you give me a moment to have another look at the figures?

B: Sure. In fact, let's take a short time-out, shall we? And meet back here in, say, half an hour?

A: OK, fine.

C: I still say we'd be better off going with Magnusson's.

5 This exercise highlights some of the nuances of expression in the language in exercise 4. Students work individually to answer the questions and then discuss their answers in pairs or small groups. Check the answers with the whole class.

Point out that the use of *seems/appears,* modifiers like *quite/a bit,* modal verbs like *may/might/would* etc are characteristic of a tendency to 'soften' language when negotiating in English. Ask students follow-up questions to compare negotiating styles in their own language e.g. *How similar is the language of bargaining in your language? Do you use any similar structures/expressions to those in exercise 4? Does the language of bargaining in English appear rather vague or too direct compared to your language?*

Ask students to categorise the language in exercise 4 under functional headings e.g. *recapping on details, asking for/checking figures, indicating that you are not satisfied, asking for a better deal, making an improved offer* etc.

Direct students' attention to the Grammar link on page 124 for more information and practice on the grammar of diplomacy and persuasion.

Showing disapproval

6 Elicit examples of how students might show disapproval and ask students to comment on how 'strong' they think these expressions are. Correct any misunderstandings in register/appropriate use of these expressions. Then ask students to complete the expressions in exercise 6. Check the answers with the class, reminding students that they should only use these expressions if they are dealing with people they know very well. Elicit more neutral alternatives for the expressions e.g.

   a   I think there must be some misunderstanding.

   b   I'm afraid I can't accept the figure of €4.

   c   Is that your best offer? I was hoping for more flexibility on (price).

   d   I'm not sure that we can reach an agreement here.

Negotiating strategy

7 🔲 **17.3** As a lead-in to the listening task, ask students to brainstorm tips for successful negotiating e.g. stay calm, be clear about what you want, be prepared to compromise etc. Collate the best ideas into a 'top ten' and write them on the board. Play the recording through once and get students to tick off any of the tips that are mentioned by the negotiators.

Check/Pre-teach: *tradeable* (in this context, something you would be willing to compromise on), *to concede, one-off deal, tough, to pause, to give away* (your strategy), *defensive, trap, to phrase.*

Ask students to read the questions in exercise 7. Then play the recording, pausing between speakers. Students check their answers by comparing with a partner. Play sections of the recording again if necessary.

Ask students which of the five speakers they agree with most and why. Elicit examples from students' own experiences which support/refute the speakers' advice.

Idioms

8 Ask students to discuss the meanings of the idioms in pairs. If necessary, refer students to the recording script on page 158 where the idioms appear in context, before checking the answers. Point out that it is useful to recognise idioms like these, but not advisable to overuse them, as this sounds unnatural to native speakers. Ask the students if similar idioms exist in their own language.

🔲 **17.3**

Speaker 1
Make your priorities clear before you begin, that's my advice. I always say remember to check your tie. Not the one you wear round your neck, your T-I-E. 'T' stands for 'tradeables'. These are the things you'll take if you can get them, but they're not that important to you and you'll concede them if it helps you to push the negotiation forward. 'I' stands for 'ideals'. These are the things you'd really like to get and will fight to get, but not if it costs you the deal. Finally, and most importantly, 'E' stands for 'essentials'. It's not that these are absolutely non-negotiable. Everything's negotiable. But if it looks like you're not going to get your essentials, then that's the time to start thinking about walking away from the negotiating table.

Speaker 2
Well, frankly, I get a bit tired of hearing people go on about win-win negotiating. I mean, let's face it, a lot of negotiations are basically win-lose, and your opponent's interests are the last thing you should be worrying about. Buying a house, a car, double-glazing – all win-lose situations. And you'd be surprised how many business negotiations are basically one-off deals as well. In my opinion, in a win-lose situation the tougher you are – without actually being aggressive – the further you'll get. That's

because your opponent takes your attitude as an indication of what's possible and what's not. And the friendlier you seem, the higher their expectations will be. It's like the old saying: **give them an inch and they'll take a mile**.

Speaker 3
'You always know who is going to win a negotiation – it's he who pauses the longest.' I forget who it was who said that but it's pretty good advice – basically, shut up! And remember that silence is very often your best weapon. It's a very difficult argument to counter. Faced with prolonged and uncomfortable silences, your opponent is liable to make another concession or give away their strategy or weaken their own position by becoming defensive. So **play your cards close to your chest**. Talk less, learn more. There's an old Swedish proverb: 'Talking is silver. But listening is gold.'

Speaker 4
I think the biggest trap less experienced negotiators fall into is to turn the whole negotiation into a debate, which it isn't. This is sometimes called 'positional negotiating'. Both sides end up arguing the whys and wherefores, rationalising their position, trying to justify themselves. It's a complete waste of time. You're not there to convince your opponent that you're right. He doesn't care if you're right or not. And neither should you. You're there to explore both sides'

interests, generate options and trade concessions – preferably giving away things that mean little to you but a lot to him and receiving the opposite in return. This is 'interest-based negotiation' – discovering the needs, desires and fears behind your opponent's position and working on those. The two phrases you need most of all are: 'If …, then …?': If I give you that, then what do I get? And 'What if …?': What if we looked at this another way? What if we did this instead?

Speaker 5
The key skill in negotiating is the ability to ask the right questions – and ask lots of them. In fact, there's an organisation called the Huthwaite Research Group, who recorded hundreds of negotiations and guess what they found? 'Skilled negotiators ask more than twice as many questions as average negotiators.' So, my advice is: phrase as many of your comments as possible as questions. You don't understand something? Don't say you don't understand – you'll look stupid. Ask a question – you'll look intelligent. You strongly disagree? Don't say you strongly disagree – they'll think you're being difficult. Ask a question – they'll think you're trying to be helpful. You have a good idea? Don't say you have a good idea – they'll wish it was *their* idea. Ask a question. They'll think it *was* their idea. Keep those questions coming and **don't take 'no' for an answer!**

5 Look back at the expressions in 4 and answer the following questions.

a Find two phrases which mean 'bad news coming'.

With respect; I'm afraid

b Explain the use of the word _seems_ in **f**. _It makes the statement less direct._

c If you change sentences **e** and **n** into the present tense, does this make them sound more or less negotiable? _less_

d Do the question tags in **i** and **k** make it easier or more difficult to disagree?

easier

e Does the negative question form in **b** make the suggestion

more persuasive? ☐ more diplomatic? ☐ both? ☑

f Why do you think the speakers use words like _slight, some, a bit_ and _quite?_

They want to soften the impact of negative information.

Grammar link

for more on the grammar
of diplomacy &
persuasion see page 124

g What is the overall effect of changing _wouldn't_ to _isn't_ in **b**, _can_ to _will_ in **e**, _could_ to _can_ in **o**, _would_ to _are_ in **q**, _might_ to _are_ in **r** and _may_ to _is_ in **t**?

They leave almost no room for manoeuvre.

Showing disapproval

6 The following expressions from the negotiations in 3 show strong disapproval, but think twice before using them yourself as they may cause offence. Complete them using the pairs of words in the box.

lot + that	joke + something	other + time	way + earth

a Is this meant to be some kind of _joke_ or _something_ ?

b There's no _way_ on _earth_ I'm paying you €4.

c Oh, come on! You'll have to do a _lot_ better than _that_ .

d Frankly, I think we're wasting each _other_ 's _time_ here.

Negotiating strategy

7 🔊 17.3 Listen to five experienced negotiators talking about strategy and answer the questions.

Speaker 1 What does T.I.E. stand for? _Tradeables, Ideals, Essentials_

Speaker 2 How can a friendly attitude be counter-productive?

It may raise your opponent's hopes and expectations.

Speaker 3 Why is silence more powerful than talking?

It makes your opponent uncomfortable and more likely to weaken their position.

Speaker 4 How do you avoid pointless debates?

focus on interests, not positions

What are the two most useful phrases in a negotiation?

If ..., then ...? What if ...?

Speaker 5 What did the Huthwaite Research Group discover?

Skilled negotiators ask more than twice as many questions as average ones.

The speaker mentions three things it's better to phrase as questions. What are they? _misunderstandings, disagreements, good ideas_

Idioms

8 Discuss the meaning of the following idioms with a partner. They were all in 7.

a Give them an inch and they'll take a mile.

If you give people a little of what they want, they will then want to take more.

b Play your cards close to your chest.

Don't tell people what you are thinking or planning.

c Don't take 'no' for an answer. _Keep pushing until you get agreement._

Negotiating a recording contract

Discussion **1** What kind of music are you into? Compare your tastes with a partner.

Pop trivia **2** Work with a partner to answer the following questions. If you've no idea, just have a guess! Then check your answers in the article.

    a Who are the world's wealthiest rock band?
    b Who are the world's five most bankable solo performers?
    c What are the two bestselling albums of all time?
    d What are the two bestselling singles of all time?
    e Which pop song has been recorded in over 2,000 versions?

Inside the
music business

The world's biggest band When Mick, Keith, Charlie and Ronnie come on stage at the Giants Stadium in New York to 40,000 adoring fans, they have the satisfaction of knowing that the Rolling
5 Stones are easily the world's wealthiest rock band. Having generated more than $1.5 billion in gross revenues since 1989, two thirds of that earned on tour, they have made more money than even fellow megastars U2, Bruce Springsteen and Sting.

10 **Financial acumen** Now firmly established rock legends, the Stones are also a rock-solid business. It was their chief financial advisor, London banker Prince Rupert zu Loewenstein, who was first to see that, whilst concerts make the most money, music rights
15 provide the steadiest income stream. And though the Stones may never have produced a real blockbuster on the scale of Fleetwood Mac's *Rumours* or Pink Floyd's *Dark Side of the Moon*, Jagger and Richards have made over 40 albums and written more than
20 200 songs. Each time they get airplay, they collect 50 per cent of the royalties. According to *Fortune* magazine, that amounts to $56 million in the past decade. Microsoft alone paid them $4 million to use *Start Me Up* in the Windows 95 commercial.

25 **Big business** The music business has come a long way since the Stones started out in the 60s. In those days record labels like Motown, Island and Elektra all had their own distinctive sound, and you could have a string of top ten hits but still barely be able to afford
30 the bus fare home from your latest sell-out gig. These days just five major music companies – UMG, Sony, Warner, EMI and BMG – control 75 to 80 per cent of all commercially released recordings and the sums of money involved are huge.

35 **Bankability** Today's most profitable solo performers are Michael Jackson, Madonna, Elton John, Celine Dion and Garth Brooks. The back catalogues of Sinatra and Elvis also bring in millions. In fact, dead Elvis started

out-earning live Elvis in 1988. Unbelievably, the world's
40 bestselling single of all time remains Bing Crosby's *White Christmas*, closely followed by the version of *Candle in the Wind* Elton John sang at the funeral of Princess Diana, and the most recorded pop song ever is The Beatles' *Yesterday*, which exists in over 2,000
45 different versions. But the real money has always been in albums, not singles. The two top-sellers are Michael Jackson's *Thriller* and Alanis Morissette's *Jagged Little Pill*. Both have sold around 30 million units worldwide.

Rights and rip-offs With this kind of money at
50 stake, it's not surprising that the relationship between artist and record company can be an uneasy one, with young up-and-coming bands often too dazzled by the prospect of stardom to look closely at the small print in their contracts. Even established performers like
55 Prince and George Michael have had well-publicised clashes with their management. Courtney Love went so far as to file a lawsuit against Geffen Records to be released from her contract. And Mariah Carey found herself in the opposite situation, reputedly being paid
60 off to the tune of £19.5 million when Virgin Records decided it didn't want to record her after all.

The future of music But soon it may be the record companies themselves who start losing out. Piracy already costs the industry $4.3 billion a year, and with
65 the arrival of MP3, only sound quality stands in the way of all music being burned onto CD on personal computers. Some 'Indie' music labels like Bombco produce albums
70 exclusively on the Internet and artists as high-profile as David Bowie have experimented with website launches of their latest recordings. Of course, the major
75 music companies have fought back by creating downloadable music services of their own, but with more direct access to the consumer, bands may yet be able to
80 fulfil their dream of being immortalised without first having to sell their soul.

Bing Crosby ▶

Negotiating a record contract

In this final section, students discuss music and test their knowledge of pop trivia. They read a text about the music business and then practise understanding vocabulary from context. A listening task about a meeting at a record label provides the background to the final fluency activity in which students roleplay a negotiation between the representatives of a new band and a record company.

Discussion

1 As a lead-in to this section, name your favourite kind of music, song and recording artist. Divide the students into pairs and ask them to compare musical tastes. Do a quick poll of the class to find out the most popular type of music, song and group or singer.

Pop trivia

2 Students work in pairs to answer the questions. If appropriate, set up this exercise as a quiz and get students to write down their answers before scanning the text to check. Establish which pair got the highest score in the quiz.

Check/Pre-teach: *acumen, music rights, airplay, rip-off* (informal for 'unfair deals'), *at stake, reputedly, piracy*. Ask students to re-read the text and then briefly summarise the main points of each paragraph, working in pairs.

3 Ask students to look back at the text to find the words and expressions a–n. Remind students to look for a word in the same form as the definition and to use the context to help them identify the meaning. Check the answers.

4 🔲 **17.4** Write the names of the people in the recording on the board: Tess, Mr Ronnie Logan, Kate, Miles. Check/Pre-teach: *A&R people* (*artist and repertoire* – people who look for new talent in the music industry), *to snap up* (to quickly take the opportunity to make a deal with an artist), *to sniff around* (in this context, to try to make contacts), *demo* (demonstration material), *inconsistent, tricky, a class act, glamorous, to tune into.*

Let students read the four questions first and get them to predict the type of language they will hear and possible answers to the questions. Play the recording through once and let students check their answers in pairs. Play the recording again if necessary before checking answers with the whole class.

As a link to the fluency task, ask students to review the strengths and weaknesses of the band (the lead singer's voice, they are musically strong, they look good; they are inconsistent, they need help with direction, the drummer isn't very good). Refer students to the recording script on page 158 and have them underline any useful vocabulary for negotiating the recording contract in exercise 5 e.g. *a demo, musical identity, a class act* etc.

Fluency

5 As a lead-in to the roleplay, write the following on the board: *song rights, royalties, advance, airplay fees, backlist.* Elicit relevant examples from the music industry e.g. artists selling their song rights early and losing a fortune.

Check/Pre-teach: *to stand to make a lot of money, vulnerable, exploitation, rumour, commitment, to commission, net receipts, the bubble bursts* (a positive situation turns negative), *split, paparazzi, to retain, to offset.*

Divide the class into AB teams. With larger groups, set up further AB teams to do simultaneous negotiations, in different rooms if possible. Refer team A to their

negotiating brief on page 137 and team B to page 139. Have students read their brief carefully, underlining the key information.

Give students plenty of time to prepare and take notes. Ask students to discuss the importance of each of the objectives 1–8 and to categorise each point as T-I-E (*tradeables, ideals, essentials*). Give students a few minutes to review the negotiating tactics on page 91 and to decide if they want to use any of them. Also refer them to the key language in the recording scripts on page 157 and have them note down useful phrases.

Arrange the seating to reflect a meeting room and if possible, have drinks on hand to add authenticity. Explain that the meeting will take place at *Starburst's* offices, so team B should be ready to welcome team A. Set a length of 45–60 minutes for the negotiation and appoint a chairperson. Write the following agenda on the board or hand it out as a photocopy:

1 Welcome and purpose of meeting
2 Discussion of potential contract for/management of *The Penitents* to cover: line-up, term, royalties, deductions, advances, territory, touring, songwriting
3 Recap on decisions in 2
4 Final decisions and action points

Monitor and take feedback notes. When the negotiation has finished, ask the students to think about what went well and what they would do differently next time. Give feedback on students' negotiation tactics and skills, and on overall fluency, before highlighting important or common errors.

If you're short of time

Leave out page 90 and start the unit with *Negotiating style* on page 91.

Omit exercises 7–8 on page 93.

Ask students to read the role cards from exercise 5 on page 95 for homework.

🔲 **17.4**

A: Tess?
B: Mr Logan. It's Kate and Miles to see you.
A: Ah, good. Send them right in.
C: Hi, Ronnie.
A: Kate, good to see you. You're looking great as usual. Miles come on in. Rough night, huh? Erm, sit anywhere you like. Can I get you a beer?
C: It's a little early for me, Ronnie. Do you have an Evian or something?
A: No problem. There you go. Miles?
D: Er, don't think I could face anything right now, man.
A: No, you certainly don't look as though you could. So, you two had quite an evening at the Marquee, so I hear.
D: You could say that.
C: Ronnie, you have to sign this band. You could hardly move for A&R people last night. If we don't snap them up, someone else will. I saw Jimmy Armstrong from Sony sniffing around.
A: Uh huh. Well, he usually is.
C: Yeah, and EMI were there as well. This band's hot. You listened to the demo I sent you, right?

A: I did.
C: And?
A: Well, …
C: Oh, come on, Ronnie. These guys are the best thing to come out of Ireland since U2 and you know it.
A: I wouldn't go as far as that, Kate. They sound a little inconsistent on the tape. They need to work on a clear musical identity, if you ask me.
C: Well, maybe they need a little help in that direction. We can work on that. But you have to admit the lead singer's voice is just amazing. In fact, they're musically really strong all round.
A: OK, I'll give you that. Apart from the drummer, that is, who's pretty second-rate. So he'd have to go.
C: She.
A: She? They have a female drummer? Interesting. Well, anyway, she's no good.
C: Could be tricky to fire. She's the lead singer's girlfriend.
A: Hm. I'm going off them already.
C: Ronnie, believe me, *The Penitents* are a class act. And I'm not easily impressed, you know that.

A: True, you're not. Miles, meet the woman who turned down *Oasis.*
D: Fine by me. I never liked them.
C: I thought we weren't going to talk about that any more.
A: OK, OK. Well, what do *The Penitents* look like? No, let me guess. Like they haven't eaten a hot meal for a week and cut their own hair, right?
C: Not at all. The lead guitarist looks like Keanu Reeves. The drummer's fabulous even if her drumming's a little off. In fact, they're all pretty glamorous. Ronnie, I have a good feeling about this one.
A: OK, call their manager and set something up. But not next week. I'm at the MTV awards.
C: OK, I'll do that. Oh, and by the way, you might want to tune in to VH1 at eight this evening. They're being interviewed live.
A: They are? Well, why didn't you say so before? Look, give me their manager's number. I might just call him myself this afternoon …

---

3 Find words and phrases in the article which mean:

a money earned before tax and costs (paragraph 1) gross revenues

b the most regular source of money (paragraph 2) steadiest income stream

c highly successful album, book or film (paragraph 2) blockbuster

d money paid to artists each time their work is sold or performed (paragraph 2)
royalties

e a series of bestselling records (paragraph 3) a string of top ten hits

f a musical performance to which all the tickets are sold (paragraph 3)
a sell-out gig

g earning more than (paragraph 4) out-earning

h likely to become popular soon (paragraph 5) up-and-coming

i excited at the chance of becoming stars (paragraph 5) dazzled by
the prospect of stardom

j the details in a contract – often limiting your rights (paragraph 5)
the small print

k angry disagreements (paragraph 5) clashes

l well-known (paragraph 6) high-profile

m becoming famous (paragraph 6) being immortalised

n do anything to win fame (paragraph 6) sell their soul

4 🔊 17.4 A major record label is considering signing a new band. Listen to an extract from a meeting between their A&R people (talent scouts) and senior management.

a Why does Kate think they have to sign the band quickly?
A lot of other record companies were at the concert and may sign them first.

b What are the band's strengths?
an excellent lead singer, musically strong, good-looking

c Why isn't Ronnie as impressed as Kate?
The band doesn't have an identity; the drummer's bad.

d Why does Ronnie sound more enthusiastic at the end of the meeting?
The band is about to get massive publicity on cable TV.

Fluency **5** Work in two teams to negotiate a recording contract between the record company and the up-and-coming rock band you heard about in 4.

Team A you are representatives from the band *The Penitents* and their managers. The high-profile record company *Starburst* is interested in signing your band. See page 137 for your negotiating objectives.

Team B you are executives from the record company *Starburst* and their lawyers. You are interested in signing the promising new band *The Penitents*. See page 139 for your negotiating objectives.

18 Shaping the future

The best way to predict the future is to invent it. *Alan Kay, director of research at Apple*

Discussion   **1** Read the following and discuss the likelihood of the predictions using the expressions in the box.

> It's already happened.
> According to this, it should've already happened, but it hasn't so far.
> I suppose it's inevitable.   It's bound to happen sooner or later.
> It might just happen.   It's pretty unlikely in the foreseeable future.
> I can't see it happening in my lifetime.   It could never happen.
> There's no way it could happen.   It's pure science fiction.

BTEXACT
TECHNOLOGIES 2001

The future is hard to predict but one thing is certain – in the distant future the world will be a very different place. The technology timeline is produced to give BT researchers and managers a view of what the operating environment may be like at any future date, so that our products and services can be better targeted to the needs of the customer. Not all these technologies will be successful in the marketplace. Some won't ever be implemented at all, but as the rest come on stream, our lives will improve in many ways.

Innovation	Date expected
• Designer babies	2005
• Cars with automatic steering	2008
• 25% of TV celebrities computer-generated	2010
• Insect-like robots used in warfare	2010
• Academic study unnecessary in the age of smart machines	2013
• First manned mission to Mars	2015
• Space hotel for 300 guests	2015
• Electronic pets outnumber organic pets	2020
• Fully functioning artificial eyes	2024
• Holographic TV	2025
• Virtual reality used extensively in retirement homes	2025
• Emotion control devices	2025
• Robots physically and mentally superior to humans	2030
• First Bionic Olympics	2030
• Direct human-to-computer brainlink	2030
• Moonbase the size of a small village	2040
• Time travel invented	2075
• Faster-than-light travel	2100

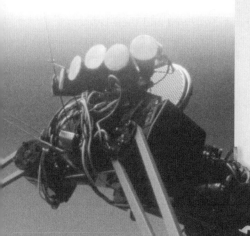

Talking points # 18 Shaping the future

The final unit in the book looks forward to the future.

Students discuss the likelihood of a number of predictions on how technology could change the future of society. They focus on the language of predicting and talking about the future before making their own predictions.

Students read different texts in which futurologists offer radically different visions of the future and then exchange information and ideas. The final section contains a recording of business people talking about their reactions to the ideas in the texts.

In this first section, students read a list of technological developments with their predicted date and discuss how likely they are to take place. They study language which can be used when discussing the future, and complete expressions used for speculating and predicting. Students then make their own predictions about the future.

Warm-up

Divide the class into small groups and get them to brainstorm the question: *What does the future mean to you?* Students then report back on three things which they feel will be part of the future. Alternatively, ask students to describe the vision of the future shown in popular films e.g. *Minority Report* or *2001: A Space Odyssey*. Examples include: *futuristic cityscape and cars, a thinking computer capable of making decisions, the ability to monitor/control human thought* etc.

Focus attention on the quotation from Alan Kay and elicit what he means (that those in Research and Development can actively engineer aspects of the future through their innovations). Ask follow-up questions e.g. *Which companies come to mind when thinking about 'inventing the future'?* Possible examples include Microsoft, Philips and Sony.

Discussion

1   Get students to compare the photos on pages 96 and 97. Ask focus questions e.g. *What do you think is shown on page 97?* (a device to enable the user to look backwards). *Do you know of any other inventions which have failed?* (e.g. Clive Sinclair's electric car).

Check/Pre-teach: *to target, to implement, to come on stream, warfare, holographic, virtual reality, bionic.* Ask students what they think the 'technology timeline' is and then get them to read the first paragraph of the text quickly to check (a set of innovations and the expected date that they will become a reality).

Focus attention on the expressions in the box and check the stress and intonation pattern for the longer ones. If appropriate, copy the phrases onto cards and hand these out for students to use as prompts during the discussion phase that follows.

Ask students to read the innovations list again and decide how likely they are to be produced by the time given. Elicit a few reactions to the innovations, using the expressions in the box. Divide the class into small groups and get students to continue giving and comparing their reactions to the list, using the language in the box. Monitor and take feedback notes.

Hold a class feedback session to establish where students agreed and disagreed most. Then hold a class vote to decide the three most likely predictions.

2 Students suggest answers to the three questions and justify their choice.

3 Ask students to add the adjectives to the timeline. Check the answers with the whole class, accepting that there may be a small degree of variation in the position of the adjectives e.g. *foreseeable* and *not-too-distant* are not precise terms, so the position of these could be interchangeable.

Check pronunciation of the adjectives. Write the following words on the board: *career, ambition, achievement* and elicit some true examples from the students using the time expressions.

4 Students complete the sentences individually with the words from the box. Check the answers before getting the students to complete the sentences with their own predictions. With weaker students, brainstorm specific questions on the following topics first: who will win a forthcoming sporting event/an imminent election/the next Oscars; what inflation will be over the next six months; what your company profitability will be next year.

5 Ask each student to read out their predictions to the class and to justify each one. Encourage the rest of the class to ask questions. With weaker groups, give each student a 'question card' (a card with a question mark on it). Explain that while each student gives their predictions, the others have to 'play' their card and ask the speaker a question.

2 Which of these technologies would

   a be the most beneficial to society?   **c** be the most controversial?
   b have the most marketing potential?

3 All the adjectives in the box can be used to talk about the future. Add them to the timeline below.

distant	near	foreseeable	immediate	not-too-distant

sooner ←————————————————————————————→ later
In the   <u>immediate</u>   <u>near</u>   <u>not-too-distant</u> <u>foreseeable</u>   <u>distant</u> future.

4 Complete the sentences with one word from the boxes. Then finish at least five with some predictions of your own concerning business, politics, the environment, leisure or life in general.

way	indications	era	possibility	possibilities	future

   a I think one industry that definitely has a bright <u>**future**</u> is …
   b Recent developments in … open up all kinds of exciting <u>**possibilities**</u>
   c All the <u>**indications**</u> are that …
   d I think we're about to enter an <u>**era**</u> of …
   e As far as I can see, … is still a very long <u>**way**</u> off.
   f As far as … is concerned, we can't exclude the <u>**possibility**</u> that …

future	outlook	brink	store	prospects	horizon

   g I think the long-term <u>**prospects**</u> for … are limited.
   h I think the part of the world facing the bleakest <u>**future**</u> is …
   i I believe we may be on the <u>**brink**</u> of …
   j The <u>**outlook**</u> for anyone involved in the … business is uncertain.
   k There seems to be political change on the <u>**horizon**</u> in …
   l It's impossible to tell what lies in <u>**store**</u> for …

5 Read out the predictions you made in 4 to the rest of the class. Be prepared to support your views.

The futurists

Discussion

1 What are the latest trends and developments in your line of business?

2 The business magazine *Fast Company* regularly features a column called *Futurist*. Work in two groups to read the predictions of six futurists they have interviewed. Group A read summaries 1–3. Group B read summaries 4–6. Choose a title for each summary, perhaps using words and phrases from the text.

1 _____

Christopher Dewdney is a fellow of the McLuhan Programme in Culture and Technology at the University of Toronto. According
5 to him, 'None of us is naturally human anymore.' At the moment we are in transition between the human and post-human – a condition he calls 'transhuman'. 'The goal of transhumanism,' explains Dewdney, 'is to surpass our current biological limitations, whether they be lifespan, physical beauty or the capabilities of our
10 brain.' Ironically, just as humans are beginning to play with their DNA structure and become more 'artificial', machines are becoming more 'lifelike'. At some point in the future 'we won't be able to differentiate between the two'. But, more significantly, the world may end up being divided into those who can afford to be genetically enhanced and those who can't, leading to 'a new class of beings
15 who will actually look and act like a different human species' – one that might even threaten conventional human beings.

2 _____

Ian Angell is Professor of Information Systems at the London School of Economics. Describing himself as 'an anarchic capitalist', he firmly believes that 'business should be running the world'. His disturbing vision of the future is one where an elite of brilliant business people and technologists will be allowed to run their own enterprises with a
5 minimum of government intervention. Indeed, the wealth-creating skills of these 'new barbarians', as Angell calls them, will be in such demand that countries will actually compete with each other to attract them as residents. But whilst these corporate free agents will be living in largely unregulated tax havens, billions of the less fortunate will be left behind living in crumbling, inefficient and crime-ridden megacities. 'Every
10 major technological shift creates winners and losers,' says Angell. 'Europe's a disaster because of a sentimental attachment to the welfare state, which is a vestige of the Industrial Age.'

3 _____

Gary Wright is a corporate demographer for the consumer products giant Procter & Gamble. Although world population, currently around six billion, is set to hit 12.5 billion by the end of the century, in the developed world it's not population growth but an ageing population that will have the most far-reaching consequences. By 2010 43%
5 of American adults will be over 50. As Wright points out, that's 97 million people. And as more and more take early retirement, fewer and fewer working people will be left to support them. Most of today's successful businesses grew up in a period of population explosion and rapid economic progress. But will business continue to flourish in the 'no-growth' or 'slow-growth' environment of the future? 'To an extent, immigration will
10 offset population declines,' says Wright, and, indeed, in many parts of the developing world the majority of people are under 35. But this could have serious cultural and political implications.

The futurists

In this section, students first discuss the future in their own sector of business. They then read and exchange ideas from texts in which futurologists offer radically different visions of the future. Finally, students listen to a series of business people talking about their reactions to the ideas in the texts.

Discussion

1 As a general lead-in, give a short presentation of some of the exciting trends in language teaching, such as the growth of online learning, virtual schools and voice recognition. (Information on these areas is available on the Internet.)

Ask students to tell you about some of the latest trends and developments in their area of business. If you have a class from the same business sector, divide the group in two and get them to brainstorm their ideas and note down key points. An individual or team from each group then presents and justifies the group's ideas.

If the students' company produces an in-house journal, or posts information on their company intranet, use this as a source of ideas. Alternatively, students can check their company website for developments, if appropriate.

2 Ask students if they have heard of the magazine *Fast Company* (a US magazine launched in by two former *Harvard Business Review* editors. It is founded on the idea that business changes the world and it aims to highlight new business practices, as well as focus on the people behind the ideas.)

Ask students what they think a *futurist* does (predict the future and write and/or give talks about what life will be like). Divide the class into AB groups. Explain that each group is going to read three texts each based on the predictions of a futurist. Students work in their groups to predict what aspects of life their texts will focus on. Group A then reads texts 1–3 and Group B reads texts 4–6 quickly to check their answers. For larger classes,

assign one text per student. With weaker classes, give students the possible titles listed below and get them to predict what they think the content will be.

Still working in their AB groups, get students to underline key words that are new in the texts and to check the meaning with the rest of the group. If appropriate, students can also use dictionaries. Then check the following vocabulary items with the whole class: *in transition, to surpass, lifespan, to enhance, anarchic, barbarian, tax haven, demographer, to flourish, to offset, to infiltrate, a precious commodity, anti-ageing, multitasking, to embrace, brain scan, gene therapy*.

Students in their AB groups read the texts again and write notes to help them summarise the content at the next stage. For weaker students, provide the following template:
Name of futurist:
Position/credentials:
Central idea:
Example(s):
Your reaction to the text:

Ask students to think of a possible title for their texts. Offer students help with strategies for selecting an appropriate title e.g. ask *What's this paragraph about?* and then analyse the answer to extract the key words; look for one phrase in the text which seems to capture the central idea.

Possible titles

1	Transhumanism; Human machine
2	The new barbarians
3	Age of the ageing
4	Electronic immigrants
5	Addicted to speed; The multitasking future
6	High-Tech, High-Touch

Recording script for page T99

Speaker 5
Well, this idea that our kids are going to be achieving a hundred times more over their working lives sounds a little improbable to me. Surely it depends on what kind of job they're doing. Everybody seems to think we all work at lightning speed these days. But, let's face it, in some jobs, things haven't changed all that much in twenty years. We're not all computer geeks. I don't think life itself is so much faster. It's just that we want so much more out of it and that's why we get so stressed trying to fit it all in. When I go on business trips to the States, it always amazes me how hyperactive everybody is. They're fixing up a time to play tennis on the phone,

having lunch at their desk while they do their spreadsheets, skim the Wall Street Journal and instant message their childminder to check their kid's doing her math homework. You want to go out for a beer with them, you need an appointment! I think what they need is to come to Mexico and relax a little.

Speaker 6
I think Naisbitt is absolutely right. As we get more technological, we also want to recapture some of the old-fashioned values of a simpler, slower, more natural age. I mean the quickest way to buy a book is through Amazon, which is a marvellous service, but it cannot really compare with the

pleasure of wandering around a good bookshop. I have a lot of fun playing computer games with my seven-year-old son, but I still want to take him ice-skating or play football in the park. I work for a design company and, interestingly, if you look at many of the most popular industrial designs of the last ten years or so, you find they all have an organic, retro look about them: the iMac, for example, the Nokia mobile phone, the Dyson vacuum cleaner, the Smart Car. No straight lines, lots of curves and bright colours. Soft, subtle technology. As Naisbitt says, high-tech, but high-touch.

3 Regroup students from group A with students from B. Students then summarise the extracts they have read and explain the title of each text, using their notes. When students have completed the information exchange, briefly review useful language for discussing implications of each vision of the future e.g. *X will open up (all kinds of exciting possibilities for …), X will create (serious divisions between …), X could lead to (new opportunities in emerging markets)*. Students discuss the implications in groups and then choose a spokesperson to feed back to the whole class. Monitor and take feedback notes.

Ask follow-up questions e.g. *Which vision of the future do you find most/least appealing? What aspects of each vision would create a best- and worse-case scenario for the future?*

4 📼 **18.1** Tell students they are going to hear a recording of six business people giving their own reactions to the extracts in exercise 2. Check/Pre-teach: *nonsense, alter, (memory chip) implant, genius, a law unto themselves, welfare state, well-off, grey dollar (spending power of older people), smart drugs, devastating, at lightning speed, computer geek, hyperactive, organic, retro, curve.*

Dictate the following statements, or write them on the board. Play the recording through once and ask students to identify the speakers' views by saying if the statements are true or false.
Speaker 1 is impressed by the idea of being post-human. (F)
Speaker 2 would be happy to live in a 'new barbarian' state. (F)
Speaker 3 is looking forward to getting old. (T)
Speaker 4 believes that human contact is important. (T)
Speaker 5 thinks we will achieve more in the future. (F)
Speaker 6 is negative about old-fashioned values. (F)

Tell students they are going to hear the recording again and they need to take notes of each speaker's opinions and attitude and any examples they give to support their view. With weaker students, write the following template on the board:
Overall opinion of the futurist's vision:
Examples to support opinion:
General tone/attitude:

Play the recording again, pausing after each speaker to allow students to make notes. Divide the students into pairs small/groups to compare their own reactions to those of the speakers. With weaker students, write focus questions on the board: *How far do you agree with speaker (1)? What do you think of the examples he/she gave? Do you share his/her overall attitude to the futurist's vision?* Monitor and take feedback notes. Hold a class feedback session and elicit examples of close agreement/strong disagreement between the students and speakers on the recording.

As a humorous end to the lesson, draw students' attention to the *Back to the future* box and elicit their reaction. Divide students into groups and get them to brainstorm strange or bizarre trends for the future. Students present their ideas to the group and then conduct a class vote for the most convincing idea.

Give feedback on overall fluency before highlighting important or common errors.

If you're short of time

Set the reading task in exercise 2 on page 98 for homework. Alternatively, omit exercise 4 on page 99.

See page T98 for speakers 5 and 6.

📼 **18.1**
Speaker 1
Well, part of me thinks this post-human thing is just a lot of nonsense, really. I mean, even if you could genetically alter people to make them stronger or slimmer, well, so what? It's just like going to the gym and working out, isn't it? I don't think we're going to be creating superhumans for a very long time yet. So it's not going to make a whole lot of difference. Erm, and I've also read those stories about giving people memory chip implants to make them more intelligent. I suppose it could be done. And it would, in a way, give people an unfair advantage in exams and job interviews and so on. But, I mean, people already have an unfair advantage if they've had a better education, haven't they? So there's nothing new about buying advantages in life. To be honest with you, they'd have to be able to make me a real genius before I'd let some doctor start doing brain surgery on *me*!

Speaker 2
Hm, I don't like the idea of these 'new barbarians' living in luxury and controlling all the world's money, while the rest of us fight it out on the streets. Sounds a bit like that film *Blade Runner* to me. But, er, we're definitely seeing businesses getting more and

more powerful. I mean, with all the corporate scandals we've had recently, I do think that companies are a law unto themselves – they just do what they like, really. So I suppose it's not too difficult to imagine certain multimillionaires forcing governments to do pretty much what they want. Er, I am, though, totally against the idea of getting rid of the welfare state. A world in which the fortunate and successful are helped to be even more fortunate and successful and the rest of us are just basically forgotten doesn't sound like the kind of world I would want to live in.

Speaker 3
Well, on the ageing population idea, I think it's one of those things everybody knows about but they're just kind of ignoring it. I mean I read somewhere that half the over-65s who've ever lived are alive *today*! Of course, in one way that's good because you've got all those relatively well-off older people with plenty of time to spend their cash – you know, the so-called 'grey dollar'. That's going to be good for travel and tourism, the leisure industry, and medical and pharmaceutical companies. And, being old might be a lot more fun in the future. What with cosmetic surgery, smart drugs and Viagra we'll be living it up well into our 80s and 90s! The problem is, we're going to need

millions of young people to run our businesses while we're all having fun. That means increased immigration from the developing world, I think. Here in Germany we have a population of about 82 million, and seven million of those are immigrants. I think that figure could double at least in the next 20 years.

Speaker 4
Well, it all sounds like a good idea at first, doesn't it? You can take your skills anywhere in the world via the Internet without actually leaving home. But it's not really practical, is it? I mean for one thing, most jobs can't be done by telecommuting, even with things like videoconferencing and stuff like that. They've been talking about it for ages, but nobody seems to like working that way. Personally, I think you need human contact in most jobs. I know I do in mine. And I can't see professionals in the EU and the US and Japan just letting people in South-east Asia and Africa take their jobs. I mean it's bad enough exploiting cheap *manual* labour in those places already. But imagine if you also had low-paid engineers and lawyers and doctors working on the Net. The consequences for the professions could be devastating, not to mention the actual quality of service you might be getting.

4

Michele Bowman is the senior vice-president at Global Foresight Associates in Boston. In her opinion, in the networked world of the future, where you live will have very little effect on where you work, and citizenship will be far less important than 'cybership'. As Bowman points out, 'Electronic immigrants, also known as cross-border telecommuters,
5   are nothing new.' In fact, with cheaper international telecommunications, many western companies already employ people in the developing world as 'back office staff' dealing with such things as customer relations. In 2002 there was a public outcry in the UK when British Telecom proposed routing domestic telephone directory enquiries via India and Pakistan. Bowman claims that: 'As the global economy becomes more
10 integrated and interdependent, the ranks of these workers will grow' – and not only in routine jobs. Electronic immigrants may 'soon infiltrate high-end technical fields such as engineering and IT'.

5

Peter Cochrane is head of research for British Telecom Laboratories. His specialism is the speed of business. Here's one of Cochrane's startling statistics: 'A generation ago, the average person had a 100,000-hour working life – 40 hours a week, 50 weeks a year, for 50 years. Today we can do everything that person did in 10,000 hours. In the next
5   generation, people will be able to do it in 1,000 hours.' In other words, what our children will be able to achieve in just six months took our parents their entire working lives. Cochrane says 'We're addicted to speed' and we'll increasingly be willing to pay large sums of money to save our most precious commodity – time. This may mean actually prolonging our lives through anti-ageing medical advances or simply packing
10 more into the lives we've got by multitasking at work and by combining several leisure activities at once in what Cochrane calls 'parallel time'. One thing's for certain: genuine free time will cease to exist.

6

John Naisbitt is one of the world's leading futurists and the author of a series of bestsellers on the subject. In his latest blockbuster *High-Tech High-Touch*, Naisbitt makes the observation that even as we rush to embrace technology that makes our lives easier, we're also starting to reject technology that makes us feel less alive, less human.
5   Neither a technophobe nor a technophile, Naisbitt sees a great future for this middle way he calls 'high-tech high-touch'. High-tech is wanting the heart transplant, the brain scan, the gene therapy. High-touch is wanting more time with the family doctor. High-tech is chatting on the Internet to someone on the other side of the world. High-touch is chatting with your neigbour on the other side of the garden fence. High-tech is the
10 dashed-off e-mail. High-touch is the beautifully handwritten letter on headed notepaper. For business the message is clear: give the technology you're trying to sell the personal touch, or fail.

3   Team up with people from the other group. Explain your choice of titles, summarise what you read and discuss possible implications and opportunities for:

- society as a whole
- the world of business
- you personally
- your company

4   [📼] 18.1 Listen to six business people's opinions on the issues in 3 and compare your views.

Back to the future

When Elvis Presley died in 1977, there were 37 Elvis impersonators in the world. Today there are 48,000. If the current trend continues, one out of every three people in the world will be an Elvis impersonator by 2010.

Mark Gibbs, *Navigating the Internet*

1 Business or pleasure?

Tense review

Practice 1 Read the e-mail and underline the best grammatical choice in each case.

From: Charles Wellcome
To: Deborah Newton, Stephen Clark, Willem Maas, Tatiana Korbutt
Cc:
Subject: this year's client hospitality event

this year's client hospitality event

Dear all

As you (1) **know/are knowing**, the annual client hospitality event (2) **is fast approaching/will fast approach** and, as yet, we (3) **did not make/have not made** a final decision on where to hold it this year. One or two of you (4) **already came forward/have already come forward** with suggestions, which (5) **are currently considered/are currently being considered**, but, as we (6) **will have to/are having to** make the necessary arrangements quite soon, I'd like everybody's input on this asap. I (7) **thought/have thought** now (8) **was/has been** as good a time as any to start the ball rolling.

What I particularly (9) **want/am wanting** to avoid is a repetition of the fiasco we (10) **had/have had** last year at the show jumping event. Apart from the fact that very few of our clients (11) **have/are having** even the remotest interest in the sport, the atrocious weather (12) **meant/was meaning** that we (13) **walked/were walking** backwards and forwards through the mud between the showring and the hospitality tent all day. The whole thing (14) **was/has been** a complete disaster. People (15) **still complained/were still complaining** about it six months later!

This year we (16) **have planned/had planned** to do something more cultural like go to the opera or even a musical, but (17) **I've wondered/I've been wondering** if this is a good idea. A musical event (18) **doesn't seem/isn't seeming** to be the best place to network. We can hardly ask the singers to keep the noise down while we all (19) **have/will have** a good chat!

I (20) **do think/am thinking**, however, that an indoor event (21) **makes/is making** most sense, so can I ask you to (22) **think/be thinking** along those lines over the next few days? (23) **I've scheduled/I'd scheduled** a meeting for next Friday to discuss the matter further. So, (24) **I'm speaking/I'll speak** to you all then.

Charles

Practice 2 Try to complete the tense quiz in under five minutes.

1 *He **leaves** at five* means
   a today **b** every day **c** either

2 *We're **having** a meeting* means
   a now **b** soon **c** either

3 *Profits **went up**.* Are profits up now?
   a yes **b** no **c** maybe

4 *Profits **have gone up**.* Are profits up now?
   a yes **b** no **c** maybe

5 *He's **gone**.* Is he here?
   a yes **b** no **c** maybe

6 *I've just **been**.* Am I back?
   a yes **b** no **c** maybe

7 *When I arrived he **was** just **leaving**.* Was he there when I arrived?
   a yes **b** no **c** we don't know

8 *When I arrived he'd just **left**.* Was he there when I arrived?
   a yes **b** no **c** we don't know

9 *I've **tried** to phone her.* Am I still trying?
   a probably **b** probably not **c** we don't know

10 *I've **been trying** to contact her all morning.* Am I still trying?
   a probably **b** probably not **c** we don't know

Summary

You use the **Present Simple** to talk about permanent facts (*I'm Spanish*), routines (*I get home at seven each evening*) and scheduled future (*The bus gets in at one*).

You use the **Present Continuous** to talk about current, perhaps temporary, activities and situations (*I'm staying at the Hilton*) or future arrangements (*I'm flying to Rome in the morning*).

You use the **Present Perfect** to talk about things that started in the past and continue up to the present (*It's rained for a fortnight*), personal experiences no matter when they happened (*I've only ever snowboarded once*) and things which have an immediate consequence (*I've lost my car keys*). Words like *already, yet* and *since* are often in the same sentence as a present perfect verb.

You use the **Present Perfect Continuous** to talk about temporary situations that started in the past and may or may not be completed (*I've been working here since January 2002*).

Photocopiable

You use the **Past Simple** to talk about finished past actions or states (*I studied engineering at Oxford*). Phrases like *last week, a year ago,* etc. make the time reference clear.

You use the **Past Continuous** to talk about an action in progress in the past (*The company was losing money*). The Past Continuous gives the background to more important events which are in the Past Simple.

You use the **Past Perfect** to emphasise that one event happened before another in the past (*By the time I left college, I'd already decided I didn't want to be a lawyer*).

Some 'state' verbs like *think, know, understand* and *seem* are not generally used in the continuous form unless the meaning is different: *I think = I believe; I'm thinking = I'm considering something.*

will is a modal verb and, amongst its other uses, one of many ways of talking about the future (*I'll see you later*).

Lexis: Conversation

A bore is a fellow talking who can change the subject back to his topic of conversation faster than you can change it back to yours. *Laurence J. Peter, creator of the 'Peter Principle'*

1 Match the sentence starters on the left to the nouns on the right to make complete statements.

a   It was a very posh   bestseller.
b   It was the trip of a   restaurant.
c   It was a very close   news!
d   That's terrific   acquaintance.
e   It's your typical Hollywood   hotel.
f   The economy's in a   blockbuster.
g   She's really just an   match.
h   I've just read his latest   lifetime!
i   It's a top-class   sell-out.
j   I hear their latest tour was a   mess.

2 Find words and phrases in 1 which mean:

a   a game in which the score is almost level
    close _match_

b   expensive and high-quality _posh_ or _top-class_

c   successful film or book _blockbuster_

d   someone you know a little _acquaintance_

e   a very bad state _mess_

f   a play or concert to which all the tickets are sold _sell-out_

3 Put the conversation in the correct order.

☐1 We were just talking about this new sports centre they're building in town. Do you play any sport at all, Kim?

☐7 Not yet, no. Why, are you doing something?

☐5 Against Real Madrid? No, I missed it. I had to go to a birthday party.

☐12 No problem. Oh, before I forget. I've got two tickets to see them in Manchester if you're interested.

☐4 No, me neither. Talking of football, did you see the match last night?

☐10 Oh, right. Thanks for telling me. Incidentally, have you still got my *Rolling Stones* CD?

☐2 Me? Well, not really. I used to play a bit of football.

☐8 No, nothing special. By the way, sorry to talk business, but did you remember to send that estimate to Clive?

☐6 Pity. It was a great game. On the subject of parties, have you made any plans for New Year's Eve yet?

☐3 Did you? Me too. I was never any good, though.

☐11 Oops! Yeah, sorry. I meant to give it back to you. I'll bring in it tomorrow. Thanks for lending it to me.

☐9 Yeah, I sent it yesterday. Oh, that reminds me. Clive said to tell you he won't be able to make Thursday's meeting. He said he'd call you.

☐13 Are you kidding? Of course I'm interested! I've never seen them live.

4 Find six expressions in 3 to guide the conversation or change the subject.

a   _Incidentally_, ...
b   _Talking_ of ...
c   _By_ the _way_, ...
d   _Before_ I _forget_, ...
e   _That_ _reminds_ me, ...
f   _On the subject_ of ...

2 Exchanging information

Conditionals

Practice Put a cross next to the ending (1 – 4) which isn't grammatically possible and then correct it. The first one has been done for you.

a As long as we're well prepared, …
1 we've got nothing to worry about ✓
2 we shouldn't have any problems. ✓
3 we couldn't go wrong. ✗
4 we'll be fine. ✓

Correction

we can't go wrong.

b I'll send them an e-mail …
1 if you'll tell me what I should say.
2 if you think it's worth it.
3 unless you'd rather do it.
4 provided I hadn't lost their address. ✗

Correction

provided I haven't lost their address.

c If you're going out, …
1 get me a newspaper, will you?
2 you're going to miss the meeting.
3 you'd better take an umbrella.
4 I come with you. ✗

Correction

I'll come with you.

d Do that …
1 and you'll regret it.
2 if it'll help.
3 if you'll get the opportunity. ✗
4 – we'll lose business.

Correction

if you get the opportunity.

e I'd stay and help you …
1 if I knew anything about computers.
2 if I'm not going out this evening. ✗
3 if I hadn't promised Jo I'd meet her.
4 if you asked me nicely.

Correction

if I wasn't going out this evening.

f I'd be grateful …
1 if you could sort this out for me.
2 if you'd keep this to yourself.
3 if you don't tell anyone about this. ✗
4 if you remembered that in future.

Correction

if you didn't tell anyone about this.

g If he actually said that to her, …
1 she'd kill him.
2 I'd have been very surprised. ✗
3 it was very stupid of him.
4 he must have been mad.

Correction

I'd be very surprised.

h I wouldn't have asked you …
1 if I didn't think you could do it.
2 unless I trusted you.
3 if I'd known this would happen.
4 if you didn't say you wanted to do it. ✗

Correction

if you hadn't said you wanted to do it.

i If it hadn't been for him, …
1 I'd still be working at Burger King.
2 I'd have got that job.
3 we might never have found out.
4 I hadn't had a chance. ✗

Correction

I wouldn't have had a chance.

Summary

You can use any tense in either half (clause) of a conditional sentence.

As well as *if, unless, as long as* and *providing/provided* (*that*), you can also use *and* as a conjunction in a conditional (*Do that **and** we'll get complaints*) or no conjunction at all (*Do that – we'll get complaints*).

Conditional clauses can come either first or second in the sentence. However, with *and* or no conjunction, conditional clauses come first.

You can put *will* or *would* in the conditional clause (*If you'll wait here, I'll go and get her for you; I'd be grateful if you'd give this matter your serious attention*), but this is unusual.

The Past Simple in a conditional can refer to the past (*Even if I **did meet** her, I'm afraid I don't remember her*), to a future possibility (*If I **resigned** tomorrow, I could get another job within the week*) or to an unreal situation (*If I **spoke** Italian, I'd phone her myself, but I don't*).

Conditionals with the Past Perfect can refer to the effects of the past on the more recent past (*If you'd **made** a backup, we wouldn't have lost the whole document*) or on the present (*If I'd **got** that job, I could be earning a fortune now*).

Lexis: Meetings

If a problem causes many meetings, the meetings eventually become more important than the problem.

Arthur Bloch, Murphy's Law

Metaphor: discussion is a journey

A lot of the language of discussion refers to journeys. Read the conversation and underline the references to movement and travel. There are 20.

Ian returns to the boardroom to find the meeting in chaos ...

Ian Sorry about that. Had to take a phonecall from Bangkok. So, are we any <u>nearer</u> a decision?

Erik Not yet, but <u>we're getting there</u>. I think we're <u>more or less on the right track</u>, anyway.

Sonia Are we? I'd say <u>we've got a long way to go</u> yet. We just seem to be <u>going round in circles</u>.

Erik Well, <u>we were making good progress</u> before <u>we got sidetracked</u>, Sonia. Now, <u>returning</u> to the question of logistics ...

Ella Sorry, but could I just <u>go back to</u> what I was saying earlier about freight charges?

Sonia Hang on, hang on. Aren't we <u>getting ahead of</u> ourselves here? We haven't <u>got as far as</u> discussing transportation yet, Ella ...

Erik We don't seem to be <u>getting very far</u> at all!

Ian The conversation seems <u>to have drifted</u> a little while I was <u>away</u> ... I can't quite see where <u>all this is heading</u>.

Erik We've certainly <u>wandered away from</u> the main topic. Now, logistics ...

Sonia I was just <u>coming to</u> that. In my opinion, this whole plan is totally impractical.

Ian I don't think I like the direction this discussion is going in. OK, look, <u>we've covered a lot of ground</u> this morning, but I think <u>that's about as far as we can go</u> at the moment.

Erik Now, just a minute! We haven't <u>come this far</u> to break off now, surely ...

Idiomatic expressions

1 In the fixed expressions below, delete the word you wouldn't expect to hear.

a So, what do you **reckon/~~guess~~**?

b I'd go **~~around~~/along** with that.

c I wouldn't go quite as **far/~~much~~** as that.

d Where do you **stand/~~sit~~** on this?

e Well, that goes without **saying/~~speaking~~**.

f I don't mind **either/~~each~~** way.

g I'm afraid it's not **~~so~~/as** simple as that.

h Any **~~responses~~/reactions**?

i The way I **~~view~~/see** it is this.

j I **wouldn't/~~couldn't~~** say that.

k Yes and no/~~No and yes~~.

l I **~~can't~~/couldn't** say, to be honest.

m I'd like us to **share/~~spare~~** our views on this.

n Oh, come **on/~~off~~** it!

o Well, I haven't **given/~~taken~~** it much thought.

p I'm **~~for~~/with** you there.

q To my **~~meaning~~/mind**, it's like this.

r To **~~a point~~/an extent** you're right.

2 Categorise the expressions in 1 according to their purpose.

a asking for an opinion
  a d h m

b giving an opinion
  e i q

c giving no opinion
  f l o

d agreeing
  b p

e disagreeing
  g j n

f half-agreeing
  c k r

3 The following are all things you might do in a meeting. Match the words in columns one and two to make an idiom. Then match the idiom to its meaning in column three.

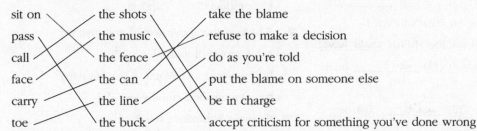

sit on   the shots   take the blame
pass   the music   refuse to make a decision
call   the fence   do as you're told
face   the can   put the blame on someone else
carry   the line   be in charge
toe   the buck   accept criticism for something you've done wrong

In general, avoid using idioms with other non-native speakers, but expect native speakers to use them quite a lot.

4 Voice and visuals

Modal verbs

Practice 1 In each of the sentences below, delete the modal verbs that are incorrect.

a We ... now, but we can if we want.
(~~mustn't pay~~/don't have to pay/~~haven't got to pay~~)

b I ... my laptop, so I left it at the office.
(~~needn't take~~/didn't need to take/~~needn't have taken~~)

c We ..., if we'd known he wasn't coming in today.
(~~didn't need to wait~~/~~mustn't wait~~/needn't have waited)

d When I was a student, I ... for hours on end.
('d study/~~would have studied~~/used to study)

e I ... quite left-wing, but I've become more conservative.
(used to be/~~would be~~/~~must have been~~)

f She ... by now – it's after twelve.
(should have left/'ll have left/~~won't have left~~)

g I took my driving test three times before I ... pass.
(~~could~~/was able to/managed to)

Practice 2 Complete the conversation using the modal verbs in the box.

can't	can't	'll	'll	must	might
shouldn't	wouldn't	won't	would have		
must have	could have	could have			
needn't have					

A Ivan, (1) __shouldn't__ Alexis be here by now? It's gone four!

B Yeah, she (2) __must have__ got held up somewhere.

A But (3) __wouldn't__ she have phoned?

B Well, you (4) __would have__ thought so.

A I mean, we're only having this meeting for her benefit. If she doesn't come soon, we (5) __needn't have__ bothered.

B Quite, though I (6) __can't__ think what (7) __could have__ held her up. I (8) __'ll__ ring her and see what's going on. That's funny, I (9) __can't__ find her number. I (10) __could have__ sworn I put it in my diary. It (11) __must__ be in here somewhere!

A Well, if you ask me, she (12) __won't__ just be coming now, anyway.

B Hang on. That (13) __might__ just be her now. I (14) __'ll__ go and check.

Summary

have to, *have got to* and *must* mean there's an obligation to do something.

don't have to and *haven't got to* mean there's no obligation to do something.

mustn't means there's an obligation *not* to do something.

I needn't have done means I did something but it wasn't necessary; *I didn't need to do* means it wasn't necessary so I didn't do it.

would do means *used to do* for repeated past actions.

She should have left means *I expect she's left* or *She's supposed to have left* or *It would have been a good idea if she'd left*.

You use *was able to* (not *could*) to talk about a specific past achievement.

That must be him is the opposite of *That can't be him*.

will is the most versatile modal verb and can be used for offers, spontaneous decisions, assumptions, predictions and to express willingness or determination.

Lexis: Presentations

Wise men talk because they have something to say; fools, because they have to say something. *Plato*

Types of presentation

1 Match the following to make nine different types of business presentation.

a conference —— pitch
b sales —— speech
c pep ——————— talk
d press ——————— conference
e after-dinner —— lecture
f academic —— speech
g project —— speech
h welcome —— demonstration
i product —— update

2 Which of the above would you give to:

a a group of journalists? d

b guests at a colleague's leaving party? e

c demotivated employees? c

d your immediate boss? g

e new recruits? h

f prospective customers or clients? b i

Photocopiable

Commenting on statistics

1 Put the following verbs and verb phrases in order from the best news to the worst.

> nearly doubled   almost halved
> quadrupled   plateau'd
> increased tenfold   more than tripled

Sales have

  a _increased tenfold_

  b _quadrupled_

  c _more than tripled_

  d _nearly doubled_

  e _plateau'd_

  f _almost halved_

Which of the above means the same as *a fourfold increase?* [b]

2 Pair up the adjectives with ones which have a similar meaning and put them in order from the biggest to the smallest.

> slight   huge   significant   modest
> massive   moderate   considerable
> reasonable

a

  a _huge_ / _massive_

  b _significant_ / _considerable_ **increase**

  c _moderate_ / _reasonable_

  d _slight_ / _modest_

3 Describe the following success rates using suitable adjectives from the box.

> phenomenal   disastrous   disappointing
> encouraging   miserable   spectacular
> unimpressive   promising

a(n)

  a _phenomenal_ / _spectacular_ 95%

  b _encouraging_ / _promising_ 65% **success**

  c _disappointing_/ _unimpressive_ 25% **rate**

  d _disastrous_ / _miserable_ 3%

Metaphor: trends and developments

1 Complete the joke by matching each noun or noun phrase on the left to a verb or verb phrase on the right. Use a dictionary to check the literal and metaphorical meaning of the verbs, if necessary.

And on the stock market today ...

mountaineering equipment — totally collapsed
military hardware — were up and down
lifts — went up sharply
kitchen knives — peaked
but the housing market — boomed

After a nervous start ...

rubber — quickly recovered
medical supplies — shot up
the automotive industry — bounced back
rifles — picked up after lunch
and vacuum cleaners also — rallied

In some of the fiercest trading seen in the City ...

swimwear — hit rock bottom
mining equipment — slumped
ice skates — plunged
alcoholic beverages — completely dried up
and the market for raisins — slipped a little

By close of trade ...

fireworks — remained unchanged
Prozac — fell dramatically
but paper products — were stationary
men's socks — reached an all-time high
and theatre curtains — skyrocketed

2 Mark the verbs and verb phrases in 1 according to the trend they describe: up (↑), down (↓), up and down (↕), down then up (↘↗) and no change (↔).

Technical hitches Complete the embarrassing situations below and match each with a possible joke you could use to save face.

> slides   feedback   transparency
> microphone   acoustics

a Your **microphone** is turned down too low.

b Your PowerPoint _slides_ won't display and the projector lead has the wrong plug.

c The room you're speaking in has terrible _acoustics_.

d The PA system is producing deafening _feedback_.

e You put your _transparency_ onto the overhead upside down.

'I was going to use PowerPoint, but we don't seem to have any power, so what's the point?' [b]

'The last time I heard a noise like that was at a heavy metal concert.' [d]

'That was for any Australians in the audience. Now, here it is again for people from the northern hemisphere.' [e]

'OK, if it's still no good after we increase the volume, I think it may be your ears that need adjusting.' [a]

'Can you hear me at the front?' [c]

5 Problems on the phone

Complex question formation

Practice 1 Polite question forms

Rewrite the requests and offers to make them sound friendlier and more polite using the words in brackets to help you. Make any necessary changes to grammar.

a Can you turn the air conditioning up a bit? (think/could)

   Do you think you could turn the air
   conditioning up a bit?

b Can you help me? (wonder/could)

   I wonder if you could help me?

c Don't mention this to anyone else. (could/ask you)

   Could I ask you not to mention this to
   anyone else?

d Can you do some overtime next week? (think/could/ask)

   Do you think I could ask you to do some
   overtime next week?

e Do you want me to put in a good word for you? (would/like me)

   Would you like me to put in a good word
   for you?

f Can you stop whistling while I'm trying to concentrate? (would/mind not)

   Would you mind not whistling while I'm
   trying to concentrate?

g Is it OK to leave early today? (do/mind/if)

   Do you mind if I leave early today?

h Do you want me to give you a few days to think about it? (would/help/give)

   Would it help if I gave you a few days to
   think about it?

i Can I ask you a personal question? (Would/mind/I)

   Would you mind if I asked you a personal
   question?

j When is Mr Alvarez coming back? (happen/know)

   Do you happen to know when Mr Alvarez is
   coming back?

k Can you lend me €50 until Friday? (don't suppose/could you?)

   I don't suppose you could lend me €50 until
   Friday, could you?

Summary

Being polite takes longer!

Modal verbs (*could, would*) soften a request that may be unwelcome.

'Type 1' conditionals (*Do you mind if I leave early?*) make requests more diplomatic.

'Type 2' conditionals (*Would you mind if I left early?*) make requests even more diplomatic.

Do you happen to know …? is useful when you're not sure the other person knows the answer to your question.

I don't suppose you could …, could you? is good way of asking people to do you a favour.

Practice 2 Question-and-answer sessions

A environmental consultant is fielding questions after his presentation. Complete the questions from the audience using the verbs in the box.

describing	telling	referred	dealt
came	pointed	mentioned	arrived
made	spoke	talking	quoted	be
explain	happen	discussing	elaborate
go	saying	believe	showing

a When you were _telling_ us about the number of species that become extinct each year, you _quoted_ a figure of 27,000. Could you tell us how you _arrived_ at that figure?

b Going back to what you were _saying_ about imposing a green tax on fossil fuels, do you honestly expect us to _believe_ that people would be prepared to pay such a tax? And, if so, would you _explain_ how it might be implemented?

c When you were _talking_ about natural resources, you _made_ the claim that American farmers draw 20 billion gallons more water from the ground every single day than are replaced by rainfall. Could you just tell us where that figure _came_ from?

d When you were _showing_ us the statistics for deforestation in Germany, you _mentioned_ in passing that 88% of conifer forests in Central and Eastern Europe are threatened by pollution. Could you _go_ into a bit more detail on that?

e When you were _describing_ the recent impact of green issues on the world of business, you _referred_ to a survey carried out by *Greenpeace*. Do you _happen_ to have a copy of that survey with you?

f Going back to the question of clean air legislation – which I thought you _dealt_ with very sensibly – you _pointed_ out that setting a standard for industrial emissions is not the same thing as setting a health standard. Could you _be_ a bit more specific?

g When you were _discussing_ the question of toxic chemicals, you _spoke_ about high levels of chemical waste in one American research facility. Would you care to _elaborate_ on that?

Summary

When you ask questions at the end of a presentation, it's a good idea to focus the presenter's attention on the context of the question before you ask it.

The **Past Continuous** gives the general context, and the **Past Simple** the more specific reference (*When you were **talking** about X, you **mentioned** Y. Could you say a bit more about that?*).

The use of *just* before a request makes it both more polite and harder to refuse (*Could you **just** expand on that a little?*).

The use of certain adjectives and adverbs can make your question sound more aggressive, even hostile (*What **real** evidence is there ...? How can you be **so** sure ...? Do you **honestly** expect us to believe ...?*).

Lexis: Phone, fax and e-mail

Taking a mobile phone into the bedroom should be grounds for divorce. *Lord Deedes, journalist*

Complete the telephone conversation using the words in the box.

on	on	on	on	on	on	up	up	up	up
out	out	out	off	off	off	down	down	in	
around	as	under	back	by	for				

A design agency office is in chaos. The phone is ringing. Tina finally answers it.

A Hello? Tina Mallon.

B Tina. Thank goodness you're there!

A Hi, Geoff. What's (1) _up_?

B Listen. I'm (2) _in_ a bit of a mess here.

A Where are you?

B I'm just (3) _on_ my way to see the people at FlexiPak and you'll never guess ... I've left the file with the visuals in it back at the office!

A Oh dear ... Well, can I fax them through to you at their office?

B No, I don't think they'd come (4) _out_ properly.

A Geoff, I'm (5) _up_ to my neck in it here. I can't access my e-mail because the server is (6) _down_ this morning and I'm rushed (7) _off_ my feet, running (8) _around_ trying to sort things (9) _out_ with IT and get those posters (10) _off_ to Milan by midday.

B Look, Tina, this is urgent. Could you go over the road to the print shop, scan the visuals and ask them to e-mail them to me (11) _as_ attachments? I'll give you FlexiPak's e-mail address.

A Geoff, I'm sorry, but I'm really snowed (12) _under_ here.

B Tina, I wouldn't ask you if I wasn't desperate. I haven't got time to come (13) _back_ and pick them (14) _up_.

A Well, maybe it would be easier just to send them (15) _by_ dispatch rider. Hang (16) _on_. Let me take (17) _down_ the details. Which visuals do you need exactly? Hello? Geoff?

B Tina?

A Geoff? You're breaking (18) _up_. Are you (19) _on_ your mobile? I can't hear you!

B Hello? Oh, what's going (20) _on_ with this phone? I can't be (21) _out_ of range. I must be running low (22) _on_ batteries. No, it's charged. Tina, can you hear me? I'll have to ring (23) _off_ and look (24) _for_ a payphone or something. Tina?

Tina bangs up, smiling

A Now, maybe I can finally get (25) _on_ with some work!

6 Leading meetings

Linking and contrasting ideas

Practice Read the meeting extracts below. For each of the words or phrases in **bold**, underline the word or phrase in brackets that is similar in meaning. Don't change any grammar or punctuation.

A Well, **in spite of** all these problems, I'd say we're still on target for a January launch.
(<u>despite</u>/even though)

B What, **even though** we've hardly completed phase one trials?
(<u>in spite of the fact that</u>/despite)

A Yes. **Although** obviously I'd have liked us to be further ahead by now, I'm confident we'll be ready in time.
(However/<u>Whilst</u>)

B Well, I admire your optimism, Sergio, but **nevertheless**, I think we should make some kind of contingency plan.
(<u>all the same</u>/however)

A I'm afraid that, **because of** the strong euro, exports are down again this quarter.
(consequently/<u>owing to</u>)

B And **as a result** our share price is falling.
(<u>consequently</u>/owing to)

A Quite. Now, **whereas** we've been able to sustain these losses so far, we clearly can't do so indefinitely.
(despite/<u>although</u>)

A Right, well, **as** nobody seems to be in favour of this proposal, I suggest we just scrap it!
(due to/<u>seeing as</u>)

B It's not that we're against it, Jakob, **although** it is an unusual idea.
(<u>though</u>/whereas)

C Yes, I'd like to support you on this one, Jakob, **but** I can't help feeling you're rushing things.
(whilst/<u>and yet</u>)

A Well, how much more time do you need? **In order to** put this before the board, I have to have your approval.
(<u>To</u>/So that)

A Now, I don't want to spend a lot of time on these new European guidelines. I do think we should go through them briefly, **however**.
(<u>though</u>/although)

B The guidelines do affect all of us, Renata.

A **Even so**, we have more important things to discuss.
(Whereas/<u>Nevertheless</u>)

A Well, everybody, **thanks to** all your hard work, the campaign has got off to a great start.
(as a result/<u>as a result of</u>)

B And **while** it's too early to say exactly how successful it will be, it's looking very good indeed.
(<u>whilst</u>/as)

A Yes. **So as to** give you a clearer idea, I've prepared copies of our sales projections for year one.
(so/<u>in order to</u>)

B The figures are broken down by country **so that** you can get the full picture.
(since/<u>in order that</u>)

A And, **since** we're celebrating, I brought along some champagne!
(<u>seeing as</u>/because of)

Summary

You can use the following words and phrases

- to make **contrasts and contradictions**:

while/whilst	though	although
even though	even so	and yet	however
nevertheless	all the same	despite
in spite of (the fact that)	whereas	but

- to express **purpose or intention**:

in order to/that	to	so as to	so (that)

- to link **cause and effect**:

because of	owing to	as a result (of)
consequently	as	since	seeing as
thanks to		

Lexis: Companies and capital

Crazy times call for crazy organizations.
Tom Peters, management guru

1 Group the following verbs according to meaning.

expand	streamline	start up	sell off
found	delayer	wind up	build up
establish	buy up	grow	liquidate
buy into	rationalise	acquire	

set up _start up_ _found_ _establish_

take over _buy up_ _buy into_ _acquire_

restructure _streamline_ _delayer_ _rationalise_

develop _expand_ _build up_ _grow_

close down _sell off_ _wind up_ _liquidate_

2 A manager is comparing business in the past with business now. Complete what he says using the words in the boxes.

1–8
economy vision customer stakeholders value global flatter outsourced

9–16
flexibility effectiveness layers learning functional total empowered networked

'Well, the most important difference, obviously, is that nowadays we're all operating in a

(1) _global_ market, rather than simply a national one – the so-called borderless

(2) _economy_. And the increased amount of competition means that this company, at any rate, has gone from being product-driven to much more

(3) _customer_-oriented. And whereas we used to focus on price, now we focus on customer

(4) _value_. And where we used to set goals, we now have something called a corporate

(5) _vision_. A lot of it is just a change in terminology but it certainly looks like we're doing something new!

'A company's chief responsibility used to be to its shareholders, but these days we prefer to talk about

(6) _stakeholders_ – not just the people with a financial stake in the company, but everyone who has an interest in the way it's run. A big change in the organisation of this company is that we now have a much (7) _flatter_ structure, instead of the old hierarchy. Everything used to be kept in-house. Now a lot of work is (8) _outsourced_.

So, we're a (9) _functional_ company now, with fewer (10) _layers_ of management. For the most part, we work in cross-(11) _networked_ teams, which gives us much greater

(12) _flexibility_. And we aim to have an

(13) _empowered_ rather than simply loyal workforce. That means we give training and development top priority. In fact, we like to think we're a (14) _learning_ company. For us, now,

(15) _effectiveness_ is a much more important concept than efficiency and we see product quality as just one part of a (16) _total_ quality mindset.'

The financial pages

1 Match the heads (a–h) and tails (1–8) of the following headlines.

a Disappointing pre-
b Venture
c $500m rights
d Kagumi plan ¥200b stock
e Fears of another rise in base
f Contex reject hostile takeover
g Government crackdown on offshore
h Record fourth-

1 rates hit housing market
2 investments
3 tax profits for Kovak
4 bid from Avalon
5 quarter earnings tipped to top €90m
6 capital dries up
7 market flotation
8 issue to finance acquisition

a	b	c	d	e	f	g	h
3	6	8	7	1	4	2	5

2 Find words and phrases in 1 which mean:
a attempted acquisition by predator company _takeover bid_
b exceed _top_
c rate of interest charged by banks _base rate_
d predicted _tipped to_
e strict new laws or measures _crackdown_
f profits for the period October to December _fourth-quarter earnings_
g badly effect _hit_
h money invested in a foreign country with lower tax _offshore investments_
i when a company goes public and issues shares _stock market flotation_
j runs out _dries up_

3 Divide the following into good (✓) and bad (✗) news.

deepening recession ✗   cash bonanza ✓
downturn in demand ✗   sales boom ✓
economic slowdown ✗   market meltdown ✗
windfall profits ✓   housing slump ✗
upswing in the economy ✓

8 Promoting your ideas

The passive

Practice 1 Make the following extracts from reports more formal by:

- using the passive
- replacing the words in **bold** with an adverb from the box
- deleting the subject.

thoroughly	unofficially	tentatively
provisionally	~~roughly~~	currently
generally	unanimously	formally

a Our site engineers estimate that construction will take **about** 18 months to complete.

It _is roughly estimated that construction will take 18 months to complete._

b They've given us the go-ahead, **but it's not official yet**.

We've _unofficially been given the go-ahead._

c We're considering several options **at the moment**.

Several _options are currently being considered._

d **Almost everyone** felt that the project was taking too long.

It _was generally felt that the project was taking too long._

e **Everyone** agreed that the proposal required further discussion.

It _was unanimously agreed that the proposal required further discussion._

f We have tested **every part** of the new software.

The _new software has been thoroughly tested._

g The company will announce the plant closure **at the official press conference** next week.

The _plant closure will be formally announced next week._

h They've OK'd the training budget **at this stage, but they may change their minds**.

The _training budget has been provisionally OK'd._

i They suggested that we could import the raw materials, **but stressed that this was only a suggestion**.

It _was tentatively suggested that we could import the raw materials._

Practice 2 Make the accusations below less personal by removing all references to 'we' and 'you' and making any necessary grammatical changes.

a But we understood that you'd agreed to this.

But it _was understood that this had been agreed._

b We assumed that you'd accept this.

It _was assumed that this would be accepted._

c We state quite clearly in the contract that you must make your payments on the first of the month.

It _was stated quite clearly in the contract that payments must be made on the first of the month._

d We presumed that you would comply with current health and safety regulations.

It _was presumed that current health and safety regulations would be complied with._

Practice 3 Rewrite the impersonal e-mail below using only active verbs and replacing some of the more formal words and phrases with friendlier-sounding alternatives from the box.

in this way	each other	get the chance
look forward	pencilled in	up to speed
seeing you there	exchange views	meet
various	from now on	

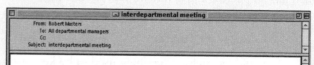

interdepartmental meeting

From: Robert Masters
To: All departmental managers
Cc:
Subject: interdepartmental meeting

It has been decided that an interdepartmental meeting will henceforth be held every month. Heads of department will thus be able to network and generally be brought up to date on recent developments in other departments. Furthermore, they will be given the opportunity to have their voice heard on a number of matters relating to overall corporate strategy.

The first meeting is scheduled for next Thursday. Your attendance would be appreciated.

Robert Masters

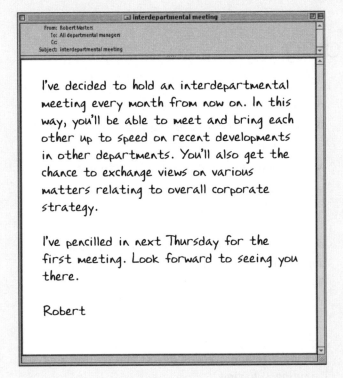

From: Robert Masters
To: All departmental managers
Cc:
Subject: interdepartmental meeting

I've decided to hold an interdepartmental meeting every month from now on. In this way, you'll be able to meet and bring each other up to speed on recent developments in other departments. You'll also get the chance to exchange views on various matters relating to overall corporate strategy.

I've pencilled in next Thursday for the first meeting. Look forward to seeing you there.

Robert

Summary

You use the **passive** when you are more interested in actions, views and decisions than in the people who actually took them. The **passive** sounds more formal and objective than the **active**. For this reason it is frequently used in reports.

If the subject of the **active** sentence is *they, you, one, people, everyone* or *no one*, it is usually unnecessary to refer to it in the **passive** e.g. *No one can do it* becomes *It can't be done by anybody*.

When using reporting verbs in the **passive**, you need to insert the word *it* e.g. *They said 'There was absolutely no corruption'* becomes ***It*** *was strongly denied that there had been any corruption*.

The **active** generally sounds more personal than the **passive**. The danger is that in criticisms it can also sound more aggressive, and so in delicate negotiations the **passive** is often preferred to depersonalise potential conflict.

Lexis: Phrasal verbs

Turn on, tune in, drop out.
Timothy Leary, 60s counterculture guru

1 The five most common verbs used in phrasal verbs are: *get, come, go, take* and *put*. Complete each set of sentences using one of these verbs in the Past Simple and a particle from the box. Use the definitions in brackets to help you.

on   on   on   into   into   out   out   through
through   off   off   over   over   around
down   across   for   in   under   up

a We <u>took</u> <u>on</u> too much work (accepted)

<u>down</u> a few details. (wrote)

<u>out</u> a bank loan. (obtained)

<u>over</u> the project. (got control of)

b They <u>came</u> <u>through</u> the recession. (survived)

<u>across</u> an accounting error. (discovered)

<u>into</u> a lot of money. (inherited)

<u>under</u> pressure to resign. (received)

c She <u>went</u> <u>on</u> to talk about training. (proceeded)

<u>over</u> the figures with us. (checked)

<u>off</u> the idea. (started to dislike)

<u>for</u> option B. (chose)

d We <u>got</u> <u>around</u> the problem in the end. (avoided)

<u>into</u> an argument. (became involved in)

<u>through</u> a ton of paperwork. (completed)

<u>on</u> well. (had a good relationship)

e They <u>put</u> <u>in</u> hours of work on it. (did)

<u>off</u> the meeting. (postponed)

<u>out</u> a press release. (issued)

<u>up</u> most of the cash. (provided)

2 Some phrasal verbs have three parts. Complete the sentences using the pairs of particles in the box.

on about + on with   round to + on to
in for + back to   out of + ahead with
up against + round to   in for + down as
along with + in with   up with + up for

a I'm afraid haven't got <u>round to</u> doing that report yet, but I'll get <u>on to</u> it as soon as I've finished these spreadsheets.

b I know there's no point going <u>on about</u> it, but I really don't get <u>on with</u> this new boss of ours.

c I'm not putting <u>up with</u> this situation a moment longer – it's time I stood <u>up for</u> myself!

d I know it's too late to back <u>out of</u> it now, but I'm really sorry we went <u>ahead with</u> this agreement.

e I'm afraid I can't go <u>along with</u> this – it just doesn't fit <u>in with</u> our plans.

f We seem to be coming <u>up against</u> a lot of opposition from marketing at the moment, but hopefully they'll soon come <u>round to</u> our way of thinking.

g I put <u>in for</u> that promotion I was telling you about but they haven't got <u>back to</u> me about it.

h I hear Jon's come <u>in for</u> a lot of criticism from the board and may have to stand <u>down as</u> chairman.

9 Relationship-building

Multi-verb sentences

Practice 1 Decide which of the verbs below precede the infinitive with *to*, the *-ing* form or both and tick the appropriate boxes. The first one has been done for you.

	to do	doing		to do	doing
agree	✓	☐	manage	✓	☐
admit	☐	✓	enjoy	☐	✓
suggest	☐	✓	hope	✓	☐
try	✓	✓	miss	☐	✓
put off	☐	✓	avoid	☐	✓
aim	✓	☐	expect	✓	☐
stop	✓	✓	promise	✓	☐
refuse	✓	☐	go on	✓	✓
carry on	☐	✓	fail	✓	☐
remember	✓	✓	dislike	☐	✓

Practice 2 Complete the conversation using the correct form of the verbs in brackets.

A Hi, James. Client meeting overran a bit, did it?

B Mm. And Lucy and I stopped __to have__ (have) a coffee on the way back.

A Oh, right.

B By the way, did you remember __to send__ (send) those invoices off?

A What invoices?

B Stuart! I distinctly remember __asking__ (ask) you to deal with the invoices. They should have gone last week.

A Well, I've been a bit busy trying __to fix__ (fix) this wretched computer!

B OK, look, stop __doing__ (do) whatever you're doing and deal with them now, would you? And what's wrong with the computer?

A No idea. It keeps crashing.

B Well, have you tried __asking__ (ask) Callum about it?

A Of course I have. I've been trying __to get__ (get) through to him all morning. But he's like you, isn't he? He's never in!

Practice 3 Complete the conversation using an appropriate preposition and *-ing* form from the boxes below.

about	about	of	of	in	on	for

being	telling	changing	wanting	making
putting	having			

A Of course, Tim succeeded __in__ __making__ a complete fool of himself at the drinks party.

B Did he?

A Oh, yes. Well, he will insist __on__ __telling__ those tasteless jokes, won't he? The president's wife was not amused.

B Well, he can forget __about__ __putting__ in for that promotion, then, can't he?

A Hm, not much chance of that here, anyway. You know I complained __about__ us __having__ to work another weekend?

B Mm, I hear Angela went mad about it.

A Yeah, she practically accused me __of__ __being__ disloyal to the company! Can you believe it?

B Sounds like her.

A Did I tell you I was thinking __of__ __changing__ jobs?

B No, but I can't say I blame you __for__ __wanting__ to get out of this place!

Practice 4 Match the three parts of each sentence below to complete the meeting extract.

A	Look, it's high time	not	putting it off, Sam.
B	OK, but I'd rather	of	made a decision.
A	Well, there's no point	we	rushing this?
B	Bill, what's the use	in	make it today.

C	OK, OK. I think	I'm	better move on.
B	Ricardo, it's	we'd	doing, Sam.
C	That's the last thing	we	end this meeting.
B	Otherwise, we might	no good	avoiding the issue.
C	OK, look. I suggest	as well	take a short break.

Summary

Some verbs can precede both the infinitive and the *-ing* form, but the meaning usually changes (*I **like to** work out twice a week* = I think it's a good idea; *I **like working** out* = I enjoy it).

Some verbs normally followed by the *-ing* form change when there's an indirect object (*I suggest **stopping** now → I suggest we **stop** now*).

When a verb is followed by a preposition other than *to*, the *-ing* form is usually used (*They apologised **for** not **getting** back to us sooner*).

Modal verbs always precede the other verbs in a sentence and are followed by the infinitive without *to* (*You **must** be wishing you'd never come to work here!*).

Certain expressions always precede the *-ing* form: ***It's no good** complaining;* ***There's no point (in)** complaining;* ***What's the use of** complaining?*

A number of expressions take the past form: ***I'd rather** you **didn't**;* ***It's time** we **went**.*

A number of expressions of intention take the infinitive with *to*: ***I'm planning to** do it later;* ***I've been meaning to** have a word with you.*

Lexis: Social English

The real art of conversation is not only to say the right thing at the right place but to leave unsaid the wrong thing at the tempting moment. *Dorothy Nevill*

1 Complete the conversation extracts from a dinner party using the pairs of verbs in the boxes.

> reckon + is   makes + think   's + be
> see + doing   is + accept   looking + ask
> think + happen   got + joking
> tells + going   mean + talking

A So, what do you (1) _think_ is going to _happen_ with this Ukrainian contract then?

B Good question. You know, something (2) _tells_ me we're not _going_ to get it.

A Oh, really? What (3) _makes_ you _think_ that? It (4) _'s_ not like you to _be_ so pessimistic.

B Well, for one thing, we've gone in way too high. My guess (5) _is_ they'll _accept_ a lower tender.

A Mm. By the way, have some more meat – there's plenty of it. You know, I don't (6) _reckon_ price _is_ really the issue.

B No?

A No. I (7) _mean_, we're _talking_ long-term here. This is a seven-year project, maybe longer.

B So?

A So, reliability is what they'll be (8) _looking_ for, if you _ask_ me. They'll pay more for that.

B You've (9) _got_ to be _joking_. This is one of the most price-sensitive markets in Eastern Europe. The way I (10) _see_ it, we'll be _doing_ well just to get part of the contract. They'll probably get a local firm in to do the main work.

A Hm, well, that's bad news ...

> knew + coming   might + known
> hear + going   stop + get   's + help
> shouldn't + saying   suppose + heard
> can't + say   had + would   is + getting

A I (11) _suppose_ you've _heard_ the news about Alex?

B About her leaving to join HP? Well, we (12) _knew_ that was _coming_, didn't we?

A I suppose so. The word (13) _is_ that Eduardo's _getting_ her job now. You know, I (14) _had_ a feeling he _would_.

B Mm. I (15) _can't_ really _say_ I'm surprised. He's had his eye on it for a while. And, anyway, if you get engaged to the executive vice-president's daughter, it (16) _'s_ bound to _help_ your career prospects, isn't it?

A He's what? I (17) _might_ have _known_! He'll (18) _stop_ at nothing to _get_ a promotion.

B Well, you didn't (19) _hear_ this from me, right, but there's a rumour _going_ around that ... well, maybe I (20) _shouldn't_ be _saying_ this, but ...

A No, no, go on! I'll go and open another bottle of wine ...

2 Underline eight new expressions in 1 that you could use yourself.

Articles

Practice Complete the text with *a, an, the* or zero article (/), as necessary.

> They say 'All's fair in / love and / war.'
> And when it comes to getting **a** good deal, **the** same is true of / business. For / example, in 1803, **a or /** half of what is now **the** USA was actually bought from **the** French for three cents **an** acre! How were they able to get such **a** bargain? At **the** time, / Emperor Napoleon was preparing to go to / war with / Britain and was desperate to sell.

Summary

The **indefinite** article is used:

- before a singular countable noun when it is unspecified and mentioned for the first time e.g. *I need **a** holiday*.

- before singular countable nouns in exclamations e.g. *What **a** day!; It was such **a** nuisance!*

- before the names of professions e.g. *She's **an** engineer.*

- before a singular countable noun where a plural could be used to mean the same thing e.g. *There's no such thing as **a** free lunch = There's no such thing as free lunches.*

- to mean *per* when talking about prices, speed, rates etc e.g. *€3 **a** kilo; three times **a** day.*

The **definite** article is used:

- before a noun that has been mentioned before e.g. *I used to have two BMWs and a Lotus, but I had to sell **the** Lotus.*

- before a noun that is later specified in the same sentence e.g. ***The** guy I met in Rio runs his own business.*

- when it is clear from the context what we are referring to e.g. *I'll drop you off at **the** hotel.*

- when the thing referred to is unique e.g. ***the** human race.*

- before an adjective referring to a group e.g. ***the** Dutch.*

The **zero** article is used:

- before mass or abstract nouns e.g. *Greed is good.*

- before the names of most countries. Exceptions include: *the USA, the UK* and *the Netherlands*.

- in certain fixed expressions e.g. *go to war.*

Lexis: Marketing and legal English

Contracts are made to be broken, but a handshake is the law of God. *JR Ewing, character in TV series 'Dallas'*

The marketplace

1 Complete the adjectives by writing in the missing vowels. The adjectives range from positive to negative.

	b**oo**m**i**ng	thr**iv**ing	☺
	h**ea**lthy	b**uoya**nt	
The market is	v**o**l**a**t**i**le	unpr**ed**ic**ta**bl**e**	
	w**ea**k	slu**gg**ish	
	fl**a**t	d**e**pr**e**ss**e**d	☹

2 Complete the sentence using some of the adjectives in 1 and information that is true for you.

The market for _____ in _____ is _____, whereas the _____ market is _____.

3 Complete the collocations by writing a noun from the box before each set of three nouns below.

> brand   market   distribution
> marketing   advertising

marketing	mix drive strategy		advertising	campaign expenditure agencies
market	forces research share		**brand**	awareness loyalty stretching
distribution	network channels costs			

4 Which terms in 3 are the following examples of?

a Omnicom   Publicis   Doyle Dane Bernbach   Dentsu

> advertising agencies

b competition   the state of the economy   political stability

> market forces

c 'the four Ps': product, place, price, promotion

> marketing mix

d wholesalers   retailers   sales reps

> distribution channels

e Virgin cola   Camel watches   Ferrari sunglasses

> brand stretching

Photocopiable

5 Listed below are some of the terms commonly used in marketing departments, but the second word in each collocation has been switched with another. Can you switch them back? The first two have been done for you.

market **outlet**
competitive **brand**
retail **challenger**
mass **sensitivity**
price **market**
leading **advantage**

subliminal **relations**
price **marketing**
niche **analysis**
public **advertising**
consumer **market**
permission **war**

6 Which of the terms in 5 refer to:

a the number two player in a market after the market leader? _market challenger_

b the importance the customer gives to prices? _price sensitivity_

c a small number of customers requiring a particular type of product or service? _niche market_

d the shop or store through which products are sold to the consumer? _retail outlet_

e a method of persuading consumers to buy by invisible, psychological means? _subliminal advertising_

f getting customers' permission before sending information to them? _permission marketing_

7 The verbs and verb phrases in the box all form strong collocations with *the market*. Put them into the most likely chronological order. One of them has been done for you.

| break back into   enter   be squeezed out of |
| dominate   compete in   target |

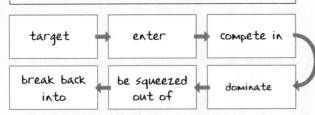

The verbs and verb phrases in the box all form strong collocations with *the competition*. Put them into the most likely chronological order. One of them has been done for you.

| take on   come up against   destroy |
| succumb to   outclass   fight back against |

come up against → **take on** → **outclass**
destroy ← **fight back against** ← **succumb to**

Business law

1 Divide the following into ten things that might lead to a court case.

taxevasion|unfairdismissal|criminalnegligence|racial discrimination|baddebt|insidertrading|insurancefraud| sexualharrassment|falseaccounting|embezzlement

Which of the above mean:

a sacking someone without good reason?
unfair dismissal

b buying shares using privileged information?
insider trading

c stealing money that you're responsible for in your job? _embezzlement_

2 Use the words in the box to make three things that might lead to legal problems.

| contract   interests   breach   funds |
| misuse   conflict |

a _breach_ of _contract_
b _conflict_ of _interests_
c _misuse_ of _funds_

Which of the above mean:

- to spend company money in an unauthorised way? [c]
- not to abide by a written agreement? [a]
- a situation in which someone cannot make fair decisions because they may be affected by the results? [b]

3 Complete the following using the verbs in the box.

| be   take   pay   bring   start |
| declare   file   settle   appeal |

a _take_ someone to court
b _start_ legal proceedings against someone
c _file_ a lawsuit against someone
d _settle_ out of court
e _be_ found liable for damages
f _pay_ compensation/a fine
g _declare_ bankruptcy
h _appeal_ against a verdict
i _bring_ an action against someone

Which of the above means to reach an agreement without asking the court to decide? [d]

12 E-mailing

Future forms

Practice 1 Present tenses for the future

Match the verbs in **bold** to their main function below.

Our train **leaves** (1) at six. So our taxi**'s coming** (2) at quarter to.

I'm not working (3) this Saturday! It**'s** (4) my wedding anniversary for goodness' sake!

an arrangement ☒2☒   an indisputable fact ☒4☒
a refusal ☒3☒   a schedule or timetable ☒1☒

Practice 2 *will*

1 Match the remarks on the left to the way they were later reported.

  a I**'ll** help you.   He promised to be there.

  b You**'ll** regret it.   He suddenly had an idea.

  c I**'ll** be there.   He offered to help me.

  d I**'ll** try it this way.   He refused to do it.

  e I **won't** do it!   He warned me about it.

2 All the sentences below refer to the future. Complete them using *'ll* (or *will*), as necessary. Use (/) if neither *'ll* (or *will*) is necessary.

  a If I _/_ see her, I _'ll_ tell her.

  b I _'ll_ say goodbye before I _/_ go.

  c We _'ll_ start the meeting as soon as they _/_ get here.

  d I expect they _'ll_ want a coffee when they _/_ arrive.

  e The people who _/_ get here early _will_ get the best seats.

Practice 3 *will be doing*

1 In each pair of sentences below tick the one you are more likely to hear.

  a We**'ll land** at Heathrow in about fifteen minutes.

  b We**'ll be landing** at Heathrow in about fifteen minutes. ✓

  c **Will** you **go** past the chemist's this morning?

  d **Will** you **be going** past the chemist's this morning? ✓

  e Give me five minutes and I**'ll call** you back. ✓

  f Give me five minutes and I**'ll be calling** you back.

  g By the way, I **won't attend** the meeting.

  h By the way, I **won't be attending** the meeting. ✓

2 Match the sentences a–d to what was said next.

  a I don't think I'll go. ☒4☒

  b I don't think I'll be going. ☒1☒

  c Will you go to the post office this afternoon? ☒2☒

  d Will you be going to the post office this afternoon? ☒3☒

  1 At least that's what they've told me.
  2 If you're not too busy, that is.
  3 And if so, could you post this for me?
  4 I certainly don't want to.

Practice 4 Lexical future

In English there are a lot of *be (+ word) to* expressions to talk about future intentions and expectations.

  a We're to
  b We're due to
  c We're about to
  d We're hoping to
  e We're aiming to   meet them to discuss the matter.
  f We're planning to
  g We're intending to
  h We're going to

Which of the sentences above refer to:

1 something which will happen very soon? ☒c☒

2 something which has been formally arranged? ☒a☒

3 something which other people are expecting? ☒b☒

4 something which has already been decided? ☒h☒

5 something we'd like to happen, but it may not?
  ☒d☒ ☒e☒ ☒f☒ ☒g☒

Practice 5 Future in the past

Put the sentences into the past and match them to what was said next.

  a We're going to fly Lufthansa.
    We were going to fly Lufthansa. ☒3☒

  b We're meeting at three.
    We were meeting at three. ☒2☒

  c I'm just about to leave.
    I was just about to leave. ☒1☒

  d I think we'll have problems.
    I thought we'd have problems. ☒4☒

  1 Can it wait till the morning?
  2 But something's come up.
  3 But there's been a change of plan.
  4 But I never expected this!

Practice 6 Past in the future

Tick the sentences which refer to the future.

a They won't have heard the news yet. ✓
b I'll have missed my chance by then. ✓
c You'll have seen our advertisements, I suppose.
d Another month and I'll have been working here for ten years. ✓

Summary

The **Present Continuous** and *be to* are frequently used to talk about fixed arrangements.

The **Present Simple** is often used either to talk about schedules and timetables or to refer to the future after words like *if, when, as soon as, before,* etc.

There's a range of expressions including *be going to* and *be hoping to* which are used to talk about plans and intentions.

Both *will* and *going to* can be used to make predictions: *will* for opinions and *going to* for more informed predictions.

'll is frequently used to make offers, promises and take initiatives.

will be doing is used to talk about something which will be in progress or which is part of a routine.

will have done and *will have been doing* are used to talk about something which will already be completed at a future time. The continuous form usually emphasises the activity rather than its completion.

Lexis: Prepositional phrases

Preposition: something you should never end a
sentence with. *Jill Etherington, journalist*

1 In each box write the preposition that precedes the words and phrases below.

at	present first least
	first glance the very most
	any rate the latest
	the same time best

on	the whole average the contrary
	second thoughts reflection
	the one hand the other hand
	no account

in	practice other words theory
	no circumstances general short
	particular effect some respects
	any case

| as | a result   a general rule |
| | a matter of fact   a last resort |

| up | to now   to a point |

| off | the top of my head |

2 Complete the meeting extracts using some of the phrases in 1.

A Well, I haven't had time to study them in detail but, at _first_ _glance_, I'd say these figures were quite encouraging.

B Yes, on _the_ _whole_, they're pretty much in line with what we were expecting. In fact, in _some_ _respects_, they're even better.

A Have you been in touch with New York yet?

B As _a_ _matter_ _of_ _fact_, I have.

A And are they in favour of this new initiative?

B One or two of them aren't, but in _general_, yes.

A Well, that's something at _any_ _rate_.

A I'm going to authorise this budget increase, but on _no_ _account_ is this project to go over budget again.

B Yes, OK.

A By the way, how much are the admin costs on this?

B I couldn't tell you off _the_ _top_ _of_ _my_ _head_, but it shouldn't be more than 30% of the budget at _the_ _very_ _most_.

A 30%! On _second_ _thoughts_, I think we'd better look at this whole budget again.

A This idea of yours is fine in _theory_, but in _practice_, I don't think it'll work.

B But you were all for it when we spoke about it last time!

A On _the_ _contrary_, I was as sceptical then as I am now. In _any_ _case_, even if I supported you, this strategy would only save us a few thousand pounds at _best_.

3 Underline the other seven prepositional phrases in 2.

13 Making an impact

Rhetorical techniques

Practice 1 Repetition

Decide which word in each statement could most effectively be repeated after a short pause and underline it. Read the statements aloud to check. The first one has been done for you.

a This is <u>very</u> important.
('This is very ... very important.')

b This is a <u>much</u> better option.

c It's <u>now</u> or never.

d There'll <u>always</u> be a market for quality.

e It is <u>here</u> in Europe that the best opportunities lie.

f And <u>today</u> we start to turn this company around.

Rewrite **a** so that you can repeat the word *important*.

This is important, very important.

Practice 2 Sound repetition

Replace one word in each sentence with a word from the box that starts with the same sound as other words in the sentence.

team	~~better~~	simpler	promotion
willing	past	dynamism	

a It's bigger. It's ~~superior~~. And it's British. *(better)*

b I'm not interested in our ~~history~~ or in our present, but in our prospects for the future. *(past)*

c We'll reach our targets together as a ~~group~~. *(team)*

d We need the right product at the right price with the right ~~advertising~~. *(promotion)*

e We have the drive, ~~energy~~ and determination to succeed. *(dynamism)*

f Are we ~~prepared~~ to work towards that goal? *(willing)*

g The new system is both more secure and significantly ~~easier~~ to install. *(simpler)*

What sound is being repeated in each of the sentences above?

a <u>b</u> **b** <u>p</u> **c** <u>t</u> **d** <u>p</u> **e** <u>d</u> **f** <u>w</u> **g** <u>s</u>

What do sentences **a**, **b**, **d** and **e** all have in common?

They are all lists of three.

Practice 3 Contrasts and opposites

Complete the sentences using the idea of contrast to help you.

a It's not a question of time; it's a qu<u>estion</u> of mo<u>ney</u>.

b If *we* don't seize this opportunity, some<u>one</u> el<u>se</u> w<u>ill</u>.

c Tackling a few minor problems now will save us a whole l<u>ot</u> of maj<u>or</u> pr<u>oblems</u> la<u>ter</u>.

d Some people are saying we can't afford to advertise, but I s<u>ay</u> we c<u>an't</u> aff<u>ord</u> n<u>ot</u> to.

e I'm not saying we're certain to succeed: what I a<u>m</u> s<u>aying</u> is we'll ne<u>ver</u> kn<u>ow</u> unt<u>il</u> we tr<u>y</u>.

f Three years ago this company was going nowhere; to<u>day</u> it's num<u>ber</u> o<u>ne</u> in the ind<u>ustry</u>.

Practice 4 Rhetorical questions

Rephrase the statements as negative questions and change the second person plural to the first person.

a This is what you need to be doing.
<u>Isn't this what we need to be doing?</u>

b You should be learning from your mistakes.
<u>Shouldn't we be learning from our mistakes?</u>

c Deep down, you all know this to be true.
<u>Deep down, don't we all know this to be true?</u>

Practice 5 Rhetorical questions + repetition

Complete the following using one word in both gaps.

problem	answer	point	result
chances	advantages		

a So much for the disadvantages, but what about the <u>advantages</u>? Well, the <u>advantages</u> are obvious.

b We're losing control of the company. So what's the <u>answer</u>? Clearly, the <u>answer</u> is to centralise.

c What are our <u>chances</u> of success? Well, frankly, our <u>chances</u> are slim.

d So what's the <u>point</u> of offering an unprofitable service? The <u>point</u> is it makes us look good.

e So what's the basic <u>problem</u> with this system? The basic <u>problem</u> is it's far too complicated!

f Three years of R&D and what's the net <u>result</u>? The net <u>result</u> is a product that doesn't work!

Practice 6 Inversion

Rephrase the statements below making any necessary changes in word order.

a This company is not only leaner, it's also greener.

Not only <u>is this company leaner,</u>
<u>it's also greener.</u>

b We mustn't under any circumstances panic.

Under no circumstances <u>must we panic.</u>
_____

c We've done better in Mexico than anywhere.

Nowhere <u>have we done better</u>
<u>than in Mexico.</u>

d We'll only be ready to launch after exhaustive tests.

Only after <u>exhaustive tests will</u>
<u>we be ready to launch.</u>
_____

Summary

In adverb + adjective phrases it is more effective to repeat the adverb (Practice 1).

If you want to repeat an adjective, it is more effective to use an adverb before repeating it (Practice 1).

It is more effective to repeat consonants than vowels (Practice 2).

Lists of three are especially memorable (Practice 2).

In a contrast it is more effective to make your main point second (Practice 3).

Asking questions (particularly negative questions) is a more effective way of getting audiences to think than making statements (Practice 4).

Talking about 'us' is a more effective way of building rapport than talking about 'you' (Practice 4).

Rhetorical questions sound more convincing when you answer them using some of the same words (Practice 5).

You can give weight and formality to what you say by sometimes reversing your word order (Practice 6).

Lexis: Metaphor

If this thing starts to snowball, it will catch fire right across the country. *Canadian politician Robert Thompson*

1 Business English is full of metaphor (describing one thing in terms of another). Match the following expressions. Then match them to their metaphorical reference.

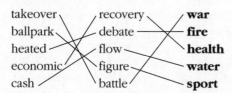

takeover   recovery   **war**
ballpark   debate   **fire**
heated   flow   **health**
economic   figure   **water**
cash   battle   **sport**

2 Complete the sentences using the words in the boxes.

growing	coming	pooling	pouring
sowing	trickling		

Money is liquid

a They're <u>pouring</u> millions of dollars into R&D.

b A small amount of cash has started <u>trickling</u> in.

c We should be <u>pooling</u> our resources – together we'd have sufficient capital to fund new research.

Ideas are plants

d After years of work, our plans are finally <u>coming</u> to fruition.

e There's <u>growing</u> support for the project – most of the people we spoke to think it's a good idea.

f They're <u>sowing</u> the seeds of doubt in the mind of the customer and, as a result, we're losing sales.

victory	attack	goalposts	guns
stakes	fight	odds	idea

Argument is war

g They shot down my <u>idea</u> before I'd even had a chance to explain it.

h We came under <u>attack</u> from the marketing team.

i He didn't put up much of a <u>fight</u>. In fact, he just seemed to give in completely.

j She stuck to her <u>guns</u> and refused to move an inch.

Competition is sport

k We've scored a significant <u>victory</u> in the home market.

l The <u>stakes</u> are high – we're risking the future of this company.

m The <u>odds</u> are against us, but there's still a chance we can succeed.

n We don't know what our objectives are supposed to be because they keep moving the <u>goalposts</u>.

14 Out and about

Narrative tenses

Practice Read the story about Pepsi A.M. and underline the best grammatical choices.

> **The Story of Pepsi A.M.**
>
> In the late 1980s Pepsi (1) **thought/was thinking** it (2) **identified/had identified** a lucrative gap in the highly competitive soft drinks market: breakfast cola.
>
> Although it (3) **wasn't conducting/hadn't conducted** very thorough market research, it (4) **seemed/was seeming** that a lot of young consumers (5) **switched/were switching** from coffee to cola for breakfast. Pepsi's R&D department promptly (6) **went away/were going away** and (7) **came up with/had come up with** Pepsi A.M., a breakfast cola 'with all the sugar and twice the caffeine'!
>
> But what the company (8) **wasn't realising/hadn't realised** was that the Pepsi drinkers (9) **were/were being** perfectly happy with the normal brand. Pepsi A.M., on the other hand, (10) **sounded/was sounding** like something you would only drink in the morning. Six months after its launch it obviously (11) **didn't sell/wasn't selling**.
>
> Marketing experts (12) **were/had been** quick to point out the company's mistake. What (13) **had it thought of?/had it been thinking of?** At a cost of millions, it (14) **had developed/had been developing** a product nobody actually (15) **needed!/was needing!**
>
> Pepsi A.M. (16) **was/had been** immediately withdrawn.

Summary

You use the **Past Simple** to talk about the main events in a story or to give factual information about the past.

You use the **Past Continuous** to talk about the things happening at the same time as these main events. Events in the **Past Continuous** are often interrupted by those in the **Past Simple**.

You use the **Past Perfect Simple** and the **Past Perfect Continuous** to look back from the time of the story to an earlier time, but the **Past Perfect Continuous** usually emphasises the activity rather than its completion. For this reason, it is not normally used with 'state' verbs like *be, know, seem, understand, mean* and *like*.

Lexis: Storytelling

> Storytelling is in the genes.
>
> *Gerry Spence, American lawyer*

Descriptive power

1   When describing things in a story or anecdote, try to avoid overusing *(not) very + neutral adjective*. Replace the dull descriptions in **bold** with more interesting alternatives from the box.

> | | |
> |---|---|
> | ~~totally pointless~~ | absolutely fabulous |
> | quite inedible | absolutely hilarious |
> | drop-dead gorgeous | absolutely filthy |
> | utterly astonished | absolutely delighted |
> | utterly furious | really fascinating |
> | utterly miserable | absolutely ancient |

a   The meeting was ~~not very useful~~.
  totally pointless

b   It was a **very interesting** book.
  really fascinating

c   They were **very happy** about the idea.
  absolutely delighted

d   The food was **not very good**.
  quite inedible

e   The weather was **very bad**.
  utterly miserable

f   Their boss was **very good-looking**.
  drop-dead gorgeous

g   Her apartment was **very nice**.
  absolutely fabulous

h   I was **very surprised**.
  utterly astonished

i   The whole thing was **very funny**.
  absolutely hilarious

j   The PCs they were using were **very old**.
  absolutely ancient

k   He looked **very angry**.
  utterly furious

l   The hotel was **not very clean**.
  absolutely filthy

2 If you do use neutral adjectives, try using a more interesting adverb to describe them. Match the following pairs of adverbs to a suitable adjective from the box.

> expensive beautiful disappointing funny
> dangerous enjoyable quiet difficult

hysterically/hilariously __funny__

stunningly/breathtakingly __beautiful__

outrageously/prohibitively __expensive__

immensely/thoroughly __enjoyable__

bitterly/terribly __disappointing__

deathly/blissfully __quiet__

highly/downright __dangerous__

exceedingly/fiendishly __difficult__

The art of exaggeration

Complete the conversation below using the words and phrases in the boxes.

> **1–7**
> ~~you'll never guess~~   like something out of
> is literally   you should have seen
> and that's putting it mildly   I'm telling you
> me tell you

> **8–13**
> I'm not exaggerating   let's just   talk about
> you'll never believe   believe me
> out of this world

(in the bar)

A Did I tell you about my trip to Sweden?

B No, I don't think so. On business, were you?

A Yeah, but (1) __you'll never guess__ the hotel the Swedes had booked us into.

B Somewhere posh, was it?

A No, not exactly. It's called *The Ice Hotel*. Have you heard of it?

B No, I don't think so.

A Well, (2) __you should have seen__ this place. (3) __I'm telling you__, it was (4) __like something out of__ a James Bond movie! Right in the middle of nowhere. And completely built out of snow and ice!

B What? You mean the walls were made of ice!

A Walls, ceilings, doors, tables, beds, chandeliers, the lot! The whole thing (5) __is literally__ made of ice!

B But, hang on. That's not possible, is it? I mean, it would just melt!

A It does. They have to rebuild it from top to bottom every summer.

B You're joking.

A No, it's true. But in the winter it's minus nine or something.

B So how come you didn't freeze to death?

A We nearly did. Let (6) __me tell you__, it was like an igloo in there. (7) __And that's putting it mildly.__ But (8) __let's just__ say we'd had plenty to warm us up in the bar before we went to bed!

B It's got a bar?

A Of course it has. (9) __Believe me__, you need a few vodkas in you if you're going to stay in a place like that!

B I can imagine.

A And they even make their cocktail glasses out of ice so you don't need any in your drink.

B Now, you're having me on.

A No, it's true. (10) __I'm not exaggerating.__ All the glasses are made of ice.

B Amazing! But it doesn't sound like the sort of place I'd want to stay in.

A Actually, it wasn't that bad once you got used to it. And it was great at night, lying in bed under a reindeer skin, looking up at the Aurora Borealis lighting up the midnight sky. (11) __Talk about__ spectacular; it was (12) __out of this world__! And, (13) __you'll never believe__ who we bumped into in the bar one night.

B Who?

A Naomi Campbell and Kate Moss!

B Oh, come on! You mean the models?

A Yeah, apparently, it's a really trendy place, this *Ice Hotel*. It's where all the cool people go.

B Yeah, very funny! So you'd recommend it then?

A Yeah, I would, but make sure you take a bottle of something strong with you, if you know what I mean. Anyway, are you about ready for another?

B Oh, yeah, thanks.

A Whisky and soda, wasn't it?

B Yes, please. No ice …

16 Teleconferencing

Reporting

Practice 1 Look at some silly things politicians have said and report each, making grammatical changes where necessary e.g. *have(n't)* → *had(n't)*, *did(n't)* → *had(n't) done, I → he, this → that*, etc.

a We have managed to distribute poverty equally.
Vietnamese Foreign Minister, Nguyen Co Thach

Mr Thach announced that *they had managed to distribute poverty equally.*

b I have opinions of my own, strong opinions, but I don't always agree with them.
US President George Bush Sr

President Bush affirmed that *he had opinions of his own, strong opinions, but (that) he didn't always agree with them.*

c I will not tolerate intolerance. *US Senator Bob Dole*

Senator Dole insisted that *he would not tolerate intolerance.*

d It isn't pollution that is harming the environment – it's the impurities in our air and water that are doing it. *US Vice President Dan Quayle*

Vice-president Quayle pointed out that *it wasn't pollution that was harming the environment – it was the impurities in our air and water that were doing it.*

e I haven't committed a crime – what I did is fail to comply with the law.
New York City mayor, David Dinkins

Mayor Dinkins denied that *he had committed a crime – what he had done was fail to comply with the law.*

f I can't believe that we are going to let a majority of the people decide what is best for this state.
US Representative John Travis

Mr Travis said that *he couldn't believe (that) they were going to let a majority of the people decide what was best for that state.*

Practice 2 Read the meeting extracts and write a summary of each using the words in brackets to help you.

Jon First of all, I'd like to hear your views on this.
(Jon/open/meeting/invite/comments/group)
Jon opened the meeting by inviting comments from the group.

Anna I don't think this training programme is necessary.
Niels Neither do I.
(Anna/question/need/training programme.
Niels/be/same opinion)
Anna questioned the need for the training programme. Niels was of the same opinion.

Anna And what about the training budget for this?
Jon I haven't made up my mind about that yet.
(Anna/raise/issue/training budget. Jon/reply/ not come/decision)
Anna raised the issue of the training budget. Jon replied that he hadn't come to a decision yet.

Niels So the board's OK about this?
Jon Absolutely.
(Jon/confirm/project/give/go-ahead)
Jon confirmed that the project was given the go-ahead.

Jon How about bringing in consultants?
Anna I don't think that's a good idea.
(Jon/wonder/if/be/good idea/bring in consultants. Anna/be/against)
Jon wondered if it was a good idea to bring in consultants. Anna was against it.

Niels Anna and I think the situation should be reviewed.
(both Anna/Niels/recommend/review/situation)
Both Anna and Niels recommended reviewing the situation.

Niels Well, I'm very much against these spending cuts.
Jon But they won't affect your department, Niels.
Anna Jon's right. These cuts won't affect us.
(there/be/some initial opposition/spending cuts)
There was some initial opposition to the spending cuts.

Anna So, you see, Niels, the new system will actually be an improvement.
Niels Hm, well, on reflection, I suppose you're right.
Jon So do I take it we're now in agreement on this?
(issue/finally/resolve)
The issue was finally resolved.

Jon I think this is an excellent proposal.
Anna So do I.
Niels Me too.
(there/be/unanimous agreement/proposal)
There was unanimous agreement on the proposal.

Summary

In reports

- it is more important to communicate the basic message than to repeat the exact words that were spoken

- we tend to use the passive when what was said is more important than who said it
  e.g. *It was suggested that ...*

- long conversations are often summed up in a simple noun phrase e.g. *There was some disagreement ...*

Lexis: Personnel and production

The most critical resource wears shoes and walks out the door around five o'clock every day.
Jonas Ridderstråle and Kjell Nordström, Stockholm School of Economics

Organisational behaviour Combine one word from the box on the left with one word from the box on the right to complete each sentence below.

human	prospects
incentive	burnout
promotion	benefits
appraisal	management
fringe	theory
track	scheme
leadership	record
executive	qualities
sickness	interview
selection	procedure
motivation	record
change	satisfaction
job	resources

a These days people talk about _human resources_ rather than personnel.

b Stress and overwork are both common causes of _executive burnout_ .

c Rates of pay, recognition and opportunities for personal growth contribute to overall _job satisfaction_ .

d Demotivated employees tend to have a fairly poor _sickness record_ and are prone to absenteeism.

e An _appraisal interview_ is one way of monitoring employee performance and personal development.

f _Fringe benefits_ include health insurance, a company car and contributory pension plan.

g For hardworking and ambitious young managers there are excellent _promotion prospects_ .

h To get into Harvard Business School you have to go through a rigorous _selection procedure_ .

i Essential _leadership qualities_ include decisiveness and the ability to get the most out of employees.

j The successful applicant must have an MBA and an excellent _track record_ in marketing.

k Many companies operate an _incentive scheme_ – commissions, bonuses, and so on.

l According to one _motivation theory_ , giving people more autonomy is better than a higher salary.

m In a global market in which nothing stays the same, _change management_ has a crucial role to play.

Operations management

1 Listed below are some of the terms commonly used in production departments, but the second word in each collocation has been switched with another. Can you switch them back? The first two have been done for you.

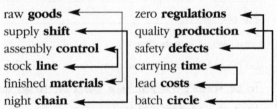

2 Which of the collocations in 1 refer to:

a unprocessed materials? _raw materials_

b the cost of storing and insuring stock? _carrying costs_

c the time between planning something and putting it into action? _lead time_

d manufacturing an article in groups rather than singly? _batch production_

e where the factory workers put the products together? _assembly line_

f factory workers who start work at the end of the working day? _night shift_

g a group of workers and managers who meet to discuss quality? _quality circle_

h a series of suppliers selling on raw materials and finished components to manufacturers? _supply chain_

17 Negotiating deals

Diplomacy and persuasion

Practice Look at the negotiation extracts. Make the direct remarks more diplomatic and persuasive using the words in brackets to help you.

Negotiation 1

A This is still too expensive.
(afraid/would still/a little out of/price range)

I'm afraid that would still be a little out of our price range.

B Well, how much do you want to pay?
(what sort/figure/did/in mind)

What sort of figure did you have in mind?

A $12 per unit.
(were thinking/somewhere/the region of/
$12 per unit)

We were thinking of somewhere in the region of $12 per unit.

B I can't go as low as that.
(be honest/not/a position/quite/low/this stage)

To be honest, I'm not in a position to go quite that low at this stage.

Negotiation 2

A You said we'd get 90 days' free credit.
(were promised/90 days' free credit)

We were promised 90 days' free credit.

B Yes, but you said you'd be placing a larger order.
(respect/was understood/rather larger)

With respect, it was understood you'd be placing a rather larger order.

A Look, this is getting us nowhere. We want free credit.
(doesn't seem/getting/very far//afraid/must insist/
free credit)

This doesn't seem to be getting us very far. I'm afraid we must insist on free credit.

B Well, I can't offer you that unless you increase your order.
(unfortunately/unable/offer/you're prepared/slightly)

Unfortunately, I'm unable to offer you that unless you're prepared to increase your order slightly.

Negotiation 3

A We need a commitment from you today.
(had/hoping/some kind)

We had been hoping for some kind of commitment from you today.

B Impossible! We're still unhappy about these service charges.
(this point/might/a bit difficult//not entirely/
service charges)

At this point that might be a bit difficult. We're not entirely happy about these service charges.

A But you said you were OK about those!
(was assumed)

But it was assumed you were OK about those.

B Not at all. Look, I think we should go over these figures again.
(afraid//shouldn't we/figures/again)

I'm afraid not. Look, shouldn't we go over these figures again?

Summary

Modal verbs (*would/might/could*, etc) are often used to soften the verb.

Modifiers are common (e.g. *a little difficult*).

Continuous forms keep your options open
(e.g. *We were wondering; We had been hoping*).

Introductory softeners (e.g. *I'm afraid*) warn that bad news is coming!

Negative adjectives like *expensive* are often avoided.

seem is common (e.g. *We don't seem to agree.*)

There's a lot of approximation (e.g. *sort of*).

Qualifying phrases are common (e.g. *at the moment*).

Alternatives are preferred to *can't* and *won't*.

The passive sounds less like an accusation
(not *You promised us ...*, but *We were promised ...*).

Suggestions are often phrased as negative questions
(e.g. *Wouldn't it be better to ...?*).

Lexis: Negotiations

A negotiator should observe everything. You must be part Sherlock Holmes, part Sigmund Freud.
Victor Kiam, CEO of Remington

Photocopiable

Sounding out your opponent Complete the questions using the prepositions in the box.

for	about	of	with	at	towards

What sort of ...

a figure were you thinking **of** ?

b terms would you be happy **with** ?

c discount were you hoping **for** ?

d delivery time are we talking **about** ?

e time-scale are we looking **at** ?

f deadline are we working **towards** ?

Discussing terms

1 These are all key points you may want to discuss in a negotiation. Write in the missing vowels.

pr**i**c**e**
d**i**sc**o**unt
cr**e**d**i**t
v**o**l**u**m**e**
tr**a**nsp**o**rt**a**ti**o**n
p**a**ck**a**g**i**ng
d**o**c**u**m**e**nt**a**ti**o**n
g**u****a**r**a**nt**e**e

c**o**ns**i**gnm**e**nts
m**a**int**e**n**a**nc**e**
d**e**l**i**v**e**ry t**i**m**e**
p**a**ym**e**nt t**e**rms
sp**a**r**e** p**a**rts
exch**a**ng**e** r**a**t**e**
aft**e**r-s**a**l**e**s s**e**rv**i**c**e**
p**e**n**a**lty cl**a****u**s**e**s

2 Complete the negotiator's proposal using the words and phrases in 1. Which one is not needed?

penalty clauses

'Well, on a repeat order of this (1) **volume** – 20,000 units – we'd be able to offer you what I think you'll agree is a very generous

(2) **discount** of 17%. I think you'd also find

our (3) **payment** **terms** extremely favourable – 120 days' (4) **credit** , of course – and we'd cover any fluctuations in the

(5) **exchange** **rate** between the dollar and the euro.

'We'd also be prepared to include in our quoted

(6) **price** all (7) **transportation** costs. That is to say, we'd handle the shipping charges, insurance and all the necessary (8) **documentation** to save you doing the paperwork yourself. We would have to use the same carrier for each delivery, however, which means the

(9) **delivery** **time** would be 14 days. I hope that's acceptable to you.

'Now, all our products come with a three-year

(10) **guarantee** which includes full

(11) **maintenance** and (12) **spare parts** . There's also a free 24-hour customer helpline, so your customers would be getting excellent (13) **after-sales service** .

'I think we could also be fairly flexible on

(14) **consignments** if you decided to increase or reduce your order from time to time.

'So, that just leaves the question of

(15) **packaging** . We normally use styrofoam containers ...'

Negotiating procedure

Complete the phases of a negotiation using the nouns in the box. Two of them have been done for you.

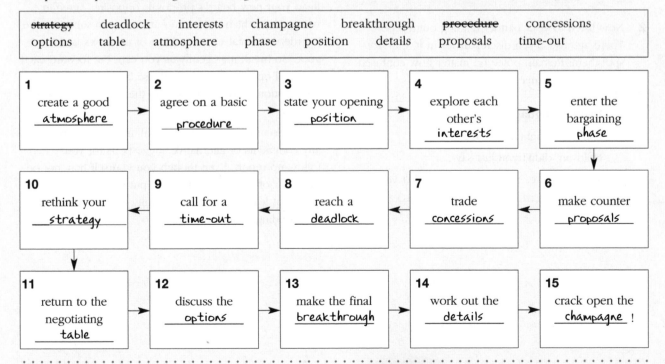

~~strategy~~	deadlock	interests	champagne	breakthrough	~~procedure~~	concessions
options	table	atmosphere	phase	position	details	proposals	time-out

1 create a good **atmosphere** → 2 agree on a basic **procedure** → 3 state your opening **position** → 4 explore each other's **interests** → 5 enter the bargaining **phase**

10 rethink your **strategy** ← 9 call for a **time-out** ← 8 reach a **deadlock** ← 7 trade **concessions** ← 6 make counter **proposals**

11 return to the negotiating **table** → 12 discuss the **options** → 13 make the final **breakthrough** → 14 work out the **details** → 15 crack open the **champagne** !

Additional material

2 Exchanging information

Fluency (p11, ex5)

Speaker A

1 Read out the following report to your partner. There are seven discrepancies in it (marked in **bold**). Can your partner spot them? If not, keep reading. Apologise for or justify any discrepancies your partner points out. If you lose your place in the text, ask your partner: 'Where was I?'

> **Report:**
> # World trade fair
>
> Our exhibition stand at the World Trade Fair in Munich was very successful again this year, attracting visitors from all over **Munich**. Although this was **our first appearance** at the Fair, our people did a great job and handed out **nearly three** brochures.
>
> We met a group of Austrian business people at the **Frankfurt** Hilton, where we were staying, and arranged a formal meeting with them by the **pool**. They were very interested in our products and said they would e-mail us as soon as they got back to **Australia**.
>
> Apparently, next year the Fair is being held outside Europe for the first time – **Paris** here we come!

2 Now listen to your partner reading out a report. There are also seven discrepancies in it. Can *you* spot them? Remain polite no matter how confused your partner seems!

> **Useful language:**
>
> Sorry, I thought you said …
>
> Hold on, didn't you just say …?
>
> Wait a minute. You just said …, didn't you?

1 Business or pleasure?

The hot buttons game (p9, ex6)

Speaker A

You're at a cocktail party with Speaker B, a very important client. You've been having a great time so far, but they don't seem to be having much fun. You don't know them very well socially, so try to find out what they're interested in – their 'hot buttons'. There's a list of conversation starters and topics on page 9. Keep changing the topic until you hit one of their hot buttons – they must be interested in something! And try to remain cheerful and positive no matter how dull and unfriendly they may seem!

The hot buttons game (p9, ex7)

Speaker A

You've just enjoyed the best annual dinner your company has ever laid on. Maybe it's because you've taken full advantage of all the delicious wines on offer, but you seem to be very talkative tonight. Look at the list of topics on page 9 and choose a favourite – your 'hot button'. Try to engage the person sitting next to you, Speaker B, in a conversation on this topic, which you're sure they must be as interested in as you. If other topics come up, just deal with them quickly and try to get back to what you really want to talk about.

2 Exchanging information

Breaking the bad news (p15, ex2)

Read your new board's proposals opposite. Agree in your group which one(s) you are going to submit at the interdepartmental meeting. Most of the news is not good, so break it as gently as you can. Put forward each proposal one step at a time. Pause between each step for questions and reactions from the other people at the meeting.

Invite discussion of each proposal and take notes on any comments or alternative suggestions for your follow-up report. Even though you yourself may not be in favour of the proposal(s) you put forward, you should at least initially show loyalty to your new bosses by sounding positive.

Proposal 1: Positive discrimination
- Board alarmed at low number of women in management positions
- Men currently outnumber women 13:1
- Plan to introduce policy of positive discrimination
- For 18-month trial period only women appointed to management positions
- No applications for promotion from male employees accepted
- Possible 'strategic demotion' of men to create more opportunities for women

Proposal 2: Work environment
- A lot of staff (35%) complaining about feeling tired and stressed
- Board thinks one of main causes may be poor work environment
- Feng shui expert called in – recommendations include radical changes to office layout
- Reception area to be turned into a water-garden to create positive 'chi' (energy)
- Internal walls to be removed to improve 'channels of communication'
- Desks ideally to be moved during the year to remain 'in harmony with the seasons'

Proposal 3: Rightsizing
- Board feels that company is overstaffed – streamlining obviously necessary
- Up to a third of current staff may have to go
- Action must be taken quickly to prevent bad work atmosphere
- No time to evaluate performance of all members of staff
- Board suggesting a LIFO (last-in-first-out) procedure
- People with the company for less than a year laid off first

Proposal 4: Travel budget
- Board deeply concerned about cost of business travel (nearly $3m last year)
- Insist on 60% cut in travel budget
- Propose three main courses of action (see below)
- All flights from now on to be economy class (no exceptions)
- Motels and two-star hotels to be used in preference to four-star
- Meal allowance to be reduced to $20 a day (no alcoholic drinks)

Proposal 5: Language training
- Board keen to market products more internationally
- English now language of international business but many staff (65%) already speak it
- In board's view, Chinese is business language of the future
- Mandarin, however, is one of world's most difficult languages
- Therefore, compulsory Chinese lessons (in employees' own time) to start immediately
- All new staff to be encouraged to accept two-year transfer to new subsidiary in Beijing

Proposal 6: Company cars
- Complaints from junior managers that sales reps get free company cars and they don't
- Board therefore rethinking whole policy on company vehicles
- Overall increase in vehicle budget not an option
- Currently reps drive Ford diesel estate cars (unnecessarily large)
- Proposal – all staff at assistant manager level and above to be issued with a company scooter
- More environmentally friendly (in line with new 'green initiative') and quicker in city traffic

Proposal 7: Customer relationship management
- Board extremely dissatisfied with amount of customer complaints
- Complaints both about products themselves and general quality of service
- In future, board would like to see staff take more personal responsibility for their work
- Rewards for fault-free production and excellent service clearly not motivating staff
- New proposal is that a system of penalties be introduced
- All product faults to be paid for by staff and bad service to result in immediate dismissal

Proposal 8: Team spirit
- Board strongly believes not enough team spirit
- Problem particularly noticeable at the production plant
- Obviously takes time to build a team, but certain things could be introduced right away
- Has been suggested a company song could be sung every morning
- The idea has proved very popular at big companies like IBM, General Electric and Mitsubishi
- Second idea is that all staff (including managers) wear a uniform in company colours – orange and green

1 Business or pleasure?

The hot buttons game (p9, ex6)

Speaker B

You're at a cocktail party with Speaker A, one of your many suppliers. You generally hate this kind of event and so far you've had a miserable evening. Look at the list of topics on page 9 and choose just two you are prepared to have a conversation about – your 'hot buttons'. If Speaker A tries to engage you in conversation on any topic apart from your hot buttons, say very little. Do nothing to change the topic, but show enthusiasm if one of your hot button topics comes up.

The hot buttons game (p9, ex7)

Speaker B

You've been at your company's annual dinner for the last five hours and are utterly exhausted. The person sitting next you seems to want to talk non-stop about the same boring topic. As they're an important client, you can't just ignore them or tell them to shut up. So, be polite, but keep trying to steer the conversation towards something more interesting. Use the list of conversation starters and topics on page 9.

2 Exchanging information

Fluency (p11, ex5)

Speaker B

1 Listen to your partner reading out a report. There are seven discrepancies in it. Can you spot them? Remain polite no matter how confused your partner seems!

> **Useful language:**
>
> Sorry, I thought you said …
>
> Hold on, didn't you just say …?
>
> Wait a minute. You just said …, didn't you?

2 Read out the following report to your partner. There are also seven discrepancies in it (marked in **bold**). Can *they* spot them? If not, keep reading. Apologise for or justify any discrepancies your partner points out. If you lose your place in the text, ask your partner: 'Where was I?'

Report:
Korean negotiations

We held our first meeting with the Koreans two months ago at their headquarters in **Osaka**. Since then we've had **twelve weeks** of tough negotiations. There were some cultural difficulties at first. Of course, we've never done business in the **Middle East** before.

They were very positive about our products, although they weren't happy with **the design, performance, price and maintenance costs**. Initially, they were demanding a discount on orders of over 10,000 units of 17%, but we finally managed to beat them down to **18**.

We haven't heard anything from them so far, but the e-mail they sent **this morning** looks promising – an initial order of **a dozen units**.

3 Material world

Quiz answers (page 16, ex1)

1 b	2 b	3 b	4 b	5 c	6 a	7 a
8 c	9 d	10 b	11 d	12 c		

Billionaire fact file

- 298 of the world's 450 billionaires are American and so are 2.5 million of the 7.2 million millionaires.
- Real estate in Eaton Square is currently worth £10,775 per m² and the average price of a flat there is £1.5m.
- Famous residents of Santa Barbara's 'Millionaires' Row' include Kevin Costner, Michael Douglas and John Travolta.
- Hiring a jumbo jet for an hour and spending a night in the Bridge Suite both work out at exactly $25,000, but a Harvard MBA would set you back nearly three times that in tuition fees.
- To get your private helicopter pilot's licence you'd need to spend around $15,000 on flying lessons.
- The Chopard watch would cost you a staggering $25m, but the Grachvogel dress a mere £1m.
- The fire-damaged Hendrix guitar went at auction for $300,000.
- British investor Joseph Lewis once paid €2.2m for a round of golf with Tiger Woods.
- The Royal Family of Qatar have a yacht as expensive as Ellison's, but theirs is not for sale!
- The Aston Martin DB5 is the car featured in the James Bond Movie *Goldfinger*.
- The record-breaking Van Gogh was the *Portrait of Doctor Gachet*, sold at Christie's in 1990.

4 Voice and visuals

Giving feedback (p22, ex4)

Speaker B: Presenter

You work for a major management consultancy and have just given a presentation to an important Taiwanese client. The presentation didn't go very well and unfortunately your boss was in the audience.

You are meeting your boss now, and are not expecting very good feedback. Make it clear that the disaster wasn't entirely your fault. Defend yourself using the following information, and assure your boss that this will never happen again.

- You've been asking your boss for a new laptop for ages – the one you've got just can't handle PowerPoint properly.
- You've been on the road for four weeks and are completely exhausted – this is your tenth major presentation. To make matters worse, the laundry ruined your best suit and left you with virtually nothing to wear.
- You've no excuse for the poor handouts. It was obviously a printer problem and you forgot to check them.
- Nobody told you your Taiwanese audience hardly spoke any English – by the time you realised you were halfway through your talk.
- Some of your jokes may not have translated very well, but you were just trying to break the ice.
- You're sure the video you were going to use was stolen from your hotel bedroom.
- No one checked the microphone: the amplifier was turned down much too low.

Useful language:

How was I supposed to know …?

It's not my fault. You should have …

Somebody should have …

It might have helped if …

Look, I'm not trying to make excuses, but …

I can hardly be blamed for …*ing*, can I?

Rest assured, it won't happen again.

---

5 Problems on the phone

Fluency (p27, ex5)

Speaker B

If you don't know Speaker A well, swap lists of the following with them before you start your telephone conversation:

- your partner's name, job and main interest
- your children's names, ages and main interests
- when and where you went on your last holiday
- your own main interest
- your favourite sport (spectator or player?)
- the name of a close colleague
- a problem you've been having at work recently

You are the sales director of Möbelkunst, a designer furniture manufacturer in Berlin. Your stylish products are getting rave reviews in the press, but business in Germany has not been good lately. Fortunately, you have recently won some very big overseas orders – one of them with Mi Casa, a large chain of furniture stores in Mexico. The only problem is Speaker A, Mi Casa's director of purchasing, who seems to like phoning you rather too often for no particular reason.

It's 5pm on Friday afternoon. You would normally be getting ready to go home soon, but today there's been a crisis to deal with – your factory in Potsdam has just turned out 1,000 leather sofas in bright pink (rather than dark red) by mistake. You're still trying to sort a solution out with your plant manager. The last thing you need now is any interruptions.

9 Relationship-building

Questionnaire analysis (pp46-47, ex5)

How you network in specific situations will, of course, be influenced by many factors, but, in general, the most effective strategy will be: **1a**, **2c**, **3b**, **4b**, **5c** and **6c**.
1c, **2b**, **5b** and **6a** could be risky.
3a and **4c** might be unfair to other people.
1b, **3c**, **4a** and **5a** may show a certain lack of assertiveness.

11 Branded planet

Discussion (p60, ex3)

Answers

a fact **b** hoax **c** fact **d** fact **e** hoax **f** fact
g fact **h** hoax

4 Voice and visuals

Quiz answers (p20, ex2)

1 12 ½ seconds
2 55% is visual; 38% is vocal; 7% is verbal
3 Mel Gibson; Julia Roberts
4 400,000; 400%; 85%
5 b is false

4 Voice and visuals

Giving feedback (p22, ex4)

Speaker A: Boss

You are a senior partner in a major management consultancy. You have just attended a presentation by one of your best consultants to an important Taiwanese client. Unfortunately, the presentation was an absolute disaster from start to finish.

You forced a smile during the presentation but are now going to tell Speaker B exactly what you thought of their performance. Base your criticisms on the following information. Try to end on a positive note by making some suggestions for future presentations.

- Speaker B was wearing a T-shirt and jeans. The Taiwanese must have felt deeply insulted.
- You could hardly hear a word Speaker B said.
- They made no attempt to modify their English for a foreign audience.
- The PowerPoint slides were not working properly – it all looked very unprofessional.
- The handouts were virtually illegible. There was no excuse for this: there was plenty of time to prepare.
- You have no idea what happened to the video you were expecting to see.
- You nearly died when they cracked a joke about China. The Taiwanese left the room in silence, clearly not amused.

> **Useful language:**
>
> Why did/didn't you …?
>
> You should(n't) have …
>
> Couldn't you at least have …?
>
> Don't you think it would have been a good idea to …?
>
> Well, anyway, in future I suggest you …
>
> And next time – if there is a next time – just make sure you …

5 Problems on the phone

Fluency (p27, ex5)

Speaker A

If you don't know Speaker B well, swap lists of the following with them before you start your telephone conversation:

- your partner's name, job and main interest
- your children's names, ages and main interests
- when and where you went on your last holiday
- your own main interest
- your favourite sport (spectator or player?)
- the name of a close colleague
- a problem you've been having at work recently

You are director of the purchasing department for Mi Casa, a large chain of furniture stores in Mexico. You like to get in touch with your suppliers from time to time – not necessarily to do business, just to maintain the relationship. It's 10am on Friday morning, most of your week's work is done and the weekend is fast approaching. Phone Speaker B, the sales director of Möbelkunst, a designer furniture manufacturer in Berlin, for a little chat.

Keep the conversation going by asking lots of questions (using Speaker B's list as a starting point). You don't really want to do any business today, but Möbelkunst's stylish chairs, tables and lamps have been very popular with your customers. If the terms were right, you might want to increase your order – even double it – for a trial period.

6 Leading meetings

In the chair (p34, ex1)

Speaker A

Meeting 1: Genetic profiling (chair)

You have been asked by head office to chair a meeting on the possible introduction of genetic testing for job applicants at all levels. Your company already insists on a medical when people apply for a job, as well as psychometric tests and checks on possible criminal records. Now they think a genetic profile would help to reduce the risk of employing or promoting people with potentially serious diseases and mental health problems. The test would probably be voluntary – this hasn't been fully discussed with the legal department yet – but refusal to undergo it may affect a candidate's chance of employment or promotion.

You have read that vulnerability to stress, alcoholism and strokes – the three main causes of people being off work for prolonged periods – are all to some extent genetically inherited, but the idea of genetic testing does seem quite drastic and is bound to provoke a certain amount of hostility.

Leader's brief: Open the meeting, inform those present of HQ's proposal, make sure everyone gets a chance to speak and no one dominates. Try to avoid digressions and keep the meeting short. Give your own opinion only after everyone else has spoken and try to reach a decision on what recommendations to make to HQ.

Meeting 2: Employee surveillance (in favour)

You have heard a rumour that head office is planning to introduce a system of checking up on employees using PC monitoring software and closed circuit television (CCTV). You are about to attend a meeting to discuss the subject. At the moment you are firmly in favour of the idea, but listen to what the other participants have to say before finally making up your mind. You are sure that huge amounts of company time and money are being wasted by employees accessing gaming and adult websites during working hours. You've even heard some of the male staff joking about it. An article you read in *Business Week* claims that employees who play computer games whilst at work cost US firms $100 billion a year – or 2% of GDP. You also remember the famous case of Chevron, who, by failing to monitor computer use, ended up being sued by four female employees who had suffered sexual harassment through the internal e-mail system. The company finally had to pay out $2.2 million in compensation.

Hidden agenda: You've heard that a junior manager in your department, who seems to have his sights set on your job, spends hours in private chatrooms on company time. In order to catch such people, you think the computer surveillance should be covert.

Meeting 3: Alternative management training (against)

You have heard a rumour that head office is planning to introduce a series of alternative management training courses for all levels of staff. You are about to attend a meeting to discuss the subject. At the moment you are not keen on the idea, but listen to what the other participants have to say before finally making up your mind. Frankly, you don't believe that 'fads' like this represent very good value for money. A friend of yours works for a firm that sent him and his colleagues to a Benedictine monastery to learn about 'Morality in the Workplace'. Predictably, it was thought to be a complete waste of time. You've also heard about weird courses offered by drama groups, orchestras, circuses, the army and even the prison service where executives spent a week in jail to build team spirit.

Hidden agenda: You have a close friend who is in charge of in-company training at a prestigious business school in the United States. If your company booked a course, you personally might get some kind of 'thank you'.

17 Negotiating deals

Fluency (p90, ex1c)

Extra information for second negotiation

You and the other speaker are ex-neighbours and very good friends. Your kids even used to play together. You both moved to different areas of the city about six months ago and meant to keep in touch, but, what with work and settling into new homes, you just haven't had the time.

6 Leading meetings

In the chair (p34, ex1)

Speaker B

Meeting 1: Genetic profiling (against)

You have heard a rumour that head office is planning to introduce genetic testing for future job applicants. You are about to attend a meeting to discuss the subject. At the moment you are strongly against the idea, but listen to what the other participants have to say before finally making up your mind. One thing you are fairly sure of is that genetic screening without consent would be illegal under civil law. You certainly consider it unethical. Also, since some of the conditions screened for (such as sickle cell disease) affect mostly black people, and others (such as breast and ovarian cancer) solely women, you are concerned that the tests could easily lead to racial and sexual discrimination.

Hidden agenda: There is a genetically inherited disease that runs in your family. Although you do not have the condition yourself, you are worried that it might show up in a genetic test and that you might be discriminated against if you applied for promotion.

Meeting 2: Employee surveillance (chair)

You have been asked by head office to chair a meeting on the possible introduction of surveillance and electronic security equipment to check up on employees of the company. In your business confidentiality is essential as many of your workers are dealing with highly classified information. Of course, a lot of your company files are encrypted, but leaks still happen. HQ is also concerned about the amount of time employees appear to be spending making personal phone calls and sending private e-mails. Details of what system to install have not yet been fully discussed, but suggestions include Internet monitoring software, random phone tapping and closed circuit television (CCTV) throughout the building.

You yourself are a little alarmed at the number of unnecessary e-mails sent back and forth over the company intranet and have overheard staff making international phone calls that were clearly not business. Monitoring Internet access and phone use is common practice in many companies these days and you don't see why anyone would object unless they had something to hide. CCTV seems a bit radical, however.

Leader's brief: Open the meeting, inform those present of HQ's proposal, make sure everyone gets a chance to speak and no one dominates. Try to avoid digressions and keep the meeting short. Give your own opinion only after everyone else has spoken and try to reach a decision on what recommendations to make to HQ.

Meeting 3: Alternative management training (in favour)

You have heard a rumour that head office is planning to introduce a series of alternative management training courses for all levels of staff. You are about to attend a meeting to discuss the subject. At the moment you are fairly enthusiastic about the idea, but listen to what the other participants have to say before finally making up your mind. You already have an MBA, but have never found what you learnt at business school much use in the real world of business. On the other hand, an ex-colleague of yours went on a course to learn about negotiating technique from an Olympic gold medal-winning judo player and says it was the best business training she's ever had.

Hidden agenda: You have a favourite cousin who runs a company that teaches business people creativity through song, poetry and drama workshops, stand-up comedy and exotic sports like Zen archery and rodeo riding. He's not doing too well at the moment and could do with more clients.

8 Promoting your ideas

Answers (p41, ex1)

USA – Extract 3
Germany – Extract 1
Japan – Extract 4
UK – Extract 5
France – Extract 6
Kuwait – Extract 2

5 Problems on the phone

Fluency (p29, ex7)

Speaker B

At the end of each conversation, give Speaker A a score out of ten for **a** helpfulness and **b** assertiveness.

1 Speaker A will phone you with a problem. You are very busy at the moment (you decide what you're doing) but try to give them some advice. If you can't, suggest someone they could phone who might be able to help.

2 You are Speaker A's boss. It's 6pm and you still have a mountain of papers on your desk to go through before the morning (you decide what sort of papers they are). Phone Speaker A and ask them if they'd mind staying on for an hour or so to help you out. Be diplomatic but don't take no for an answer – unless they can suggest someone else.

3 Speaker A has just been promoted and you are now their boss. But a colleague from an overseas division of your company (you decide who) is going to spend the next three months working on an international project in your division and they need to be provided with a suitable office. Speaker A's office would be ideal (you decide why). Phone them and try to get their agreement without causing any bad feeling.

4 You have been working on an important report for nine months. Because of a lot of unforeseen difficulties and complications (you decide what) you are a month behind schedule and now need six, rather than two, more weeks to finish it. On completion of the report you are due to present your findings to senior management and you think they will be impressed. Much to your annoyance, however, you think your boss, Speaker A, is going to try to speed things up by bringing in someone else to help you finish the job and take half the credit for all your hard work.

9 Relationship-building

Fluency (p47, ex6)

Speaker B

You are

- the chief purchasing manager for MacGregor Sports Goods, based in St Andrews, Scotland
- responsible for 37 stores in Scotland, selling sports equipment but specialising in golf and fishing supplies
- at an international conference in Dublin, which has been quite enjoyable so far – apart from the lashing rain!
- staying at the Fitzwilliam Hotel until tomorrow afternoon – you're flying back to Scotland at 6pm

You have

- a lot of experience in the golf business, having previously run a golfing holiday company in Edinburgh
- a relative who is a famous sports personality (you decide who)
- met Speaker A before at the Golf World Expo in Marbella, Spain, but you're not sure what they do

You think

- Speaker A is based in the USA – California, perhaps?

You want

- to reintroduce yourself to Speaker A and find out what they do

> **Useful language:**
>
> Hello. I don't know if you remember me, but …
>
> What do you do, by the way?
>
> Well, in that case, perhaps …

9 Relationship-building

A dinner invitation (p51, ex1)

Host: Ulterior motive

You're considering promoting your guest to a more senior post (you decide what) at your company's subsidiary in Melbourne. You are very impressed with your guest's work record and general management ability, but you haven't made up your mind yet about the promotion. So, drop a few hints during the evening and see what the reaction is. Don't be too specific at this stage and be ready to change the subject if things don't go according to plan!

6 Leading meetings

In the chair (p34, ex1)

Speaker C

Meeting 1: Genetic profiling (in favour)

You have heard a rumour that head office is planning to introduce genetic testing for future job applicants. You are about to attend a meeting to discuss the subject. At the moment you are basically in favour of the idea, but listen to what the other participants have to say before finally making up your mind. You know that 350 million working days are lost each year in the EU alone through illness – stress being the cause of 41 million of those. UK companies lose £13 billion annually because of employees going off sick. If people with potential social problems (such as alcoholism or drug abuse) could be screened out at the job application stage, it would make for a healthier workforce and could save the firm millions.

Hidden agenda: Your department has been particularly affected by people taking sick leave. At the moment you are trying to cope without three of your key managers – one of them, you suspect, has a drink problem.

Meeting 2: Employee surveillance (against)

You have heard a rumour that head office is planning to introduce a system of checking up on employees using PC monitoring software and closed circuit television (CCTV). You are about to attend a meeting to discuss the subject. At the moment you are very much against the idea, but listen to what the other participants have to say before finally making up your mind. You firmly believe that a good work atmosphere is built on trust and that such security measures should only be taken when there is strong evidence to suggest that company facilities are being abused. Moreover, you suspect that phone taps, video cameras and PC monitoring may just be the thin end of the wedge. You've heard in some companies workers have also been videotaped in toilets and locker rooms and investigators have even been hired to follow them home. What next? Electronic tagging devices? Implants?

Hidden agenda: You often surf the Internet on your office PC during coffee and lunch breaks (never during working hours, however) and regularly log on to chatroom channels. You see this as valuable networking and not an abuse of company Internet access. Still, if Internet monitoring was introduced, you'd prefer the company to announce the fact and not investigate past use.

Meeting 3: Alternative management training (chair)

You have been asked by head office to chair a meeting on the possible introduction of a series of alternative management training courses. In the past, your firm has sent junior members of staff on practical office skills courses and middle and senior management on executive courses at several top business schools. But the feedback has sometimes been rather negative. As people at all levels in your company require a high degree of creativity, HQ is proposing to hire the services of a number of 'arts and business' companies to help employees 'think outside the box'.

Suggestions so far include: working with a renowned artist to produce a 5m x 30m company mural to be displayed at HQ; putting on a variety show with the help of professional actors with all members of staff taking part in song, dance and comedy routines; choreographing a modern ballet to dramatise the challenges facing the company; and music lessons from professional musicians leading to an end-of-year company jazz session. Many big-name companies have found similar training to be highly enjoyable and successful – why not your company too?

Leader's brief: Open the meeting, inform those present of HQ's proposal, make sure everyone gets a chance to speak and no one dominates. Try to avoid digressions and keep the meeting short. Give your own opinion only after everyone else has spoken and try to reach a decision on what recommendations to make to HQ.

11 Branded planet

The name game (p61, ex1)

(the author's suggestions)
Your choice of name will principally depend on:
- the sound of the name (and if there are different ways of pronouncing it, could that be a problem?)
- the appearance of the letters (some letters have proven customer appeal: Zs and Xs, for example)
- linguistic and cultural associations (does the word look or sound like another word in your language or the target market's language?)

For an English-speaking market, the following names would be effective:
1 Zyex – visually attractive combination of letters; sounds quite masculine and 'techie'
2 Ios – short and simple; sounds pure, classical and feminine (Eos was the Ancient Greek goddess of the dawn)
3 Areon – suggests lightness, speed and mobility
4 Zantis – has exotic associations (By**zanti**um, Atl**antis**) but, if said quickly, sounds quite like 'scientist'

5 Problems on the phone

Fluency (p29, ex7)

Speaker A

At the end of each conversation, give Speaker B a score out of ten for **a** helpfulness and **b** assertiveness.

1   You are having problems with your computer – it either won't do something you want it to or it's just done something you definitely didn't want it to (you decide which). Phone Speaker B and see if they can give you any advice. If not, ask them who you should phone instead.

2   Speaker B, your boss, will phone you with a problem. It's 6pm and you are just on your way out of the office when the phone rings. You've arranged to go out with a few colleagues this evening (you decide when and where). This is the fifth time this month your boss has held you up right at the end of the day.

3   You have just been promoted and Speaker B is now your boss. You particularly like your great new office (you decide why), which is exactly what you need to do your new job (you decide why). Someone told you today that a colleague from an overseas division of your company may be coming to work at your division for a few months and you are waiting for your boss to phone and give you the details.

4   Speaker B is usually a star member of your team, but at the moment they are a month behind with an important report and you are under pressure from head office get it completed on schedule (within the next two weeks). You think the best idea is to bring someone else in (you decide who) to help get the report finished in time and team present the final results to senior management with Speaker B. Phone and make your suggestion as tactfully but forcefully as you can.

9 Relationship-building

Fluency (p47, ex6)

Speaker A

You are

- the sales director for Fairways, a golfing equipment manufacturer based in Florida
- at an international conference in Dublin, which you are really enjoying so far – great place, excellent talks
- staying at the Fitzwilliam Hotel for the next two days – you have a meeting tomorrow at 10am
- currently looking for new agents and distributors in Northern Europe

You have

- just come back from a disappointing business trip to Scotland – you didn't find any suitable agents
- met Speaker B before, but can't remember where – a trade fair in Portugal?

You think

- Speaker B runs some kind of golfing holiday agency
- Speaker B is related to a famous sports personality – a tennis player, maybe?

You want

- to talk to Speaker B about running a joint promotion with their travel company

---

Useful language:

Haven't we met somewhere before?

Aren't you … or am I mistaken?

I thought you might be interested in …

---

9 Relationship-building

A dinner invitation (p51, ex1)

Guest: Ulterior motive

You've secretly applied for and been shortlisted for a better job (you decide what) at another company in San Francisco. You've been fairly happy in your current job and you don't want to upset your host, so break the news gently at some point during the evening and try to see if they'll write you a good reference. Be careful what you say and be ready to change the subject if things don't go according to plan!

13 Making an impact

Fluency (p73, ex4)

Group A: Bhutanese Preservation Party

1 The success of our current gradual development programme

Since 1993 life expectancy has increased from 49 (for women) and 46 (for men) to 66 (for both).

In the same period infant mortality has halved.

78% of the population now have access to safe drinking water.

Adult literacy has increased from 4% to 54%.

95% of people who leave Bhutan to work or study abroad return.

2 The risks of overdevelopment

Alaska, Bali, Mongolia and Tahiti once enjoyed a lifestyle like that in Bhutan and have suffered irreparably from too-rapid development.

The arrival in Bhutan of the Internet and cable and satellite television stations like MTV is causing envy and dissatisfaction among Bhutan's young people.

3 The natural environment

The Bhutanese forests are home to many species of flora and fauna, which have as much right to be here as we have – 60% of Bhutan should remain virgin forest and 26% as parkland.

Many of Bhutan's indigenous species are on the endangered list: the red panda, snow leopard and tiger (now the third most endangered animal on Earth).

The mountains are sacred and must be kept off-limits to tourists and climbers, who would disturb the spirits.

We welcome respectful tourists but their number must be restricted to the present quota of 7,000 a year.

4 Our religion

Our historic monasteries and temples are places of worship, not tourist attractions.

The teachings of the Buddha show that what matters is our long-term karma or spiritual development, not short-term gain and profit margins.

14 Out and about

Fluency (p76, ex11)

Speaker A

Hold short conversations with a fellow passenger, Speaker B, on three different international flights.

Use the information below to get you started, but invent any extra information you need to keep the conversation going for a minute or two.

1 Flight BA1311 from Dubai to London Heathrow, business class (9pm)

You are an engineer travelling back from Dubai, where you have been working for Royal Dutch Shell (Emirates) for the last five years, to take up a senior position at head office in London. Your three-year-old son is accompanying you on the flight, but your partner won't be joining you in the UK for another couple of weeks. You're not looking forward to the flight much because your son is quite a hyperactive child and you can never sleep on planes anyway. Try to start a conversation with the person sitting next you, Speaker B. They seem to be playing with their hand-held computer at the moment.

2 Flight AF6001 from Paris to Rio de Janeiro, economy class (3am)

You are a product manager for Pfizer Pharmaceuticals on your way from a project meeting in Paris to another meeting in Rio. You have an appointment with a group of Brazilian research chemists with whom you are collaborating on a new kind of miracle travel sickness pill, which, if all goes well, could be on the market in six months. So far your journey has been a nightmare. Your original flight was cancelled due to bad weather and the only seat you could get was in economy class on the red-eye leaving at two-thirty in the morning. To top it all, it looks like it's going to be a bumpy flight. You can't sleep, so you might as well try and read your book, a crime novel you picked up in the airport called *The Pentangle* by A. J. Bell. Seems quite good.

3 Flight LH1706 from Los Angeles to Munich, first class (2pm)

You are a film producer for Touchstone Pictures flying from a meeting with Oscar-winning actor Al Pacino in Los Angeles to a casting meeting in Munich. You are looking for a German- and English-speaking actor to play the part of an environmental activist in your latest film and would prefer to choose an unknown rather than a big box-office star. You've just enjoyed your second glass of complimentary champagne, when you notice that the passenger sitting next you looks perfect for the part! You can't believe your eyes, but remind yourself they are probably a business executive with no acting ability whatsoever. At the moment they are watching the in-flight movie on their headphones, but try to find an excuse to get talking to them.

17 Negotiating deals

Fluency (p90, ex1a)

Speaker A

It's 6pm on Christmas Eve and you're still at the office. You've been so busy lately, you've hardly had a moment to spend with your family. You even had to miss your young son's first match for the school football team last week to attend an important meeting. Apparently, you were the only parent not there.

Fortunately, you have a chance to put things right. You know there's something kids are all going mad for this Christmas – the Z-Cube Gaming System. At $189, it's a little more than you were planning to spend, but it would be great to see the look on your son's face when he opens it. After phoning seven stores without success, you finally find one that has three left. You try to reserve one, but the shop assistant says 'Sorry, only my boss can do that and she's not here. But if you hurry, you should be OK. We're open till 6.30.'

You fly out of the office and into a taxi. You get to the store just before it closes. To your horror, you see there's only one Z-Cube left. It has a big label on the box saying 'LAST ONE'. But as you head for it, you see another person with the same idea (Speaker B) coming in the other direction. You both reach the box at the same time and grab opposite ends …

17 Negotiating deals

Fluency (p95, ex5)

Team A: The Penitents (band and management)

Obviously, you are delighted that a record company as high-profile as *Starburst* is interested in signing your band. If the deal goes through, you stand to make a lot of money. You are aware, however, that relatively unknown artists are vulnerable to exploitation by the big labels and should take this into account in your dealings with them.

Read your negotiating objectives opposite and then work with your team to plan your overall strategy. In particular, make sure you know which of your objectives are:

1 tradeables (things you'll concede to get what you really want in return)
2 ideals (things you'd really like to get, but not if it costs you the deal)
3 essentials (things you absolutely have to get or the deal's off)

1 **Band line-up**
The four members of the band – the lead singer and rhythm guitarist, lead guitarist, bass guitarist and drummer – all met at college in Dublin and have played together through good times and bad for five years. You've heard a rumour that *Starburst Records* may want to make changes to the line-up – perhaps sacking the drummer, who is also the band's female backing vocalist.

2 **Term**
You'd like a three-year commitment from *Starburst*. It can often take several albums before band members make a profit, so you'd like them to commission at least two albums during that time. If, after three years, the contract is terminated, you'd prefer to keep the rights to all the songs you have recorded – otherwise you would have to pay *Starburst* a fee to perform or re-record your old material.

3 **Royalties**
You think a 15% royalty on net receipts from album sales would be fair. If the band's current popularity does not last, you'd like to make as much as money as possible before the bubble bursts.

4 **Deductions**
You expect *Starburst* to cover all the costs of packaging and promotion, including any TV advertising. Accessing marketing power is one of the advantages of signing to a major label.

5 **Advances**
You are more interested in a good long-term relationship with *Starburst* than instant cash. Nevertheless, a $200,000 non-repayable advance would allow band members to cover living costs, purchase of equipment and stage costumes, etc.

6 **Territory**
You're happy for *Starburst* to have 'universal rights' to your material globally, provided the terms are right. Otherwise, you'd like to be able to approach other labels in the States and Asia.

7 **Touring**
Touring is an essential part of building a band, especially in the early stages of its development. But some of the band members have other jobs and family commitments. They wouldn't want to take on more than 20 weeks' touring (not consecutively) in the first year unless the financial rewards were high – say, 50% of ticket sales.

8 **Songwriting**
The lead singer, Rick Harlow, writes all the band's songs. He says he wants the usual 50:50 split with the music publisher on fees for airplay on radio and TV and other public performances.

13 Making an impact

Fluency (p73, ex4)

Group B: Progress Party of Bhutan

1 The need to speed up the rate of progress

22% of the population still have no access to clean drinking water.

40% of children are malnourished.

33% of them are unable to attend school.

Almost half the population remains illiterate.

2 Infrastructure and communications

The 'last paradise on earth' image is counter-productive – Bhutan is exactly the kind of country that could benefit most from the Internet economy for both commercial and educational purposes.

Until 1999 Bhutan was without TV and there was only one cinema. More needs to be spent on the Bhutan Broadcasting Service (BBS) and Sigma Cable Service.

Bhutan's Internet ISP DrukNet, though popular, is still too expensive (seven cents per minute), but the use of websites and e-mail has reduced international phone bills by 90% and should be promoted.

3 Bhutan's enormous potential as tourist resort

Many of the current improvements in Bhutan are the result of foreign investment, principally from India and Singapore. Why shouldn't other countries be encouraged to invest as well?

Bhutan's superb wildlife and fabulous mountain scenery would be ideal for ecological tourism and adventure holidays.

Limiting the number of tourist visas to just 7,000 a year and insisting that 86% of the land area remain undeveloped is missing a huge opportunity.

Druk Air, the world's smallest commercial carrier, consists of just two planes flying six or seven times a week.

4 The youth of Bhutan

45% of the population of Bhutan is under 15 years of age – it is time to respond to the needs of the younger generation instead of living in the past.

14 Out and about

Fluency (p76, ex11)

Speaker B

Hold short conversations with a fellow passenger, Speaker A, on three different international flights.

Use the information below to get you started, but invent any extra information you need to keep the conversation going for a minute or two.

1 Flight BA1311 from Dubai to London Heathrow, business class (9pm)

You are the partner in a small software company specialising in computer-assisted engineering applications for the oil industry, and are travelling back home from a series of meetings with potential clients in Dubai. It's been an exhausting trip and not as successful as you would have liked. Frankly, you'd just like to skip dinner and try and get some sleep. First, however, you think you'll order a martini while you update your client files on your PalmPilot. You are not pleased to see that the person sitting next to you, Speaker A, has a young child with them. There goes your relaxing flight.

2 Flight AF6001 from Paris to Rio de Janeiro, economy class (3am)

You are a financial speculator who specialises in medical, pharmaceutical and biotech stocks. You are coming back from a meeting in Paris to Rio where you live with your American partner, the crime novelist A. J. Bell. Due to the cancellation of your business class Varig flight, you've ended up in economy class on an early morning Air France flight instead. And you are already regretting this – there's barely room to move and, to make matters worse, the plane seems to be experiencing some turbulence. You've never been a great flyer and are starting to feel a bit sick. Perhaps talking to the person sitting next to you would take your mind off it. But they seem to be reading a book. Actually, the book looks quite familiar …

3 Flight LH1706 from Los Angeles to Munich, first class (2pm)

You are a highly paid German-English interpreter based in Munich and travelling back from LA, where you've been assisting at the American launch of the new BMW sports car. When you arrived for your business class flight this morning, you were delighted to find that it was overbooked and that you had been upgraded to first class. You've had quite an exciting, if stressful, week in LA and are now thoroughly enjoying the flight home. You've had an excellent lunch and have just tuned into the in-flight movie on your personal video screen. You've already seen the film, but don't mind seeing it again as it stars your favourite actor, Al Pacino. And anyway, the person sitting next to you looks like some big millionaire business type.

17 Negotiating deals

Fluency (p90, ex1a)

Speaker B

It's Christmas Eve and you and your family are placing the last few presents under the tree. Your partner turns to you and whispers how excited your young son is: 'Thank goodness you bought him that new gaming system back in November. Apparently, the stores have completely sold out, and it's all he's talked about for months. You remembered to get him the blue one, didn't you?'

You feel a sudden surge of panic. Oh, no ... the Z-Cube Gaming System! How could you have forgotten? You meant to get one months ago, but you've been so busy it completely slipped your mind. You mumble something to your partner about going out to get some better lights for the tree and spend the next three hours searching every store in town. But nobody has one. One shop offers to order it for you, but it will take at least a fortnight ...

In desperation, you try a tiny shop in a side street. It's just about to close as you walk in. To your relief, you see they have one Z-Cube left – and it's a blue one. You can't believe your luck. It has a big label on the box saying 'LAST ONE'. But as you head for it, you see another person with the same idea (Speaker A) coming in the other direction. You both reach the box at the same time and grab opposite ends ...

17 Negotiating deals

Fluency (p95, ex5)

Team B: Starburst Records (executives and lawyers)

You are very excited about this band's prospects. *The Penitents* are musically exceptionally strong with proven song-writing abilities. What's more, they have already generated a lot of media interest. However, the risks with a new signing are always high. Fashions change quickly in your business and you should bear this in mind in your dealings with the band's management.

Read your negotiating objectives opposite and then work with your team to plan your overall strategy. In particular, make sure you know which of your objectives are:
1 tradeables (things you'll concede to get what you really want in return)
2 ideals (things you'd really like to get, but not if it costs you the deal)
3 essentials (things you absolutely have to get or the deal's off)

1 **Band line-up**
Three of the four members of the band – the lead singer/rhythm guitarist, lead guitarist and bass guitarist are exceptionally talented, though the lead guitarist has a reputation for hitting members of the paparazzi and was recently involved in an unpleasant incident aboard an airliner that resulted in his being banned for life. The weak link is the drummer, who simply must be replaced.

2 **Term**
You are prepared to offer a one-album deal, but would like to retain an option on at least two subsequent albums, if the first is successful. You'd also like to keep the performing and recording rights to all the songs – otherwise, if you don't renew their contract and they later become successful with a different label, you won't be able to profit from their backlist of songs.

3 **Royalties**
You think a 10% royalty on net receipts from album sales would be fair. This might be renegotiable after the first three albums, but you'd like to offset the initial risk of taking on the band by maximising profits in the early stages.

4 **Deductions**
If sales of the first album are good (at least 200,000 units), you may want to run a TV campaign. In this case you would like to deduct the cost of 20% of this from the band's royalties.

5 **Advances**
Since advances are normally non-repayable, you'd prefer to offer a relatively modest one on the first album (say $80,000) and promise higher ones on later albums once the band is established.

6 **Territory**
As you'll be spending a substantial amount of time and money on promoting *The Penitents*, you require total 'universal rights' to sell their music globally.

7 **Touring**
With a band like *The Penitents* touring is a key part of building a fan-base. The band is particularly strong live and you would like to capitalise on that. You'd expect them to tour for at least eight months in their first year. Your preferred schedule would be: release two singles, record the first album and do the tour. You'd want 80% of the revenue from ticket sales but will pay for hotels, coach travel and food while on tour.

8 **Songwriting**
The standard songwriter-music publisher split on fees for airplay on radio and TV is 50:50. You're quite happy with this arrangement as long as you retain the rights (see item 1).

Contents: Resource materials

Worksheet & author	Timing	Aim	Task
9b **Socialising with confidence** Rosemary Richey	30–40 minutes	To practise social English	To re-phrase negative language and roleplay awkward situations
10a **Survival** John Allison	30–45 minutes	To practise the language of meetings and decision-making	To play a survival game
10b **No U-turn?** Chris Murray	30–45 minutes	To practise the language of decision-making	To read a case study on a failing company and decide on a way forward
11 **Blurring and stretching** John Allison	1 hour	To promote fluency in discussing products, brands and the marketing mix	To read about two marketing techniques and apply these to a product development task
12a **Who's first?** Jeremy Taylor/Jon Wright	30–40 minutes	To promote discussion on the handling of e-mail and to raise awareness of register	To prioritise a set of e-mails, discuss how to respond to them and choose a writing/roleplay follow-up
12b **Manager on the move** Pete Sharma	45 minutes–1 hour	To practise writing e-mails	To write and respond to e-mails based on a series of problems
13 **Patently absurd** Chris Murray	45 minutes–1 hour	To practise giving presentations	To present a new invention using a high-impact opening
14a **Flight to Rubovia** Paul Emmerson	45 minutes	To raise awareness of cross-cultural issues	To discuss what you need to know about another country to do business there
14b **Business humour** Nicholas Sheard	45 minutes	To practise telling jokes/anecdotes	To discuss humour in the workplace, and read and re-tell a joke
15 **Buzzword Bluff** John Allison	1 hour	To practise bluffing, and explaining complex terms and concepts	To play a game giving true and invented definitions of business buzzwords
16a **Reporting activities** Anne Watson	30 minutes	To practise reporting, using indirect speech	To find out and report information on future and past business activities
16b **Can you see me?** Jeremy Taylor/Jon Wright	30 minutes	To practise the language of videoconferencing and using equipment	To reorder a jumbled dialogue and match collocations
17a **Spin doctors** Jeremy Taylor/Jon Wright	30–40 minutes	To practise diplomatic language	To match sentences to ways of making language diplomatic and complete dialogues
17b **Traffic trouble** Pete Sharma	1 hour	To practise the language and skills of negotiating	To take part in a negotiation
18 **21st-century business** Nicholas Sheard	40 minutes–1 hour	To practise reading for information and summarising main ideas	To read and exchange ideas from a text on future business trends

1a All about you

Overview

To review tenses and verb structures by completing questions about jobs, and asking and answering these questions. This worksheet could be used as a 'getting to know you' activity.

Preparation

One copy of the worksheet for each student.

Procedure

1   Hand out copies of the worksheet to each student. Ask them to complete the stems in any way they like in order to form questions about their classmates' jobs. Remind students to think carefully about the tenses and verb forms they use.
2   Divide the class into pairs and get students to ask and answer each other's questions. They can write a brief answer in the spaces provided. Encourage them to ask follow-up questions to find out as much information as possible. Ask the students to feed back anything interesting from their discussions.
3   As an optional follow-up, ask the students to walk round the classroom asking and answering their questions. They should try to talk to as many people as possible. Encourage students to ask their classmates what their job is to give a context to the questions.

Alternative procedure

1   Hand out copies of the worksheet to each student. Ask them to write the names of all their classmates at random in the spaces next to the question stems. (In smaller classes, students can use classmates' names more than once.)
2   Ask the students to complete each question specifically for the student whose name corresponds with the question. Remind students that the questions should all be about jobs and work and that they should think carefully about the tenses and verb forms they use.
3   The students then walk around the classroom, asking and answering the questions. Encourage them to ask follow-up questions to find out as much information as possible and to ask their classmates what their job is to give a context to the questions. Ask the students to feed back anything interesting from their discussions.
4   As an optional follow-up, ask the students to work in pairs and to ask and answer all of their questions.

1b Getting connected

Overview

Students focus on useful language in social situations and then roleplay networking at a social function.

Preparation

One copy of the worksheet for each student.

Procedure

1   Divide the class into pairs/small groups. Hand out copies of the worksheet to each student. Have them discuss the question in exercise 1 and encourage them to give examples. Ask them to tell an anecdote that illustrates their behaviour as a host or guest.

2   Explain that students need a range of language in high-frequency situations to avoid sounding repetitive. Encourage them to find two (or more) ways of saying the same thing for each situation in exercise 2. Then check the answers, writing the key language on the board.
3   Divide the class into several small groups or ask students to stand in a line around the room until you signal the start of the roleplay. Remind students to keep their score as they network and that they only have 15 minutes. Encourage them to conduct the roleplay briskly but without appearing rude.

Possible answers

a   Hello, are you here for (name of function/event)? / Good afternoon, welcome to the (name of function/event).
b   Hi there, I'm … and I work for … / Hello, my name's … and I'm a … with (name of company). / Good to meet you. I'm … and I work in (name of sector) at (name of company).
c   Is this your first time at a function like this? / This is quite an event, isn't it? / Have you been to a (name of function/event) before?
d   Could I have your business card? I'd like to keep your details on record. / Can you let me have your business card? / Do you have a business card on you?
e   What do you think of the (name of function/event) so far? / Are you enjoying yourself here? / Are you having a good time?
f   Would you like something to drink? / Can I get you something from the bar? / Can I get you a top-up?
g   Can I introduce you to X? This is Y from (name of company). / (Paul), this is … He/She's a … with (name of company). You both have something in common.
h   Would you excuse me? I've seen someone I must talk to./ It's been nice talking to you. See you later, I hope. / If you'll excuse me a moment. I'll be right back.

2a The language of meetings

Overview

Students study possible collocations for a wide range of 'meetings' language and decide which word in each group does not collocate. Then they review some of the collocations in a gap-fill task.

Preparation

One copy of the worksheet for each student.

Procedure

1   As a warmer, introduce the idea of verb + noun collocations by writing on the board: *to reach a/an …* . Elicit as many nouns collocations as possible, using prompts such as definitions, providing a few letters on the board etc. (Possible answers: *an agreement/a compromise/a conclusion/a consensus/a dead-end/a decision/a verdict.*) Clean the board when you finish, as some of these words appear on the worksheet.
2   Hand out copies of the worksheet to each student. Explain that students have to focus on the words in italics in exercise 1 and cross out the ones that do not collocate. Students work in pairs and complete the exercise. Check the answers with the whole class and deal with any problems of wrong collocations. Where appropriate, point out what the other italicised words can collocate with.

3 In pairs, students do exercise 2. Check the answers.

4 As an optional follow-up, students can write the closing comments to a real meeting they have attended recently.

Answers

Exercise 1

The following words do *not* collocate:

a the situation b make; anticipate it c halt; a promise
d advance; material e viable; a concord f soon; take
g full; study h treat; hostilities to i feel; small j have; register

Exercise 2

a discussion b issues c decision d implications
e conclusions f study g opinion h account

2b If ...

Overview

Students practise and consolidate conditionals by playing a board game.

Preparation

One copy of the worksheet, enlarged to A3 if possible, for each group of two to four students. One copy of the worksheet for each student to be given out at the end of the activity. Each group will also need a die and counters for each student.

Procedure

1 Divide the class into groups of two to four and hand out copies of the game. Explain the rules as follows:
- Each student places their counter on the 'Start' square. Player A rolls the die, moves to the appropriate square and completes the sentence with anything he/she likes which is grammatically correct and is true for the student. He/She then continues to talk about this statement giving further information/details/explanation/justification for 30 seconds. The other students can ask questions.
- The other players then roll the die and the process is repeated.
- If a student lands on a question square (beginning with *What ...?*), he/she asks the other group members a question of his/her choice beginning with the words given. Each group member must answer the question in turn.
- The game is over when the first player reaches the 'Finish' square.

2 Monitor the game to help with any language queries.

3 After the game, ask students to report back anything interesting from their discussions.

4 As an extension or homework exercise, ask the students to complete (some of) the sentences in writing.

3 Quote, unquote ...

Overview

Students work with and discuss famous quotations on the subject of success and money (as a possible lead-in to Unit 3 *Material world*). They then prepare and deliver a short team presentation on one of the themes in the quotations.

Preparation

One copy of the worksheet per student. Alternatively, cut the quotation halves into individual slips (see *Alternative procedure* below).

Procedure

1 Hand out copies of the worksheet to each student. Learners work individually to complete the well-known quotation 'If at first you don't succeed, ...' in three different ways. (The proverbial version is, of course, 'try, try again', but other popular versions have included 'find someone who knows what they're doing', 'destroy all evidence that you tried', 'failure may be your style' and 'quit – what are you trying to prove?'). Allow a few minutes for comparison. If appropriate, have the class vote for the best ending.

2 Divide the class into pairs and get them to match the beginning and endings of the quotations. Check the answers with pairs as they finish and then have them choose the quotation that they like.

3 When each pair of students has done the matching task and chosen a quotation that they like, ask them to prepare a 90-second presentation on it. They should try to open with a rhetorical question e.g. *How important are success and money? What does success mean to you?* and finish with the quotation itself. Encourage both students in each pair to contribute, but allow them to organise the preparation stage how they like.

4 The pairs of students give their presentations and the rest of the class can ask questions if they want to.

Alternative procedure

1 Cut the quotation halves into individual slips before the class and hand them out to the students. With a large group, give the students one or two slips each, making sure there is an ending for every beginning. (It doesn't matter if some people have two slips and some only one.) With smaller groups, give the students more slips. The students then mingle trying to find 'their other halves'. When they do so, encourage them to chat about the quotation they share for a few seconds and then go in search of another match. Tell them it's fine to interrupt or join pairs who are already talking to see if they have a match.

2 At the team presentation stage, see if the groups can predict which quotation the presenters are talking about before they complete their talk. This encourages them to listen to each other's talks more closely.

Answers

a8 b4 c11 d9 e10 f12 g2 h3 i5 j1 k6 l7

4a There was a ...

Overview

Students read a series of limericks to identify and practise stress, weak forms and linking. They then unscramble the words in a limerick about Richard Nixon.

Preparation

One copy of the worksheet for each student. Hand out the copies after the dictation in step 2.

Procedure

1 Tell students that they are going to do a worksheet on aspects of pronunciation. Explain that they are going to use some humorous poems called limericks, which illustrate stress, weak forms and linking. Point out that these features of spoken English are especially important when giving a presentation.

2 Tell students you are going to dictate a five-line limerick and they should write down what they hear. Emphasise that the dictation is not a test and the aim is to help students with stress, weak forms and linking. Check/Pre-teach *doze* and write the surname *Creek* on the board. Dictate the limerick at normal speed, then line by line.

3 Hand out copies of the worksheet to each student and have them check their dictations. Demonstrate the stresses in the first line and then ask students to identify the stresses in the other four lines by marking a dot or circle above the appropriate syllable. Encourage students to try beating a regular rhythm with a finger as they read. Check the answers and then have students read the limerick aloud, focusing on the stressed syllables.

4 Demonstrate the weak forms in the first line and remind students of the schwa /ə/. Ask students to identify and mark weak forms in the rest of the limerick by lightly crossing out the relevant word/syllable. Check the answers and then have students practise reading the limerick aloud again.

5 Mark the links in the first line and then ask students to find the links in the rest of the limerick by joining the appropriate letters at the base of the words. Check the answers. Check students understand elision (the disappearance of a sound that is linked to another) and then ask them to find two examples of elision – *ol(d)* and *pitche(d)*. Students practise reading the limerick aloud one final time.

6 Check/Pre-teach: *snorter* (an old-fashioned word for an alcoholic drink) and *porter* (an old-fashioned word for a dark brown beer). Students mark stress, weak forms and linking, and practise reading the second limerick. Check the answers by writing the limerick up on the board with the appropriate marks in place.

7 Ask students what they know about Richard Nixon and his unsuccessful TV debate with John F. Kennedy in 1960. (He participated in a TV debate with JFK as part of his presidential campaign and came across badly. Elected President in 1968 and re-elected in 1972, he was forced to resign in 1974 over the Watergate scandal after the burglary of the Democrat Party HQ; his 'economy with the truth' earned him the nickname 'Tricky Dicky'). Check/Pre-teach: *stubble*, *sticky* (here meaning 'difficult') and *tricky* (here meaning 'untrustworthy'). Students re-order the limerick and then check the answers.

8 If students are enthusiastic about limericks, give them the 'formula' in the table below to help them write their own. (Remember that it is difficult even for native speakers to write limericks that rhyme and scan correctly, so this should be an optional follow-up.)

Person	There was a	(adjective)	(noun)	called	(name)	(rhyme A)
				from	(place)	
Background	who					(rhyme A)
Problem (1)						(rhyme B)
Problem (2)						(rhyme B)
Resolution						(rhyme A)

Answers

Exercises 1, 2 and 3

There was an old salesman named Creek,

who pitched to his clients in Greek.

He said, 'While they doze

it's much easier to close,

and I do love to hear myself speak.'

Exercise 4

A young Irish chemist from Cork

was nervous when giving a talk.

She concocted a snorter

from whiskey and porter,

and now she can talk but not walk.

Exercise 5

An old politician called Ricky
found TV appearances sticky.
His five o'clock stubble
got him into trouble,
and Ricky became Tricky Dicky.

4b Business language

Overview

Students roleplay working for a consultancy. They prepare and deliver presentations on the pros and cons of different language training providers. Students then hold a meeting to choose the school they wish to recommend.

Preparation

One copy of the worksheet for each student. Cut the worksheet into four.

Procedure

1 Ask students which language course they would prefer: three hours a week all year, five courses of three days in a year or two weeks studying in the country of the target language. Ask them to give reasons for their choices.

2 Hand out the role card and client information to each student and ask them to read the details. Check students understand the scenario.

3 Divide the class into three groups, A, B and C. Hand out copies of the correct advert to each group. Have students read the information and check vocabulary as necessary. Ask each group to prepare a detailed presentation on their language provider. They should outline the pros and cons of recommending their school/programme to the client. Ask them to support their arguments with costs if appropriate. Allow about 15 minutes for this stage and monitor the activity. (With larger classes, the three groups can be sub-divided with one group of students presenting the pros, the other the cons.)

4 Students give their presentations. Set a time limit for each one of about 10 minutes.

5 Students then hold a general meeting to decide which school/programme to recommend to their client. This should last about 15 minutes.

5a Problems, problems

Overview

To practise and consolidate the language of dealing with problems, and of making and dealing with complaints.

Preparation

One copy of the worksheet for each pair of students. Cut the worksheet into cards. One copy of the complete worksheet for each student to be given out at the end of the activity.

Procedure

1 With the whole class, brainstorm areas of problems/complaints that people experience both at work and outside work e.g. *in a hotel, at an airport, hiring a car, making a telephone booking, phoning customer services, in a restaurant, a faulty product, an incorrect invoice, a delayed delivery, an inaccurate report, a difficult meeting, a badly organised business trip.* Write the ideas on the board.

2 Divide the class into pairs and give each one a copy of the cut-up cards, shuffled and face down. Tell the students that they are going to roleplay some of the problem situations on the board. As well as trying to reach a satisfactory agreement, the aim is also to use the expressions on the cards as part of their roleplays.

3 For each roleplay, the students should decide who will be the complainant and who will deal with the complaint. They then choose a scenario from the board and spend a short time thinking about what they will say. Encourage the students to be imaginative.

4 Each student takes one of the cards from the top of the pile. The students begin the roleplay and as quickly as possible they should use the expression on the card in a complete sentence and in a natural way. When they have done this, and while continuing the roleplay, they take another card and repeat this process. The aim is to use as many of the expressions as they can during the roleplay.

5 The students choose a new situation, swap roles and repeat the process.

6 Hand out a complete worksheet to each student at the end of the activity.

Alternative procedures

1 Instead of taking the cards one by one, the students could take six cards per roleplay and try to use them in any order they like.

2 Instead of cutting up the cards, give the students a complete copy of the worksheet. They refer to this and cross off the expressions as they use them.

5b Effective phoning

Overview

Students rephrase unhelpful phone language and then roleplay customer complaint situations.

Preparation

One copy of the worksheet for each student.

Procedure

1 Students brainstorm their own positive and negative experiences of customer service on the phone. Establish what general problems/frustrations students have experienced.

2 Hand out copies of the worksheet to each student. They can work in pairs or small groups to complete the flow chart.

3 Elicit possible phrases to improve the tone of the language for each stage of the call. Write them on the board.

4 Divide the class into pairs and have them roleplay the situations in exercise 2. Encourage students to refer to the flowchart to help them and remind them to swap roles for each situation. Monitor the activity.

5 As an optional follow-up, ask students why a good telephone manner is importance in business (projecting a professional image that takes care of customers; the key to keeping customers and finding new ones). Students can brainstorm a checklist for making the right impression on the phone e.g. *be prepared, make/take the call with customer information on hand, be polite, use an enthusiastic tone of voice and intonation, show interest in the caller, don't eat/drink/chew gum during the call, confirm/read back information, agree on action points.*

Possible answers

1 How can I help you today?
   What seems to be the problem?
   I'll just make some notes as you are speaking.

2 Could I just go over/check (your order) again?
   I can suggest/recommend …
   Would you mind sending me a copy of your receipt?

3 I can see how this creates a problem for you./ I agree wholeheartedly.
   I don't blame you for being angry./ If I were you, I'd feel the same way.
   We do pay serious attention to all customer comments.

4 I'll call you back on …/I'll get back to you on …
   I'll look into it straightaway.
   I'm sure we can sort this out for you.

5 Could I help with anything else today?
   Is there anything else I can help you with?
   Do ring us again if you need further assistance.

6a The missing million

Overview

Students discuss the characteristics of a typical chairperson of a meeting and then hold an informal discussion to solve a logic puzzle in which a million dollars has gone missing. A brief feedback session raises awareness of different roles within group discussion.

Preparation

One copy of the worksheet for each student. Cut up the information cards.

Procedure

1 Hand out copies of the worksheet to each student. Ask them to think about the profile of a typical chairperson. (This will point students in the right direction when identifying the culprit in the case.)

2 Have students read the scenario in exercise 2. Tell them the aim of the activity is to use the information you will give them to identify the profile of each person at the meeting and decide who was in the chair.

3 Divide the class into groups. Hand out the 12 information cards equally among the students (four per group of three, three per group of four etc. If you only have two students, you can take part yourself to provide a more realistic 'meeting'.) Tell students not to show their cards to each other and to memorise the information on each one. Stress the importance of this or they may not be able to solve the case. When they have memorised all the details, collect in the cards. (This stops students putting all the cards on the table, which decreases the authenticity and the length of discussion.)

4 Students pool and analyse their information to solve the case. Don't appoint a chairperson at this stage. Most groups will realise that they need a chairperson and probably a secretary – wait to see if and how this happens. Monitor the activity. If students are struggling with the case, suggest they use a table to organise the information (see below). We are not told specifically who chaired the meeting, but most people will conclude that it was Charles, especially as he's an accountant. If students can justify a different suspect, so much the better!

5 Students discuss their roles within the group during the discussion. If students feel defensive about their role, remind them that a silent thinker/evaluator is as important to the group as a talkative hypothesiser.

Answers

Anne	23	secretary	always scoring points
Brian	45	production	time waster
Charles	52	accountant	always pulls rank
Dianne	55	personnel	rarely contributes
Ellen	26	sales	always late

6b A meeting on meetings

Overview

Students prepare for and participate in a meeting on how to improve the meetings they have in their workplace.

Preparation

One copy of the worksheet for each student.

Procedure

1 Ask students to give examples of what they like and dislike about the way meetings are run where they work.

2 Explain to the students that they are going to participate in a meeting on meetings! Hand out copies of the worksheet to each student. Check they understand that they have to complete items 2–5 of the agenda in order to prepare for their meeting. Refer students to the task hints to help them. Allow about 15 minutes for the preparation stage. (With larger groups, have students prepare in pairs.)

3 Divide the class into small groups and appoint or allow the students to choose a chairperson. Set a time limit of about 30 minutes for the meeting. Monitor the activity.

4 After the meeting, ask students to complete the evaluation checklist. Ask them to reflect on the meeting and evaluate their group's performance against the targets they set for an effective meeting. Students then compare their evaluation with other members of their group.

5 Hold a short feedback session on the most popular suggested changes for meetings in the students' workplace.

7 Information overload

Overview

Students predict figures from a text on information management and read the text as preparation for a ranking exercise and follow-up discussion.

Preparation

One copy of the worksheet for each student.

Procedure

1 As a warmer, ask students how much information they have to handle on a daily basis. Ask if they think it's too much and what can be done about it. Note down students' ideas on the board.

2 Check/Pre-teach: *to handle, to restrict, bombardment, to filter, distracted, thorough, to nurture, hierarchy.*

3 Hand out copies of the worksheet to each student. Have them cover the text when doing exercise 1. Students complete the prediction exercise based on their own experience and then discuss with a partner.

4 Have students read the first paragraph of the text to check their answers to exercise 1. Ask if they were surprised by any of the figures. Students then read the rest of the text and compare their experiences with those described by the writer and with a partner/rest of the group.

5 Individually, students rank the six skills in order of usefulness/feasibility for dealing with information overload. They then work in pairs/small groups to compare rankings and discuss. Hold a short feedback session.

6 If appropriate, ask students to relate the skills to their learning of English and choose the most useful tips for managing the information they receive both inside and outside the classroom.

8a Options and choices

Overview

Students review phrasal verbs for presenting options and choices. In pairs, students hold a meeting to decide which choices to make for a new business and then present their decisions to the rest of the group.

Preparation

One copy of the worksheet for each student.

Procedure

1 Students complete the phrasal verbs in exercise 1. Check the answers.

2 In pairs, students hold a meeting to evaluate the alternatives for the scenario in exercise 2. Remind them they need to choose just one solution for each point on the agenda. Monitor the activity.

3 Refer students back to the useful verbs in exercise 1. In pairs, students present their choices to the rest of the class, who play the part of business coaches. The coaches should query the decisions and give feedback on the feasibility of the plans.

Answers

a into b out c with d away e for f up g for
choose – plump for, go for; not to choose – rule out, stay away from

8b A radical proposal

Overview

Students prepare and give presentations on a controversial scheme. They then ask/answer searching/difficult questions.

Preparation

One copy of the worksheet for each pair of students. Cut the worksheet into two.

Procedure

1 Ask students if they have ever had to make a difficult presentation, or persuade somebody to do something that was unpopular or controversial.

2 Check/Pre-teach: *emissions, greenhouse gases, global warming, scheme, ration, quota, to issue, to allocate, smart card, to debit, register, to bury, reservoirs, to recover, to dispose of.* Model the pronunciation of difficult words as necessary.

3 Divide the class into AB pairs. Hand out the correct half of the worksheet to each student and have them read the information. Monitor and give further help with vocabulary as necessary. Ask students for initial reactions to the ideas, and check that the information about the schemes is clear.

4 Ask students to prepare their presentation and make notes on the key questions. Allow plenty of time for this. Monitor, helping with vocabulary and the organisation of the presentation as necessary.

5 Students give their presentations to a partner/small group. (Alternatively, students can give team presentations.) Allow enough time for both the A and B students/teams to give their presentations. Ask the 'audience' to make notes and to prepare key questions. Feed in language from the box below to help students with this. Students have a question and answer follow-up after the presentations.

> **Presentations: asking questions**
>
> Could you just explain/describe how X will work?/how you will deal with the problem of …?/how you will organise …?
>
> I'd be very interested to know …
>
> Could you just give us a bit more information about …?
>
> You mentioned … in your presentation. I'd like to know …
>
> You used a phrase, …, that I am not familiar with. What exactly does it mean?
>
> Can I just pick up on the point you made about …?
>
> I was very interested in what you said about … . Could you tell us a little more?
>
> Are you seriously suggesting that …?
>
> If I understand correctly, you're saying that … . How would that work in practice?

9a First impressions last

Overview

Students read a text as a springboard for discussion of the significance of corporate colour.

Preparation

One copy of the worksheet for each student.

Procedure

1 Divide the class into pairs or small groups. Ask the students to discuss the importance of corporate colour and to give examples of colour associations with different products and services. Hold a short feedback session.

2 Hand out copies of the worksheet to each student. They work individually to think of companies/products and associated colours. Students read the text to check the appropriateness of the colours and then compare examples and ideas in pairs.

3 Hold a short feedback session and then encourage discussion with the students in pairs or small groups. You could ask some of the following questions: *Do the colours of the companies in the text appropriately reflect their products and services? Do the colours mentioned in the text have any other or different connotations and associations in your country or culture? What is your company's corporate colour? Is it appropriate for your company's products and/or services? What colour associations do other organisations, for example political parties, sports teams, in your country have?*

4 Students work in pairs or small groups to do exercise 2. If appropriate, allocate five items from the list to each pair/group for them to discuss. Ask the students to feed back anything interesting from their discussions.

5 As an optional follow-up, ask students to imagine that their company is going to change its corporate identity and to decide what the new colour(s) should be. The students then prepare a two-minute presentation to the board outlining the new identity. If you have students from the same company, they could give team presentations.

9b Socialising with confidence

Overview

Students practise polite language in awkward social situations.

Preparation

One copy of the worksheet for each student.

Procedure

1 Ask students to give examples of social settings in business e.g. corporate entertaining including lunch, dinner, drinks, parties/receptions and business-related events/functions like meetings, seminars, conferences, presentations, telephoning and trade fairs.

2 Elicit examples of students' own experience in uncomfortable social situations.

3 Hand out copies of the worksheet to each student. Students rephrase the language in exercise 1, working individually or in pairs. Remind students to think of two ways of rephrasing the language for each situation and that in English people expect an explanation/justification for refusing an invitation, leaving an event early etc.

4 Elicit answers from the class and write up key phrases on the board:
Making requests: *Excuse me, …, Would you/Could you +* infinitive without *to, Would you mind + -ing, Do you mind if + clause, If you don't mind, + clause, Would it be possible (for me) + to-infinitive*
Introducing a negative point: *I'm afraid …, Unfortunately …, This seems to be …, It seems that …, I believe/think that …*
Apologising: *I'm really/very/terribly/awfully sorry.*
Thanking: *Thanks so/very much, It's very kind of you + to-infinitive*
Moving away from a conversation: *Would you excuse me?*
Stating something you believe to be true: *I understand …, Am I right in thinking that …*
Also highlight the use 'softening' modifiers such as *so/very/really/terribly*.

5 Have students perform the roleplays in exercise 2 in pairs. Encourage them to act out the situations as realistically as possible e.g. sitting together as if at the dinner table. Get students to change partners and practise the situations twice.

Possible answers

a I know a lot of people like (sushi), but I'm afraid it's not my favourite. Would it be possible for me to order something else? / I'm sure this is delicious, but I don't usually eat (squid). Do you mind if I have something else?/If you don't mind, I'd like to order something else.

b Excuse me, but I believe this is/this seems to be a no-smoking area. / Would you mind putting out your cigarette? This restaurant has a no-smoking policy.

c I know we've met before, so would you mind telling me your name again? / I'm sure we've met before, but could you remind me of your name?

d Would you excuse me? There's someone over there I'd like to talk to. / I'm really/very sorry, but I've just seen someone I need to talk to. Would you excuse me?

e I'm terribly/awfully sorry but I'm afraid/unfortunately I'm extremely tired after (the journey here). / I really appreciate/Thanks so much for the invitation, but I'm really tired from (the flight). / It's very kind of you to invite me, but I think I'd be too tired to enjoy (the performance). It was a very long flight.

f I understand you are no longer with the company. / Am I right in thinking that you've moved on from your previous job?

10a Survival

Overview

Students hold meetings to decide which items to choose in a survival situation and then discuss which personalities they would like to be with in the same situation.

Preparation

One copy of the worksheet for each student.

Procedure

1 Ask students to suggest what they would need to survive for 48 hours cut off from the rest of the world.

2 Hand out copies of the worksheet to each student and have them read the scenario. Emphasise that there is no prospect of escaping from the lift before Monday morning, so students must focus on surviving.

3 Give students a few moments to choose their eight objects, working individually. Then divide the class into groups (ideally groups of four, but other numbers are also possible). Set a time limit of about 15 minutes for the discussion and remind students that they have to agree on all eight objects. Monitor the activity.

4 If a group finishes early, ask them to justify their choice – this will usually restart the discussion. If you have time, you can ask groups to report back on their decisions.

5 Students decide which one additional object they would like to have and give reasons.

6 Students discuss who they would like to be stuck in the lift with them and give reasons.

10b No U-turn?

Overview

Students read a case study on a takeover in the auto industry to provide background information for a meeting roleplay. Using role cards, they reach a decision on company strategy.

Preparation

One copy of the worksheet for each student. Cut up the role cards. With smaller classes, reduce the number of role cards by leaving out first F, then E, then D.

Procedure

1 Find out if any students work in companies that have been part of a merger/takeover recently and ask what happened. Hand out copies of the worksheet to each student. In pairs/small groups, have students discuss the questions in exercise 1. Hold a short feedback session (possible answers: cultural differences, unequal power issues, resentments of outsiders 'taking over', poor communication etc.)

2 Check/Pre-teach: *niche market, brand consolidation, ailing, past their best, to diversify, synergy, hands-off, reluctant, doomed.*

3 Students read the case study. Make sure everyone understands the situation by asking some short check questions: *Which company has taken over which? Why? What are the main problems for each company?*

4 Explain that the students are going to roleplay a meeting between members of the company to agree on a way forward. Depending on class size, try to form groups of six students for the roleplay. If necessary, reduce the number of roles as described in *Preparation*. Hand out the role cards and give students time to prepare their arguments for the meeting.

5 Students roleplay the meeting and come up with a proposal for the way forward. Remind them to take notes of the key decisions. Monitor the activity.

6 Hold a short feedback session where students report and explain their decisions. If you have more than one group, ask the class to compare the decisions and choose the best way forward for the company.

11 Blurring and stretching

Overview

Students read an article about two marketing techniques and then brainstorm and present new product concepts by mixing and matching existing products, brands and packaging. Students feed back on each other's ideas.

Preparation

One copy of the worksheet for each student.

Procedure

1   Check/Pre-teach: *to blur* and *to stretch*. Hand out copies of the worksheet to each student. Ask the question in exercise 1 and have students read the article and find the answer. Students discuss the questions in exercise 2 and feed back to the class.

2   Divide the class into two teams and focus attention on exercise 3. Ask students to recall/suggest guidelines for productive brainstorming e.g. *suspend judgement – no idea is too crazy, suspend constraints – nothing is impossible, produce as many ideas as possible, record all ideas* etc.

3   Write an example on the board of a new product concept made by mixing brand, product and packaging e.g. Nike chocolate in a toothpaste tube. Set a time limit for the brainstorming session and monitor the activity.

4   Ask students to choose their three best ideas, and to give the information in the list in exercise 3. They should present their ideas as a product overview e.g.
New product: soft chocolate
(New) brand name: Nikolate
Packaging: in a toothpaste tube
Positioning: high-energy food for athletes during sport
Promotional idea: sponsor tennis players to use product during matches

5   Ask each team to give their ideas to the other group. Each group should decide how many marks out of ten to award to each idea.

6   Students then cross-pair to give feedback and justify the marks awarded.

12a Who's first?

Overview

Students read and prioritise a series of e-mails and then discuss how they would like to respond to each message. As a follow-up, they choose to write a reply to the most important message or roleplay one of the situations.

Preparation

One copy of the worksheet for each student.

Procedure

1   Ask students some general discussion questions about e-mails e.g. *Do you remember life before e-mail? How many messages do you send every day? Do you send jokes etc. or do you stick to business matters?* If appropriate, tell the students the following anecdote: An author once sent an e-mail to a publisher apologising for being a little 'busty' recently. He didn't notice his error until after he had sent the message and the spell check didn't pick it up!

2   Check/Pre-teach: *frost, to go through the roof, asap, shop floor, shift, to leak, damp, packaging plant*. Hand out copies of the worksheet to each student. Have them read the e-mails and prioritise them. Monitor quietly but don't interfere at this stage. Have students compare their order of priority in pairs.

3   Elicit answers and see how far different students agree. (There are no right or wrong answers here, though a quick response to Angela would be a good idea and the Polish project can probably wait.) Focus attention on the greetings and closing phrases for each e-mail and ask students which are formal and which are informal and why. Elicit examples of less formal language than would be found in a letter (*go through the roof, get my hands on, asap, Interested?*)

4   Have students discuss the questions in exercise 2 and elicit a range of answers.

5   Allow students to choose a task in exercise 3. The roleplay can be done either as a telephone call or as a face-to-face meeting and the writing task could be given for homework.

12b Manager on the move

Overview

Students participate in an e-mail project. They write and respond to e-mails based on a series of problems. The project can be done in two ways:

• the students write the e-mails by hand on the photocopiable template on page 184. The messages are then 'delivered' by the teacher or by the students themselves.

• students with access to a computer network with internal e-mail can type their messages and send them across the network. The teacher can also ask learners to print out the e-mails in order to correct them later.

Preparation

• One copy of the worksheet for each pair/small group of students. Cut the worksheet into two.

• For students doing the e-mails by hand, three copies of the e-mail template on page 184 for each student; for students working on computers, check you know the e-mail address of the computers they are sending the messages to/from.

Procedure

1   Ask students if they can pick up e-mail remotely and if they find this convenient or if it just creates more work.

2   Students should ideally draft the e-mails in pairs/small groups but, in smaller classes, they can work individually. Divide the class into AB pairs/small groups. Hand out the correct half of the worksheet to each student/group. Give students time to read the role card and the problem cards. Check vocabulary as necessary and that each student/group knows the name of the person they will be e-mailing.

3   Give students time to compose and send their e-mails. Tell them to keep the e-mails short and to focus on the main information in the problem cards. (You could set a time limit of five minutes per e-mail to keep the e-mail exchange moving.) Remind students that they may need to write more than three messages if they need to clarify something or to ask for additional information. Monitor the activity and be prepared to 'deliver' the messages across the classroom.

4   Take the e-mails in for marking if appropriate. Students working on a network can print off the e-mails.

13 Patently absurd

Overview

Students match techniques for opening presentations to examples and then give a short, high-impact presentation of a new invention. The class vote for the best invention to back financially.

Preparation

One copy of the worksheet for each student. Cut up the invention cards. Depending on class size, either give an invention to each student in groups of four or with larger groups, have students work in pairs/small groups to present their invention.

Procedure

1 Elicit from students any techniques for creating high-impact presentations. Hand out copies of the worksheet to each student. Have them match the openings with the relevant technique. Ask which they think are the strongest/weakest, or in which situations they could be used.

2 Explain that the students are going to prepare a 3–5 minute presentation on a new invention to persuade venture capitalists to give them financial backing. Depending on class size, have the students work in groups of four and give one product card to each student. If there are more than four students, have them work in pairs to prepare a team presentation.

3 Ask the students to read the product cards. Use the pictures of the inventions to help them with vocabulary. Give the students time to prepare their presentations. Encourage them to use one of the presentation openings from the matching exercise and to make up any details about function, materials etc. Remind students they need to show how their invention will make money for investors. Monitor the activity.

4 Students give their presentations to the rest of the group/class. When they are not presenting, they should take the role of the venture capitalists and be prepared to ask tricky questions about the inventions' market chances.

5 Ask the class to choose the invention they would back and to give reasons.

Answers

a4 b5 c6 d2 e7 f1 g3

14a Flight to Rubovia

Overview

As an exercise in inter-cultural awareness, students think of questions to ask about the culture of 'Rubovia' – an imaginary country. They compare with other students' ideas, and also with a set of given suggestions.

Preparation

One copy of the worksheet for each student with the bottom section of suggested questions folded under.

Procedure

1 Before handing out the worksheets, read out the first line from the box: *You are on your first business trip to Rubovia.* Pause and look up, waiting for students to realise that it is an imaginary country. Perhaps play them along a little: *You know, it's next to Kabalia.*

2 When students realise that Rubovia is an imaginary country, continue reading the text in the box, pausing at each full stop for dramatic effect and the students' comments.

3 Hand out copies of the worksheet, with the bottom part folded under. Make sure the students understand that they shouldn't look at this part yet.

4 In pairs, students write their eight questions in the spaces provided. Make it clear that there are no 'right' answers, and the point of the exercise is awareness-raising for doing business in another culture.

5 Ask students to read out their questions to the class. (With larger classes, students can do this stage in small groups.) Write any interesting questions on the board and encourage discussion.

6 Ask students to look at the questions at the bottom of the page. Point out that these are just suggestions, and are not necessarily better or worse than the students' own ideas. Again, encourage comments and discussion.

7 Regroup the students into new pairs/threes and ask them to choose the ten most important/useful questions. If you have time, try to agree on the top ten questions for the whole class.

14b Business humour

Overview

Students discuss humour in the workplace and then read and re-tell a joke in pairs.

Preparation

One copy of the worksheet for each pair of students. Cut the worksheet into three.

Procedure

1 If you know a good joke, tell it to the students. Discuss their reactions to it. Ask them if they thought it was funny.

2 Divide the class into pairs/small groups and hand out the top of the worksheet. Students discuss the questions. Monitor, helping with vocabulary if necessary. Hold a short feedback session.

3 Explain that students are going to each read a different joke and then tell it to their partner. Divide the class into small groups (all A students working together and all the B students working together) to prepare to re-tell their joke. (In a small class, students can be divided in two equal AB groups.)

4 Hand out the correct part of the worksheet to each student. Monitor as students read their joke, helping with vocabulary as necessary. In joke A, make sure students understand the pun in *You have risen to where you are due to a large quantity of hot air* – literally hot air in the balloon and 'to talk hot air' means to sound impressive but to be meaningless.

5 Ask individual groups if they found their joke funny, Then ask students to memorise their joke, focusing on the key points in the text in order to be able to re-tell it. Encourage students to note down key words to help them or to sketch out the joke in diagram form. Model the pronunciation of difficult words as necessary.

6 Remind students they need to make the joke as engaging for the listener as possible. Focus on techniques for telling jokes/anecdotes like repetition, pausing for dramatic effect at key points, using a different tone of voice (or even accent!) for different speakers. Emphasise that good clear delivery of the punchline (if there is one) is essential.

7 Students then cross-pair and tell their joke to a new partner. Remind them not to look at the text of the joke but to re-tell it as best they can from memory. Hold a short feedback session to find out students' reactions to the jokes and if they enjoyed the re-telling.

15 Buzzword Bluff

Overview

Students play 'Buzzword Bluff' – a game of bluffing and persuasion – by giving real and made-up definitions of business buzzwords.

Preparation

One copy of the worksheet for each student. Cut off the buzzwords and definitions for team A and team B.

Procedure

1 In pairs, students read the definitions of *bear* and *heavy hitter* and decide which is the true definition (*bear* – a timid or pessimistic investor; *heavy hitter* – a top-class salesman).

2 Students underline useful phrases for bluffing in the sample definitions: *As you know, …/Well, as a matter of fact, …/Oh really, how absurd!/No, in reality, …/You've heard of …/Take it from me, …/What nonsense! Actually, …/Obvious, isn't it?/No, come on, let's be serious.* Elicit other useful expressions e.g. *You're kidding/Trust me/Would I lie to you?*

3 Divide the class into AB teams. Explain that the objective of the game is to fool the other team by giving convincing bluffs and perhaps making the true definition less obvious by adding distracting details.

4 Hand out the correct buzzwords and true definitions to each team. Help each team with vocabulary as necessary. Give students time to prepare their bluffs and decide who will give the true definition. (If there are fewer than three students per team, students will have to give more than one definition.) Encourage students to develop the definitions in their own words, and not just to read out what's on the paper.

5 Chair the game, encouraging the 'listening' team to discuss the three definitions they have just heard before announcing their choice.

6 Invite students to give examples of the categories of people in the game, from their own experience or from the news.

16a Reporting activities

Overview

Students practise reporting by interviewing each other about business activities and then reporting back to the rest of the class.

Preparation

One copy of the worksheet for each pair of students. Cut the worksheet into two.

Procedure

1 Divide the class into AB pairs. Hand out the correct half of the worksheet to each student. Give them a few moments to read their cards and think about the questions they need to ask. If students work in the same company and know each other well, they should be encouraged to add questions appropriate to their functions in the company, or to adapt the questions to their real business activities. With a weaker class, you could elicit the wording of the questions before students interview each other.

2 Student A asks student B questions using the cues on the card and takes notes of B's answers. Students then swap roles. Set a time limit of 15 minutes for this stage. Monitor and check for correct question forms.

3 When pairs have finished the activity, each student reports their partner's activities to the rest of the class. If your class is very large, group three or four pairs together for the reporting stage.

4 As a follow-up or for homework, you could ask students to prepare a short written report of their partner's activities.

16b Can you see me?

Overview

Students order a jumbled dialogue based on a videoconference and then match verb–noun collocations connected to using equipment. As a follow-up, students discuss the pros and cons of videoconferencing.

Preparation

One copy of the worksheet for each student.

Procedure

1 As a warmer, ask students some general questions to establish the topic e.g. *Have you ever used chat programs on the Internet? Was it for pleasure or business purposes? Have you ever tried videoconferencing? What was it like? Was it easy to use?*

2 Check/Pre-teach: *pretty* (used as a modifier to mean 'quite'), *to bear with someone, to adjust* and *lousy*.

3 Hand out copies of the worksheet to each student. Give them time to do the re-ordering task. Then check the answers.

4 Have students do exercise 2 and then check the answers. (Both volume and the focus can be adjusted but only volume can be turned up.) Divide the class into pairs and elicit further possible collocations.

5 Divide the class into groups and ask them to discuss the pros and cons of videoconferencing. If appropriate ask focus questions e.g. *Do you think that videoconferencing could reduce the amount of business travel? What about other applications? Could doctors use webcams to look at a patient many miles away? Who else could benefit from the technology?*

6 If your students have access to the Internet in the classroom or in their workplace, you could ask them to roleplay helping someone who has never used a chat program to have their first videoconference. This could be an entertaining exercise, though check first it is acceptable for in-company classes to use chat programs.

Answers

Exercise 1
j1 i2 b3 d4 g5 o6 l7 k8 m9 e10 n11 c12 a13 h14 f15

Exercise 2
a4 b5 c8 d7 e3 f6 g2 h1

Possible collocations
adjust: the brightness, the volume/sound, the height of your chair, the position of your webcam
click on: an icon, 'OK', the right mouse button
open: a file, a folder, a new document
turn up: the volume/sound, the brightness
install: software, programs, virus protection
connect: cables, video, computer peripherals, the power
download: programs, software, e-mails, games, music
turn on: a computer/printer, a television, the lights, the power

17a Spin doctors

Overview
Students match sentences to ways of making language more diplomatic/persuasive and then complete dialogues in awkward situations in a positive way.

Preparation
One copy of the worksheet for each student.

Procedure
1 Elicit anecdotes from students of when they handled an awkward situation well or badly. Establish what techniques they would repeat and what they would do differently in the future.

2 Hand out copies of the worksheet to each student. Have them do the matching task in exercise 1, referring to the Grammar link on page 124 of the Student's Book as necessary. Check the answers.

3 Have students read the dialogues in exercise 2 and deal with any vocabulary problems. Remind them that apologising/explaining in English generates quite a lot of language and it's often not enough just to say 'I'm sorry.'

4 Divide the class into AB pairs and ask the students to complete the dialogues. Monitor the activity. Then check the possible answers.

5 Ask students to roleplay each situation, working from memory if possible to avoid reading the dialogues off the page.

Answers/Possible answers

Exercise 1
a6 b3 c5 d1 e2 f4

Exercise 2

Dialogue 1

A I'm sorry to hear that but I'm afraid that might present a problem.

A I'm afraid all our rooms are taken tonight. However, I'll send the maintenance man and room service to your room immediately to put everything right. In the meantime, can we offer you a complimentary meal in our restaurant while we sort out the problems? I shall personally ask the other guests not to make any noise, and we can move you to another room tomorrow morning.

Dialogue 2

B I'm extremely sorry to hear that. What seems to be the problem?

B I'm sorry about that. I'm afraid our offices were flooded during the recent storms. We lost a lot of important paperwork.

B I'm terribly sorry. I'll find out what's happened and get the quote to you by the end of today. In the meantime, can I fax/e-mail you our latest catalogue? It shows a new range you might be interested in. We do value your custom, so I'm sure we can offer you a 5% reduction in price on your next order by way of apology.

Dialogue 3

A I'm so sorry for the delay in sending you our brochure and price list.

A I'm sorry to hear that. We are normally very accurate with these things, but I know we have had printing problems and it may be the person you were talking to had the wrong figures. As for our materials, it is very important to us and our customers that we use only the best materials for all our products. They are fully guaranteed and if you are not completely satisfied with them, we'll refund your money immediately.

Dialogue 4

B I see what you are saying but it's been a very difficult year. As you know, the market has been depressed for six months and everyone is suffering as a result of the price of oil.

B I honestly believe that we have invested in the best team possible; everyone is highly qualified, well trained and very motivated. I understand your position, but I don't feel that reducing staffing levels is the answer.

B I am confident that we have the skills and ability to turn the situation around. The latest figures show things are getting better and orders are up. I feel sure that we are in a good position to exploit this upturn in the market.

17b Traffic trouble

Overview

Students take part in a negotiation between a consortium who wants to develop a city's shopping centre and the local city council. They present proposals for a reduction in traffic congestion before any building work can take place.

Preparation

One copy of the worksheet for each group of students. Cut the worksheet into three. If possible, allow students to prepare for the negotiation in separate rooms so that they don't hear each other's plans.

Procedure

1   Ask students if they know any cities that have congestion charging e.g. London. Ask if they would pay the transport charge for driving into the city, or if they would use public transport. Get them to give reasons for their answers.

2   Divide the class into two groups, A and B. (With larger classes, divide the class into a series of AB groups.) Hand out copies of the background information and report findings. Give students time to read and assess the information. Ask check questions e.g. *What do the council want? What do the consortium want? What are the four suggested solutions?*

3   Hand out the correct negotiation brief to each group. Give students time to prepare their proposals, working in separate rooms if possible. Monitor the activity.

4   Bring the A and B groups together for the negotiation stage. Remind students of any relevant negotiations skills they may have worked on in the Student's Book e.g. *Is there a common or long-term interest?*

5   Appoint a chairperson if appropriate or allow students to choose one. Students conduct the negotiation. Set a time limit of about 30 minutes.

6   Hold a short feedback session in which students discuss how the negotiation went and assess what they would do differently next time.

18 21st-century business

Overview

Students read a short text on future business trends and present the ideas in the text to other students. They then discuss the trends in relation to their own business/industry.

Preparation

One copy of the worksheet for each pair of students. Cut the worksheet into two.

Procedure

1   Ask students how they think business will be done in the 21st century. Ask focus questions e.g. *Will 50% of the workforce be working from home and will a four-day week be the norm? Will there be three months' paid paternity leave and an equal number of men and women in top management positions?*

2   Check/Pre-teach: *to supersede, core business, to prosper, to struggle, to commute, hierarchy, alliance.*

3   Divide the class into AB pairs. Hand out the correct half of the worksheet to each student. Give them about five minutes to read their text. Monitor, giving further help with vocabulary as necessary.

4   In pairs, students then present and discuss the themes in their respective text. Remind students not to look at the text when they give their summary.

5   Students do exercise 2 in pairs or small groups. Then hold a short feedback session to discuss the themes in the texts.

6   As an optional follow-up, ask students to prepare and write their own report about business in the 21st century, choosing from the following titles: *Green is good, Globalisation, Quality, not quantity, Manufacturing, Education and training, Service industries, Will the customer be king?, Brands, Sustainable development, Business ethics, Employee relations.*

1a All about you

Jon Hird

a _____ your job? _____

b What exactly _____? _____

c How long _____? _____

d _____ before your current job? _____

e _____ other jobs _____? _____

f Why _____? _____

g How often _____? _____

h _____ abroad? _____

i _____ your colleagues? _____

j _____ the best and worst _____? _____

k _____ at the moment? _____

l _____ recently? _____

m _____ ever _____? _____

n _____ in the next few months? _____

o _____ in ten years' time? _____

p _____ English? _____

1b Getting connected   Jeremy Taylor/Jon Wright

1   Are you more naturally a host or a guest? Work in pairs or small groups and discuss.

2   You are attending a social function at an important business conference. Decide what
you would say in each of these situations and think of two different ways of saying it.

  a   Welcoming new arrivals:

  1 _____

  2 _____

  b   Introducing yourself and your company:

  1 _____

  2 _____

  c   Starting a conversation with people you don't know:

  1 _____

  2 _____

  d   Asking for someone's business card:

  1 _____

  2 _____

  e   Finding out someone's opinion about the event:

  1 _____

  2 _____

  f   Offering to get someone a drink:

  1 _____

  2 _____

  g   Introducing someone:

  1 _____

  2 _____

  h   Ending a conversation:

  1 _____

  2 _____

3   You are attending a social function for your company. You have 15 minutes to network
successfully. In that time you must perform the tasks in the table and try to score as many
points as possible. Keep a note of your score as you go!

Action	Points	Your total
Welcome someone to the event	5	
Introduce yourself	10	
Start a conversation with someone new	10	
Ask for someone's business card	10	
Find out someone's opinion about the event	5	
Offer to get someone something	10	
Introduce someone to new people	20	
End a conversation	10	

2a The language of meetings Paul Emmerson

1 Delete the word(s) that do not form natural collocations.

a I'd like to raise *an important issue/the situation/an objection/the matter later*.

b When are we going to *call/hold/have/make/arrange/organise* the next meeting? Do you think we could *put it back/delay it/postpone it/anticipate it/bring it forward*?

c It's getting late, and I think we should *halt/close/finish/adjourn/end* the meeting. It looks like we've reached *a promise/a conclusion/a decision/a dead-end*.

d I'd like to *give/advance/express/put forward* my own opinion on this *issue/material/topic/subject/question*.

e We've had a *full and frank/constructive/viable/fruitful* discussion on this issue, and I'm sure we can reach *a decision/an agreement/a compromise/a consensus/a concord*.

f It would be *dangerous/risky/premature/soon/a mistake/wrong* to *draw/take/reach/jump to* any conclusions at this stage.

g This decision is going to have *wide-ranging/far-reaching/full/serious* implications, and we need to take into *account/consideration/study* a number of different factors.

h I'd just like to *clarify/deal with/treat* your *doubts about/objections to/hostilities to* this proposal.

i I *see/feel/appreciate/understand* what you're saying, but I think you're taking a very *narrow/small/short-sighted/short-term* view.

j Before we can *make/take/have/come to/reach* a decision, we'll have to *make/undertake/register/carry* out a detailed study.

2 Complete the chairperson's closing comments with the words in the box. There are two words you don't need to use. All the words appeared in 1.

account	conclusions
decision	discussion
implications	issues	opinion
promise	study	topic

Well, colleagues, I think we've had a very constructive
(a) _____ this afternoon, and a number of very important
(b) _____ have been raised. But it's getting late, and I
can see that we're not going to come to a (c) _____
today. I don't think that presents a problem because any decision we
take will have far-reaching (d) _____ and it's important
not to jump to any (e) _____ at this early stage.
Before the next meeting we need to carry out a detailed
(f) _____ of all the options involved, and circulate
it amongst everyone present. And if I can express my own
(g) _____ ,
I think that the report needs to take into (h) _____
the financial costs as well as the marketing aspects of the project.
Well, unless there's any other business, I think we can finish there.

2b If …

Jon Hird

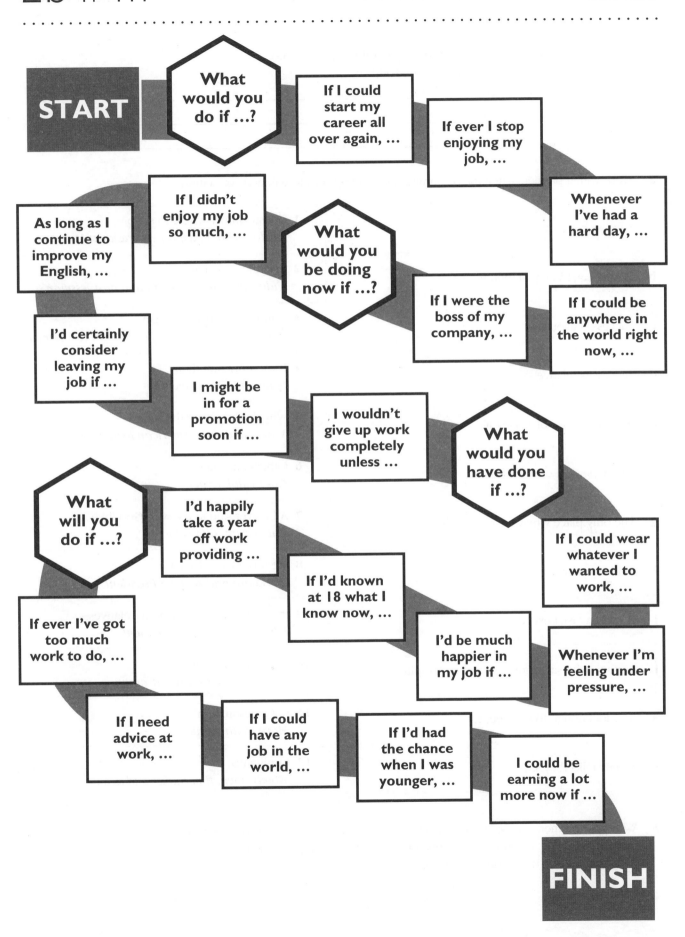

START

What would you do if …?

If I could start my career all over again, …

If ever I stop enjoying my job, …

Whenever I've had a hard day, …

If I didn't enjoy my job so much, …

As long as I continue to improve my English, …

What would you be doing now if …?

If I were the boss of my company, …

If I could be anywhere in the world right now, …

I'd certainly consider leaving my job if …

I might be in for a promotion soon if …

I wouldn't give up work completely unless …

What would you have done if …?

If I could wear whatever I wanted to work, …

What will you do if …?

I'd happily take a year off work providing …

If I'd known at 18 what I know now, …

I'd be much happier in my job if …

Whenever I'm feeling under pressure, …

If ever I've got too much work to do, …

If I need advice at work, …

If I could have any job in the world, …

If I'd had the chance when I was younger, …

I could be earning a lot more now if …

FINISH

3 Quote, unquote ...

Mark Powell

1 Think of three different ways to complete the following quotation.
Then compare with other people in your group.

'If at first you don't succeed, _____ ,

_____ ,

_____ ,

2 Work with a partner. Match the beginnings and endings of these famous quotations.

a Success comes to those who ...	**1** doesn't know where to shop. *Imelda Marcos, wife of ex-President Marcos*
b Money can't buy you friends.	**2** is in the dictionary. *Vidal Sassoon, hair stylist and businessman*
c Success is a journey, ...	**3** stands a surprised woman. *Maryan Pearson, wife of Canadian ex-Premier*
d Success is relative – ...	**4** It can only rent them. *Spike Milligan, comedian*
e What is the use of money if ...	**5** why do they keep the score? *Vince Lombardi, American football coach*
f Eighty percent of success is ...	**6** Others must fail. *Gore Vidal, writer*
g The only place where success comes before work ...	**7** All it ever said to me was 'Goodbye'. *Cary Grant, film actor*
h Behind every successful man ...	**8** are too busy to look for it. *Benjamin Franklin, US President*
i If winning isn't everything, ...	**9** the more success, the more relatives. *John F. Kennedy, US President*
j Anyone who says money can't buy happiness ...	**10** you have to work for it? *George Bernard Shaw, dramatist*
k It is not enough to succeed. ...	**11** not a destination. *Mark Twain, writer*
l Money talks they say. ...	**12** turning up. *Woody Allen, film-maker and actor*

3 With your partner, choose one of the quotations in 2 and prepare a 90-second team presentation on it. Open your presentation with a rhetorical question and close it with your chosen quotation: *As ... said, '...'*

4a There was a ...

John Allison

> *There was an old salesman named Creek,*
> *who pitched to his clients in Greek.*
> *He said, 'While they doze*
> *it's much easier to close,*
> *and I do love to hear myself speak.'*

1 Underline the stressed syllables in each line of the above limerick. Then practise reading the limerick aloud with the correct stress and a regular rhythm.

2 Now mark the weak forms in each line. Read the limerick again paying attention to stress, rhythm and weak forms.

3 Mark the linking (words beginning with a vowel are linked to the previous word). Find two examples of elision where the final 'd' of a linked word disappears. Read the limerick again with the correct stress, rhythm, weak forms and linking.

4 Repeat the procedure in 1–3 with the following limerick.

> A young Irish chemist from Cork
> was nervous when giving a talk.
> She concocted a snorter
> from whiskey and porter,
> and now she can talk but not walk.

5 Put the words in each line in the correct order to make a limerick about Richard Nixon.

> Ricky called an old politician
> TV found sticky appearances.
> five his stubble o'clock
> trouble got into him,
> Ricky and Dicky became Tricky.

4b Business language

Pete Sharma

Read the role card and client information.

Role: You work for a consultancy, advising corporate clients on effective language learning programmes. Your client has asked for help in planning next year's programme. You have short-listed three major providers interested in tendering for the contract.

Client information: a large bank in Germany based in Frankfurt with branches worldwide. They have a large budget for training, but want tangible results. Potential students around 300: mid-level management (about 140), sales force (about 160). Range of levels from elementary to upper intermediate. Previous problems encountered:
'We used a CD-ROM program but it was boring.'
'The students went to lessons early in the morning or after work and they were tired.'

Group A

Bizlangue

Bizlangue is the world's premier business and professional English language training organisation, offering both individual and small group courses. Participants obtain maximum benefit from our residential centres in the US and the UK. Use and practise the language every hour of the day!

The benefits of taking a course with us are many, and include the opportunity to meet and study with professionals from all over the world. Our client list is impressive and includes students from 35 countries. We provide a truly international environment!

All centres, three in the US and two in the UK, are externally inspected and we guarantee the highest standards in professional training. If you are serious about learning English for business, choose Bizlangue.

Costs: around $1,750 per week, including materials.

Group B

COL
(Courses Online)

Learn from the convenience of your workplace or home. In the start-up lesson in our virtual classroom, you meet your personal tutor online. He or she will work with you throughout the course.

Study online or download the material and study offline at home, at work – wherever, whenever you want. 24/7 is our motto. Send e-mails and voicemails to your tutor and then receive corrections and comments. Chat to other students on your course, post messages. Practise speaking with your tutor in every module by phone.

Our business material is always up-to-date. It is written by experienced and qualified teachers.

Competitive prices. Full technical support available during the course. €500 per person annual licence fee.

Group C

Languages Worldwide

Established 35 years ago, we are the world's largest training organisation for business English, with schools in 50 countries.

We come to your workplace to provide a full language audit. We do an individual language needs analysis and a full placement test.

Both one-to-one and group training are available. We organise lesson times to suit you. One- to five-day seminars focus on business skills: presentations, meetings, negotiations.

All course materials provided and all our teachers are fully qualified.

Competitive prices available: £450.00 per person for a 10-week module.

5a Problems, problems

Jon Hird

Do you think you could …?	I don't suppose …?	Could you give me …?
Do you happen …?	Would it help …?	Is there anything else …?
Is there any chance …?	I wonder if you could …?	Are you absolutely …?
Would you mind …?	Would it help if …?	Is there any point …?
Will you/I'll check …	Leave it with me and …	Do you mind …?
Will you/I'll get on to …	Will you/I'll look into …	Will you/I'll see if …
Not to worry, I'll …	No problem. I'll …	OK, what I'll do is …

5b Effective phoning

Rosemary Richey

1 Look at the examples of unhelpful phone language from a customer services training session. For each stage of the call, rewrite the phrases to produce a flow chart of useful expressions.

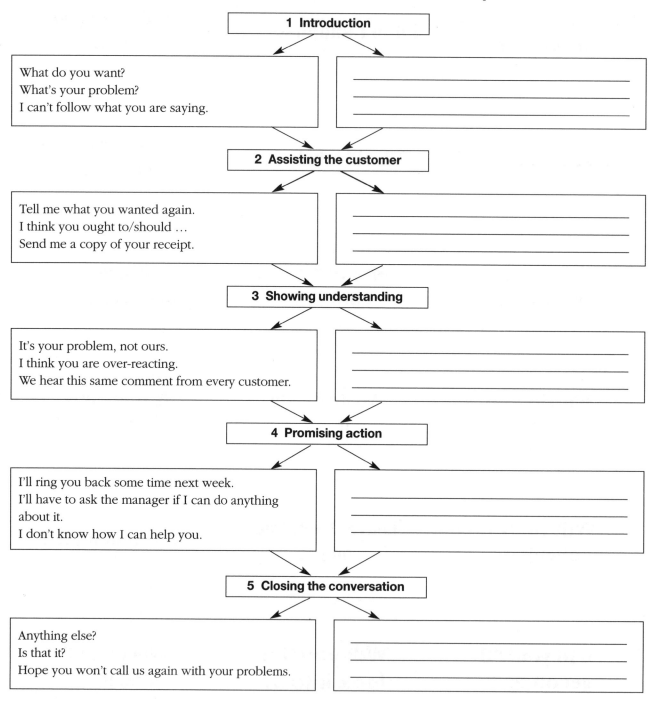

1 Introduction

What do you want?
What's your problem?
I can't follow what you are saying.

_____
_____
_____

2 Assisting the customer

Tell me what you wanted again.
I think you ought to/should …
Send me a copy of your receipt.

_____
_____
_____

3 Showing understanding

It's your problem, not ours.
I think you are over-reacting.
We hear this same comment from every customer.

_____
_____
_____

4 Promising action

I'll ring you back some time next week.
I'll have to ask the manager if I can do anything about it.
I don't know how I can help you.

_____
_____
_____

5 Closing the conversation

Anything else?
Is that it?
Hope you won't call us again with your problems.

_____
_____
_____

2 Roleplay the following customer complaint situations. Take turns to be the caller and the customer services adviser. Use the flow chart in 1 to help you.

- a new customer complains about a delayed order
- a client reports a mistake in his/her invoice
- a hotel guest's room is too noisy
- the helpdesk line is always engaged
- the customer care staff is rude and unfriendly

In Company Upper intermediate Teacher's Book © Macmillan Publishers Limited 2004

6a The missing million

John Allison

1 What are the characteristics of a typical chairperson of a meeting? Think about gender, job, age and personality.

2 One million dollars has gone missing from Costapack Corp. The police suspect the chairperson of a recent meeting, but the five attendees refuse to say who it was. Can you deduce who was in the chair? Use the following expressions in your discussion.

Perhaps we can come back to this later.

We seem to be getting sidetracked here.

Can we go back to what we were discussing earlier?

Perhaps we could speed things up a little.

OK, so just to summarise what we've said so far.

I'm not so sure, but maybe I'm missing something here. Run me through it again.

I don't quite agree with you there. However, you've given me another idea.

(Marek), could (Luis) just finish what he was saying?

Hold on a minute (Ana), you'll get your chance in a moment.

(Tanya), what's your position on this?

(Oscar), I think what (Eva) is trying to say is …

Does anybody have anything they'd like to add?

3 How easy was it to solve the case? Why? What roles did the members of your group play in the discussion – chairperson, secretary, hypothesiser, critic?

The five attendees are between 23 and 55 years old.	The person who works in production is 45 years old.
The time-waster is not an accountant.	The secretary is always trying to score points.
Ellen works in sales.	Charles is the oldest apart from Dianne.
Dianne rarely contributes to the discussion.	Anne is the youngest.
Neither Anne nor Dianne works in production.	The person who works in personnel is 10 years older than Brian.
The person who is always late is 26 years old.	The person who always pulls rank is twice as old as Ellen.

6b A meeting on meetings

Pete Sharma

1 You are going to take part in a meeting to decide how to improve meetings in your own place of work. Look at the agenda below and make notes.

Agenda

»Task Hints

1	Aim	To create an action plan for best practice in meetings.	
2	What do you like about our meetings now?	relaxed and informal	» Think about relationships, setting, and outcome.
3	What is wrong with our meetings now?	time-wasting	» Be thorough without being personal.
4	What makes an effective meeting?	Circulate agenda beforehand.	» What makes 'the perfect meeting'?
5	What changes would you like to make to the way we hold meetings?	Set a time limit.	» Brainstorm ideas and choose your top 3.
6	Action plan	Draw up the action plan. Review the meeting and summarise. Close.	

2 Now have your meeting, using the agenda in 1 to help you.

3 Complete the evaluation of the meeting. Compare your responses with other members of your group.

Evaluation checklist

The meeting was successful.	yes ☐	no ☐	partly ☐
The meeting kept to time.	yes ☐	no ☐	nearly ☐
The attendees kept to the agenda.	yes ☐	no ☐	partly ☐
All attendees participated successfully.	yes ☐	no ☐	quite ☐
The meeting was chaired effectively.	yes ☐	no ☐	quite ☐
An appropriate action plan was drawn up.	yes ☐	no ☐	partly ☐

7 Information overload

Chris Murray

1 How many of the following types of information/communication does a typical office worker have to deal with daily? Discuss with a partner.

a phone calls _____   **e** inter-office memos _____

b e-mails _____   **f** faxes _____

c voicemails _____   **g** mobile phone calls _____

d items of post _____

2 Read the first paragraph of the text and find the answers to 1. Do any of them surprise you? Then read the rest of the text. Which of the points in the text are most relevant to you. Discuss with a partner.

Another day in the office, which, according to one recent study, consists of handling 46 phone calls, 25 e-mails, 16 voicemails, 23 items of post, eight inter-office memos, 16 faxes and nine mobile phone calls.

Enough to send you crazy? You may be right. Gerry McGovern, who is writing a book on information overload, is in no doubt the huge quantity of information has led to increasing stress levels and results in a downturn in productivity.

'I think that, to some degree, long-term or medium-term strategic thinking is being restricted by the necessity to react to the continual bombardment of short-term data,' he says. 'A lot of managers are spending so much of their time coping with the data that's coming through today that they don't have as much time as they should to properly analyse it and put it in perspective.'

Les Posen, a psychologist who has written numerous articles on technology and psychology, says information overload can lead to people losing control of what material is important and what isn't. 'Our filtering systems get overloaded, so the good stuff gets left out as much as the useless stuff, and we might find ourselves not able to easily differentiate between quality material and non-quality material,' he says.

'Someone who spends hours sorting e-mails and getting distracted by unimportant details may be suffering from information overload,' Posen adds. Other signs include switching off completely. He says the key to avoiding information overload is to find a middle ground that recognises the importance of technology to our working and social lives while ensuring it doesn't eat up all our time.

3 Gerry McGovern put forward a list of six skills for dealing with information overload. Rank the skills according to their degree of effectiveness (1 = most effective). Compare your ranking with the rest of your group/class.

Six skills to avoid information overload

a ☐ Learn to think better. More decisions aren't necessarily better decisions. You might make better decisions if you make fewer decisions.

b ☐ Learn to plan better. Don't simply react to short-term data. Make sure you are also thinking about the medium and long term.

c ☐ Learn to research better. Be thorough about what you do. According to a survey conducted last year, only one in 20 people will scroll to the second page of search results.

d ☐ Learn to organise better. Nurture the architect in you.

e ☐ Learn to collaborate better. Work towards common goals. McGovern quotes author Frances Cairncross from his book *The Company of the Future*: 'The most widespread revolution in the workplace will come from the rise in collaboration and the decline of hierarchy.'

f ☐ Learn to network better. People are the network.

8a Options and choices

John Allison

1 Complete the phrasal verbs with the appropriate preposition. Which two verbs mean 'to choose'? Which two verbs mean 'not to choose'?

away	for	out	into	with	for	up

a When deciding on our new premises, we looked _____ location, cost and transport.

b We decided to rule _____ using a consultant for the first year.

c We wanted a modern office, but we concluded we could live _____ an older property.

d Due to quality issues, we wanted to stay _____ from second-hand equipment.

e We were tempted to plump _____ designer furniture, but cost was a problem.

f After weighing _____ the pros and cons, we finally rejected taking on a big bank loan.

g As for staff, we decided to go _____ experienced people.

2 You and your partner are starting a new business – SOS PC. Your new company will guarantee to send a computer expert to solve your customers' PC problems within two hours. Hold a meeting to decide on one solution only for each item on the agenda below.

SOS PC　　Agenda for partners' meeting

1 Capital
- a bank loan of $20,000 at 15% interest
- an overdraft facility for $30,000 at 23%
- venture capital of $50,000 in return for 49% of the company

2 Positioning
- quality and fast service at high prices
- low prices but slow service
- reasonably fast service at medium prices

3 Staff
- a student from your local business school – will work for nothing for 3 months
- a relative – will do 5 hours/week administrative work for nothing
- an unemployed friend – will work 8 hours/day for food and lodging

4 Premises
- a tiny office in a new building in the city centre – $750/month
- two rooms above a café near the railway station – $400/month
- a relative's garage in the suburbs – free, but no heating

5 Transport
- a 15-year-old scooter
- a new mountain bike
- a one-year bus pass

6 Consultant
- a friend who is a lawyer
- a friend who is an accountant
- a friend who was president of the Chamber of Commerce 20 years ago

7 Sales literature
- a website
- 500 brochures
- 10,000 fliers

8 Advertising
- a full-page advert in the local football club magazine
- five 15-second spots per day for one week on local radio
- a 5cm advert on page 27 of a specialist computer magazine for six months

---

3 Present your decisions to the rest of the class. Use the verbs in 1 to present your options and choices.

8b A radical proposal

Nicholas Sheard

Student A

1 You have been asked to give a presentation about the following topic. Read the information below.

Domestic Tradable Quotas

- At a recent climate conference it was agreed that countries must cut emissions of greenhouse gases by 12.5% over the next 10 years. Greenhouse gases, largely created by human activity, contribute to global warming.
- Your company, QuotaCo, has developed a new scheme – Domestic Tradable Quotas (DTQ). Under the scheme, everyone in the country would receive a ration of carbon units (CUs) each month. The quota would be based on present emissions and gradually reduce. The government would issue the CUs, and would therefore know if targets were being met. About half the units would be auctioned to companies, and the other half would be divided equally between everyone in the country.

- Everyone would be allocated a smart card. Your carbon account would be debited whenever you used fuel with a carbon content, at a petrol station or when paying the gas bill, for example.
- Once the CUs had been issued, the market would operate. People who used less than their quota could sell their surplus on the open market to those who wished to have more. A central register would monitor who had used what.
- The DTQ scheme would not interfere with people's freedom to choose their lifestyle, but there would be economic incentives for businesses and individuals to be energy-efficient and help the environment.

2 Make notes for your presentation. Think about these key questions.

- Who are you?
- Who is your audience?
- What is the problem?
- What is the cause of the problem?
- What is your proposed solution?

Student B

1 You have been asked to give a presentation about the following topic. Read the information below.

Burying carbon dioxide

- At a recent climate conference it was agreed that countries must cut emissions of greenhouse gases by 12.5% over the next 10 years. Greenhouse gases (carbon dioxide is one of these), largely created by human activity, contribute to global warming.
- Your company, GasBed, has created a new technique: burying carbon dioxide emissions from industrial processes beneath the sea in huge underground reservoirs.
- The technique can also be used to pump millions of tonnes of carbon dioxide into oilfields, and so help bring out any remaining reserves of oil. The value of the recovered oil would probably make this a cheaper way of disposing of the pollution than just pumping it down and storing it.

- An extensive network of underground pipes would need to be set up to carry the waste gas large distances to the coast, and the huge cost of setting up the infrastructure would require a partnership between oil companies, power generators and national governments.
- Critics say that the scheme is dangerous and expensive and that the money should instead be spent on investments in cleaner, renewable forms of energy.

2 Make notes for your presentation. Think about these key questions.

- Who are you?
- Who is your audience?
- What is the problem?
- What is the cause of the problem?
- What is your proposed solution?

9a First impressions last

Jon Hird

1   Think of two or three companies/products that you associate with each of the colours below. Then read the text and decide if the colour is appropriate for these companies/products. Say why/why not.

First impressions last. And in terms of corporate identity nothing creates a more powerful first impression than colour. But what do the different colours say to us? Read on and find out.

Red

Red means power and energy and suggests a bold, competitive, go-getting attitude. Red excites us. It is particularly prevalent on anything designed to appeal to men. In the Far East, the colour also symbolises good luck and is consequently used by many Asian companies such as Canon, Sharp and HSBC. It is no surprise that arguably the world's most recognisable logo, Coca-Cola, predominantly features red.

Blue

Blue is the world's favourite corporate colour and evokes coolness, calmness and authority. It also denotes intellect, trustworthiness and dependability, which is why it is a favourite with sectors such as banking and insurance. Over 60% of all company logos are blue. Well-known corporate blues include IBM, General Motors, Ford, Pepsi, Wal-Mart and Microsoft.

Purple

Purple has been the colour of leadership and luxury since the Roman Empire, when only the imperial family were allowed to wear it. Although Yahoo! and the telecommunications company NTL pair it with yellow and green, purple is rarely used on its own as a corporate colour. The big exception to this is the confectionery giant Cadbury, who originally chose purple in the late 19th century because it was said to be Queen Victoria's favourite colour.

Yellow

Yellow is a youthful and fun colour. For this reason, it is perhaps the perfect colour for the photographic company Kodak. Many countries' business telephone directories are yellow and the colour is also popular with construction companies.

Green

Green is the colour of money, nature and, in many cultures, jealousy. While its money connotations are exploited by companies such as Britain's biggest bank Lloyds TSB, the colour is also used by petroleum giant BP, for whom it represents an environmental stance. Green now generally stands for something quite specific and often very political.

Brown

Brown suggests solidity, neutrality and straightforwardness. Perhaps the most recognisable corporate brown is that of the United States delivery company UPS. However, the company actually started using the colour in 1917 for the simple common sense reason that brown vehicles didn't show the dirt picked up from dusty roads.

Orange

Being bold, bright and lively, orange catches the eye. It's young, fresh, energetic and dynamic. The phone company previously known as Microtel was so dedicated to the colour that it simply renamed itself after it. Other notable oranges include budget airline easyJet and the drugs giant GlaxoSmithKline. Pentium and Reuters have both incorporated orange into their existing blue colour scheme.

---

2   Choose some of the following businesses and discuss what corporate colour(s) would be most appropriate for them. You could also discuss other businesses.

- investment fund
- electronic goods
- fast food restaurant
- upmarket restaurant
- car hire

- courier service
- health food products
- estate agent
- fitness club
- music shop

- waste disposal
- clothing for teenagers
- energy supplier
- DIY company
- supermarket

- beauty salon
- toyshop
- airline
- advertising agency
- language school

9b Socialising with confidence
Rosemary Richey

1   Look at each awkward situation and think of two ways of rewriting the negative language.

2   Roleplay the following situations, using as much polite language from 1 as you can.

Situation 1

Student A

You are the sales manager at a meeting with an important client. The negotiation for a valuable new contract is going very well but then you spill coffee on the client's white shirt. What can you say to apologise and to make amends?

Student B

You are a client negotiating an important contract at a meeting with the sales manager. You're about to sign when the sales manager spills coffee on your white shirt. It's an expensive designer label and one of your favourites. What do you say?

Situation 2

Student A

You are a guest at a dinner with a VIP client. The restaurant is noisy and smoky and you think the food and service are awful. You want to get out of the place as quickly as possible. How can you politely excuse yourself?

Student B

You are the host of a dinner at your favourite restaurant. One of your guests looks uncomfortable and approaches you about leaving early. It bothers you that he/she wants to leave, but you can't force him/her to stay. How can you handle the situation diplomatically?

Situation 3

Student A

You applied for job with another company with higher pay and better promotion prospects. You didn't get the job because you failed a test in the interviewing process. How can you explain this to your colleague?

Student B

You see your colleague in the canteen. You've heard he/she applied for a better job, but didn't get it. How can you diplomatically ask what happened?

10a Survival

John Allison

You and your colleagues are stuck in the office lift on the top floor of the building; the emergency alarm doesn't work, and there is no signal for your mobile phones. It's Friday evening, and nobody will come to the office before Monday morning. Have a nice weekend!

1 You can have only eight of the objects below to help you survive the weekend – decide together which eight objects you will choose.

- a giant 1kg packet of potato crisps
- a large pot of cold coffee
- a bottle of cheap white wine from last year's office party
- some balloons, also left over from the office party
- a laptop computer
- a spare battery for the laptop
- a lab coat

- a pencil
- a telephone directory
- a packet of dried milk
- a pair of scissors
- a CD player with a Frank Sinatra CD
- a first-aid kit
- a cigarette lighter
- a roll of adhesive tape

2 Choose a ninth object to help you survive the weekend – but everyone in the group must agree!

3 Who would you like to be stuck in the lift with you? Choose one person from each category:

- a business leader
- an actor/actress
- a sports personality
- an artist or musician

10b No U-turn?   Chris Murray

1 What are some of the problems that can arise in international mergers and takeovers? Why do so many of them appear to fail? Discuss in pairs/small groups.

2 Read the following case study of a troubled auto industry takeover.

Elite Motors is a German niche market producer of luxury sports cars. It is long-established and successful but quite small. Three years ago, during a series of brand consolidations in the auto industry, the CEO pushed through a controversial takeover of Empire Motors, an ailing British producer of middle-range cars. Empire's products and facilities were long past their best, but they had a good brand name and a complementary range that potentially offered a quick way to diversify Elite's products. 'Synergy' was the word on everyone's lips and the vision was to support the development of a new model range at Empire but in a fairly hands-off way, allowing the existing management to run the company.

Unfortunately, things are not going according to plan. Despite investing more than €600 million, Empire Motors is continuing to make bigger than expected losses, and it's still 18 months before the new product range will be launched. Meanwhile, although Elite is still making good profits, the diversion of financial and engineering resources is threatening to delay the development of its own new models. The group's share price is starting to fall, and there are rumours that it could itself be the target of a takeover from one of the big Japanese companies.

The British government, criticised for not preventing the takeover of a proud national symbol in the first place, is under pressure to save jobs at Empire, but reluctant to invest more money in what many see as a doomed enterprise. Something needs to be done.

A Group CEO
This was your big idea in the first place. You believe in Empire Motor's management. They just need more time (and a lot of cash) to turn things around. Stringent cost cuts at Empire together with a nine-month delay in replacing products at Elite should solve the problem. You're sure you can persuade the British government to come up with some cash too.

B Group Finance Director
You knew all along this would be a disaster. Another two years of these losses and the company will be in danger of going bankrupt. The only solution is divorce! The problem is that finding a new partner for Empire won't be easy. Still, you have to get out of this disastrous relationship whatever it takes. You believe that niche markets are the future, and that Elite should concentrate on its strengths and forget about diversification.

C Empire Managing Director
Your reputation and job are under threat here. The problem is the resistance of the trade unions to radical change, but now there's not much choice. Deep cuts in the workforce and new German working practices are needed. You're sure the new models will be a success, but why are those German engineers so fussy about quality? You would have had the new model in the showroom by now, even if there were still a few minor defects.

D Group Marketing Director
At first enthusiastic about the broadened product range, the poor quality and performance of the Empire models is beginning to have an impact on your company's market image. The new models look like winners, but it might be too late to reverse the damage. You're now not really sure that your company needs a full model range.

E Group Engineering Director
You've invested a lot of time and energy in renewing Empire's model range, and would hate to see it scrapped now. You're determined to produce a top-quality product for Empire. On the other hand, many of your engineers are complaining about the lack of resources for their own projects at Elite. They want to ditch Empire and go for their own medium-range models (three-year development time), based on Elite's engineering excellence. It would require big investment but in the long term might make more sense.

F Empire Trade Union Leader
You're in a weak position, but must try to protect the jobs of your members. The company is pressing for salary cuts and redundancies to improve productivity. Your members have already accepted a two-year wage freeze. They won't take much more. The problem is lack of investment and lack of communication between the two management groups.

11 Blurring and stretching

John Allison

1 Why would you pay more today than you paid yesterday for the same product?
Read the article and find out.

Manufacturers of consumer goods are finding new ways to increase prices and profits. Blur marketing is the process of bypassing established price references by using packaging and presentation borrowed from apparently unrelated products. Milk in a spray bottle, chewing gum to clean your teeth, and yoghurt drinks are some of the products being offered to persuade consumers to part with more cash. Brand stretching allows the manufacturer to transfer the added value of a recognised brand to a new product outside its normal territory: think of Marlboro sportswear, Nestlé mineral water, and Adidas aftershave.

Creative marketing can persuade consumers to adopt new patterns of behaviour in order to open up new markets. Champagne producers Pommery have positioned their 20 cl mini-bottle as the fashionable drink in pubs and clubs. Served with a straw, it can cost up to 50% more than old-fashioned champagne in a glass. Pernod-Ricard's new pre-mixed aperitif saves consumers the trouble of adding water – and it can command up to three times the price of the original, undiluted Pernod!

2 What is the advantage for manufacturers of 'bypassing established price references'?
Why not just create a new brand for a new product?

3 Divide into two teams. Brainstorm new product concepts by blurring and stretching products,
brands and packaging. Use the product information below and your own ideas.

Brand	Product	Packaging
Anchor	butter	individual portions
Cadbury's	chocolate	foil-wrapped bar
Chanel	perfume	spray
Coke	cola	33 cl can
Häagen-Dazs	ice cream	frozen in plastic box
Disney	video cassettes	plastic box
Glenfiddich	whisky	1 l bottle in tin
Marlboro	cigarettes	pack of 20

Brand	Product	Packaging
Mercedes	cars	none
Nike	sports shoes	cardboard box
Nutella	chocolate spread	glass jar
Penguin	paperbacks	none
Colgate	toothpaste	plastic tube
Sony	discman	blister pack
?	?	?
?	?	?

4 Choose the three best ideas from 3 and present your new products. Give the following information:
- the new product
- the (new) brand name
- the packaging
- the positioning strategy
- a promotional idea to raise brand awareness

12a Who's first?

Jeremy Taylor/Jon Wright

1   You are the manager of a small chocolate factory and one morning you receive five e-mails.
Put the messages in order of importance (1= most important) and then compare with your partner.

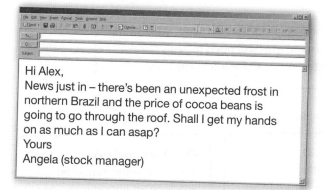

Hi Alex,
News just in – there's been an unexpected frost in northern Brazil and the price of cocoa beans is going to go through the roof. Shall I get my hands on as much as I can asap?
Yours
Angela (stock manager)

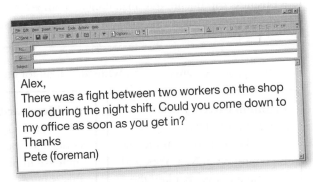

Alex,
There was a fight between two workers on the shop floor during the night shift. Could you come down to my office as soon as you get in?
Thanks
Pete (foreman)

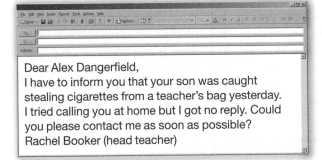

Dear Alex Dangerfield,
I have to inform you that your son was caught stealing cigarettes from a teacher's bag yesterday. I tried calling you at home but I got no reply. Could you please contact me as soon as possible?
Rachel Booker (head teacher)

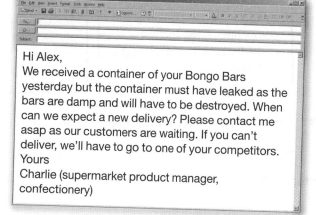

Hi Alex,
We received a container of your Bongo Bars yesterday but the container must have leaked as the bars are damp and will have to be destroyed. When can we expect a new delivery? Please contact me asap as our customers are waiting. If you can't deliver, we'll have to go to one of your competitors.
Yours
Charlie (supermarket product manager, confectionery)

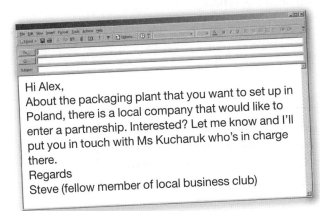

Hi Alex,
About the packaging plant that you want to set up in Poland, there is a local company that would like to enter a partnership. Interested? Let me know and I'll put you in touch with Ms Kucharuk who's in charge there.
Regards
Steve (fellow member of local business club)

2   Now discuss which of the messages you would respond to (a) by e-mail (b) by phone or
(c) in a face-to-face meeting. Give reasons for your answers.

3   Choose one of the following tasks:
  • write an e-mail in reply to the message you thought was most important.
  • roleplay one of the situations with a partner.

12b Manager on the move
Pete Sharma

Student A

1 Read the role card below.

> **Profile:** You are the plant manager of Bio-pharm, a pharmaceuticals company. You are on a business trip but are in e-mail contact with your assistant. You will need to send him/her tasks while you are away and you will receive messages, requests for information etc.

2 Read the 'problem cards' below. Write an e-mail for each situation and send it to your assistant.

> **Problem card (1)**
> You have suddenly remembered that the trade fair is coming up in New York and you have not yet booked the hotel or flights. Get your assistant to send you a rough estimate of costs based on competitive fares and mid-range hotels for yourself and a colleague.

> **Problem card (2)**
> Your usual supplier has contacted you demanding an increase in prices. They say this is necessary due to the recent rise in fuel costs. You need your assistant to draft a brief, tactful letter rejecting the new terms and conditions and e-mail you the draft asap.

> **Problem card (3)**
> You have come across an article in an important trade journal that raises the possibility that your latest product, an antihistamine drug, is potentially dangerous and demands it be recalled by Bio-pharm. E-mail your assistant asking for any reaction/thoughts before you write your own press release.

3 You will receive three e-mails from your assistant which will need answering.

Student B

1 Read the role card below.

> **Profile:** You are the assistant plant manager of Bio-pharm, a pharmaceuticals company. Your boss is on a business trip but is in e-mail contact with you. You will need to inform him/her of problems at the plant and also reply to messages, requests for information etc.

2 Read the 'problem cards' below. Write an e-mail for each situation and send it to your manager.

> **Problem card (1)**
> There are problems with the computer network. You think it's a virus but have no idea what action to take or who to contact. Ask your boss what to do.

> **Problem card (2)**
> The report from the latest health and safety inspector has just arrived. In a strongly-worded attack, it condemns conditions in the laboratory. He wants to arrange a meeting asap. How should you reply?

> **Problem card (3)**
> The transportation company that distributes your products in central Europe has gone on strike, demanding higher wages. You do not know how to get supplies out to Poland and Hungary on time. Ask your boss what to do.

3 You will receive three e-mails from your manager which will need answering.

13 Patently absurd

Chris Murray

Match the presentation openings to the techniques they exemplify.

Presentation openings	Technique
a How many of you here today have ever been in the situation where you wanted to get cash from the bank on a Sunday?	**1** Making a topic statement
b I remember the time when I was asked a difficult question in an interview and had no idea what to say.	**2** Giving an amazing/surprising fact/statistic
c What's the biggest problem that car drivers face today?	**3** 'Visualisation' of statistics
d We have found that four out of every five homeowners don't have adequate insurance cover.	**4** Personalisation through rhetorical/genuine questions about audience's experiences
e With this product you'll be able to slash 35% off your fuel bills.	**5** Personal anecdote
f Today I'm going to talk to you about the new staff training programme.	**6** Stating a problem/personalisation through rhetorical/genuine questions about general issues
g Did you know that Americans on average eat 18 acres of pizza every day?	**7** Showing the benefits and opportunities of your product/service etc.

a   The ski propeller
Description: For independent skiers. Rucksack unit with small petrol engine (e.g. chain saw motor), propeller for thrust. Throttle controls on ski sticks or on supports attached to motor unit. No more expensive ski passes and lift queues.

b   The full-body motorcycle airbag
Description: Lifesaver for all motorcyclists (could be adapted for bicycles?) Special suit, like a car airbag, attached to bike by a cable which breaks when rider is thrown off – inflates suit. Reusable if checked by service company.

c   The motorised ice-cream cone
Description: For kids and adults. Motorised revolving ice-cream cone, electric motor, variable speed control, batteries. Two versions – hand-held or on table/body strap for hands-free use (possibly in-car entertainment?) Small cooler built in to prevent melting.

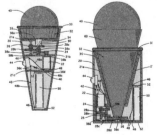

d   The ball boat
Description: Revolutionary water-based transport system. Rolls over water, less friction, higher speed (3x faster than conventional boat), fuel economy, comfort. Powered by propeller engines on cabins attached to each side (can detach in emergency and travel independently).

Images from www.totallyabsurdinventions.com

14a Flight to Rubovia

Paul Emmerson

(Adapted from an exercise in 'The Cross-Cultural Business Pocketbook' by John Mattock)

> You are on your first business trip to Rubovia. You board the flight and the cabin crew and passengers are all speaking Rubovian. You don't understand a word. A Rubovian sits next to you and greets you in excellent English. Over the next few hours you have a wonderful opportunity to find out about Rubovia and its culture. What questions will you ask the friendly passenger at your side?

1 Write down four questions about general culture in Rubovia, and four about business culture. When you have finished, read out your questions and listen to other people's ideas.

General culture	Business culture
1	1
2	2
3	3
4	4

2 Look at the sample questions at the bottom of the page. How many are similar to the questions you thought of? Which questions would you ask if you only had time for ten questions in total?

-------- fold --- fold ----------

General

How do you say 'Hello', 'Please', 'Thank you', 'Sorry', 'Cheers' and 'Goodbye' in Rubovian?

How do people greet each other, by shaking hands or kissing?

What's good to eat and drink?

Are there any religious taboos I should know about?

What are the common mistakes that foreigners make in Rubovia?

What's the population of Rubovia?

What's the most popular sport?

What's the geography of the country like?

Are there big regional differences inside the country?

How have things changed over the last ten years?

What do Rubovians think about my country?

What is everybody talking about at the moment?

Business

How should I address people? When do people use first names?

Are personal relationships important in business?

How important are punctuality and deadlines?

Is decision-making quick and decisive, or slow and cautious?

Is documentation important, or is 'my word' good enough?

Is it normal to openly disagree with people in meetings?

If not, how should I show that I'm not happy with something?

Do people continue the business discussion at lunch?

Is it expected that you offer a gift at the end of a visit?

If so, what is appropriate?

14b Business humour

Nicholas Sheard

How much humour is there in your workplace? In which of the following places or situations are you most likely to hear or tell jokes to colleagues/business contacts?

- a lift
- a business lunch
- a formal meeting
- a negotiation
- a presentation
- a coffee break
- an informal in-company meeting
- the work canteen
- a pub/bar after work
- at your desk in the office

Student A – The engineer and the manager

A man in a hot-air balloon realised he was lost. He reduced altitude and noticed a woman below. He descended a bit more and shouted, 'Excuse me, can you help me? I promised a friend I would meet him an hour ago but I don't know where I am.'

The woman below replied, 'You are in a hot-air balloon approximately 30 feet above the ground. You are between 40 and 41 degrees north latitude and between 59 and 60 degrees west longitude.'

'You must be an engineer,' said the balloonist. 'I am,' replied the woman, 'how did you know?' 'Well,' answered the balloonist, 'everything you told me is technically correct, but I still have no idea how to interpret your information, and the fact is, I am still lost. Frankly, you haven't been much help so far.'

The woman replied, 'You must be in management.' 'I am,' replied the balloonist, 'but how did you know?' 'Well,' said the woman, 'you don't know where you are or where you are going. You have risen to where you are due to a large quantity of hot air. You made a promise which you can't keep, and you expect people below you to solve your problems. The fact is you are in exactly the same position you were in before we met, but now, somehow, it's my fault.'

Student B – The engineers and lawyers

Three lawyers and three engineers were going to a conference by train. At the station, the three lawyers each bought tickets and watched as the three engineers bought only one. 'How are three people going to travel on only one ticket?' asked one of the three lawyers. 'Watch and you'll see,' answered one of the engineers.

They all got on the train. The lawyers took their seats but all three engineers crammed into the toilet and closed the door behind them. Shortly after the train departed, the inspector came round checking tickets. He knocked on the toilet door and said, 'Ticket, please.' The door opened slightly and an arm appeared with a ticket in its hand. The conductor checked it and moved on.

The lawyers saw this and agreed it was a clever idea. So, after the conference, the lawyers decided to copy the engineers and save some money on their tickets. When they got to the station, they bought just one ticket for the return trip. To their surprise, the engineers didn't buy a ticket at all. 'How are you going to travel without a ticket?' asked one confused lawyer. 'Watch and you'll see,' said one of the engineers.

When they got on the train, the three lawyers crammed into a toilet and the three engineers crammed into another one nearby. The train departed. A few moments later, one of the engineers left his toilet and walked over to the toilet where the lawyers were hiding. He knocked on the door and said, 'Ticket, please.'

15 Buzzword Bluff

John Allison

1 Read the three definitions for each business buzzword; only one is correct, the other two are bluffs. Which is the true definition?

BEAR

a 'As you know, a "bear" is a large, heavy animal with enormous, strong, hairy arms. In business, a "bear" is a guy who has been promoted from a manual job to management – he can be very intimidating!'

b 'Well, as a matter of fact "bears" are actually very timid animals – they prefer to avoid risks like human beings. So on the stock market, a "bear" is a timid or pessimistic investor; someone who expects the market to go down.'

c 'Oh really, how absurd! No, in reality, a "bear" is a term used to describe a company or a person from Russia or from Eastern Europe. More and more companies are relocating their production facilities to Eastern Europe, where the "bears'" salaries are much lower than in the West.'

HEAVY HITTER

a 'When business is tough, some managers keep a bottle of Scotch in their desk. You've heard of "hitting the bottle"? Well, take it from me, a "heavy hitter" is a manager who "hits the bottle" several times a day.'

b 'What nonsense! Actually, the true definition of a "heavy hitter" is the bad guy in a negotiating team; he's aggressive and threatening, so his partner appears friendly and flexible and gets agreement. Obvious, isn't it?'

c 'No, come on, let's be serious. The "heavy hitter" is the big guy in a baseball team who hits home runs, picks up huge bonuses, and pulls all the girls. So in business, a "heavy hitter" is a good-looking, top-class salesman.'

---

2 Divide into two teams. Your teacher will give you the true definition of the buzzwords in the lists below. Invent two bluffs for each word and then take turns to give the three definitions. If you bluff the other team, you score a point; if not, they get the point.

Team A	**Team B**
GHOSTBUSTER	HIP-SHOOTER
WHISTLE-BLOWER	VULTURE CAPITALIST
MARZIPAN SET	EMPTY SUIT
GREATER FOOL	GONNABE

3 Have you encountered any of these categories of people? Can you give examples?

Team A

GHOSTBUSTER: a tax investigator who catches 'ghosts' (businessmen who avoid paying tax)
WHISTLE-BLOWER: an employee who leaks information about their company's illegal activities
MARZIPAN SET: middle management – between the workers and the executives like marzipan between the cake and the icing
GREATER FOOL: a person who buys shares on the stock market at a higher price than you paid

---

Team B

HIP-SHOOTER: a manager who acts too fast, like a cowboy who shoots without taking careful aim
VULTURE CAPITALIST: an investor who leaves no profit for the business
EMPTY SUIT: a middle manager in a large company with no real power
GONNABE: an ambitious young manager who is sure he is 'gonna be' CEO

16a Reporting activities

Anne Watson

Student A

1 You are going to attend a monthly departmental meeting. Your colleague, Student B, won't be able to attend, so you will have to report their business activities since the last meeting. Ask Student B questions, using or adapting the cues below, and make notes of the answers.

Activities since the last meeting

Decisions taken:

One objective reached:

One objective not reached:

Trips abroad:

Meeting(s) attended:

Outcome of meetings:

Other activities:

2 Now report your partner's activities to the other members of the meeting.

✂ ....

Student B

1 You are going to attend a monthly departmental meeting. Your colleague, Student A, won't be able to attend, so you will have to report their business activities for the coming month. Ask Student A questions, using or adapting the cues below, and make notes of the answers.

Activities for the coming month

Projects:

Problems/emergencies to deal with:

People to visit:

Trips abroad:

Planned meeting(s):

Holiday/days off:

Other activities:

2 Now report your partner's activities to the other members of the meeting.

16b Can you see me? Jeremy Taylor/Jon Wright

1 Sophie wants to set up a videoconference to show Jimmy some new products. To do this, they are using a simple chat program on their computers. Put the sentences of their conversation in the correct order.

a ☐ Video icon … ah, there it is. Wow, I can see something … a sort of big pink ball … but the picture isn't very clear. Is it one of your new toys?

b ☐ No, actually, it's been pretty sunny for the last three days.

c ☐ Well done! Right, the next stage is to click on the 'video' icon in the top left-hand corner of the chat program.

d ☐ Wow, that's good news. OK, I have some new toys for the Christmas market I'd like to show you. Are you ready to start our videoconference?

e ☐ That's good! Now find my name and then double-click on it.

f ☐ Ooops! Sorry about that Sophie! I told you I was lousy at using new technology!

g ☐ Er, sure. I've never done this before though. You'll have to bear with me if I'm a bit slow.

h ☐ Er, no, that's my face, Jimmy. I'll have to adjust the focus …

i ☐ Fine thanks, Jimmy. Is the weather still miserable in London?

j ☐ Hello, Sophie! Good to speak to you! How are things in Paris?

k ☐ Right, last time I was in London I installed a chat program so all you have to do is to click on the 'chat' icon at the bottom of the screen.

l ☐ Yes, it is, I know that much!

m ☐ Hold on, hold on, 'chat' icon … there it is … The program is opening and there's a list of names in a sort of box.

n ☐ Here you are, 'Sophie–Paris'! Now double-click … Wow, a dialogue box just appeared out of nowhere! Let me key in H-e-l-l-o S-o-p-h-i-e.

o ☐ Don't worry, Jimmy. It's very easy. Now, is your computer switched on?

2 Match the verb and nouns/phrases. Then work in pairs and think of other collocations with these verbs.

a	adjust	**1**	your computer
b	click on	**2**	the chatroom software from a reliable website
c	open	**3**	the chatroom software on your computer
d	turn up	**4**	the focus if necessary
e	install	**5**	the chat program icon
f	connect	**6**	your computer to the Internet
g	download	**7**	the volume if necessary
h	turn on	**8**	your webcam

3 Work in groups. Discuss the pros and cons of videoconferencing using a chat program on your computer.

17a Spin doctors

Jeremy Taylor/Jon Wright

1 Match the sentences to the ways of making language more diplomatic/persuasive.
If necessary, use the Grammar link on page 124 of the Student's Book to help you.

a The price rise might create a problem for us.	**1** introductory softeners to warn that bad news is coming
b We're rather concerned about the new contract.	**2** passive to avoid sounding accusatory
c We were wondering if we could negotiate the deal.	**3** modifiers to soften the message
d I'm afraid that we are behind schedule.	**4** suggestions
e We were told that the delivery would be on time.	**5** continuous forms to keep your options open
f Wouldn't it be better to come to a decision now?	**6** modal verbs to soften the verb

2 Work in pairs. Read and complete the dialogues in a positive/diplomatic way, using the information given in brackets.

Dialogue 1

A Is everything all right with your room, sir?

B Actually it isn't. I want to change it immediately.

A _____ .
(Apologise but explain that might be difficult.)
Could you tell me what's wrong with your room and I'll see if I can put it right for you?

B It's terrible and I won't spend another minute there. It's small – there's almost no room to move. The lights don't work, the bathroom is dirty and I can hear everything the people in the next room are saying!

A _____ .
(Explain why you can't move him/her to another room. Suggest a solution to make him/her happy. Be firm but polite and persuasive.)

Dialogue 2

A I'm not at all satisfied with the service I've received from your company.

B _____ ?
(Apologise and ask about the problem.)

A Everything! You said you would send me a detailed quote for the building work weeks ago.

B Ah yes, _____ .
(Apologise again and explain the reason for the delay.)

A When I rang to complain, the person who answered left me waiting for ten minutes. He promised the manager would call me immediately – and he didn't. I'm going to take my business to another company.

B _____ .
(Apologise again, sympathise with the caller, suggest a solution and try to make sure he/she remains your customer. Can you make him/her a special offer?)

Dialogue 3

A _____ .
(Apologise for not sending the client your brochure and price lists earlier.) We had

problems with the company that prints our material. I hope it all arrived safely.

B Yes, I got it, thank you.

A I hope it showed you all you needed, and that you can see exactly how we can meet your needs.

B Actually, I was surprised to find that the figure in the brochure is very different from the one you had given me over the phone. It's almost 40% more! And I'm not convinced the materials you plan to use are the right quality for what we need. They look pretty cheap to me.

A _____ .
(Apologise again, explain the reasons for the change in price. Give assurance about the quality of your materials and a guarantee.)

Dialogue 4

A I've called you here because I am not very happy with the report you sent me. The figures are terrible and something's got to be done about it. Your department's results are over 15% lower than we expected. I need an explanation!

B _____ .
(Acknowledge the problem and explain it has been a difficult year. Outline what external factors have caused this.)

A Every year is difficult. We have to make a profit, even in difficult years – especially in difficult years. With figures like these, I can't see how I have any choice but to cut staff numbers. You're just not performing. We need some new blood, new ideas in the department …

B _____ .
(Tactfully explain why cutting staff is not a good idea, but show you understand A's position.)

A Well something's got to change. It can't go on like this.

B _____ .
(Be positive about the outlook for the future and explain why. Convince A that the situation is getting better.)

17b Traffic trouble

Pete Sharma

Read the background information and the report.

> **Background:** Newville is a busy town (population 500,000) on a major supply route.
> A consortium of business people want to develop the city's shopping centre, investing a
> huge amount of money ($300m). The local city council is happy at the prospect of
> creating new jobs, and at the resulting increase in prosperity.
>
> **The problem:** transport congestion – approximately 10,000 vehicles enter the town on
> weekdays, there is poor traffic flow at peak times and high levels of air pollution.
> A consultancy firm has examined and costed solutions for dealing with traffic. This issue
> must be resolved before any building on a new shopping centre can begin.

Consultancy report findings				
Options	**Set-up costs**	**Traffic reduction**	**Breakeven**	**Other information**
1 Congestion charging	$15m	25%	7 years	10% of costs paid by government if target reduction achieved in 3 years.
2 Park and ride	$10m	17%	10 years	Proposal uses electric buses. An alternative with tram costs $10m more.
3 Ring road	$50m	5%	never	The reduction affects through traffic only. Total time for a government enquiry and construction is 6–8 years.
4 Underground car park	$30m	2%	9 years	Costs to be shared between council and consortium. Extends shopping centre construction time by 6 months.

Group A

Negotiation brief: Local council

- You want to minimise traffic in the town centre, but you also want the consortium to invest as much money in the area as possible. You are keen for any project to be a partnership.
- You like option 2 (reduces private cars) and option 3 (excludes through traffic). Option 1 is the most cost effective but is difficult to set up and manage.

Task

Prepare for the negotiation with the consortium. Consider the advantages and disadvantages of all the options for reducing traffic. You may have other proposals.

Agenda

1 Aim: to agree a proposed course of action for traffic reduction
2 Proposals: Local council/Consortium
3 Negotiate an agreement
4 Review/action plan

Group B

Negotiating brief: Consortium

- You want to maximise profits and are aware that this type of project tends to go over budget. You do not want customers to be discouraged from visiting the new shopping centre.
- You are quite keen on option 4, provided the council shares costs. You see option 1 as being too complicated to work successfully.

Task

Prepare for the negotiation with the local council. Consider the advantages and disadvantages of all the options for reducing traffic. You may have other proposals.

Agenda

1 Aim: to agree a proposed course of action for traffic reduction
2 Proposals: Local council/Consortium
3 Negotiate an agreement
4 Review/action plan

18 21st-century business
Nicholas Sheard

Student A

1   Read the following vision of the future. Then summarise and present the themes in your text to a partner.

Cultivating the customer

In the next century, people will have more information and less time. What customers want will continually evolve. It's easy to predict some individual products of the future such as intelligent fridges, mobile internet phones, e-banking, but most new ideas cannot be anticipated. The only thing we know for sure is that new products will be superseded sooner rather than later. In this environment, the success of a company will not be based on the individual products or services that they provide, but on the customers that they cultivate. The worth of the future company will be measured by the hold it has on these customers. The companies that offer their customers a 'total experience' will survive. This means all the products and services related to their core business, a complete offer that saves their customers time and effort. So rather than buying gas, electricity, water and telephone services from different companies, consumers will be choosing one provider for all these services to save them time and money. The companies that provide this 'total experience' will win customers. Any company that expects to prosper in the old way, by focusing on its core products alone, will struggle.

---

2   Discuss the following questions in pairs or small groups.

   a   Which predictions do you think will come true?

   b   Which ones are you sceptical about?

   c   Which ones would be beneficial/harmful to your business/industry?

   d   How is your business preparing to respond to the conditions described in the predictions?

   e   What other trends do you predict for the world of business in the future?

Student B

1   Read the following vision of the future. Then summarise and present the themes in your text to a partner.

Mobile future

Mobility is the key to the future. Mobile in terms of where people and companies are based, and flexible about the way work is done at every level. People will no longer have to *go to* work to work. The technological revolution that has enabled this to occur is already here. People can work online from home, only having to go into the office for occasional team meetings. This will increasingly reduce the need for office space and help to make individuals more efficient; they will no longer have to waste huge amounts of time commuting to and from work. Traditional company hierarchies are likely to disappear. In this environment, only results matter, not the number of hours you put in at the office. Employees will no longer stay with one company for their whole career or think in terms of a 'job for life'. Think in terms of co-operative networks of highly-skilled individuals forming strategic alliances and working on short- or medium-term projects. The knowledge-based industries will take over, particularly in the developed world. Manufacturing jobs will be mobile in a different way too. High tech, specialist manufacturing will be done in developed countries, with lower-level manufacturing done in developing countries where labour and manufacturing costs will be cheaper.

---

2   Discuss the following questions in pairs or small groups.

   a   Which predictions do you think will come true?

   b   Which ones are you sceptical about?

   c   Which ones would be beneficial/harmful to your business/industry?

   d   How is your business preparing to respond to the conditions described in the predictions?

   e   What other trends do you predict for the world of business in the future?

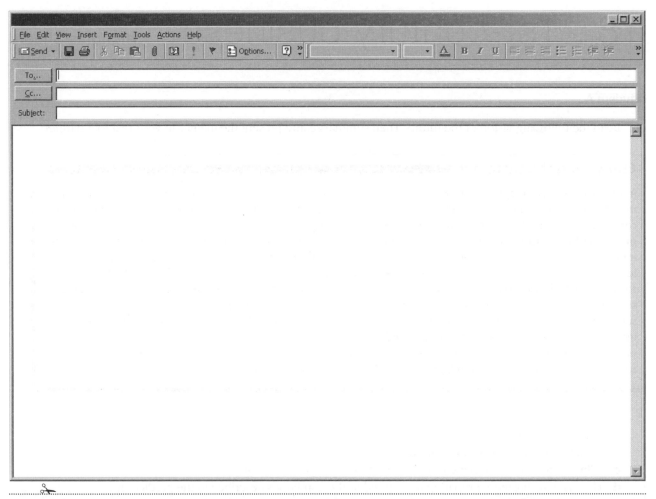

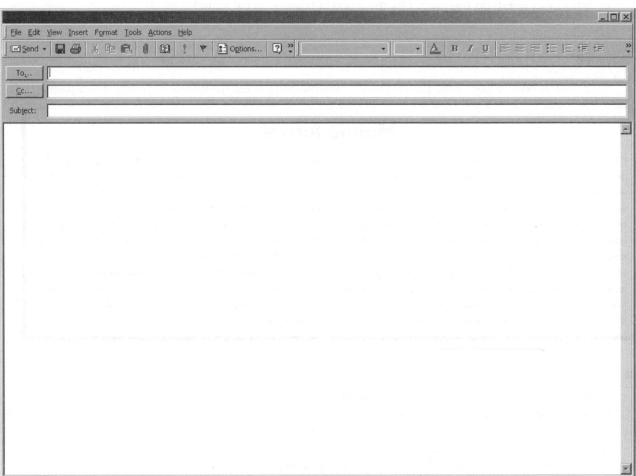

Feedback sheet

Name: _____	Date: _____	Activity: _____

Good use of language:

Language to be corrected:	**Possible correct version:**

Macmillan Education
Between Towns Road, Oxford OX4 3PP
A division of Macmillan Publishers Limited
Companies and representatives throughout the world

ISBN 0 333 95738 5

Text © Macmillan Publishers Limited 2004
Design and illustration © Macmillan Publishers Limited 2004
First published 2004

Note to teachers

Photocopies may be made, for classroom use, of pages 100–125 and
154–185 without the prior written permission of Macmillan Publishers
Limited. However, please note that the copyright law, which does not
normally permit multiple copying of published material, applies to the
rest of this book.

Text by Pete Sharma

Resource materials by John Allison; Paul Emmerson; Jon Hird;
Chris Murray; Mark Powell; Rosemary Richey; Pete Sharma;
Nicholas Sheard; Jeremy Taylor; Anne Watson; Jon Wright

Designed by eMC Design, www.emcdesign.org.uk
Illustrated by Mike Stones icons (research photos Photodisc);
Julian Mosedale pp156, 169; Val Saunders pp154, 170
Original cover concept by Jackie Hill at 320 Design
Cover illustration by Mike Stones (research photos Photodisc)

The authors and publishers wish to thank the following who have kindly
granted permission to use copyright material: **Gerry McGovern** for
adaptation of 'Seven Deadly Skills' © article in Sydney Morning Herald
(www.gerrymcgovern.com); **David Adams** author of adapted extract
from article 'Spinning around' © David Adams which appeared in *The Age*
20/5/03; **John Mattock** author of 'Cross-cultural Business Pocketbook' for
granting us permission to use adapted material; **Ted VanCleave** for
granting permission to use adapted extracts from website
www.totallyabsurd.com; **Lynn Shepherd** for granting permission to use
adapted material from Business Life article 'Any colour you like as long as
it's orange' © Lynn Shepherd in July/August 2003 edition; **M. Etienne
Gless** author of adapted article 'Blurring and stretching' from Magazine
L'Entreprise, dated December 2002, Extracts No. 206/207 used with kind
permission; **Louis Garnade** for granting permission to adapt material in
'The Internet in Business English' © Summertown Publishing, 2003.

Student's Book acknowledgements

Text © Mark Powell

Design and illustration © Macmillan Publishers Limited 2004
Designed by Jackie Hill at 320 Design
Illustrated by Mike Stones icons (research photos Photodisc); Kim
Williams pp73, 79; Julian Mosedale p92
Photo research by Sally Cole

The publishers would like to thank Bob Ratto, Byron, Rome; Angela
Wright, British Council, Rome; Norman Cain, IH Rome; Fiona Campbell,
Teach-In, Rome; Sue Garton, Lois Clegg and Irene Frederick, University of
Parma; Simon Hopson and Gordon Doyle, Intensive Business English,
Milan; Dennis Marino, Bocconi University, Milan; Mike Cruikshank,
Advanced Language Services, Milan; Christine Zambon, Person to Person,
Milan; Fiona O'Connor, In-Company English, Milan; Peter Panton, Panton
School, Milan; Colin Irving Bell, Novara; Marta Rodriguez Casal, Goal
Rush Institute, Buenos Aires; Elizabeth Mangi and Silvia Ventura, NET
New English Training, Buenos Aires; Graciela Yohma and Veronica Cenini,
CABSI, Buenos Aires; Viviana Pisani, Asociación Ex Alumnos, Buenos
Aires; Claudia Siciliano, LEA Institute, Buenos Aires; Cuca Martocq, AACI,
Buenos Aires; Laura Lewin, ABS International, Buenos Aires; Charlie
Lopez, Instituto Big Ben, Buenos Aires; Alice Elvira Machado; Patricia
Blower; Valeria Siniscalchi; Carla Chaves; Virginia Garcia; Cultura Inglesa,
Rio de Janeiro; Susan Dianne Mace, Britannia, Rio de Janeiro; John
Paraskou, Diamond School, Sèvres; Dorothy Polley and Nadia Fairbrother,
Executive Language Services, Paris; Claire MacMurray, Formalangues,
Paris; Claire Oldmeadow, Franco British Chamber of Commerce, Paris;
Ingrid Foussat and Anne James, IFG Langues, Paris; Karl Willems, Quai
d'Orsay Language Centre, Paris; Louis Brazier, Clare Davis, Jacqueline
Deubel, Siobhan Mlačak and Redge, Télélangue, Paris; John Morrison
Milne, Ian Stride, Gareth East and Richard Marrison, IH Madrid; Gina
Cuciniello; Helena Gomm; Paulette McKean.

The authors and publishers would like to thank the following for
permission to reproduce their material: **Bloomsbury Publishing Plc** for
dictionary extracts from the *Macmillan English Dictionary* © Bloomsbury
Publishing Plc 2002; **PFD** for extracts from 'A Night to Remember' by
Dolly Dhingra, first published in *The Guardian* 03.12.01; **Tate
Enterprises** for adapted extracts taken from www.tate.org.uk/britain/
hospitality/rooms.html copyright © Tate, London - first published online

www.tate.org.uk 2003; **Vicefund** for extracts from
www.vicefund.com/docs/ViceProspectus.pdf; **Copyright Clearance
Centre, Inc** for extracts from *Artful Persuasion: How To Command
Attention, Change Minds, and Influence People* by Harry A Mills
(AMACOM, 2000) copyright © AMACON 2000; **Random House Group
Limited** for extracts from *The Ultimate Business Presentation Book* by
Andrew Leigh (Random House Business Books, 1999); **Macmillan
London, UK** for extracts from *How To Argue And Win Every Time* (Pan
Books, 1995); **Copyright Clearance Center** for extracts from 'You have
to start meeting like this!' by Gina Imperato first published in *Fast
Company* April 1999 Issue 23 (www.fastcompany.com); **N I Syndication
Limited** for extracts from 'Should genetic tests decide job prospects?' by
Margaret Cole, copyright © Times Newspapers Limited 1999, first
published in *The Sunday Times* 24.01.99; **Tribune Media Services
International** for extracts from 'In a high-tech world, it's a clinch for
employers to spy on workers' by Liz Stevens first published in *Knight
Ridder* Newspapers 12.06.02, copyright © Knight Ridder/Tribune Media
Services International 2003; **Francis Beckett** for extracts from 'Creative
way to better management' by Francis Beckett first published in *Financial
Times* 08.11.99, copyright © Francis Beckett 1999; **Kogan Page** for
extracts from *Great Myths of Business* by William Davis (Kogan Page,
1997); **Gifford and Elizabeth Pinchot** for extracts from
www.intrapreneur.com; **Lesley Everett** for extracts from 'Dress for success
and walk into a topline career', copyright © Lesley Everett first published in
The Guardian 22.06.02; **McGraw Hill Companies Inc** for extracts
from 'Golf and business: a perfect couple' by Mark Nelson, taken from
www.businessweek.com/lifestyle/content/nov2001/1s2001116.3182.htm,
copyright © McGraw Hill Companies Inc 2001; **Quirk Books** for extracts
from 'The Worst-Case Scenario Survival Column' by David Borgenicht
taken from www.worstcasescenarios.com/mainpage.htm; **John Adair** for
extracts from *Effective Decision-Making* by John Adair (Pan Books, 1985);
Book House Publishing AB for extracts from *Funky Business* by Jonas
Ridderstråle and Kjell Nordström (ft.com, 2000); **The Adbusters Media
Foundation** for extracts from 'Buy nothing day' taken from
www.adbusters.org; **Guardian Newspapers Limited** for extracts from
'No Logo: Naomi Klein review' by Katherine Viner, copyright © The
Guardian 2000, first published in *The Guardian* 23.09.00; **The Economist**
for extracts from 'Going global' first published in *The Economist* 06.12.01,
copyright © The Economist Newspaper Limited, London 2001; **Lexicon
Naming** for extracts from www.lexiconbranding.com/contact.html;
Sandra Harris for extracts from 'Deliver us from e-mail', copyright ©
Sandra Harris 2000, first published in *Business Life* Magazine September
2000; **John Wiley & Sons Limited on behalf of Capstone Publishing
Limited** for extracts from *The Ultimate Book of Business Quotations* by
Stuart Crainer (Capstone Publishing Limited, 1997), copyright © Capstone
Publishing Limited 1997; **Margaret Thatcher Foundation** for extracts
from *Speech to Conservative Party Conference* 10.10.75; **Atlantic
Syndication** for extracts from 'Bad spelling is the key to success' by Molly
Watson, first published in *Evening Standard* 10.04.01; **Hilary Rubinstein
Books** for various extracts taken from *The Penguin Book of Twentieth
Century Speeches* edited by Brian MacArthur (Viking, 1992); **Random
House Group Limited** for extracts from *The Accidental Tourist* by Anne
Tyler (Chatto & Windus, 1985).

Whilst every effort has been made to trace owners of copyright material in
this book, there may have been some cases when the publishers have
been unable to contact the owners. We should be grateful to hear from
anyone who recognises copyright material and who is unacknowledged.
We shall be pleased to make the necessary amendments in future editions
of the book.

The authors and publishers would like to thank the following for
permission to reproduce their photographs: Action Plus/G.Kirk p49;
Alamy/Stockfolio p14, Pictor p20, J.Ward p27, R.Llewellyn pp31(t), 40, 63,
D.Delimont p51(m), T.Payne p52, TH Foto p58, C.Ehlers pp74, 87, Robert
Harding p89; Anthony Blake/T.Robins p5, M.Brigdale p51(b), S.Atkinson
p57; Car Photo Library p56; Corbis/D.Turnley p6, Bettmann pp10, 21, 82,
N.Rabinowitz p16, Pandis Media p18, F.Cevallos p25, P.Corral p36, P.Ward
p37, J.Feingersh p42, 83, Left Lane Productions p44, G.Mendel p46,
A.Schein p59, Hulton-Deutsch p69, J.Miele p71, S.Prezant p78, D.Laine
p81(t), R.F p81(b), T.Svensson p95; GettyImages/Chabruken p13,
M.Oppenheim p17, R.Brimson p22, S.Battersby p35, R.Lockyer p47,
Photodisc Blue p48, R.Melnychuk p51(t), C.Hawkins p54, Photodisc
Green p56, Amwell p62, T.Yamada p64, D.Madison p68, H.Grey p77,
J.Bradley p91, Hulton Archive pp32, 94, 97; Panos Pictures/Alain le
Garsmeur p73; Photonica/F.Cantor p90; Press Association/EPA pp39, 66;
Rex Features/J.Sutton Hibbert p60; Science Photo Library/B.Frisch p96, US
Dept of Energy p98; Vin Mag Archive p37; Zefa pp4, 84.

Cartoons on p23 reproduced with permission from the New Yorker/© The
New Yorker Collection 2000 Frank Cotham from cartoonbank.com. All
Rights Reserved; p59 Calvin and Hobbes © 1995 Watterson. Reprinted
with permission of Universal Press Syndicate. All Rights Reserved.

Printed and bound in Spain by Edelvives SA

2008 2007 2006 2005 2004
10 9 8 7 6 5 4 3 2 1